CW01249764

MALTA AND BRITISH STRATEGIC POLICY
1925–1943

CASS SERIES: MILITARY HISTORY AND POLICY
Series Editors: John Gooch and Brian Holden Reid
ISSN: 1465-8488

This series will publish studies on historical and contemporary aspects of land power, spanning the period from the eighteenth century to the present day, and will include national, international and comparative studies. From time to time, the series will publish edited collections of essays and 'classics'.

1. *Allenby and British Strategy in the Middle East, 1917–1919*
   Matthew Hughes

2. *Alfred von Schlieffen's Military Writings*
   Robert Foley (ed. and trans.)

3. *The British Defence of Egypt 1935–1940: Conflict and Crisis in the Eastern Mediterranean*
   Stephen Morewood

4. *The Japanese and British Commonwealth Armies at War, 1941–1945*
   Tim Moreman

5. *Training, Tactics and Leadership in the Confederate Army of Tennessee: Seeds of Failure*
   Andrew Haughton

6. *Military Training in the British Army, 1940–1944: From Dunkirk to D-Day*
   Tim Harrison-Place

7. *The Boer War: Direction, Experience and Image*
   John Gooch (ed.)

8. *Caporetto 1917: Victory or Defeat?*
   Mario Morselli

9. *Postwar Counterinsurgency and the SAS, 1945–1952: A Special Type of Warfare*
   Tim Jones

10. *The British General Staff: Reform and Innovation, c.1890–1939*
    David French and Brian Holden Reid (eds)

11. *Writing the Great War: Sir James Edmonds and the Official Histories, 1915–1948*
    Andrew Green

12. *Command and Control in Military Crisis: Devious Decisions*
    Harold Høiback

13. *Malta and British Strategic Policy, 1925–1943*
    Douglas Austin

Malta and British Strategic Policy 1925–43

Douglas Austin

Foreword by David French

FRANK CASS
LONDON • NEW YORK

First published in 2004
by Frank Cass
11 New Fetter Lane, London EC4P 4EE

Simultaneously published in the USA and Canada
by Frank Cass
29 West 35th Street, New York, NY 1001

Frank Cass is an imprint of the Taylor & Francis Group

© 2004 D. Austin

British Library Cataloguing in Publication Data
Austin, Douglas
Malta and British strategic policy, 1925–43. – (Cass series. Military history and policy; 13)
1. World War, 1939–1945 – Malta 2. World War, 1939–1945 – Campaigns – Malta 3. Great Britain – Military relations – Malta 4. Malta – Military relations – Great Britain 5. Great Britain – Military policy 6. Malta – History 1798–1964 7. Great Britain – Foreign relations – Mediterranean Region 9. Great Britain – Foreign relations – 1910–1936 10. Great Britain – Foreign relations – 1936–1945
I. Title
945.8'5'03

Library of Congress Cataloging-in-Publication Data
Austin, Douglas, 1934–
Malta and British strategic policy, 1925–43/ Douglas Austin; forword by David French.
p. cm. – (Cass series – military history and policy; ISSN 1465-8488)
Based on author's doctoral thesis (University of London).
Includes bibliographical references and index.
1. Great Britain – History, Military – 20th century. 2. Great Britain – Defenses – History – 20th century. 3. Malta – Foreign relations – Great Britain. 4. Great Britain – Foreign relations – Malta. 5. British – Malta – History – 20th century. 6. World War, 1939–1945 – Great Britain. 7. Great Britain – Military policy. 8. World War, 1939–1945 – Malta. I. Title. II. Series.
DA566.5.A97 2004
355'.03354585'09041–dc22

ISBN 0-7146-5545-7
ISSN 1465-8488

All rights reserved. No part of this book may be reprinted or reproduced or utilised in any form or by any electronic, mechanical, or other means, now known or hereafter invented, including photocopying and recording, or in any information storage or retrieval system, without permission in writing from the publishers.

Typeset in ClassGarmnd by Frank Cass
Printed and bound in Great Britain by MPG Books Ltd, Bodmin

To the memory of my parents

Contents

List of Illustrations ix
List of Maps x
List of Tables xi
Series Editor's Preface xiii
Foreword by David French xv
Acknowledgements xvii
Abbreviations xviii

Introduction 1

1 The Base at Malta in the 1920s 6

2 The Failure to Strengthen Malta's Defences, 1930–35 20

3 Malta in the Abyssinian Crisis, 1935–36 35

4 Prelude to War, 1936–39 49

5 Final Preparations for War 64

6 The Threat of Invasion 76

7 The Initial Onslaught 91

8 The German Intervention in the Mediterranean in 1941 107

9 Malta's Contribution to 'Crusader' 123

10 The 1942 Siege of Malta 143

11 Malta's Contribution to the Recovery of North Africa 159

| 12 | Conclusion | 181 |

Appendix: Axis Supply and Shipping Losses   191
Notes   193
References   215
Index   225

Illustrations

1 Aircraft over the Grand Harbour, Valletta, 1931
2 Submarine base at Manoel Island
3 Hurricanes at Takali airfield
4 Tunnelling work in Valletta
5 Air attack on HMS *Illustrious*, January 1941
6 Bofors AA position in Valletta
7 Wellington bomber at Luqa airfield
8 Albacore torpedo bomber at Hal Far airfield
9 Air attack on SS *Talabot* in the Grand Harbour
10 Bomb damage in Valletta, 1942
11 General Dobbie, Air Marshal Tedder and Sir Walter Monckton at Valletta in April 1942
12 The visit of the Prime Minister, Winston Churchill, to Malta, November 1943

All prints reproduced courtesy of the Imperial War Museum. Crown copyright.

Maps

		pages
1	Malta, showing airfields in April 1942	13
2	Radius of action of aircraft from Malta, 1942	126
3	Axis air and sea transport routes, October 1942–May 1943	163

Tables

		pages
1	Heavy anti-aircraft guns on 1 February 1940	68
2	Number of air raid alerts in 1940	103
3	Proportion of Axis ships sunk by Malta forces, January–May 1941	115
4	Axis supplies landed and percentages lost, January–May 1941	115
5	Number of bombing and strafing attacks on Malta, January–May 1941	116
6	Aircraft serviceable within 14 days, June–December 1941	127
7	Proportion of Axis ships sunk by Malta forces, June–October 1941	134
8	Axis supplies landed and percentages lost, June–October 1941	134
9	Proportion of Axis ships sunk by Malta forces, November–December 1941	135
10	Axis supplies landed and percentages lost, November–December 1941	136
11	Axis supplies landed in North Africa, June–December 1941	138
12	Axis supplies landed and percentages lost, January–May 1942	150
13	Proportion of Axis ships sunk by Malta forces, January–May 1942	151
14	Bomb tonnage dropped on Malta, 1942	152

15	Axis supplies landed and percentages lost, June–October 1942	164
16	Proportion of Axis ships sunk by Malta forces, June–October 1942	166
17	Axis supplies landed and percentages lost, November 1942–May 1943	177
18	Proportion of Axis ships sunk by Malta forces, November 1942–May 1943	178
19	Axis supply and shipping losses in the central Mediterranean, 1940–1943	188

Series Editor's Preface

INTRODUCTION

The role played by the island of Malta, and more particularly by the aircraft, ships and submarines based there, in the Mediterranean war has been and remains a controversial one. Historians have divided sharply on the impact made by the operations of those forces on Rommel's campaign in North Africa, some believing them to have made a crucial contribution to the Axis defeat and others claiming that their role was secondary at best. The controversy has been a lively one in Italy too, where the failure to attempt Operation C3 and knock the island out of the war has generated a considerable literature, as has the question of whether the interdiction of supplies to North Africa was or was not a central fact in explaining the outcome of the desert war. In a related field, Malta has by contrast been conspicuous largely by its absence. In all the work which has now been published on British defence policy in the inter-war years, Malta has figured little – and then all too often simply as an example of neglect, justifiable or not according to the outlook of the author.

The pre-history of Malta before 1939, as Douglas Austin shows in this book, goes back at least to 1923. Within eight years, the authorities envisaged the possibility of a massed air attack by Italy's Regia Aeronautica – whose strength and capability they considerably over-estimated. In the intense competition for limited resources in the early 1930s, the island had to compete with Singapore but although it was accorded a low priority, it was by no means ignored altogether. Its misfortune, as will become apparent in the pages that follow, was to fall between two stools as Great Britain rearmed for war against Germany and sought to defend its Far eastern interests against Japan. Although it was not, as Lord Chatfield acknowledge, of critical importance the Mediterranean crisis of 1935 and its aftermath raised important considerations about its potential role in war and particularly about its function in relation to the defence of Egypt. Without the understanding of the defence debates which both preceded and followed the Abyssinian war and which is provided here it is impossible fairly to judge whether myopia, distraction or simply the more pressing nature of other difficulties best explains the attitude taken by the authorities to the island at the time.

Malta's war-time history is closely bound up with Winston Churchill, who made his first important intervention when he was instrumental in rejecting the First Sea Lord's proposal in June 1940 to withdraw the Mediterranean fleet to Gibraltar. Its importance as an active piece on the strategic chessboard came when Marshal Graziani invaded Egypt in September 1940, when it immediately presented an ideal base from which to interdict Italian and later Axis supply lines. The sharp differences between the Royal Navy and the Royal Air Force in the months and years which followed about which service should do what and whether either was bearing more than its share of the burden provide an important insight into the difficulties of inter-service collaboration. The disputes on the Axis side, if briefer, were more fundamental and perhaps in the long run more important as the Germans made it plain that they did not want to occupy Malta while the Italians concluded that they could not do so. Douglas Austin's conclusion that, had Malta been in Italian hands by the autumn of 1942, 'a better supplied Axis force in North Africa might have fought the 8th Army to a standstill' is a thought-provoking example of the illumination that modest but well-founded counterfactual history can provide.

The award of the George Cross to the island on 16 April 1942 made Malta a symbol of resistance against the odds. Keeping the island going until its siege ended in December of that year is an important facet of this study. Resistance demanded a lot of the islanders, and a lot also of the officials responsible for running it and fighting from it, at least one of whom was quite understandably worn down almost to collapse by the strain. There was much heroism in Malta's war-time story – but properly to analyse its contribution requires dispassionate examination of the evidence of its activities, much of which is embedded in the graphs and tables of ships sunk and planes downed and in calculations of cargoes destroyed and petrol undelivered. With all this evidence now laid before us, we can see the force of Douglas Austin's conclusion that without Malta's contribution the conquest of North Africa might have taken at least a year longer.

John Gooch

Foreword

'Since the acquisition of Malta the position of the British Empire as a leading Mediterranean Power has never been questioned either in peace or war, and the possession of the two fortresses of Gibraltar and Valetta fixes the hold upon the waters of Southern Europe which Charles II dreamt of, and which Rooke and Leake and Stanhope, instigated by Marlborough, first definitely secured. Naval warfare is not a war of posts. But its true object, the breaking of the enemy's power at sea, cannot be achieved without posts. And the history of the Mediterranean since the days of Blake shows how greatly maritime preponderance depends upon the possession of bases whither fleets can repair to make good damages, to replenish stores and ammunition, and to rest during periods when conditions of the campaign permit them to lie in port.'

C. E. Callwell, *Military Operations and Maritime Preponderance: Their Relations and Interdependence* (London, William Blackwood, 1905), pp. 73–4

Charles Callwell was a soldier, but he knew how important base facilities were to the successful exercise of naval power. Historians have sometimes fallen into the fallacy of measuring the relative naval strength of the powers simply by counting battleships. They have forgotten that fleets cannot maintain themselves at sea for very long without safe harbours where their ships can be repaired and re-supplied and their crews rested. Malta fulfilled this role for Britain's fleet in the central Mediterranean.

But when Callwell wrote his assessment of the importance of the Mediterranean to Britain's status as a great power, and of Malta to Britain's power in the Mediterranean, air power was hardly even in its infancy. Thirty years later, it had developed so rapidly that it called into question not only Britain's ability to use Malta as a base for offensive operations against the Axis powers, but also its ability to maintain it as a garrison outpost. Yet, as Douglas Austin makes apparent in this meticulously researched study, the British never seriously considered abandoning the island. The advent of air power did make Malta vulnerable to attack in a way that it had not been in the eighteenth or nineteenth centuries. But by the same token, air power also offered

Malta the opportunity both to defend itself and to strike back against its assailants.

The role of Malta both before and during the Second World War is frequently alluded to in books about British defence policy between the wars and British strategy in the Mediterranean and North Africa during the Second World War, but it is rarely discussed in detail. Austin has done an important service by filling this gap and by demolishing two powerful and misleading myths. He has produced the first detailed assessment of the debate that was conducted between the British service ministries and the Cabinet about the role of Malta in a future Mediterranean war. In doing so, he has undermined the notion that the Admiralty was ready to give up the island as being indefensible. What was lacking was not resolve to defend the island, but the resources to do so. Secondly, he has revised the revisionists; his careful analysis of the extant evidence shows conclusively that Malta-based forces did indeed play a vital role in interdicting Axis supply lines to Rommel at vital moments during the war in North Africa. This book shows why Malta mattered to the British, and what they were prepared to do to retain it.

David French
University College London

Acknowledgements

My thanks are due first to Professor David French of University College London who has kindly written the foreword to this book. It was under his supervision that the University of London Doctoral thesis, from which this book is derived, was researched and written, and I am indebted to him for his expert guidance over many years. I am also indebted to Professor Kathleen Burk for valuable advice and insights during the course of this work.

Much of the research for this study was carried out at the Public Record Office at Kew, and I am grateful, as all researchers at Kew must be, to the efficiency and helpfulness of all the PRO staff. The official documents held there are Crown Copyright and permission to quote from these documents is hereby acknowledged. The three maps reproduced in this book are taken from The Official History of the Second World War, *The Mediterranean and Middle East*. These too are Crown Copyright material and are reproduced with the permission of the Controller of HMSO and Queen's Printer for Scotland.

I am grateful to Sebastian Cox, Director of the Air Historical Branch of the Ministry of Defence, London, for allowing me to read through several documents still held in the Branch. My thanks are due, too, to the Trustees of the National Maritime Museum, Greenwich, for permission to include several quotations from the Papers of Admiral of the Fleet Lord Chatfield in their possession. The photographs included in this volume are all held by the Imperial War Museum, London. I am grateful to the staff of the Photographic Archive for their help in choosing a few of the many hundreds which depict aspects of Malta before and during the Second World War. These are also Crown Copyright and permission to reproduce these is hereby acknowledged.

Last, but by no means least, my thanks are due to my wife and family for constant encouragement and support, and for their valiant attempts to interest themselves in events long past. Visits to the warm and welcoming island of Malta were but a partial reward.

Abbreviations

AA	anti-aircraft
ACM	Air Chief Marshal
ADGB	Air Defence of Great Britain
AHB	Air Historical Branch
AM	Air Marshal
AOC	Air Officer Commanding
AOC-in-C	Air Officer Commanding-in-Chief
A/S	anti-submarine
ASV	Air-to-Surface Vessel radar
AVM	Air Vice-Marshal
BEF	British Expeditionary Force
CAS	Chief of the Air Staff
CID	Committee of Imperial Defence
CIGS	Chief of the Imperial General Staff
C-in-C	Commander-in-Chief
CNS	Chief of the Naval Staff
CO	Colonial Office; Commanding Officer
COS	Chiefs of Staff (Committee)
CSS	Chief of the Secret Service
CU	Consumption Unit
DAK	*Deutsches Afrika Korps*
DBFP	Documents on British Foreign Policy
DCAS	Deputy Chief of the Air Staff
DCNS	Deputy Chief of the Naval Staff
DCOS	Deputy Chiefs of Staff (Committee)
DDI	*Documenti Diplomatici Italiani*
DDMOI	Deputy Director of Military Operations and Intelligence
DDNI	Deputy Director of Naval Intelligence
D/F	direction finding
DGFP	*Documents on German Foreign Policy*
DMOI	Director of Military Operations and Intelligence
DNI	Director of Naval Intelligence
DOP	Defence of Ports Committee; Director of Plans

ABBREVIATIONS

DP(P)	Defence Plans (Policy) Committee
DPRC	Defence Policy and Requirements Committee
DRC	Defence Requirements Committee
EDS	Enemy Documents Section
FAA	Fleet Air Arm
FM	Field Marshal
GC&CS	Government Code and Cypher School
GOC	General Officer Commanding
HMSO	His/Her Majesty's Stationery Office
HQ	headquarters
JDC	Joint Oversea and Home Defence Committee
JIC	Joint Intelligence Committee
JPC	Joint Planning Committee
JPS	Joint Planning Staff
KOMR	King's Own Malta Regiment
Lt-Gov.	Lieutenant-Governor
MCC	Military Co-ordination Committee
MEDC	Middle East Defence Committee
MEIC	Middle East Intelligence Centre
MRA	Marshal of the Royal Air Force
MTB	motor torpedo boat
NID	Naval Intelligence Division
ODC	Oversea Defence Committee
OKW	Oberkommando der Wehrmacht (German High Command)
PR	photo-reconnaissance
PRO	Public Record Office
RAF	Royal Air Force
RDF	radio direction-finding (later 'radar')
RMA	Royal Malta Artillery
R/T	radio telephony
SAC	Strategical Appreciation Committee
SASO	Senior Air Staff Officer
Sigint	Signals Intelligence
SIS	Secret Intelligence Service
SO(I)	Staff Officer (Intelligence)
SLU	Special Liaison Unit
USMM	Ufficio Storico della Marina Militare
VA	Vice-Admiral
VAM	Vice-Admiral Malta
VCAS	Vice-Chief of the Air Staff
VCIGS	Vice-Chief of the Imperial General Staff
VCNS	Vice-Chief of the Naval Staff
W/T	wireless telegraphy

Introduction

Much has been written about Malta's experiences during the Second World War, and, 60 years later, new books and articles about Malta continue to find publishers and readers. The great majority of these publications deal with specific aspects of the air and naval warfare that centred on Malta between June 1940 and the end of 1943. Most begin with some review of pre-war decisions and preparations, or the absence of them, in order to provide a strategic framework that explains Malta's condition at the outbreak of the war with Italy. Most also point out that the island's anti-aircraft (AA) gun defences in June 1940 were limited, and, in particular, that there were no modern fighter aircraft stationed on the island. The Royal Air Force (RAF) in Malta could only put up three obsolete Gladiators – the famous 'Faith', 'Hope' and 'Charity' – to meet the early Italian air raids.

These undisputed facts about Malta's defences in 1940, coupled with the departure of the Mediterranean Fleet to Alexandria, have led to a widespread acceptance of the view that the British government had decided not to defend Malta should Italy attack the island. For example, in a recently published book about the campaign in Tunisia Alan Levine writes of Malta: 'Surrounded by enemy bases, it had been written off as untenable.'[1] In the same vein, Charles Jellison concluded that 'although no official document says as much, it is clear that sometime during the years immediately preceding the war the British government reached the decision not to defend Malta in the event of a conflict with Italy'.[2] However, in the summer of 1939 Malta was the first British overseas base to be provided with still highly secret radar equipment. Furthermore, in the ten months between the outbreak of war with Germany and Italy's declaration of war in June 1940, 18 more AA guns, of which there was a desperate shortage in England, were shipped to Malta. Finally, on 16 May, *after* the German breakthrough in the Ardennes, the British government authorised the despatch of a fifth battalion of infantry to strengthen the island's garrison. These facts alone are sufficient to raise doubts about the validity of the judgements quoted above.

1

As to the wartime years, differing assessments have been offered about the actual benefits that Britain gained from the retention and sustenance of Malta. One group holds the view that the Mediterranean war, sometimes even the whole war, could not have been won had Malta been lost. Captain Donald Macintyre, for example, has written that on the struggle to maintain Malta 'depended, absolutely, the success or failure of the campaigns in North Africa and hence, it can be said, of the whole war'.[3] Opposed to them is a somewhat smaller group that endorses the view, first propounded by Martin Van Creveld in 1977, that Rommel's ultimate defeat in the desert owed almost nothing to the loss of sea-borne supplies, the interruption of which was Malta's primary strategic task. Rather, his supply problems were due, principally, to inadequate transport resources and limited port capacity in North Africa.[4] Accepting this interpretation, Correlli Barnett concluded that the damage caused to Axis convoys by Malta's limited forces 'can in no sense be said to justify on objective strategic grounds the grievous losses incurred . . . in keeping the island going'.[5] Italian naval historians have also reached differing conclusions. Commander Bragadin regarded Malta as 'the principal factor' in Allied victory, whereas Dr Giorgerini considered Malta to be a serious menace in only three months of a conflict that lasted three years.[6]

These divergent opinions about Malta's condition in 1940 and its contribution to the war in the Mediterranean stem largely from the absence of an analysis that focuses on the strategic debates and decisions that affected Malta during the inter-war period and what Malta's forces actually achieved during the war. The first part of this study seeks to correct this by tracing from the mid-1920s the continual consideration given by the British authorities to the role that Malta might be called upon to play in a future war, and how it should be equipped to carry out that role. It then considers the decisions that were taken as war with Italy grew nearer, and what was done, and not done, to implement those decisions. The impact of internal developments in Malta on the island's strategic value is also examined. Italian government support for the Maltese Nationalist Party, which had in 1933 pursued policies that led to the suspension of the constitution, raised the possibility that the naval dockyard might become unusable if the Maltese were no longer prepared to accept British colonial rule. The measures taken in Whitehall and Valletta to deal with this problem need to be examined to determine whether the military value of Malta was jeopardised by a failure to retain Maltese support for British policies.

The second part of this study examines and weighs Malta's contribution to the fighting that began in June 1940 and ended with the clearance of North Africa in May 1943. The central task given to its naval and air commanders was to destroy, damage or delay the seaborne flow of men, equipment and supplies to the Axis armies in North Africa. Consequently, the degree to which this task was accomplished is an important and the most visible yardstick of Malta's value. It was not, however, the only advantage that Britain derived from the retention of Malta and a correct overall assessment of the island's wartime value requires due consideration of these frequently ignored benefits.

Since a number of questionable interpretations and judgements have become embedded in the historiography concerning the island, the analysis presented in these pages is based primarily on the contemporary records of those who weighed the problems posed by Malta, and took the decisions. Those who believe that Malta's needs were neglected in the pre-war period might be astonished at the enormous number of documents in the British Public Record Office (PRO) that relate to Malta. These range from the Papers and Conclusions of the Cabinet, through the records of the Colonial Office and the Service departments, to those of the Committee of Imperial Defence (CID), the Chiefs of Staff Committee (COS), and of the many standing or ad hoc sub-committees that dealt with specific problems. For our purposes the records of the Joint Home and Oversea Defence Committee (JDC) are essential reading. The defence of Malta appears on the JDC agenda on hundreds of occasions between 1925 and 1939, and this committee's deliberations generated the papers that went up to the COS, CID and, on occasions, to the Cabinet for final debate and decision.

Malta is no less prominent in the wartime records, particularly after Italy entered the war in June 1940. The daily, or often twice daily, meetings of the COS or Defence Committee, together with the supporting work of the Service departments, gave rise to another enormous archive of Malta-related material. The Prime Minister's files about Malta, for example, run to no fewer than 1,000 pages. This archive has, in recent years, been further expanded by the deposit of a great many of the thousands of Italian and German signals, whose interception and decryption played such a large part in the attacks launched by Malta's forces on Italian supply convoys. These are complemented by the post-war records of the Historical Branches of the Admiralty and Air Ministry, which went to great lengths to compile accurate records showing the loss of each enemy ship in the Mediterranean, and the cause of her loss. These analyses, which draw on official Italian and German records, are indispensable for any attempt to assess Malta's contribution to the Mediterranean war.

The secondary-source material bearing on the first part of this study is limited. This is not because there have not been valuable studies of British inter-war military strategy, but because the particular place of Malta in strategic planning has attracted only sporadic attention. An illustration of this occurs in the period of the Abyssinian crisis between mid-1935 and mid-1936. The sudden threat of a war with Italy has merited a full chapter in most of the histories of the pre-war years. Typical is Professor Gibbs's account in Chapter VI of the first volume of the *Grand Strategy* official history series.[7] Apart from the discussion in this chapter, however, Malta makes few appearances in the rest of this lengthy review of pre-war strategic planning.

Based on then unpublished official documents General Playfair's six-volume official history of the war in the Mediterranean and Middle East is indispensable for an understanding of the course of the war in that very large area.[8] However, the first volume devotes only 40 pages to the period before August 1939, of which only two pages relate to Malta. The treatment in those pages hardly does justice to the complexity of the problem posed by Malta in the event of war with Italy. A further page briefly refers to Malta just before the first Italian attack, but, unusually, errs in implying that no additional AA guns were sent to the island between August 1939 and the outbreak of the war with Italy. In the official British naval history of the war, *The War at Sea*, Captain Roskill wrote that 'Malta was considered indefensible against Italian air power and no serious attempt was made to defend it until it was almost too late'. This in itself is a questionable statement but Roskill was simply incorrect when he wrote in the subsequent one-volume history that he produced for the United States Naval Institute that 'the British Government [had] accepted the Army and Air Force view that Malta could not be defended against Italian air power'.[9] On the contrary, as we shall see, the British government in 1939 came to the opposite conclusion when they authorised a major strengthening of Malta's defences. Much detail about the gun defences of Malta is contained in Denis Rollo's encyclopaedic *The Guns and Gunners of Malta*, recently published in Valletta.[10] This draws on War Office records to illustrate the renovation of Malta's coastal artillery in the 1930s and the establishment of the AA defences.

For the wartime period the secondary sources are extensive and continue to grow. Much of this, however, is mainly of operational interest, such as Tony Spooner's *Supreme Gallantry*.[11] The six volumes of Playfair's official Middle East history, already mentioned, cover the ground in great detail, but were written before the appearance of Hinsley's official intelligence history.[12] The Middle East was a fruitful field for the interception and decryption of enemy signals since nearly all the communications were 'on the air'. Moreover, the code breakers at Bletchley Park were, by mid-1942, able to read almost all of the cyphers used by the enemy, including several relating to supply matters and Italian supply convoys. These were invaluable in enabling the commanders at Cairo and Malta to plan attacks, particularly on tankers.

INTRODUCTION

The detailed analysis contained in Hinsley's volumes, supported by the deposit of many of the related intercepts in the PRO, is essential for a correct assessment of Rommel's recurrent supply difficulties, and of Malta's contribution to them.

A thorough analysis of the Mediterranean war from the German perspective is contained in the third and sixth volumes of *Germany and the Second World War,* with sections by various writers.[13] The German view from 'the other side of the hill' can also be seen in various books and articles written by senior German officers. *The Rommel Papers* is uneven, being a post-war edited collection of Rommel's diaries and papers.[14] The book nevertheless records the frequent occasions when supply difficulties endangered or limited his operations. Rommel's assessment of Malta's contribution to these difficulties is contained in a famous phrase: 'Malta has the lives of many thousands of German and Italian soldiers on its conscience.' Finally, Italian historians have devoted much attention to the war in the Mediterranean, although very little of this has been translated into English. Commander Bragadin's book, mentioned above, draws on the 19-volume official Italian naval history of the war published by Ufficio Storico della Marina Militare (USMM).[15] A number of these volumes contain material relevant to this study, including, in particular, three volumes devoted to the defence of the convoys to the Axis armies in North Africa.

These and the many other secondary sources consulted in the preparation of this study are identified in the relevant footnotes and references. However, as noted earlier, greater attention has been paid to official records and other contemporary evidence. The still growing volume of British official records, particularly intelligence files, allows more balanced judgements to be made about the pre-war planning related to Malta and the contribution made by its forces to the war in the Mediterranean than was possible in earlier post-war years.

1

The Base at Malta in the 1920s

MALTA'S ROLE IN IMPERIAL STRATEGY

It is not easy now to appreciate the value attached to Malta by the British government in the period between the two world wars. Malta, after gaining its independence in 1964, became a republic in 1971, and although British and NATO forces continued to use the island's military facilities for several years, the last British naval, army and air force units left the island in April 1979. The first task, therefore, is to understand why Malta was held to be of such importance in the pre-war years, and to seek the reasons for this we need to return to the 1920s.

After the end of the First World War, one of the many decisions facing the Admiralty was the distribution of the fleet, and, in particular, the strength and composition of the force to be stationed in the Mediterranean. There was, however, no question about the most suitable base for such a force. Since Malta had become a British colony in 1814, and especially after the opening of the Suez Canal in 1869, the island had become the Royal Navy's main base in the Mediterranean. Valletta's fine harbours had docks capable of handling the navy's largest ships, and its extensive repair and storage facilities had been continually modernised and expanded to meet the navy's changing requirements. Moreover, the position of Malta in the centre of the Mediterranean made it a natural base from which to watch over British interests in the area. Prior to the First World War, therefore, the Malta-based Mediterranean Fleet had at times included as many as 14 battleships, although all of these were steadily withdrawn before 1914 to meet the threat posed by Germany.[1] The post-war decision about the Mediterranean Fleet became the more urgent because attempts to support anti-bolshevik armies from the Black Sea in 1918–20, and the subsequent British involvement in the Greek conflict with Turkey which led to the Chanak crisis of 1922, had already compelled the Admiralty to transfer additional ships to the eastern Mediterranean.[2]

Practical considerations of this kind, as well as broader issues of naval policy, confronted the Board of Admiralty in the early 1920s when it was considering where to place its fleets. In resolving this matter the Board had to take account of two new post-war developments. First, by virtue of financial pressures that saw the naval estimates fall from £158 million in 1919–20 to £58 million in 1923–24,[3] and the effects of the Washington Naval Treaty of 1922, the total number of the navy's ships, and particularly its battleships, was very significantly reduced. Second, the Admiralty had, since 1919, felt it necessary to consider the possibility of war with Japan.[4] The Anglo-Japanese Treaty, which had made Japan an ally in the First World War, was not renewed in 1922, and although she had accepted a 60 per cent limitation on her capital ships compared with the United States and Great Britain,[5] the Admiralty felt it could not ignore the potential threat posed by Japan's fleet of ten capital ships. It was this concern which led to the decision by the Cabinet, in June 1921, to authorise the construction of a new naval base at Singapore, albeit at a pace which would preclude its completion for many years.[6]

In its post-war deliberations about fleet distribution, the Admiralty adhered to what it considered to be the correct principles of naval strategy. These were set out clearly in a memorandum prepared by the Oversea Defence Committee (ODC), paragraph 10 of which pointed out, 'Our naval strategy . . . is based on the principle that a fleet of adequate strength, suitably disposed geographically and concentrated against the enemy's fleet, provides the "cover" under which security is given to widely dispersed territories and trade routes.'[7] The vital importance of fleet mobility was also emphasised, and, in order to maintain this mobility, 'defended bases are necessary at strategic points throughout the Empire'. With these precepts firmly in mind, the Board of Admiralty in 1923 decided, as part of its post-Washington Treaty strategy, to strengthen the Mediterranean Fleet at Malta.[8] It gave two reasons for so doing. First, the Mediterranean was a vital area in terms of British and imperial interests. Through it ran the principal trade route to India and the eastern empire, and although plans were made to divert shipping around the Cape in an emergency, this would add considerably to the costs of imperial trade.[9] Furthermore, the incipient bellicosity of fascist Italy, demonstrated in the Corfu incident in 1923, although as yet an irritant rather than an immediate danger, could not be wholly ignored. In addition, Britain needed to ensure the safety of the Persian Gulf and Iraqi oil fields, now that its economy and armed services were becoming increasingly dependent on oil. Nevertheless, these interests might have been safeguarded by basing at Malta a squadron of battleships and support ships, to be reinforced as necessary from the Atlantic Fleet, as was the policy in the immediate post-war years.

It was, however, the second reason that had the greater influence on the decision to position a major fleet at Malta, and this was the intention that this fleet would proceed to the defence, or relief, of Singapore should this become necessary.[10] A fleet based in Malta could reach Singapore ten days earlier than one sailing from home waters, and this time saving was regarded as critical.[11] At first sight this may seem a strange decision, since Malta is over 6,000 miles from Singapore, and it was estimated that it would take at least six weeks even for a Malta-based relieving force to reach Singapore. There was, however, little choice in this matter simply because the navy's ports east of Suez could not accommodate its modern battleships. Prior to the First World War docking facilities at Singapore, Hong Kong and Colombo were adequate for the battleships of that era, but the increasing size of more recently built capital ships had not been matched by a comparable increase in dock size at those ports. Although the Admiralty maintained a force of cruisers and destroyers at Hong Kong, Britain had agreed, by the terms of the Washington Treaty, not to expand facilities at this port, while other ports on the route to Singapore, such as Bombay, Trincomali and Rangoon, could only be developed as supply and refuelling stations. It was this very problem which had prompted the decision to build a completely new base at Singapore, but, until it was completed, Malta was the closest fully equipped fleet base. Even at Malta there were difficulties. In the first place, Valletta's harbours were not large enough to accommodate all the ships allocated to the expanded Mediterranean Fleet, and Gibraltar had to be used as an 'overflow' base.[12] Second, Malta's graving docks would not be wide enough to take the fleet's largest capital ships once anti-torpedo bulges had been added to their sides. This problem was met in part by towing a floating dock out from England, but it was also agreed that half of the fleet would return to home ports each year to refit.[13]

Despite these unavoidable difficulties, Malta was chosen as the base for what was soon to be designated the 'Main Fleet', and this decision was reinforced in 1924–25 when the Admiralty's Far East plans were affected by major changes in government policy. The initial shock was the decision of the first Labour government in 1924 to cease work at Singapore.[14] Although this decision was reversed later in that year when Baldwin was re-elected, the new Chancellor, Churchill, then launched a vigorous attack on the financial implications of the Admiralty's strategic plans. To help them in these discussions the Cabinet invited the CID to assess the current and foreseeable risk posed by Japan, and the CID, in April 1925, endorsed the judgement of the Foreign Secretary, Austen Chamberlain, that 'aggressive action . . . on the part of Japan within the next ten years is not a contingency seriously to be apprehended'.[15] The upshot was a Cabinet decision which effectively deferred completion of the Singapore base until 1935.[16]

In the course of these discussions the Cabinet had enquired what the Admiralty's interim war plan was 'in the event of war occurring before the base at Singapore was capable of sustaining a British fleet superior to the Japanese navy'. Admiral Beatty, the First Sea Lord, responded to this at a meeting of the CID in April 1925,[17] and although no notes were taken of his statement, the Admiralty's plans of August 1924[18] show that virtually all of the Mediterranean Fleet, except possibly the older, coal-burning, *Iron Duke* battleships, were to proceed to Singapore. Although the Admiralty reserved its decision about the command of the Main Fleet when it reached Singapore, it ordered that 'the C-in-C Mediterranean will, during peace time, be responsible that the arrangements for the rapid passage of the Fleet to the East are kept fully prepared'.[19] In compliance with these instructions, Admiral Sir Roger Keyes, the Commander-in-Chief (C-in-C) of the Mediterranean Fleet at that time, carried out a number of exercises with this object in mind.[20]

The importance of Malta in the mid-1920s should, therefore, be seen in a global context rather than simply in Mediterranean terms. Although the defence of area interests was an immediate and important task, the Malta-based Main Fleet also bore the ultimate responsibility for protecting India and the whole eastern empire. The continued postponement of work at Singapore inevitably placed great weight on the strength and mobility of the Mediterranean Fleet and made it all the more important that Malta, with its vital docking and repair facilities, should be secure from attack. As the Director of the Admiralty's Operations Division pointed out in 1923: 'One bomb on the floating dock would be fatal.'[21]

THE DEFENCE OF OVERSEAS PORTS

Malta, however important, was only one of Britain's many naval ports around the world, and the system that operated in the 1920s to ensure that these bases were effectively defended now needs to be examined. The CID, which advised pre-war governments on all defence matters, in turn appointed various sub-committees to investigate particular problems. However, even before the CID was constituted in 1904, the ODC was charged with the responsibility for the defence of overseas ports, while the Home Defence Committee kept under review the defences of ports in the British Isles. Although the ODC retained a prime responsibility for the overseas ports, particular matters were increasingly considered by a joint committee of the Home and Oversea bodies, referred to in brief as the Joint Defence Committee (JDC). This committee first met in March 1920, when it decided to set up a Technical Sub-Committee to examine, in the light of war experience, the defensive needs of each port.[22] The planning staffs of the three services supplied the members of this sub-committee, and it is usually referred to as the Defence of Ports Committee (DOP). It is with the proceedings, papers and reports of the JDC and the DOP that we will be most concerned in the following pages, although some questions continued to be dealt with by the ODC.[23]

When the Chiefs of Staff were preparing their first Annual Review of Imperial Defence Policy in 1926, Sir Maurice Hankey, Secretary of the CID, produced his own memorandum about the many matters that had been considered since 1920, and Part II of this described the work carried out in the preceding five years by the committees considering the defence of ports.[24] As he explained it, the initial work of the JDC was 'overhauling, in the light of war experience, the general principles on which our coast defences are based'. This led to the presentation to the CID in July 1923 of a memorandum entitled 'Coast Defence. Forms of Attack and Forms of Defence', and this was subsequently revised in November 1927.[25] Assessments of the 'Scale of Attack' that might be expected at each port were the responsibility of the relevant service, and these were continually revised to reflect changing circumstances. The result of all the discussions about a particular port was the preparation of a 'Defence Scheme', which was a very detailed manual specifying how attacks were to be met, and in which the roles of all three services were clearly set out. The 1935 Malta Defence Scheme, for example, runs to over 300 typed foolscap pages.[26]

The obvious need to conserve resources and allocate them efficiently led to the production of two further documents. The first was an 'Order of Priority for Installation of Armament', in which Malta was placed sixth after Singapore, Hong Kong and the ports east of Suez, while the second was a 'Classification of Ports', which the JDC recommended to the CID in June 1928.[27] This second paper divided all the many defended ports into three categories, within which 'Category A' ports were those 'at which adequate defences should be installed in peace time to be fully manned and efficient before the outbreak of hostilities'. Malta was placed in this category. It was within the terms set out in this elaborate but flexible conceptual framework that the various committees charged with the updating of port defences began their work in the 1920s. In early 1926 the attention of the DOP was directed to the Mediterranean ports, that is Malta and Gibraltar.[28]

Although the navy was the principal beneficiary of ports defence, its doctrines of mobility and concentration of force precluded its taking a significant part in the defence of any port. The basis of the Admiralty's strategy was that, if any port were subjected to attack, an appropriate force would be concentrated and sent to its relief. Consequently, the 'period before relief' became an important element in the planning of a Defence Scheme. The result of this thinking was that the navy's only committed contribution to port defence was the provision of light coastal forces, and such passive measures as harbour booms, anti-torpedo baffles and anti-submarine nets. It was the army that was primarily responsible for the defence of overseas ports. First, it provided a garrison of a size and composition determined by the port's strategic importance and its vulnerability to potential attack. This might include one or more battalions of the regular army, supported in some cases, as at Malta, by local militia under British officers. Its second obligation was to provide guns and their crews. Before the First World War this meant heavy, fixed, coastal artillery capable of engaging enemy warships at long range, together with some mobile field artillery to support the anti-invasion role of the garrison. To this was added, after the war, a growing requirement for anti-aircraft guns.

However, it was the contribution of the RAF to the defence of Malta that was to present the greatest difficulty, and indeed dispute, throughout the inter-war period. This will be traced in the following chapters, but it will be useful at the outset to introduce two major strands in the doctrine established for the RAF by its first Chief of the Air Staff (CAS), Sir Hugh Trenchard. First, Trenchard, in his fight to maintain the independence of the RAF, insisted that the proper function of an air force was to attack the enemy's sources of production and supply. He did not believe that fighter defence against bomber attack was possible and defensive measures were taken, in the main, only to meet public and political demands.[29] One consequence of this thinking was that the RAF's limited resources were devoted to bomber development and production at the expense of fighters. When a 52-squadron Home Defence Air Force was agreed in 1923, Trenchard proposed that the bomber squadrons should outnumber fighters in the ratio of two to one.

A second element in Trenchard's thinking was his insistence that the RAF could and should take over certain imperial defence responsibilities from the other services. Among these was his claim that the RAF should play a larger role in the defence of ports. His basic thesis was that, in many cases, the RAF could more effectively, and *more economically*, defend a port such as Malta from sea attack than coastal artillery because its aircraft, armed with bombs or torpedoes, could sink or drive off a bombarding or invading force well beyond the range of the heaviest coastal guns. Moreover, defence costs could be pared since, whereas heavy artillery at each defended port was expensive to install and maintain, and might never come into action, the aircraft substituted for these guns would not be tied to any particular port, but could be moved to a point of danger on the same principles as were applied by the Admiralty. It was not difficult for Chancellors to see attractions in such a policy.

This particular dispute came to a crisis in July 1926 when the Chiefs of Staff were trying to reach agreement on the defences to be installed at the new base at Singapore. Trenchard was vehemently opposed to the planned installation of 15-inch guns there, and refused to accept the equally adamant views of his two colleagues. However, after a personal appeal from Admiral Beatty, the First Sea Lord, Trenchard eventually relented and accepted that the first three such guns should be installed, provided that the whole question of substituting aircraft for guns was reviewed again before the second stage of the Singapore defence plan was implemented.[30] His final statement on this long-running battle with the other services was contained in a memorandum that he submitted directly to the Cabinet when he retired in 1929.[31] In one of several attached supplementary memoranda, Trenchard set out again his argument for the employment of aircraft in coast defence, concluding that 'a share in the responsibility for coast defence should be allotted to Air Forces in substitution for guns of calibre greater than 6-inch'.

The RAF's doctrinaire aversion to fighter-based defensive operations, and its particular opposition to heavy coastal artillery, was at times to make it an awkward contributor to discussions about Malta's defences in the pre-war years.

MALTA'S DEFENCES IN THE 1920S

At this juncture it may be helpful to describe briefly the mid-1920s defence establishment at Malta in order to provide a background to the review of the DOP discussions (see Map 1). Valletta's two harbours, the Grand Harbour to the south and Marsamuscetto to the north, were, after additional dredging in 1925, just large enough to accommodate most of the expanded Mediterranean Fleet and its support vessels.[32] The docks, repair yards and storage facilities were spread around the inner part of the Grand Harbour, and gave direct employment at times to as many as 14,000 Maltese workers. The C-in-C Mediterranean Fleet, when not at sea, maintained his headquarters (HQ) at Valletta. The army garrison in 1925 comprised two understrength regular battalions of the British army, with detachments of gunners, sappers and support units. Its C-in-C was the Governor, always a senior military appointment, and in his military role he came under the direct orders of the War Office. The British battalions were supplemented by the King's Own Malta Regiment (KOMR), a locally recruited militia unit that was

MAP 1
MALTA, SHOWING AIRFIELDS IN APRIL 1942

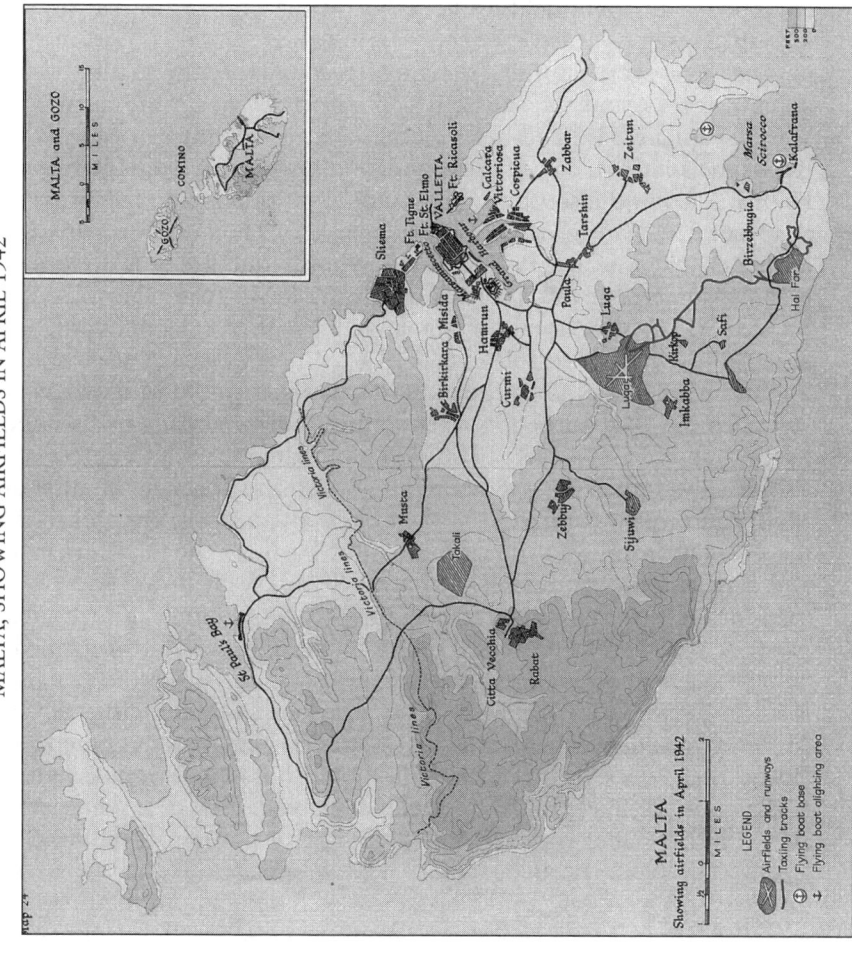

Source: *The Mediterranean and Middle East*, Vol. II, p. 279, Map 24.

converted to a territorial unit in 1928,[33] and by another local unit, the Royal Malta Artillery (RMA), which was a part of the regular army but only available for service in Malta. This unit was also reorganised in the 1920s and it helped to man the coastal artillery located around Valletta and at other key points in the island.[34] These guns were of various calibres up to 9.2-inch, but were all of pre-1914 design with ammunition of equivalent vintage and quality. The garrison was also equipped with some field artillery, but in the mid-1920s had no anti-aircraft guns.[35]

The RAF was naturally the most recent addition to the island's defence forces, and the smallest in numbers.[36] During the First World War a seaplane base had been established at Kalafrana in Marsaxlokk Bay at the southern end of the island, and, in 1923, a landing ground at Hal Far, also in the south of the island, to accommodate the aircraft of the Fleet Air Arm (FAA) when not embarked. The only RAF aircraft at Malta in 1925 were six seaplanes, whose function was to provide reconnaissance, convoy escort, and spotting for the coastal artillery. The RAF at Malta was usually commanded by an Air Commodore, but under the direct control of the Air Ministry. Malta was also an important staging post on the imperial air route to the Middle East.

When the DOP turned its attention to Malta it already had a Report by the ODC to consider.[37] In 1924 the Admiralty had expressed its concern about the vulnerability to air attack of its bases at Gibraltar and Malta, and this was referred to the ODC. An appreciation prepared by the Air Staff in February 1925 formed the basis for the ODC discussion and this assumed an attack by Italy.[38] It observed, however, that the 'present inefficiency' of the Italian air force would limit it to dropping no more than 7 tons of bombs on Malta per day, which it described as 'almost negligible'. Nevertheless, on the assumption that the Italian air force in future years was likely to gain in both size and efficiency, the Air Staff considered the possibility of strengthening aircraft defences to ensure that 'work in the dockyards should not cease'. It asserted that Malta could be made into an 'excellent air base, though at considerable cost', but the paper concluded by arguing that no immediate provision against air attack need be made. This appreciation was not in fact discussed by the ODC until December 1925, when both the Admiralty and War Office members dissented from the view that the air threat was 'negligible'.[39] As a result, the ODC Report, while accepting the main thrust of the Air Staff paper, concluded with a recommendation that 'detailed plans for the aerial defence of Malta should be drawn up at an early stage'. This Report was then referred to the DOP for further consideration.

The DOP held two meetings in early 1928, at which it considered 15 papers prepared by the service staffs. Ten of these related to Malta, mostly dating from 1927 and early 1928. For the review of gun defences a War Office paper set out details of all the existing coastal guns, which comprised 16 9.2-inch, 17 6-inch and 12 12-pounders.[40] It was proposed to reduce the number of 9.2-inch and 6-inch to ten and 12, respectively, but, as the army member pointed out, the reduced number of 9.2-inch were to be converted from Mark V 15° to Mark VII 35° mountings, which would more than double their range from 14,000 to 29,000 yards and also increase their arc of fire. The War Office paper also proposed the installation of 16 3-inch anti-aircraft guns to protect the dockyard, but the navy member objected that this was inadequate given the limited range and ceiling of this weapon. He was told that it was hoped to replace these in due course with a new 4.7-inch gun, although this was still in the experimental stage.

The threats to Malta from air attack and invasion were considered at the DOP's second meeting on 19 July 1928. For this the Air Staff produced a revised estimate of the potential weight of Italian air attack, showing a marked increase from the appreciation made in 1925.[41] It was now thought that the increased strength of the Italian air force in Sicily was such that up to 50 landplanes and 18 seaplanes might be available for an attack on Malta, and that these could deliver up to 25 tons of bombs each day. The memorandum noted Malta's current 'air garrison' of six naval co-operation aircraft, but made no proposals about a strengthening of this, confining its recommendations to that of reserving suitable sites for additional airfields. However, at the DOP's meeting Squadron Leader Bottomley expressed the Air Staff's opinion that it would be desirable 'in order to make effective counter-attacks, to have at Malta three squadrons of bombers, or torpedo-bombers, two squadrons of fighters, and two flights of seaplanes'. Nevertheless, 'even with this force', he warned, 'Malta would be very vulnerable to air attack', and the employment of more aircraft was limited by the lack of landing grounds. The preponderance of bombers in this proposed force reflected the prevailing RAF doctrine noted earlier. There was no suggestion of an all-fighter defence force.

The escalation of the assumed air threat provoked a review of the earlier discussion about anti-aircraft guns, and led to the recommendation that an additional eight should be provided for aerodrome defence. Finally, the DOP took a War Office paper on the defences against invasion.[42] This began with the assumption that the Italian navy could land as many as 12,000 troops in one night with more to follow. To contain this force in the assumed ten-day period before relief arrived, a garrison of four regular battalions was proposed, in addition to the KOMR, and these troops would have substantial field artillery and machine gun support, plus a company of armoured cars. However, before any further meetings could be held, or a report prepared, discussions about Malta, and indeed all other coast defence enquiries, were suspended while bombardment trials were carried out at Malta and Portsmouth. These were designed to test the effectiveness of existing coast defences, and the initial results were so poor that additional trials were undertaken in 1929 and 1930. The consideration of the defences at Malta was, consequently, left in abeyance for a further three years.

This provides a convenient point at which to make an assessment of the state of Malta's defences in the mid-1920s and of the plans that were then being discussed for their improvement. The first point worth noting is that, although appreciations of a possible French attack continued to be produced by the planning staffs, it was Italy that was identified as the potential attacker against which plans were to be made. This was not simply due to the proximity of Sicily, but was also a response to Mussolini's militant fascism that was at that time directed at British interests in Malta, as discussed in the next section. The second point of interest is that, while the purpose of the defence planning was to ensure the security of the naval base, the navy proposed to make only a limited contribution to its defence. It fell to the army, therefore, to provide the island's principal defences against invasion. It recognised that a garrison of two understrength battalions, plus local militia units, was inadequate to counter an invasion threat, and the proposed doubling of this force, together with the modernisation of the coastal artillery, offered a more plausible defence until relief arrived.

Nevertheless, it was increasingly recognised that the most likely future threat was air attack. Against such attack there was at that time no defence at all, and the War Office could only offer 24 3-inch guns. Although the other services objected to the limited performance of this weapon, it would have been of some value in the conditions prevailing at that time. It had a rapid rate of fire and its effective ceiling of about 20,000 feet was also the height that was then considered to be the maximum at which effective bombing could be carried out.[43] Moreover, the introduction in the mid-1920s of the Vickers Predictor, an instrument designed to meet the problem of hitting a fast-moving aircraft, had led to a significant improvement in anti-aircraft shooting.[44]

It is, however, the RAF's contribution to the discussions that deserves particular notice in view of later developments. Consistent with its prevailing doctrines the Air Staff recommended an air garrison of 5½ squadrons, which included only two fighter squadrons, and was confident that, despite some inevitable bomb damage, this force could help to ensure that the work of the dockyard could continue. It did not say how it proposed to employ the strike aircraft, but later plans suggest that enemy warships and Sicilian airfields would have been primary objectives.[45] The Air Staff at that time was determined to play a larger role in the defence of Malta, and there was no suggestion then that the RAF might not be able to ensure the use of the dockyard, or that the navy should seek an alternative Mediterranean base.

It seems fair, therefore, to conclude that if the proposals being considered by the DOP in 1928 had been accepted and implemented while the coast artillery problem was being investigated, the defences of Malta would have been significantly strengthened. However, nothing was in fact done at this time, and the explanation for this can be sought in two factors, each powerful and, in conjunction, decisive. Financial constraint was the first reason for delay. Although the Chiefs of Staff in their 1926 Annual Review had made the defences of ports between England and Singapore their second most important priority, they had then recommended that the defences of Malta should be postponed 'in the present financial position'.[46] The Baldwin government of 1924 was committed to a programme of reduced taxation and social reform. To finance these objectives, without adding to the already high level of the national debt, the Cabinet gave full support to Churchill's attack on the service estimates. This powerful financial pressure was made irresistible by the second factor, and this was the government's growing confidence in a peaceful world outlook. The signing of the Locarno Treaty in 1925, the admission of Germany to the League of Nations in 1926, the Kellogg–Briand Pact of 1928, and the preparatory work towards the Disarmament Conference, were all seen as evidence of an increasingly benign international climate in which the Cabinet found it difficult to see where, and by whom, the empire was threatened. Not even Japan was considered a threat within the next ten years, and the completion of the Singapore base was postponed. Although this reasoning increased the importance of Malta as the base of the Main Fleet it also postponed the modernisation of its defences.

THE IMPACT OF MALTESE NATIONALISM AND ITALIAN INFLUENCE

The question for consideration here is not how Malta developed in political, social or economic terms in the 1920s, but rather whether the British authorities came to the view that these developments might adversely affect the security of the naval base. Was there any risk that the Maltese might, actively or passively, hinder or prevent its efficient operation?[47]

Prior to the First World War the British government generally regarded Malta as a 'fortress colony', where naval and military interests were paramount. In 1902, Joseph Chamberlain, then Colonial Secretary, asserted that 'we hold Malta solely and entirely as a fortress essential to our position in the Mediterranean', and he added that 'in a fortress anything like open agitation is a thing that cannot be tolerated'.[48] However, in the post-war climate of self-determination the British government yielded to mounting pressure from Maltese political leaders for a measure of self-government, and a new Constitution was granted in 1921. This was a diarchy that gave to an elected Legislature control over domestic affairs, while reserving certain matters, such as defence, to the Governor as representative of the Crown. The first three administrations formed under these new arrangements seemed to work reasonably well, but in the 1927 elections the Constitutional Party, led by Sir Gerald (later Lord) Strickland, gained a small majority, and Strickland formed a government with the support of the four members of the Labour Party. However, in the following three years there ensued a conflict of increasing intransigence between Strickland and the Catholic Church in Malta, ostensibly about Church interference in political decisions. When the Church then effectively forbade its members from voting for the Constitutional Party at the forthcoming 1930 election, the British government felt it had no alternative but to cancel the election and suspend the Constitution. L. S. Amery, who as Under-Secretary of State for the Colonies in 1919, and later Colonial Secretary, had much to do with the framing of the 1921 Constitution, subsequently blamed 'the vehemence of Maltese internal quarrels' for this breakdown.[49]

Into this domestic antagonism there was then introduced an external element which seemed to carry rather more worrying implications for the security of the island. This was the willingness of the Italian government to be used by certain elements in the Nationalist Party to further their political objectives. Although the great majority of the people spoke only Maltese, Italian was the language of the law courts, of the Church, and of the more politically conscious professional middle class. Within this relatively small, but active, group some chose to stress Italian cultural and political links as a counterpoise to British influences. This group naturally looked to Italy for support, and the Italian government was prepared to give its assistance in various ways.[50]

Nevertheless, at this time the Governor's reports and the minutes of the Colonial Office suggest irritation rather than alarm, and irritation as much directed at Strickland as at the Nationalist Party. There is no expression of concern about the security of the naval base. Despite this, in early 1930 Lieutenant Kenneth Strong, who was later to become Eisenhower's Chief of Intelligence, was appointed to the new position of Defence Security Officer at Malta, and this implies that by that time the War Office, at least, were somewhat more concerned about security. Although Strong's intelligence reports are still in closed files, he recorded in his autobiography that, although many regarded the Nationalist Party as being 'covertly subsidized by Italy and intent on leaving the British

Empire', his own conclusion was that Nationalist attitudes 'did not seem to me to be as dangerous for Britain as many alleged'. On the other hand, he made the comment that, after listening to a speech in Sicily by Mussolini, he felt 'distinctly apprehensive for the future'.[51] Potentially more worrying was a large increase in unemployment in the dockyard as the Admiralty sought to meet the reduction in the naval estimates by reducing repair and refit work at Malta. There were over 2,000 discharges in 1926 and the Lieutenant-Governor warned the Colonial Office that 'these men are likely to become a cause of unrest'.[52] Emigration to other Commonwealth countries was officially encouraged to ease this unemployment problem.

The picture that emerges from a reading of the official reports and analyses of Maltese affairs in the late 1920s is one of relative unconcern about the security of the naval base there, despite Italian encouragement of anti-British groups. Nevertheless, the late 1920s breakdown in the political machinery was worrying. Although it began as a local dispute between Strickland and the Church in Malta, it eventually escalated to a wider conflict between the British government and the Vatican, thus creating a situation from which only Italian irredentists and the pro-Italian Nationalist Party were likely to benefit. Sensing, therefore, that the suspension of the 1921 Constitution and a reversion to direct Whitehall rule after nine years of self-government might lead to a more serious deterioration that might adversely affect security, the British government appointed a Royal Commission in 1930 to conduct a full inquiry.

2

The Failure to Strengthen Malta's Defences, 1930–35

THE 'GUN *v.* AIR' CONTROVERSY

In the years following their first annual review of Imperial Defence in 1926,[1] the Chiefs of Staff expressed mounting concern about the dilapidated state of the defences at naval bases. In 1930, having pointed out that, as a result of the London Naval Conference, 'the reduction in the size of the Navy . . . tends, if anything, to increase the importance of adequate bases and fuelling stations', their view about Malta was:

> The armament of the coast defences is, generally speaking, in a pre-war state and totally inadequate to meet an attack by modern naval forces. In particular, the anti-aircraft defences are almost non-existent and are insufficient to meet even the weakest of air attacks.[2]

Faced, however, with aggregate defence estimates that, as a result of the economic crisis of 1931, reached their lowest level in 1932,[3] the Chiefs took the view that other demands had a greater claim on their diminished resources.

But there were other, more technical, factors that contributed to the deplorable state of all coast defences, including those of Malta. In its May 1929 annual review of ports defence, the JDC recorded:

> Not only has no improvement been made in the coast defences of the Empire, but our whole coast defence policy has been subjected to criticism, and the investigations of the Committee into the defences of particular ports abroad have necessarily had to be suspended.[4]

As we saw in the first chapter, this suspension occurred when the DOP was half way through its review of Malta, and its immediate cause was the unsatisfactory results of bombardment trials conducted in the summer of 1928 that cast doubt on the effectiveness of the heavy coastal artillery. This was, in turn, an element in the wider 'Gun *v.* Air' controversy between the Air Ministry and the other two services, which had only been temporarily suspended by the agreement about Singapore reached in 1926.[5] Both of these problems clearly had to be resolved before plans could be made about the defences to be installed to counter the threat of naval bombardment. Concern about the effectiveness of existing coastal guns and their ammunition had emerged in 1924,[6] and after inconclusive trials in 1927, a more elaborate programme took place in the summer of 1928 at Malta and Portsmouth.[7] It will not be necessary to follow these trials in detail but inevitably they caused considerable delay, and it was not until April 1931 that the War Office felt able to state that 'our coast defence guns, with improved mountings and instruments, can fulfil their role as a deterrent to bombarding squadrons'.[8]

Although the resolution of the artillery problem took time, it was, nevertheless, a clear War Office responsibility. By contrast, the 'Gun *v.* Air' controversy was a confrontation between Trenchard, his successor as CAS, Sir John Salmond, and the War Office. The essence of this dispute has already been described in the preceding chapter, and since there was no indication that the Chiefs of Staff could resolve the matter among themselves, an ad hoc CID Sub-Committee was established in December 1931, under Baldwin's chairmanship, to decide the matter. Its appointment at that time was clearly prompted by the recent Japanese aggression in Manchuria, which posed a worrying threat to Singapore where the installation of the three 15-inch guns agreed in 1926 had been delayed by this long-running dispute.[9] The Committee considered 19 memoranda at six meetings before presenting its Report on 24 May 1932.[10]

In the course of this lengthy investigation two factors emerged that appear to have carried special weight with the Committee. First, the gun was a well-tried coastal defence method, and to that extent offered a degree of certainty, especially after the improvements which resulted from the bombardment trials. By contrast, the substitution of aircraft for guns was a novel alternative supported only by theoretical argument. Second, and perhaps decisively, Salmond, the CAS, was unable to give a guarantee that the necessary aircraft would be in the vital place when danger struck. When he was asked if coast defence aircraft might be withdrawn in response to 'emergency calls for them from other theatres of war', leaving important bases unprotected, Salmond could only say, 'The Air Staff assume that authority for acceding to, or refusing emergency calls for aircraft in other theatres will be given, not by the Air Staff, but by the War Cabinet, or other supreme controlling body.'[11]

He went on to say that the Air Staff would 'strongly oppose' such a diversion, but had to admit that the War Cabinet might take the view that 'the successful prosecution of the war might be jeopardized less by a reduction of the defences of one or more bases than by an adverse air situation in a decisive theatre'. The Committee recognised the force of this argument in favour of the gun by quoting Admiral Mahan's remark that 'permanent works . . . have the advantage that they cannot be shifted under the influence of panic'.[12]

After these extensive deliberations the Committee appears to have had little difficulty in recommending that the gun should continue to be the main deterrent to naval attack. It added, however, that the co-operation of aircraft, particularly at major naval bases, was essential. A measure of the intensity of this long-running controversy is seen in the Committee's 'strongest possible appeal to all concerned to carry out our recommendations in a spirit of constructive co-operation'.[13] In retrospect it can be seen that this protracted dispute, by focusing on defence against naval attack, diverted attention from the growing threat from the air. The continued failure even to make a start on providing AA defences can only be ascribed to the prevailing mood of unconcern noted in the first chapter. A second consequence was that, despite the plea for inter-service co-operation, the secondary role given to aircraft was to make it more difficult henceforward for the RAF to argue its case for strengthened air defences. Marshal of the Royal Air Force (MRA) Sir John Slessor, who was a member of the Air Planning section at the time, later wrote that the decision that ports be defended by both guns and aircraft meant, in practice, 'there would not be enough of either'.[14]

THE JOINT DEFENCE COMMITTEE INQUIRY, 1933-34

The resolution of the 'Gun *v.* Air' dispute enabled the JDC to reopen its suspended investigation into the defence requirements at Malta.[15] Hankey took the chair at most of the meetings, and the other members were provided by the planning staffs of the three services, among whom Group Captain Portal represented the Air Staff. An invaluable 'behind the scenes' commentary on the deliberations of the JDC in this period is provided in Colonel Pownall's diary entries for these months.[16] Pownall joined Hankey's staff in January 1933 and became Secretary of the JDC and the ODC.

To be secure Malta needed defences against naval attack, possibly carried out as a prelude to invasion or a raid designed to destroy the naval dockyard, and against air attack. The threat of naval bombardment and the appropriate deterrent to such assault had been exhaustively investigated by the Coast Defence Inquiry, and its decisions established the framework for the War Office's revised gun defence scheme. This new scheme also incorporated the lessons learned from the bombardment trials, with the result that the heavy guns were to be reorganised into batteries of three or four guns to permit controlled salvo firing. Some improved mountings and control instruments were planned in order to increase range and accuracy. The War Office proposed to make a start by regrouping the existing guns, converting one 9.2-inch battery to 35° mountings, and one 6-inch battery to 45° mountings, and by modernising the range finders.[17]

The second, and newer, army responsibility was the provision of anti-aircraft guns, 24 of which had been proposed during the DOP inquiry.[18] Captain Moore repeated the Admiralty's earlier objection to the limited range and ceiling of the proposed 3-inch guns, but the army at that time had no alternative to offer. Colonel Haining reported that the 4.7-inch gun which had been undergoing trials was unlikely to be satisfactory, due to its weight and slow rate of fire, and that a 3.7-inch was being designed as a successor to the obsolescent 3-inch.[19] The slowness of the War Office to develop effective anti-aircraft guns during the inter-war period was one of the least satisfactory features of the rearmament programme. Postan, Hay and Scott are critical of pre-war anti-aircraft gun development, and, in particular, 'of the leisurely process of pre-war design'.[20] They point out that the 3.7-inch gun, although first mooted as early as 1920, did not go into production until April 1937. Liddell Hart, too, writing in 1939 of the War Office attitude to anti-aircraft defence, observed that there was 'a tendency in high quarters to talk of money devoted to air defence as if it were money taken from "the Army"'.[21]

The Admiralty had been more energetic and successful in developing anti-aircraft guns, but when Admiral Sir William Fisher, the C-in-C of the Mediterranean Fleet in 1933, suggested that some of the navy's older 4-inch guns be used for the defence of the Valletta dockyard, the Admiralty replied that they 'do not see their way to suggest to the War Council that naval 4-inch AA guns should be mounted at Malta'.[22] The result was that, in 1933, the best that could be offered by the War Office was a scheme to install 24 increasingly obsolescent guns whose only value was that they *might* deter hostile aircraft from bombing at less than 20,000 feet.

The importance attached to anti-aircraft defences reflected the growing conviction that air attack was the more obvious threat to Malta. As long as the Mediterranean Fleet was based there an Italian naval bombardment was highly unlikely, but in the case of an air attack the odds seemed increasingly to favour Italy. RAF Intelligence in 1931 reported that the *Regia Aeronautica* had almost 1,000 aircraft of modern design. Moreover, operational efficiency was judged to have improved and the Italian preference for massed bombing tactics was noted.[23] Consequently, by the early 1930s, the Air Staff's appreciation was that, for an attack on Malta, the Italian air force would have no difficulty in deploying at least 100 aircraft, capable of delivering 30–35 tons of bombs per day.[24] This compared with estimates of only 7 tons in 1926, and 25 tons in 1928. Nor did the Air Staff expect such an attack to be deterred by the proposed anti-aircraft defences. When asked about the value of anti-aircraft fire during the Coast Defence Inquiry, the CAS, Salmond, said: 'I am strongly of the opinion that, in spite of all modern improvements, anti-aircraft fire alone will not prevent well-led squadrons from delivering most effective attacks.'[25]

Largely as a result of reservations of this kind, it had always been accepted that aircraft would provide the main defence against air attack. The 1927 version of the memorandum, 'Forms of Attack and Forms of Defence', was quite clear about this, affirming that 'bombing and fighting aircraft provide the most effective form of defence – bombing aircraft to destroy and harass hostile air bases within range, and fighting aircraft to secure and maintain local air superiority'.[26] As we have seen, the RAF in 1925, and again in 1928, were ready to accept this responsibility for the air defence of the Malta dockyard. While acknowledging that some bomb damage could not be avoided, the Air Staff view was nevertheless quite sanguine, and it proposed to provide a mixed force of 5½ squadrons for this purpose.

By 1931, however, it was having second thoughts about the RAF's ability to limit damage to the dockyard, and these doubts were expressed in a paper submitted by Salmond to the Chiefs of Staff in July of that year.[27] How, the CAS asked, could an effective air defence be mounted against the full potential strength of a major air power from a small island that could only accommodate 60 aircraft? Malta, moreover, was only 60 miles from the nearest Sicilian air bases, allowing little possibility of early warning or defence in depth. Salmond concluded by saying that the air defence of Malta was a 'problem of the greatest difficulty', and he urged the Admiralty to seek an alternative base for the Mediterranean Fleet.

This paper was not in fact discussed by the Chiefs until April 1933, by which time Admiral Sir Ernle Chatfield had become the First Sea Lord. Chatfield, whose previous appointment had been C-in-C of the Mediterranean Fleet, attacked the CAS's position from several directions. He pointed out, first, that there was no other base in the Mediterranean capable of taking the whole Fleet, and, in any case, the abandonment of Malta would 'imply the loss of control of the whole of the central Mediterranean' and 'we should lose our opportunity for attacking Italy'. He, second, challenged the assumption about the scale of attack, arguing that this would be reduced by actions which the

British air and naval forces would take in the event of a war with Italy. He accepted that 'it might come about that the Fleet were forced to leave Malta, but he was strongly of the opinion that this should not take place until it was driven out and we should certainly make every effort to remain'. After a prolonged discussion, the Chiefs of Staff concluded 'it was very desirable that the defence of Malta . . . should be sufficient to constitute a strong deterrent both to bombardment from the sea or attack from the air'.[28] It will be seen from this discussion that, despite the growing doubts about the RAF's ability to protect the dockyard, none of the Chiefs suggested that Malta be 'written off as indefensible'.

Moreover, in reaching their conclusion the Chiefs rejected a suggestion made by Hankey. This deserves closer attention since it was to re-emerge later in the year with far-reaching consequences. The JDC, Hankey advised, in studying the defences of Malta, 'inclined to the view that the Italian Air Forces were numerically so strong that it was practically impossible to defend Malta on an adequate scale'. He likened the position to that at Gibraltar where defence against Spain was based on the deterrent effect of 'military measures of wider scope', rather than on the strength of its own defences. In reply to a question by Admiral Chatfield whether the JDC had decided that Italian attack on Malta should be disregarded, Hankey said that no conclusion had yet been reached, but 'it was his own opinion that a really adequate defence against Italy was beyond our powers'.

It is not clear from the record of this meeting whether Hankey believed that adequate defence was simply impossible on technical grounds, such as those advanced by Salmond, or whether Britain could not afford the required scale of defence, given her other commitments. However, what is clear from the JDC minutes is that the suggestion that the risk of Italian attack be left out of account and reliance placed on 'military measures of a wider scope' was his own, and that it received little support from other members. Group Captain Portal said that, although the exclusion of Italy would permit the reduction of Malta's air garrison from five to two squadrons, the Air Staff could not take responsibility for such an approach. At the following meeting, he reported the Air Staff's view that the exclusion of Italy would require CID approval.[29]

In April 1933, however, further consideration of Malta was interrupted by more pressing concerns. When Admiral Chatfield became First Sea Lord in January 1933 his first concern was for the position in the Far East.[30] Concern turned to alarm upon receipt of intelligence that, as early as January 1932, the Japanese had prepared a naval and army task force of divisional strength for the specific purpose of attacking Singapore. This force was believed to be still in existence, and could reach Singapore in 8–10 days, long before naval help could arrive.³¹ These dangers were reviewed by the Chiefs of Staff in February 1933, and, in the following month, they recommended, *inter alia*, that the construction of the defences at Singapore be accelerated to ensure their completion in 3½ years rather than five.³² This plan would, according to the CIGS, now General Sir Archibald Montgomery-Massingberd, cost an additional £750,000 in 1934–35, and a further £700,000 in the two subsequent years. The CID and the Cabinet accepted these recommendations.³³

At the JDC meeting on 27 April 1933, Colonel Haining referred to the problems that would be caused by the Chiefs' Singapore recommendation. He said that he had hoped 'to get a provision of £100,000 for Malta in 1934–35, to be followed in successive years by other amounts until 1939'.³⁴ This would now be very difficult. Hankey undertook to raise the matter with the Chiefs of Staff during their discussions on their 1933 annual review, and he did so on 2 May 1933. He pointed out that a defence scheme for Malta was being drafted, adding that he had been 'impressed . . . by the size of the plan'. This included Air Staff proposals for two squadrons that he thought would need to go to the CID eventually. In the discussion that followed, Montgomery-Massingberd remarked that, in view of the additional £750,000 now sought for Singapore, it was difficult for him to see 'how they could also provide anything appreciable for Malta'. Chatfield then agreed that the Chiefs should concentrate on the Far East, adding that 'he felt it would be very ill advised, in addition to Singapore, to put forward in isolation further demands which could not be implemented in the immediate future'. This prompted Hankey to suggest that he might 'go slow' on Malta and not report to the CID 'at the present moment'. After further discussion, the Chiefs accepted the need to put forward an order of priority in their forthcoming annual review, and, in the meanwhile, resolved that 'the submission of proposals for the defence of particular ports should be reserved'.³⁵ In his diary Pownall noted that 'the Malta defence business has been temporarily shelved, the COS agreeing that in present circumstances it is useless putting up a bill for £2 or £3 million, having just got the Singapore bill passed'.³⁶

While these matters were being debated in London, the view from Malta was being vigorously expressed by Admiral Fisher, Chatfield's successor as C-in-C Mediterranean and a close personal friend. He analysed the vulnerability of Malta and the fleet to Italian air attack in an official despatch of 20 June 1933.³⁷ He supplemented this with a personal letter to Chatfield in which he expressed the hope that, having got Cabinet agreement to Singapore, '*now* might be the time to "go on hitting"'.³⁸ Chatfield's official reply was not sent until 3 October when he advised that the 'entire inadequacy' of Malta's defences was realised, but 'in view of even more serious defence commitments elsewhere, financial considerations may preclude the installation of defences at Malta on the full scale at present'.[39]

To return to London, Hankey, in response to the Chiefs' instructions, could only advise the JDC that the time for a full report on Malta was 'inopportune', but he did suggest an Interim Report which 'might deal with any steps which could usefully be taken by Departments within the next few years for modernizing existing equipment'.[40] The War Office and Admiralty concurred in this suggestion, since it embraced most of their proposals, but Portal for the Air Staff strongly disagreed because the RAF's plans envisaged *new* measures, that is, two squadrons of aircraft and two additional airfields. Eventually, and with marked reluctance, Portal agreed to re-consider what might be done on an interim basis.[41] Whatever difficulties the Air Staff may have seen in the air defence of Malta, they were surely right in their repeated assertion that aircraft were no less important than anti-aircraft guns, and that the first priority ought to be the construction of additional airfields to accommodate such aircraft. A draft Interim Report incorporating these recommendations was then being prepared by the Secretaries when the Malta defence planning process suffered yet another setback.

THE DEFENCE REQUIREMENTS COMMITTEE INQUIRY, 1934–35

The year 1933 marked a significant watershed in the inter-war defence planning process. Until then Japanese aggression in China, and the consequent threat to British interests in the Far East, had preoccupied the Chiefs of Staff. In 1933, however, the year in which Hitler became Chancellor, and Germany withdrew from both the Disarmament Conference and the League of Nations, the re-emergence of a potentially more dangerous threat in Europe compelled the government and its military advisers to re-examine priorities and plans. The Chiefs of Staff had already anticipated the failure of the Disarmament Conference when they presented their 1933 annual review in October,[42] and the CID considered this on 9 November.[43] At this crucial meeting the CID accepted and recommended to the Cabinet the priorities advocated by the Chiefs, that is, the Far East, Europe and India, but then added the further recommendation: 'No expenditure should *for the present* be incurred on measures of defence required to provide exclusively against attack by the United States, France, *or Italy*'[44] (emphasis added). The inclusion of Italy in this stipulation was clearly a major setback to defence planning for Malta, since it was difficult to see against what dangers defences were to be prepared if threats from Italy as well as France were to be ignored. This requires closer examination.

The Chiefs of Staff, at their meeting in May 1933, had decided that, since their forthcoming annual review would be the first comprehensive review since that of 1930, the advice of the Foreign Office should be sought. This was met by a particularly detailed memorandum,[45] which argued that, in view of the possibility that the Disarmament Conference would collapse, leaving Germany free to continue its increasingly overt re-armament, British relations with 'the leading European States have, therefore, become a problem of decisive importance'. Consequently, 'our policy should be to cultivate the most friendly relations with the United States, France, and Italy'.[46] The memorandum then went on to examine Italian policies, motives and actions at some length, observing that 'Italian propagandist and cultural activities in Malta' might lead to the emergence of a 'Malta question', if not checked. The Foreign Office, nevertheless, repeated the judgement it had consistently reached since the Chiefs' first review in 1926, that the likelihood of war with Italy was remote, 'save in virtue of our obligations under the Covenant of the League of Nations'. It summed up by asserting that 'Italy, in a word, is still to be had for a policy of prudence and precaution, despite the tendencies and activities noted in the Italian section of this memorandum'.[47] This memorandum carries the stamp of Sir Robert Vansittart, the Permanent Under-Secretary at the Foreign Office, who was convinced that in a resurgent Germany lay the principal danger, and that policy towards Italy, as well as France, should be framed accordingly.[48] The Foreign Office advice, therefore, was no more than a re-affirmation of existing policy, since at that time, and indeed as late as the Stresa Conference of April 1935, Italy was allied with Britain and France in opposing German expansion and any attempt to gain control of Austria.

The Chiefs, with their military responsibilities, were not bound to accept the Foreign Office's advice. As we have seen, Malta defence planning had long assumed attack by Italy and the validity of this planning hypothesis was strengthened by the rapid growth of the Italian armed forces. In February 1931 Field Marshal Sir George Milne, then CIGS, had forwarded to the CID a detailed memorandum on 'The Military Tendencies of Italy'.[49] This examined the development of fascist military training, the growth of the armed forces, and the expansion of Italy's war industries. Although he accepted that Italian hostility was then directed at France and Yugoslavia, rather than at Britain, he took the view that Italy's sympathies and interests lay with those states seeking to overturn the Versailles agreements. He concluded that Italy would continue to be a 'focus of European unrest and a potential danger to European peace'.

Nevertheless, whatever the concerns the Chiefs may have had about Italy's long-term objectives, they accepted the advice of the Foreign

Office, and in their review made Japan and Germany their first two defence priorities, placing third the defence of India against Soviet aggression.[50] They recorded that the defences of the Mediterranean ports had been under review, but concluded:

> At the present time, in view of our good relations with France and Italy, and the greater urgency of our defensive requirements elsewhere, this aspect of Imperial Defence cannot occupy a high order of priority. But we feel bound to mention that our defensive arrangements in the Mediterranean are in many respects obsolete and have not been adjusted to the development of the French and Italian navies, and the increasing range and strength of French and Italian military aircraft.[51]

The review concluded with a request for a new guiding principle to replace the 'Ten Year Rule' that had been effectively abandoned in 1932.

When this review came before the CID on 9 November 1933,[52] it was the Chancellor, Neville Chamberlain, who, seizing on the references to Italy in both the Foreign Office memorandum and in the review itself, made the suggestion that the Chiefs' difficulties might be eased by leaving certain powers out of their calculations altogether. He then proposed that France and Italy might be eliminated in this manner, and the United States was later added to this group. No objection was raised to this approach to the problem, nor to the inclusion of Italy in this group, and the Prime Minister, Ramsay MacDonald, accordingly proposed the recommendation quoted at the beginning of this section.

Although Hankey made no contribution to this CID discussion it seems probable that he had some influence on the decision to exclude Italy from immediate defence planning. The minutes of the meeting record that the Prime Minister proposed the wording of the resolution adopted, but Hankey's draft of this, bearing MacDonald's rather hesitant notation, 'This seems to be all right', survives in the Cabinet records.[53] More significantly, this decision echoes the suggestion made by Hankey earlier in the year to both the JDC and COS committees. The most likely explanation of his motives is that he, perhaps more than most Ministers, was aware of the large gap between Britain's defensive needs and the resources available to meet them. His solution to this problem was to apply all of these resources to the two principal dangers and to rely on the concept of general deterrence to meet the Italian threat if diplomacy failed. What is more surprising is that the Chiefs of Staff made no objection, publicly at least, to this novel approach to the defence of Malta. Although they had accorded this a low priority in their May review, this was not the same as ignoring the island's defences altogether. Indeed, in April they had urged that Malta's defences be made strong enough to permit the Main Fleet to use the Valletta dockyard. One is left to assume that they accepted the risks entailed by such a policy because risks were inevitable somewhere, and, at that time, were persuaded that Italian enmity was a lesser risk. The phrase 'for the present' in the CID formula may have helped to gain their compliance.

The new guidance thus agreed was, nevertheless, couched in very general terms, and its interpretation and application to the question of Malta's defence planning was to exercise the JDC in the following months. The first body to wrestle with this problem was the Defence Requirements Committeen (DRC), which had been set up at the same CID meeting in November 1933 'to prepare a programme for meeting our worst deficiencies'.[54] Hankey chaired this committee and its other members were the Chiefs of Staff and Sir Robert Vansittart and Sir Warren Fisher, representing, respectively, the Foreign Office and the Treasury. The first DRC report was signed on 28 February 1934.[55] It proposed an interpretation of the condition eliminating the United States, France and Italy from defence preparations, and this was eventually endorsed by the Cabinet. With respect to this element in their terms of reference the DRC report stated:

> We recommend that this should not be interpreted to rule out the provision in certain localities of a limited amount of modern equipment required to enable personnel to be trained and exercised with modern weapons. . . . It would also be unsound to allow any of our Naval bases to fall to so low a degree of efficiency that it would be impossible to bring them up to a suitable standard within a reasonable time should changes in the political situation in Europe make this necessary.[56]

With this limited relaxation of the condition set by the CID to allow training in the use of modern weapons, the JDC once more resumed its deliberations about Malta in April 1934, since Hankey had resolved to press on with the completion of an Interim Report. The plans of the Admiralty and the War Office were left largely unscathed by the new conditions since they involved modernizing existing though outdated equipment. Consequently, attention focused on the Air Staff's new proposals.[57] The memorandum presented by the Air Staff is crucial for a correct understanding of their planning, then and later, for the defence of Malta. The paper was signed by Air Vice-Marshal (AVM) Ludlow-Hewitt, later to become C-in-C, Bomber Command. He first made the assumption that, in order to eliminate a base as important as Malta, the Italian Air Force might employ a large proportion of her 1,000 first-line aircraft. He then argued that, against an attack on this scale, Malta could not be defended '*from Malta alone*'. His judgement was, 'It is not a feasible operation, *without effective support from other air bases*, to defend a small island area within effective range of the metropolitan air force of a great Power' (emphasis added). However, he made the assumption that allied air bases would be available and, in consequence, attack by only 100 enemy aircraft needed to be considered. To counter this he recommended a 'nucleus' of two squadrons permanently based at Malta, and an additional airfield to permit rapid reinforcement of this nucleus. To comply with the JDC's request for 'initial measures', he proposed a composite squadron of torpedo-bombers and fighter-bombers, as part of the 'nucleus' force, and a new aerodrome at Takali in the centre of Malta.

The key aspect of this document was the concept that Malta's defence would best be secured by counter-attack from outside the island. This would reduce the weight of attack on Malta to a level that could be met by a five-squadron air garrison, of which the composite squadron was the initial component. Since there was no British territory within supporting range, it was assumed without question that air bases in France or, perhaps, Yugoslavia would be available from which to launch the counter-offensive. The Air Staff recognised that a defence on these lines would be difficult, and although they did not feel able to guarantee that the dockyard could remain in operation, they were determined to make a full contribution to the overall defence of Malta against invasion. The Air Staff certainly did not consider that the air defence of the island was impossible.

It now fell to Group Captain Arthur Harris, who had succeeded Portal as the RAF member of the JDC, to argue the case for the composite squadron and the additional aerodrome. The Treasury representative was not convinced that proposed expenditure of more than £½ million could be squared with the CID's directive prohibiting expenditure against Italy, while Hankey urged that the Air Staff's proposals be framed to meet the training requirement that the Cabinet had accepted. For this purpose the army member requested a flight of spotter aircraft. With considerable reluctance, after pointing out that 'there was no provision for the aircraft defence of Malta', Harris eventually put up another paper[58] that recommended the addition of a further flight of spotters to the composite squadron. He continued to insist that this squadron and the additional aerodrome were essential and consistent with the committee's brief. The JDC accepted this amended proposal.

All to no avail, however, since the Cabinet committee appointed to consider the DRC report, upon which the JDC had been basing its plans, decided in July that the DRC proposals were 'impossible to carry out', and that 'we have had to devise a new programme'.[59] Two elements in this new programme adversely affected Malta. First, the DRC proposal that the army should spend £200,000 a year for five years on the gun defences of the Mediterranean and Cape ports was simply cut in half, thus putting back the completion of Malta's gun defences to the indefinite future; second, and of much greater significance, no provision was made to station a squadron of aircraft in Malta. Although 41½ new squadrons were to be raised, only four were intended for overseas employment and all of these were to be sent to the Far East.[60] The Cabinet accepted these recommendations at the end of July 1934.[61]

Thus when the long-delayed Interim Report on Malta was finally signed on 1 October 1934 the only recommendations it contained were the provision of some harbour nets and booms, the installation of the previously agreed 24 3-inch anti-aircraft guns over an extended period, and the modernization of one 9.2-inch and one 6-inch coastal battery. No aircraft were to be added to the existing flights of four flying boats and four communications aircraft, but a second aerodrome was recommended. In its conclusion the report, after quoting the DRC's injunction that the defences of naval bases should not be permitted to fall into such neglect that recovery could not be achieved in a reasonable time, stated, 'It is the view of the Committee that in its present condition Malta is perilously close to that condition; that, indeed, in the matter of air defence it has already reached it.'[62] The growing risk to Britain's Mediterranean interests of a defenceless Malta was serious enough, but, as was shown in the first chapter, Malta was also a vital part of the Admiralty's plans to deal with a crisis in the Far East. If Malta succumbed to attack the relief of Singapore might also be in jeopardy. This risk was recognised in the Malta Interim Report:

> If it became necessary to send reinforcements from Europe to Singapore, it would be essential that they should be able to use the Suez route and should not be deflected round the Cape of Good Hope; the latter alternative, if forced upon us, might well cause the reinforcements to arrive too late to serve our purpose.[63]

The Interim Report on Malta was considered by the CID on 22 November 1934. Despite the stark warning that the island's air defences could not be put right within a reasonable time, its recommendations were approved with almost no comment, on the assumption that the proposed expenditure on the airfield fell within existing approvals.[64] When, however, in January 1935, the Air Ministry wrote to the Treasury requesting that an amount of £59,000 be provided in the 1935/36 air estimates to finance the acquisition of the Takali site and runway construction, the Treasury demurred.[65] Treasury officials argued that the CID intended that this amount should be provided out of the deficiency sum allocated to the Air Ministry as a result of the DRC inquiry. The Air Ministry was also reminded that priority had been given to the defences of Singapore, and that Malta must take second place.

THE STATE OF MALTA'S DEFENCES IN 1935

This chapter has followed the well-meaning attempts of the JDC to renovate the defences of Malta and the many obstacles that frustrated these efforts. The early problems were of a technical nature and were considerable. Long overdue modernization of coastal artillery was essential, and it was the delay in dealing with this problem that left the 'Gun *v.* Air' dispute unresolved for so long. The steady growth in the size of the Italian air force and the assessment of its improving standards also raised concerns which caused the Air Staff, firmly convinced of the bomber's supremacy, to have second thoughts about the air defence of the island and of the Valletta dockyard in particular. Nevertheless, its proposed response to this, to construct new aerodromes to accommodate a garrison of two permanent squadrons that could be reinforced as required, and to develop a counter-offensive capability from Malta and adjacent territories, reflected contemporary RAF thinking. The state of Malta's defences at the beginning of 1935 was not, therefore, the result of a lack of concern, or a decision that Malta was indefensible, although no one underestimated the difficulties this presented. If, then, the blame for Malta's weak defences is not to be laid at the door of the JDC and the service planning departments, where is the explanation for such neglect to be found?

Three factors which contributed to the condition of Malta's defences can be identified. First, although in 1934 there were signs of economic recovery, the National government was, as the Prime Minister pointed out in June 1934, 'committed in their next Budget to a restoration of the cuts in pay and also to a further reduction in the Income Tax, and so on'. It was the commitment to these objectives that led to the truncation of the DRC's deficiency programme, the suggestion that larger expenditure might be financed by a Defence Loan being curtly dismissed by the Chancellor, Chamberlain, as the 'broad road which led to destruction'.[66] Financial risks were still perceived to be the greater and this meant that moneys were available for only the most pressing defence needs. The zeal with which the Treasury implemented this policy was exemplified by their response to the financing of the Takali aerodrome. Second, when external dangers re-emerged in the 1930s, initially in China and then in Germany, these could scarcely be seen as a direct threat to Britain's Middle East interests. Rather, the Japanese and German threats led, respectively, to the 1933 decision to accelerate the defensive works at Singapore and to the 1934 programme for the expansion of the RAF in Britain at the expense of other claims. Among these lay the plans for Malta.

The third obstacle to the Malta planners was the Cabinet decision to rule out, 'for the present', expenditure to provide against attack by Italy. Faced with mounting dangers and a dilapidated defence structure, the government concluded that it had little choice but to take risks somewhere. Judging Germany and Japan to pose the greatest threats, Ministers decided to apply all of the resources they felt a still convalescent economy could afford to meet these dangers. The least likely threat from Italy was to be managed by diplomacy, backed up by a general deterrence of war should Italy attack British interests. But if that should fail it was recognised that Malta would be largely defenceless. That was the risk that the Cabinet accepted in 1934–35.

It may be asked, however, why the government's military advisers also accepted without stronger protest a decision that left Malta without adequate defences. Field Marshal Milne had earlier warned of the dangers of fascist policies, but in 1933 the Chiefs of Staff chose to accept the assurances of the Foreign Office that Italian enmity was remote, and endorsed the decisions that flowed from that premise. If the Chiefs of Staff are to be criticised, it is because they failed to re-insure against a policy based on diplomacy and general deterrence. In 1940 Admiral Chatfield wrote that 'the failure was to plan for the future, to insure against miscalculation'.[67]

The miscalculation about Italy was soon exposed. In their 1935 review of defence policy, signed on 29 April, the Chiefs of Staff wrote:

> The situation in Europe is such that no attack on Gibraltar or Malta is contemplated in the near future. Consequently, the modernisation of coast defence armaments, and the provision of anti-aircraft defences, are being carried out gradually in order that they shall not fall too far below modern requirements.[68]

Within two months the Chiefs of Staff were hurriedly making preparations for war with Italy that might begin with a surprise attack on Malta.

3

Malta in the Abyssinian Crisis, 1935–36

THE DECISION TO DEFEND MALTA

On 5 July 1935, to their consternation and barely suppressed anger,[1] the Chiefs of Staff were advised by Hankey of the Prime Minister's request that 'they keep in mind the military implications' of the possible application of sanctions against Italy.[2] Admiral Chatfield, as chairman of the Chiefs of Staff Committee, immediately responded to this unwelcome development by insisting that, since sanctions meant war, the services must be given adequate time to make preparations, 'if only to prevent Italy taking the opportunity of our unpreparedness to strike a military blow in some form against us at her own selected moment'. Right from the beginning of the crisis, therefore, it can be seen that the Cabinet and the Chiefs were concerned about the possibility of what came to be referred to as a 'mad dog attack'.[3] This was a worry that was to have a major influence on British planning and decision making throughout the emergency, and especially in relation to Malta.

While most of the Mediterranean Fleet returned to England to participate in the Jubilee Review at Spithead on 16 July, the planners, accordingly, set to work, and at the next COS meeting on 30 July Chatfield tabled an Admiralty appreciation which formed the basis for an Interim Report of 2 August.[4] This reiterated the need for time to prepare, and for the active co-operation of the French, but it left open the question of the defence of Malta, pending discussions with the War Office and the Air Ministry. This Interim Report was considered on 6 August at a Meeting of Ministers attended by only the Prime Minister, Stanley Baldwin, the Foreign Secretary, Sir Samuel Hoare, and Anthony Eden, Minister for League of Nations Affairs. The upshot of this was a further request from the Prime Minister that the Chiefs of Staff examine 'what the position would be if Italy took the bit between her teeth', and what immediate steps should in consequence be taken. Hoare added that the Foreign Office would not object to relatively quiet steps being taken, such as raising the AA defences of Malta to the previously agreed scale, even if this should become known.[5] Eden believed that this gave the Chiefs authority to send out reinforcements to Malta, but nothing was done until September.[6]

Although this implied growing anxiety about Mussolini's intentions, it did not prevent the Cabinet and many senior officers going off on their summer holidays. Hoare, one of the few Ministers left in London, felt somewhat abandoned, complaining in a letter to Chamberlain of 18 August, 'I have received little or no help from other quarters. Stanley [Baldwin] would think of nothing but his holiday and the necessity of keeping out of the whole business almost at any cost.'[7] It was during August, however, that critical naval and military decisions had to be taken, including the question whether Malta could, or should, be defended. A more detailed analysis was circulated on 9 August, and this was based on an appreciation prepared by the Joint Planning Committee (JPC) of the Chiefs of Staff.[8] The most pressing decision was whether the Mediterranean Fleet, on its return from the Spithead review, should remain at its Malta base, or move elsewhere. On this question there was disagreement. Admiral Fisher, the Mediterranean C-in-C, confidently asserted, 'on receiving suitable reinforcements from Home Fleet any situation at sea could be dealt with', and urged 'the provision of every available high angle gun, naval if necessary, for Malta and despatch of fighters and bombers up to the limit that can be operated there'.[9] Chatfield, however, decided otherwise. The ships of the Mediterranean Fleet were simply too few and too valuable to be exposed in Malta's virtually defenceless harbours to the threat of surprise air attack from Sicilian bases only 60 miles away, however unlikely that risk might be. It was, in consequence, declared in the 9 August report that the Mediterranean Fleet would proceed to Egyptian waters by the end of August.[10]

The more contentious problem, however, was whether, and, if so, how, Malta itself could be defended. The JPC analysis was pessimistic. Assuming the co-operation of the French, the planners considered it unlikely that the Italians would attempt a landing, 'but it is well within Italy's power to concentrate a heavy scale of air attack on Malta'.[11] The JPC considered what could be done to strengthen the island's defences. The War Office could rush out the additional 16 AA guns previously authorised, and bring all the coast defence artillery to full manning levels. It could also send two additional battalions of infantry, bringing the total to four, although it was thought that these would be required 'primarily for internal security'. The value of such reinforcements was, however, strictly limited. As General Anderson, the Deputy Director of Military Operations and Intelligence at the War Office, told the Foreign Office: 'The CIGS hoped that he had not misled [the Foreign Office] into believing that by sending a few AA guns and searchlights Malta can be put into a satisfactory state of defence.'[12] The neglect of many years was not so easily to be repaired.

But if the War Office saw great difficulties in defending Malta, the Air Ministry maintained the position stated by Ludlow-Hewitt in early 1934, that the island could not be defended from Malta alone. The Cabinet decisions of 1934 had precluded the stationing of any front-line aircraft at Malta, and, as late as 2 August 1935, the Treasury confirmed their refusal to provide additional funding for a second aerodrome at Takali.[13] It was only after Air Staff objections,[14] and an urgent meeting between the Deputy Chief of the Air Staff (DCAS), Air Vice-Marshal Courtney, and the Permanent Under-Secretary at the Treasury, Sir Warren Fisher, that, on 12 August, Fisher gave approval after saying that his only objection had been, 'that an overt move of this kind would exacerbate Italy at a time when His Majesty's Government were inclining towards a policy of conciliation'.[15]

Nonetheless, however important it might be for the future, the Takali decision did not meet the immediate difficulty. As the Air Staff had explained in 1934, this was much more fundamental. The Italian metropolitan air force was believed to comprise 700 first line aircraft, of which 400 were bombers, all capable of reaching Malta from Sicily. The only way to defend Malta, they contended, was to divert the Italian air force by counter-attacks on Italy.[16] Such attacks launched from French North Africa on Sicilian airfields would serve to reduce the air assault on Malta. Better still would it be for the RAF to support the French air force by strikes from southern France on the Italian aircraft factories around Turin where 400 bombers of an advanced design, the Savoia S.81, were being built.[17] The Air Staff plans, therefore, envisaged, first, operations in conjunction with the French against Sicily and the Italian mainland as being 'the only effective method of employment for our air forces calculated to achieve an Italian defeat'. Second, any air forces that could be based on Malta's single airfield would only serve as a deterrent, 'and to provide ocular proof to the local population that the enemy Air Forces are being opposed'. For this secondary purpose it was initially suggested that a mixed force of one torpedo-bomber, one light bomber, and two fighter squadrons be despatched to Malta.[18]

These preliminary and only loosely co-ordinated appreciations and proposals were distributed to Ministers who were summoned back from their holidays for an emergency Cabinet meeting on 22 August. Sir Robert Vansittart, the Permanent Under-Secretary at the Foreign Office, had already taken the precaution of advising Admiral Little, Chatfield's deputy, that the Cabinet might decide to lift the embargo on sales of arms to Abyssinia, and that any such decision was bound to cause anger in Rome. Consequently, on 21 August Little cabled to Fisher in Malta warning of the possibility of 'precipitate action in the form of air attack on the Fleet', and instructing that the Fleet should be at 24 hours' notice to sail after noon on 22 August.[19] However, at a five-hour meeting on that day the Cabinet quickly decided not to lift the arms embargo.[20] The principal naval decisions were to endorse the proposed move of the Mediterranean Fleet from Malta after 29 August and its reinforcement by an aircraft carrier, destroyers and submarines. The Home Fleet was to assemble at Portland on the same day and then proceed to Gibraltar. With regard to Malta, however, the Cabinet could not make up its mind. It authorised the despatch of only one squadron of aircraft 'if the Admiralty should so desire', and rejected the War Office plan to send two extra battalions 'if this involved the calling up of reserves for them'. It then remitted the matter, including the proposal to send out additional AA guns, to the recently established Defence Policy and Requirements Committee (DPRC) of the CID, with the request that the Committee 'consider with the Chiefs of Staff whether it was worth while to increase the armament of an island so exposed as is Malta to attack from Italy'.

The published minutes do not record the discussion that led to this decision, but it is difficult to escape the suspicion that the Cabinet, or at least some of its members, was at this point thoroughly alarmed by the possibility of a 'mad dog attack'. This was certainly Hoare's worry. In a letter of 17 August to Cunliffe-Lister, the Secretary of State for Air, he wrote:

> We are dealing with a monomaniac and no one can tell what he may or may not do. My fear is not that we shall drift into a war with Italy but rather that Mussolini and some of his wilder Fascists may commit some mad dog act against us.[21]

On the following day the DPRC, with Baldwin in the chair, considered the matters referred to it by the Cabinet.[22] It authorised the despatch of 16 AA guns and 12 searchlights, 900 personnel to man this equipment, and additional personnel and ammunition for the coastal artillery. On the other hand, it thought 'in present circumstances [it was] not necessary to despatch additional battalions to Malta'. These limited measures suggest that senior Ministers remained undecided about the wisdom of adding further to Malta's defences. Nor was this unreasonable. Although any decision not to defend Malta would ultimately be a political one, it was in the first place a matter for the government's military advisers to consider, and in this respect it must have become clear that the Chiefs of Staff were themselves uncertain. It was, therefore, quite reasonable for the DPRC to ask the Chiefs to make up their minds first on the strategic questions involved in the defence of Malta.

Before considering the COS meeting it will be useful to review the lines on which the thinking and plans of the Admiralty and the Air Ministry were developing. On 24 August the Admiralty sent to Fisher and other C-in-Cs the first of several summaries about recent events.[23] Chatfield elaborated on this in a long private letter to Fisher on 25 August. In this he set out his reasons for many of the decisions that he had taken, and he had this to say about Malta:

> Malta is a minor matter in the long run. . . . If Italy is mad enough to challenge us, it is at the ends of the Mediterranean she will be defeated and, knowing that her communications with Abyssinia are cut, you yourself will have a freer hand in the Central Mediterranean and Malta, even if it is demolished, will come back again.[24]

For the forthcoming COS meeting Chatfield then set out his intended strategy for a war with Italy.[25] The reinforced Mediterranean Fleet in the eastern Mediterranean and the Red Sea would cut off the large Italian army and air forces in Eritrea, while the Home Fleet, based at Gibraltar, would enforce an economic blockade from the west. To force the issue, however, it was essential to engage and destroy the Italian Fleet, and this necessitated control of the central Mediterranean where, Chatfield conceded, Italy was in a strong strategic position. For this purpose the Fleet might not be able to use Malta, but even if Malta were forced to surrender, 'this would not be a vital consideration'. Rather, Chatfield based his plans on the use of a makeshift base in Navarino Bay ('Port X'), on the west coast of the Peloponnese. This was further removed from Italian air bases, from which Fisher had expressed the opinion that only occasional attacks need be anticipated.[26] Although there would be no docking or repair facilities at Port X, its possession would enable the Fleet to pursue an aggressive forward policy against the Italian fleet and mainland targets.

At the Air Ministry, the CAS, Air Chief Marshal Sir Edward Ellington, after reading Chatfield's naval plan, at once wrote to his Minister, Cunliffe-Lister, expressing the view that Port X could not be defended against air attack, and arguing the case for an air campaign against northern Italy. He pointed out, too, that the Chiefs had not yet discussed the overall strategy to be pursued.[27] He and the other Chiefs had also received a further JPC appreciation on the air aspects of the naval plan, and the practicability of using Port X.[28] This report, however, simply highlighted the divergent views of the Naval and Air Staffs, not only about the viability of Port X, but about the employment of the 25 squadrons available to the RAF in England. The Admiralty had requested that about half of these be sent to support the Fleet, but the Air Staff were now prepared to offer only one squadron plus 15 flying boats for this purpose. On this point the report concluded, 'the Admiralty requirements cannot be met except by neglecting the requirements of the concurrent air campaign'.

The 149th Meeting of the Chiefs of Staff on 6 September was a critical one, not only for the overall strategic plans, but also for the defence of Malta.[29] On the main strategic issue Ellington was adamant that a large proportion of the RAF's limited squadrons in England should be employed in the south of France to support French attacks on the Italian aircraft factories. Chatfield naturally preferred an air strategy of attacking the Sicilian airfields where large Italian forces were now concentrated. 'It was not very satisfactory,' he remarked, 'to leave these alone and tell their victims that their replacements were being attacked.' As far as Malta was concerned, Ellington was equally clear that purely local air defence was impossible. His view was that it would be 'a comparatively simple matter' for the Italian air force, by attacking the one available aerodrome, 'to neutralise any counter action by our aircraft', and they would then concentrate heavy attack on the dockyard area. His pessimistic judgement was that all the aircraft sent to Malta would be lost, and that Malta would have to be abandoned.

Chatfield would have none of this. Although the retention of Malta was not strategically essential, it was simply not possible to evacuate the island, for the defence of which he had left a force of destroyers and submarines. He urged that 'all efforts must be sacrificed in the interests of the Mediterranean'. The CIGS, General Sir Archibald Montgomery-Massingberd, generally sided with Chatfield. With regard to the gun defences of Malta he admitted that, 'we were caught at a very unfortunate time' since the coastal guns were being changed and new signals systems laid. He made a plea for spotter aircraft to assist the guns, and torpedo aircraft as additional defence against naval attack. On the other hand, he was reluctant to send two further battalions of infantry but 'would not oppose this if pressed'. At first Ellington would not be budged from his central strategic conception, but, bowing to pressure, conceded that 'if it was the policy to defend Malta', he would provide an additional squadron of torpedo bombers, and a flight of spotters. Hankey then intervened to say that, since the Cabinet's position was far from clear, the Chiefs should enquire 'whether it is the intention of His Majesty's Government that Malta should be defended'. Assuming an affirmative answer, the Chiefs recommended the reinforcement of torpedo bombers and spotters, and asked the ODC to examine the question of army reinforcements.

It was Hankey's task to express these still divergent views in a report to the DPRC.[30] As regards Malta the report stated that 'from a purely strategical point of view the role of Malta as the principal naval base of the Mediterranean Fleet ceases in the event of hostilities with Italy'. This, 'if pressed to its logical conclusion', might justify the 'virtual abandonment of the Island to its fate'. On the other hand, there were valuable stores and facilities in Malta, such as the floating dock, and, moreover, 'the abandonment of Malta without an effort to defend it, even though temporary, would inflict a resounding blow on the prestige of this country'. This fell short of being a firm recommendation, but the Chiefs could hardly do this, since, on strategic grounds alone, even Chatfield had concluded that Malta was not of critical importance. The Chiefs could only, therefore, offer an essentially political reason for defending the island. The DPRC considered this report on 11 September,[31] by which time the ODC had also submitted its recommendation that the Malta garrison be reinforced by two battalions at full strength, or three on peace time establishment.[32] The DPRC then ruled:

> All plans . . . should be made on the assumption that it is the policy of His Majesty's Government in no circumstances to abandon Malta without every effort to defend it, unless they are advised by the Chiefs of Staff that our general objects in the war would be frustrated by defending that base.

They then sanctioned the despatch of the recommended aircraft, together with three battalions on peace establishment. The proviso to the DPRC's consent returned the matter once more to the Chiefs of Staff for a final decision.[33] The Chiefs debated this at their next meeting on 13 September and concluded:

> The defence of Malta is not, in our opinion, likely to have any adverse effects on the general result of the war. On the contrary, the air attacks that the Italians are likely to make on the Island will be equivalent to a diversion favourable to the operations of the Fleet.[34]

It had taken almost two months for the Cabinet and its military advisers to decide to defend Malta, and it was finally as much a political decision as a military one. The Air Staff remained unshaken in their view that air defence by local forces alone, especially with only one airfield, was simply not feasible, but their own strategy to reduce the scale of attack on Malta by counter-action against Sicily and northern Italy collapsed in December when the French made clear that they had no intention of attacking Italy unless France were attacked first.[35] Despite the threat posed by the S.81 bomber, it was the Admiralty's position that 'only war experience can prove what the risk of air attack really amounts to'. On these grounds, the Admiralty planned to use Port X to control the central Mediterranean unless and until experience showed that the risks were too great. But this confidence in Port X was founded in part on its 250-mile distance from the nearest Italian air bases, and Malta lacked this protective distance. With considerable reluctance, therefore, even Chatfield was forced to acknowledge that Malta could not be the base for the Mediterranean Fleet in an early conflict with Italy.

Nevertheless, despite the acknowledged inadequacy of Malta's existing defences to resist a determined Italian assault and the island's limited military value, the Cabinet in 1935 resolved that everything possible be done to defend Malta. When the same question was put in later years the same answer was given.

THE FEAR OF A 'MAD DOG' ATTACK

If war between Britain and Italy actually broke out, geography made air attack on Malta almost inevitable, as the events of 1940 were to show, and it was the possibility of such an attack that prompted Baldwin's instruction to the Chiefs of Staff in July 1935. Any rational calculation of the consequences for Italy of an attack on Malta would have ruled it out, but the essence of British anxiety was the fear that a man like Mussolini might well be capable of an irrational 'mad dog' act if he became desperate. What was quite rational, however, about his campaign of rumours indicating the possibility of an attack on Malta was the calculation that the British government, preoccupied with the greater dangers posed by Germany and Japan, would ultimately decide not to risk the potentially severe losses which a conflict with Italy might entail. The conduct of such a strategy of threats was made easier by Mussolini's almost certain knowledge of the information and instructions flowing between the Foreign Office and the British embassy in Rome. After many suspicions about lax security at the embassy, an enquiry in 1937 concluded that the Italian intelligence service could easily have removed and copied the embassy documents and ciphers,[36] and in 1944 it was finally established that a long-serving Italian employee at the embassy had been responsible for thefts of embassy documents.[37] It seems clear, therefore, that, from an early stage, Mussolini was well informed about the Cabinet's growing reluctance to risk war with Italy should he refuse to be deterred by the possibility of sanctions. His campaign of threats was designed to encourage this reluctance.

Nevertheless, threats, in order to be convincing, had to be supported by visible military preparations. As early as May 1935 the Italian navy had, on Mussolini's instructions, prepared plans for an attack on Malta, and on 13 August the Italian Chiefs of Staff discussed at length the actions each service could take if war with Britain arose.[38] The Chief of the Italian Air Force, General Valle, said that his forces would be able to drop 100 tons of bombs a day on Malta, but Admiral Cavagnari, for the Italian navy, thought that an attack on Malta would serve little strategic purpose since the Royal Navy would concentrate at Gibraltar and Alexandria. Cavagnari also expressed the opinion that the Italian forces could only give the impression of action in order to make the British hesitate. Nevertheless, despite the gloomy tenor of the meeting, General Badoglio, the head of the Italian Chiefs of Staff, reported that the services had taken steps to be ready for war by 30 August.

The misgivings of the Italian Chiefs of Staff were unknown in London as the British authorities assessed the probability of a 'mad dog' attack. To help them in this work there was no shortage of 'information'. As Admiral Chatfield later wrote to Vansittart: 'If I believed all the stories I heard at the time of the Abyssinian crisis I should now be in a lunatic asylum.'[39] Rumours began to circulate in July alongside stridently anti-British articles in the Italian press. Many of these rumours were repeated and embellished in the British press, and although most could be ignored, others demanded closer attention. Mussolini himself gave many interviews to journalists, while his speeches to army units leaving for east Africa were intended for a wider audience. Increasingly in August, these mentioned the possibility of war with Britain. During a meeting on 13 August with the French Ambassador in Rome, Charles de Chambrun, Mussolini said that, if the Suez Canal were closed against Italy, 'out of desperation I would not hesitate, if it were necessary, to make war on [the British]'.[40]

In order to put these proliferating rumours into perspective Chatfield would have turned to his secret intelligence sources, such as they were at the time. The British intelligence records for this period have not been released, and we have only Professor Hinsley's limited observations, and some of the papers of Alastair Denniston, Head of the Government Code and Cypher School (GC&CS) in the pre-war years, and of William Clarke, who was in charge of the Naval Section. The first two chapters of Hinsley's British intelligence history describe the limited resources of GC&CS in the early 1930s, and the shortage of trained cryptographers and clerical staff. Despite this he recorded:

> By 1935 GC&CS had broken . . . some of the high-grade cyphers used by the Italian services and colonial authorities and was beginning to make progress with Italy's diplomatic cyphers. The resulting intelligence threw useful light on Italy's intentions before and during the Abyssinian crisis and the Spanish Civil War.[41]

Unfortunately, he does not elaborate on this, but his phrase 'useful light' does not connote conclusive evidence about Italian plans and intentions. More informative are several items in a collection of Clarke's papers.[42] In March 1935, the Italian navy introduced two new book codes, and in August Clarke advised Admiral Sinclair, who was in overall charge of both GC&CS and the Secret Intelligence Service (SIS), that although 'the most important of these books is well on its way to legibility ... work on it is hampered by lack of clerical staff'. He pointed out that 'work at this date is confined to messages already six weeks old ... and the position is getting worse every day'. Two days later, after a meeting with the Deputy Director of Naval Intelligence, he recorded the view that 'I doubt very much if the present location of the main units of the Italian Fleet is known with any accuracy.'[43] By September, however, after a significant increase in the staffing of his section to cope with intercepts which had grown from 100 per month in March to 600–700 in August, he was able to provide the Admiralty with more up-to-date information, notably the 'first news of Italian concentrations of submarines at Tobruk and Leros', and the establishment of a patrol line of submarines between Malta and Alexandria.[44] Denniston confirms this record of success in deciphering Italian naval signals.[45]

Nevertheless, although invaluable for operational purposes, intelligence of this kind was of little help to Chatfield in trying to assess the risk of a surprise attack on the Fleet at Malta, since such attack, although perhaps supported by submarines, would be carried out by aircraft. For this reason it was essential to monitor the build-up of Italian air forces in Sicily. Fortunately, this presented less difficulty since ferries and commercial traffic continued to operate in the normal way between Valletta and Syracuse. Fisher said in a letter to Chatfield that he was continuing to send officers 'to picnic in Sicily',[46] but it seems unlikely that any SIS agents were involved in espionage in Italy during this period. Although Hinsley noted that such operations were not forbidden, he also quoted the Chief of the Secret Service (CSS) as saying that financial stringency 'had long ago forced the SIS to abandon its activities in several countries which would have been good bases for obtaining information about Italy'.[47]

Confirmation of Italian air reinforcements would have been provided by photo reconnaissance. Hinsley recorded that the RAF photographed Eritrea, Abyssinia, Cyrenaica and Sicily in 1935, but has given no details of the frequency or results of these flights. Their value in relation to inland airfields would, in any case, have been limited by the need to take photographs at an oblique angle from outside the three-mile limit.[48] An RAF intelligence report of September 1935 records a 'training cruise' carried out by two flying boats of the Malta-based 202 Squadron between 21 and 24 August. Their route took them from their Kalafrana base via Sicily and southern Italy to Corfu and then to Navarino Bay, before returning to Malta. The timing and route of this flight almost certainly indicates an intelligence-gathering mission.[49] All of this would have confirmed that, by August, the Italians had concentrated forces in Sicily and southern Italy capable of attacking Malta, and Chatfield referred to this at the COS meeting on 6 September. However, as Hinsley has pointed out, 'Sigint, even when in plentiful supply, is less revealing about a government's intentions than is sometimes supposed.'[50] If an attack on Malta was to be launched in August it is more likely that the planning for this would have been carried out in Rome, and instructions sent to local commanders by hand or secure landlines.

All this evidence, as well as the continuing flow of Italian troops through the Suez Canal, strongly suggested that not only would Mussolini not be deterred from an attack on Abyssinia, but also that he might even attack Malta and other British targets if military sanctions were imposed on Italy. Faced with this prospect, the British Cabinet, rather than suffer the loss of ships needed to meet the growing threat from Germany and Japan, decided to support only mild economic sanctions that would not provoke Italian attack. To be sure that this was understood, Sir Eric Drummond, British Ambassador in Rome, was instructed to explain to Mussolini, at an interview on 23 September, that British actions in the Mediterranean were purely precautionary, and that such matters as the closing of the Suez Canal or military sanctions had not been discussed in London.[51]

It is idle to speculate whether, if military sanctions had been imposed on Italy, Mussolini would have attacked Malta. In a diary entry of 21 December 1937 the Italian Foreign Minister, Ciano, recorded:

> I remember his wanting to make a surprise attack on the Home Fleet [sic] at Alexandria and Malta in August 1935. He said to me then, 'In one night the course of history can be changed.' However, he didn't do it, because we had no precise information about the efficiency of the English fleet and because our navy put on the brakes.[52]

In 1935 the need for decision did not arise. The military measures that Mussolini had ordered, allied to the fear in London that he might act irrationally, sufficed to ensure the success of his strategy.

THE RESPONSE TO THE CRISIS IN MALTA

Whether or not Mussolini had any intention of attacking Malta, none had any doubts about the consequences for the island and its people of any such attack. Recovering from an operation in London in August 1935, the Governor of Malta, General Sir David Campbell, wrote to the Colonial Office that, in the event of war, 'Malta would be utterly defenceless against such an air attack as Italy could launch against it. In a short space of time it would be a veritable shambles.'[53] Baldwin was reported as saying in early 1936: 'If Mussolini broke out there would be more killed in Valletta in one night than in all the Abyssinian campaign up to date.'[54] But was there not also the possibility that the Italian government would seek to render the base ineffective by persuading the Maltese people to prevent, or at least, hinder, the use of the island for operations against Italy, either by passive non-cooperation, or even by acts of sabotage? Given the presumed strength of the pro-Italian faction in Malta, this was well worth attempting. Moreover, the Italian authorities began with the considerable psychological advantage that the island had recently reverted to autocratic colonial rule from Westminster.

The reasons for this further breakdown are complex and beyond the scope of this work, but the main elements need to be briefly stated in order to explain the public mood in Malta in 1935.[55] After the suspension of the Constitution in 1930, a Royal Commission was established, and in January 1932 it recommended measures to promote the use of Maltese and English, at the expense of Italian, in the courts and in the schools. It also recommended the restoration of the Constitution. The last-minute withdrawal by the Bishops of Malta of the anti-Strickland Pastoral letter, which had caused the 1930 suspension, allowed new elections to be held in June 1932, and in a record poll the Nationalist Party was returned to office with a commanding majority in both houses. Unwisely, the new administration took this as a mandate to reverse the language changes enacted in London in May, and to restore the teaching of Italian alongside English in the elementary schools. It thus embarked on a policy of confrontation with London of which there could be only one outcome. In November 1933 the Ministry was dismissed, and the Constitution once more suspended. As a consequence, when the Abyssinian crisis developed in the early summer of 1935, supreme authority in Malta rested with the Governor, who was also the C-in-C of the garrison. For a fortress island threatened with attack this autocratic form of government had practical advantages, but there were offsetting drawbacks in that the Maltese Nationalist Party's pro-Italian bias was strengthened. This naturally attracted the suspicion of the authorities, thus further increasing the tension.

Many threatening Italian press articles were reprinted in *Malta*, the Italian-language Maltese daily newspaper edited by Enrico Mizzi, a former Nationalist Minister. Nightly broadcasts from Rome and Naples, aimed at Malta, propounded the Italian case against Abyssinia, and the threat of bombing attacks on Malta soon arose.[56] The Lieutenant-

Governor, Sir Harry Luke, was initially sceptical about the impact of this propaganda, expressing the view in a despatch of 6 August that Italian sympathisers were 'more noisy than numerous'.[57] By 4 September he was less complacent. Enclosing a report from his Defence Security Officer, which now put the number of Italian sympathisers 'at nearer to four figures . . . and constantly gaining adherents', he warned: 'The body of feeling against us is much larger than was anticipated . . . and in the event of war with Italy, sabotage may be attempted both in the Dockyard and elsewhere.'[58]

Luke's assessment of the public mood in Malta was echoed in a letter to Chatfield from Vice-Admiral Sir Wilfrid French, who became the naval commander in Malta after Fisher's departure to Alexandria. In a letter of 3 September he wrote that 'even educated Maltese are beginning to lose confidence in us', and were 'depressed in our apparent lack of readiness, and that our tiny garrison and air force have not been reinforced'.[59] Potential trouble in the dockyard, French thought, was more likely to stem from pay grievances than political motives, and both he and Fisher recommended the restoration of an earlier reduction in pay. Fisher thought that this would remove '80 per cent of the Anti-British feeling in the Dockyard'.[60] In this propaganda war of nerves, as in the military sphere, the Italian government had clearly stolen a march on the British authorities.

However, a more positive British response in Malta gradually emerged in September. The plans of an enterprising Valletta merchant to import and sell British-made anti-gas respirators led, after a long debate, to a decision that respirators should be provided free of charge to all who needed one.[61] A further problem was the proposed evacuation of the wives and children of British servicemen living in Malta. These numbered about 5,000, and it was proposed that they should return in the troopships taking reinforcements to the island.[62] This matter was referred for decision to the DPRC, which decided on 17 September that the evacuation should be postponed. Malcolm MacDonald, the Colonial Secretary, argued that such an evacuation would cause 'considerable alarm', and Hoare agreed that this would be a sign of weakness.[63] These decisions were supplemented by a more effective news organisation, using both the newspapers and radio, to counter the pro-Italian reports, while in September three new Ordinances were enacted to control the Maltese press and 'to repress the spreading of false reports'.[64] The most tangible evidence of British resolution, however, was the arrival in mid-September of substantial reinforcements, and this would have been instantly known throughout the island and in Rome.

The potentially more dangerous threat to the British forces in Malta lay in espionage and acts of sabotage, the prevention of which was the responsibility of the Defence Security Officer. In 1935 this position was held by Major Bertram Ede, who was part of Colonel Vernon Kell's MI5 organisation, which had been given responsibility for counter-espionage in the colonies in 1919.[65] Ede's zeal for the detection of the King's enemies did not always attract the approval of the Foreign Office, where he was variously described as a 'spy maniac' and as one 'aiming at a kind of secret service dictatorship in Malta',[66] but his work was more highly appreciated at the Colonial Office.[67] Ede had access to the full resources and counter-espionage techniques of MI5, and the Colonial Office files contain transcripts of conversations that suggest the use of hidden microphones. Ede also appears to have established an extensive network of informers.[68]

A number of arrests, including that of a British subject, had been made for espionage activity in 1934, and in March 1935 an Italian factory owner, Belardinelli, was sentenced to three years hard labour for passing military information to the Italian Consul in Tripoli.[69] More seriously, in early 1936 Ede began to receive evidence to confirm his suspicion that the Italian Consul General, Ferrante, was instigating espionage. In March he reported that Ferrante had been involved in attempts to bribe dockyard employees to obtain plans of the navy's Asdic submarine detection equipment.[70] This was confirmed in May when two Maltese, one of whom was Professor Delia, a former Nationalist Member of Parliament, were arrested and confessed that they had received their instructions and payment from Ferrante. He was expelled in July and the recently appointed Governor, General Sir Charles Bonham-Carter, reported that this 'was welcomed by the vast majority of the population'.[71] Ede's attention was also drawn to several Maltese citizens. He reported adversely on the pro-Italian sympathies of the Chief Justice, Sir Arturo Mercieca, but although these led to Mercieca's arrest and detention in Uganda during the Second World War, no action was taken against him in 1935.[72]

This brief review of developments within Malta shows the extent to which the British and Maltese authorities had, in 1935, under-estimated potential anti-British sentiment in the island. Despite the ill will caused by the suspension of the Constitution – and even the pro-British former Prime Minister, Lord Strickland, opposed the reversion to colonial rule[73] – the authorities in London and Malta had made little attempt to maintain Maltese support for British interests. It was, consequently, an unpleasant shock to discover the extent of sympathy for the Italian position in the summer of 1935. However, once the authorities decided to take firm measures against Italian propaganda and espionage, the risk of internal disruption diminished. Nevertheless, there was left unanswered the question of how Maltese support for, rather than just acquiescence in, British rule was to be recovered.

4

Prelude to War, 1936–39

THE INITIAL RESPONSE TO THE ABYSSINIAN CRISIS

Speaking in the House of Commons on 18 June 1936, Anthony Eden, who had succeeded Sir Samuel Hoare as Foreign Secretary in December 1935, after foreshadowing the government's intention to vote at the forthcoming League Assembly meeting for the lifting of sanctions against Italy, went on to say that 'the Government have determined that it is necessary to maintain permanently in the Mediterranean a defensive position stronger than that which existed before this dispute began'. On the previous day, to a more specific question about Malta, Hoare, recently restored to the Cabinet as First Lord of the Admiralty, denied rumours that Malta was to be abandoned. The island would continue to be the navy's principal base in the Mediterranean, and 'we shall certainly take every practicable means to make its defences secure against any possible attack'.[1]

However, behind these reassurances the reality was quite different. By early July, following the League of Nations decision to lift sanctions against Italy, almost the entire defensive structure hurriedly put together during the crisis was being dismantled. The Mediterranean Fleet, less the reinforcements received from the Home Fleet, and further reduced by ships returning home for re-commissioning, resumed its station at Malta. At the same time, the army and air force units that had been despatched there in the previous September were sent back to England. These measures reflected not only the urgent need to return to normal conditions, but, more significantly, the firm conviction of the Chiefs of Staff that 'our interests lie in a peaceful Mediterranean and this can only be achieved by returning to a state of friendly relations with Italy'.[2]

Brushing aside proposals by the JPC designed to strengthen the position in the Mediterranean, the COS affirmed that 'the first desideratum is a secure Mediterranean. . . . No action should be taken which is liable to prejudice this primary consideration.'[3] This statement reinforced the recommendation of the third DRC report of November 1935, which, while warning that 'we must not under-estimate Italian capacity for mischief if we were in conflict with Germany', went on to say:

> Our defence requirements are so serious that it would be materially impossible, within the [3-year] period with which this Report deals, to make additional provision for the case of a hostile Italy. We take the view, therefore, that, for the moment at any rate, it is neither urgently necessary nor feasible to make provision for the contingency of a permanently hostile Italy.[4]

This recommendation clearly echoes the decision taken in November 1933 that virtually all of Britain's limited resources should be concentrated against Japan and Germany. But after 1935 it was no longer possible to assume that Italy was a friendly power and to rule out defensive preparations against her for a further three years was to take a significantly higher risk. Nonetheless, the DRC report was endorsed by the Cabinet, and formed the basis for the 1936 Defence White Paper.[5]

Diplomacy was, in consequence, the only means to fill the vacuum left by the withdrawal of British armed strength from the Mediterranean in the summer of 1936. This was a task that Eden and the Foreign Office undertook with considerable reluctance, especially after Italy's early armed intervention in the Spanish Civil War that erupted in July. The focus of this study will not permit detailed examination of Eden's cautious approach to the restoration of friendly relations with Italy, but it is evident from his statement to the House quoted earlier that he believed that diplomacy conducted with Mussolini should have the backing of armed strength.

However, a more practical ruling about the military preparations to be made at Malta in the aftermath of the Abyssinian conflict was necessitated by a report from the Governor in September 1936.[6] In his capacity as C-in-C, General Sir Charles Bonham-Carter, who had succeeded General Sir David Campbell after the latter's death in June 1936, set out proposals by the three local service commanders for the rearmament of the island, the details of which will be described later. Before considering these recommendations, and certain other proposals that had been put to them, the JDC wanted to know if they were still to be bound by the 1933 formula that prohibited expenditures against Italy. This question was referred to the CID, who debated the matter at a meeting in February 1937. The discussion that followed revealed widely divergent views. Hoare, the First Lord, whose statement to the House has been noted above, held strongly to the opinion that 'it was impossible to exclude the possibility of war with Italy', and urged that 'a start must be made on the modernisation of the defences'. The Secretary of State for War, Duff Cooper, while agreeing in principle, argued against 'very heavy expenditure'. Chamberlain, the Chancellor, thought that, although Italy could no longer be considered a reliable friend, 'the probability of her positive enmity was small'. After an untidy discussion, a new formula was agreed which stated:

(1) (ii) Italy cannot be counted on as a reliable friend, but in present circumstances need not be regarded as a probable enemy.
(2) In the above circumstances no very large expenditure should be incurred on increasing the defences of these [Mediterranean] ports, but that at the same time some steps should be taken to bring them up to date and to increase their efficiency.[7]

Gibbs considers this as little more than a repetition of the DRC recommendation quoted above that what was not practicable was not necessary.[8] It was certainly heavily qualified, but it at least removed the notion embedded in the 1933 formula that no expenditure at all was to be undertaken. The problem was now seen to be one of priorities. Moreover, this first tentative step was soon to be followed by another. At the first meeting of the newly established Defence Plans (Policy) Committee (DP(P)) in April 1937,[9] Eden opened the discussion by suggesting that 'the dangers to be apprehended from Italy required reassessment', and he presented his own views about this in a memorandum that he circulated to the CID in June. His paper catalogued the mounting evidence for assuming Italian hostility, laying particular emphasis on the transfer of Italian naval, air and army forces to southern Italy and Libya. He concluded that there was 'clear evidence of a definite ill will in the whole trend of Italy's present foreign policy', and recommended, consequently, a new formula which stated that 'Italy cannot be considered as a reliable friend and must for an indefinite period be regarded as a possible enemy'.[10]

Eden's proposal was analysed by Hankey in a memorandum of 3 July 1937 that he addressed to Chamberlain, who had, in May, succeeded Baldwin as Prime Minister.[11] As chairman of the DRC, and author of its third report, Hankey was firmly aligned with the Chiefs of Staff in their wish for improved relations with Italy. In an earlier memorandum to Baldwin, while recognising the potential danger posed by Italian 'imperial ambitions in the Mediterranean', he nevertheless urged that 'we should grasp the hand of friendship held out by Signor Mussolini, however repugnant it may be, and do our best to get back to cordial relations with Italy'.[12] What worried him about Eden's proposed formula was that expenditure on defences against Italy would 'dissipate our limited resources if we adopt now the Mediterranean as a third decisive area'. He offered an alternative formula, but also recommended that final decisions on the matter be postponed until the completion of a new review of the Mediterranean.

The CID discussed Eden's memorandum at two meetings in early July.[13] Once again the Foreign Secretary's views gained only modest support from his colleagues. Even Chatfield observed that, were the formula to be changed, it would be a 'long time before it would be possible to take any definite measures on that basis'. He referred, however, to the current investigation of Mediterranean strategy being undertaken by the JPC, and Chamberlain, following Hankey's suggestion, seized on this to propose a slightly modified form of words, the application of which would be governed by the decisions arrived at after consideration of the new review. The result was that, although Italy was removed from the 1933 list of countries against which no defensive expenditure was to be incurred, the February ruling against 'very large expenditure' was reaffirmed. Further decisions were to await the new Mediterranean review. For our purpose the relevance of this latest formula is that, although it still left Mediterranean rearmament firmly in third place, the need for it had now been recognised. Nevertheless, those responsible for the defence of Malta had to make do with very limited resources, a restriction which was bound to affect the use which could be made of the island as a naval base.

RECONSIDERATION OF MALTA'S STRATEGIC ROLE

Before examining the steps taken to strengthen Malta's defences, it will be useful to consider briefly the changing strategic context that governed decisions about the island. The removal of the Mediterranean Fleet to Alexandria in 1935 reduced the role of Malta to that of a possible repair base for the main units of the Fleet. However, a force of destroyers and submarines remained there to help defend the island, to support Main Fleet operations and to disrupt Italian sea communications. This secondary role as a central Mediterranean base for light forces was in itself a sufficient reason to warrant retention of the island.

After the Abyssinian crisis, nevertheless, the Admiralty searched the Mediterranean for a suitable alternative base for the Fleet. Cyprus was examined in detail, but the cost of establishing a new base there was estimated at a colossal £24½ million.[14] Finally, in March 1937, the Chiefs of Staff reached the conclusion, despite considerable misgivings, that additional repair facilities and the construction of a new graving dock at Alexandria would make that a more satisfactory, or, at least, a less exposed, war station in the event of a war with Italy.[15] However, the construction of these new facilities would take many years, and the graving dock was not completed before the outbreak of war. The result of this enquiry was to leave the Mediterranean Fleet, as Chatfield admitted, in a strategically unsound position. In practice, Malta remained the Fleet's main base throughout the period before the outbreak of war, and until a floating dock was towed to Alexandria in 1939, it was still the possessor of the only docking facilities capable of accommodating capital ships. Consequently, throughout the pre-war period the Admiralty pressed strongly for strengthened defences at Malta to permit its use as a Main Fleet base.

Malta's strategic role was also influenced by decisions about the Far East. Papers prepared for the Imperial Conference that met in London in May–June 1937 repeated a declaration that the Chiefs of Staff had previously made in their Annual Review in February. They reaffirmed: 'the principle that no anxieties or risks connected with our interests in the Mediterranean can be allowed to interfere with the despatch of a fleet to the Far East'.[16]

In other words, if the hopes for a restoration of friendly relations with Italy proved misplaced, and she were to threaten British interests while Britain was engaged with Japan, a fleet would nonetheless be despatched to Singapore leaving only light naval forces in the Mediterranean.

However, within weeks of this declaration, those Mediterranean interests were being subjected to pressures that compelled the government to re-examine their strategic value and to consider how they were to be defended. Despite the CID decision of 5 July not to regard Italy as a probable enemy, relations between the two countries quickly deteriorated again to a near-crisis level. In July, Lord Perth, the British Ambassador in Rome, warned that anti-British propaganda had risen to levels that were 'unpleasantly reminiscent of the technique used in the early months of 1935'.[17] In August, 'pirate' submarines, known by the Admiralty to be Italian,[18] intensified their attacks on Spanish-bound shipping. This quickly led to reinforcement of the British naval forces in the area, while at the Nyon Conference in mid-September an Anglo-French patrol system was agreed. Tension was also raised by the Italian announcement of its intention to increase its forces in Libya to a total of 60,000 troops. Against this force stood a British garrison in Egypt which was restricted by the Anglo-Egyptian Treaty to 10,000 troops.

In this deteriorating situation, the JPC rushed out in late July, 'in the event of a sudden emergency arising', an Interim Draft of a Mediterranean and Middle East Appreciation, which considered a single-handed war with Italy breaking out suddenly before reinforcements could arrive.[19] Should such a conflict develop the planners expected that there would be an immediate Italian assault on Egypt, accompanied by air attacks on the Mediterranean Fleet 'with the object of preventing it from operating in the central and eastern Mediterranean'. The main focus of this appreciation was the defence of Egypt against a possible attack from Libya, but with regard to Malta the JPC concluded:

> The proximity of Malta to Italy, its value to us as a base for light forces, and the increase in prestige which Italy would gain by its capture, make it certain, however, that Italy would give full consideration to the possibility of operations against it.[20]

Since the 1936 withdrawals had left the Malta garrison under strength, and the only aircraft at Malta were a flight of flying boats, the JPC thought that a well-planned Italian *coup de main* would probably be successful. If, on the other hand, Italy decided not to invade the island, air attack might quickly render the naval base useless. Nevertheless, the desirability of retaining Malta as a base for light forces led the JPC to recommend a reinforcement of two infantry battalions, the raising of the two battalions presently in the island to war strength, the full manning of all coastal and AA guns, and the completion of the approved 24-gun AA scheme. It also recommended the provision, when available, of an additional 24 AA guns. No aircraft were proposed for Malta, but it was recommended that, in an emergency, three squadrons should be sent to Egypt by aircraft carrier.

In this analysis of a single-handed war with Italy it was felt that, if the recommended reinforcements arrived, Malta could be held and would then play a valuable role in the defeat of Italy. However, the remaining two parts of the Appreciation, which the JPC prepared later, and which considered, first, a war in alliance with France against Italy and Germany, and, second, the addition of Japan as a third enemy, led the planners to assume, without quite saying so, the loss of Malta.[21] In the first case the Mediterranean 'would become a secondary theatre', and 'a very considerable period may elapse before reinforcements can arrive at Malta'. In the latter case, 'a commitment which neither the present nor the projected strength of our defence forces is designed to meet', the Appreciation repeated the statements quoted earlier that the despatch of a fleet to the Far East would take precedence over Middle East risks and anxieties. Naval control of the Mediterranean would, in consequence, be surrendered and the capture of Malta was even more likely. In the final version of this report, which was circulated in January 1938, only one additional battalion was required, since the other had already arrived, but all the other recommendations were retained. The report was finally approved by the CID in March 1938 'as a basis for plans', it being recognised that the additional 24 AA guns proposed were simply not available.

The impact of this analysis on Malta's strategic role in the unlikely event of a single-handed war with Italy was considerable, since the Chiefs of Staff had concluded that, with its existing below-strength garrison, the island was likely to be seized by Italy at the outset of any such conflict. But a reinforced garrison should enable it to resist a *coup de main* and play a valuable part in the defeat of Italy. Doubts persisted, nevertheless, about Malta's position in the two other, more probable, eventualities considered by the JPC. The relegation of the Mediterranean to 'a secondary theatre' in a war with Italy and Germany, and its virtual isolation were Japan also to become involved, implied that the chances of Malta's survival, even with a strengthened garrison, were bleak. Even if the island were not invaded, surrender might be forced by the inability to re-supply the island with the five shiploads per month that were essential to its survival.[22] These 1937–38 discussions about Mediterranean security showed a heightened awareness of the need to strengthen the defences of Egypt, the core of Britain's Middle East position. At that time, however, the retention of Malta continued to be seen as an asset rather than a strategic necessity. As Chatfield remarked at a CID meeting in July 1937, repeating the position he had taken in 1935: 'Malta might be lost for the time being; we should rely on regaining possession after our ultimate victory. It would be essential, however, to keep control of Egypt and the Middle East.'[23]

The Munich crisis in late 1938 provoked a further review of British global strategy and led to the preparation by the Chiefs of Staff of a new European Appreciation.[24] This was a comprehensive document designed to provide a strategic framework for Anglo-French staff talks due to take place in March–April. In the initially defensive strategy that it outlined, stress was laid on the need for self-sufficiency in the Middle East in order to avoid the risks of reinforcement in war conditions. But what if a fleet were required to sail to Singapore? Was this still to have precedence over Mediterranean 'anxieties'? The Appreciation acknowledged the commitment given to the Dominions to provide such protection, but hedged this by adding that, 'the strength of that fleet must depend on our resources and the state of the war in the European theatre'. When, at a CID meeting in February, the Prime Minster asked whether the Dominions should be advised of this qualification, Lord Stanhope, the First Lord of the Admiralty, remarked that he was 'disturbed at the prospect of the Mediterranean being denuded of capital ships'. He thought that only two battleships should, in an emergency, be sent east. Chatfield, who was now the Minister for the Co-ordination of Defence, strongly disagreed, and the whole question was referred to a new Strategical Appreciation Committee (SAC), chaired by Chatfield.[25]

The SAC held six meetings in March and April to decide and recommend to the CID the overall war plan to be presented at the forthcoming Anglo-French staff talks. The Naval Staff had for some time been considering a strategy of striking first at Italy, should it declare war on Britain and France, in order to knock it out of the war. This policy also had the support of Churchill, who sent a memorandum to Chamberlain on this point in March.[26] When Chatfield enquired how such offensive action could be taken against Italy if a fleet had to be sent to the Far East, Admiral Backhouse, the First Sea Lord, replied that 'if we struck a series of hard blows at the start of hostilities she might be counted out and the whole course of the war turn in our favour'.[27] After much debate, and a protest by Chatfield that this was a reversal of previous policy, an Interim Report was submitted stating: 'The object of the Allies would be to secure their interests in the Mediterranean and Middle East, and to knock Italy out of the war as soon as possible.'[28]

When, however, the Chiefs of Staff were asked to consider how the attack on Italy should be carried out they were reminded that French concern about Spanish Morocco meant that, even if Spain remained neutral, it would take at least two months before French forces could attack Libya.[29] Further analysis by the JPC, who had previously considered the plan to knock out Italy impracticable, led the Chiefs to reverse their earlier position and recommend that the neutrality of Italy, should Britain be at war with Germany, would be more advantageous. This amended advice was accepted by the CID, with some consternation, on 24 July.[30]

This far-reaching 1939 re-evaluation of strategy, despite the last-minute decision to encourage Italian neutrality, effectively removed the 1937–38 planning assumption that Mediterranean interests would necessarily be secondary to the needs of the Far East. Moreover, although its implementation was by no means clear, the concept of offensive action against Italy had gained considerable support. Consequently, should Britain and France in due course decide to force the issue in the Mediterranean, the retention of the base at Malta, which seemed to be of limited value in 1937, appeared much more important. Its value as a light forces base had always been recognised, but the growing probability of conflict with Italy reinforced the Naval Staff's persistent demands that the island be sufficiently strongly defended to allow its use as a main operational base

THE RE-ARMAMENT OF MALTA

With these strategic developments in mind, we may now return to the deliberations of the JDC to see how the new CID ruling of July 1937 affected defence planning at Malta. Two matters came before the JDC in the latter half of 1936. The first was the question of building a third aerodrome at Luqa to supplement the older airfield at Hal Far and the newer one at Takali that the Treasury had, rather grudgingly, approved at the height of the Abyssinian alarm in August 1935.[31] The Air Staff had first made this request in 1934 and now, in July 1936, argued that it was essential in order to accommodate the two squadrons that the third DRC Report had recommended. The CID approved the purchase of the land in July, and in the following April authorised the necessary construction work.[32] The importance of these decisions is considered later, but it should be noted that the Treasury authorised the escalating construction costs on Malta's airfields with only minor grumbles about poor planning.[33] Luqa, unlike Takali, was to be an all-weather airfield capable of operating medium bombers and facilitating the passage of transit traffic (see Map 1).

The second matter that claimed the attention of the JDC was a detailed report from General Sir Charles Bonham-Carter, the Governor of Malta, setting out the proposals of the three service commanders for the improvement of the island's defences.[34] Most of the earlier discussions about Malta had focused on its defences but the Governor's report of September 1936 emphasised the strategic purpose for providing such defences. In his view Malta was a base for offensive action that could be applied from no other place and naval and air force units based there 'could be expected to fix forces greater than those needed in Malta'. Naval operations, he recommended, could be carried out by submarines and motor torpedo boats (MTBs), while an air force of 60 aircraft, some of which might be float-planes, could be based there to 'serve as an effective thorn in the side of the enemy'. This was only feasible, however, if the island was properly defended, and for this to be achieved there were three essential military prerequisites. These were modern coastal guns and an adequate garrison to repel any attempt to capture the island, the 'fullest possible scale of anti-aircraft defence, using the most modern and most powerful equipment', and, finally, bomb-proof shelters for the naval and air units to be based there. Were these measures to be taken, the Governor declared, 'the considered opinion of the three Services here [is] that Malta can be made almost impregnable'. In addition, he urged, 'it is essential that the civil defence organisation should be maintained at a high standard'.

The more far-reaching of the Governor's recommendations were debarred by the 1933 ruling, but it was this report that provoked the debate in the CID in February 1937 that has been discussed above. Unfortunately, as we have seen, the revised July formula, while conceding that 'some steps should be taken', maintained the prohibition on 'very large expenditure'. This, for the moment at least, ruled out the more ambitious recommendations that the Governor had submitted. Nevertheless, much of the work on modernising the island's gun defences went slowly ahead. Although none of the reduced number of 9.2-inch guns was put onto the Mk VII 35° mountings, as planned in 1934, most of these and the 6-inch guns were re-sited, given new barrels, and provided with modern ammunition. Lights, range finders and communications were also replaced.[35]

Meanwhile, however, the issue that had always been the most contentious aspect of Malta's defence problem had resurfaced. In early 1937 the Naval Staff once again renewed their demand that their only fully equipped Mediterranean naval base be provided with adequate defences against air attack. It had long been recognised that the only satisfactory defence scheme was one that combined AA guns and fighter aircraft, and, in the following pages, it will be convenient to deal, first, with the AA gun defences of Malta, before examining the question of an air garrison.[36] The (CID) had agreed in 1934 that Malta should be provided with 24 AA guns but, after the removal of most of the additional guns sent to the island in the autumn of 1935, Malta, in mid-1936, was still protected by only 12 3-inch AA guns. The first of the more powerful 3.7-inch AA guns, which had taken so long to develop, were not issued until the summer of 1938, and, more importantly, Ministers ruled in November 1937 that Home Defence was to have absolute priority in the matter of AA equipment.[37]

It was against this background of a desperate shortage of modern AA artillery that the General Staff, in January 1937, put to the JDC their proposals for an order of priority in the installation of AA guns at overseas ports.[38] Malta, they recommended, should be placed a lowly eighth, after Freetown and Penang. When these proposals were reviewed by the COS in April, Chatfield lodged a strong protest, saying that he was 'appalled by the prospect of leaving . . . Malta with only twelve guns for a considerable time'. However, General Sir Cyril Deverell, the Chief of the Imperial General Staff (CIGS), explained that, since 600 AA guns were required for the Air Defence of Great Britain (ADGB) programme, little more could be done about overseas ports.[39] At the Admiralty's request the General Staff undertook a further examination of the overseas position, but, at a JDC meeting on 7 July, Colonel Pargiter, while conceding that 48 guns would be 'desirable' at Malta, could only undertake the completion of the 24-gun scheme in view of the CID ruling prohibiting 'very large expenditure' two days earlier. Speaking for the Admiralty, Captain Syfret immediately rejected this proposal, and the upshot was that the JDC referred the disagreement back to the COS, where, at a meeting on 4 November, Chatfield again took up the argument.[40]

By that time, as we have seen, Mediterranean dangers had escalated, and the reinforcement of Middle East garrisons was being vigorously urged by the local C-in-Cs, led by Admiral Pound. The draft Mediterranean Review of early July had also recommended the provision of 48 heavy AA guns. The thrust of Chatfield's argument to his colleagues was that the defence of Malta was essential to enable the Fleet to operate in the central Mediterranean. 'HM ships', he said, 'when in harbour should be able to rest under the secure protection of the shore defences.' He also argued that 'the Chiefs of Staff should not be influenced by consideration of the cost involved; that was a matter for the CID to decide'. Deverell disagreed with this latter argument, but, in any case, pointed out that a severe shortage of both men and material, as well as the absolute priority accorded to the ADGB programme, precluded any early improvement at any of the Mediterranean ports, including Malta. Finally, and more fundamentally, 'he doubted very much whether a large increase in the AA defences of the ports would in fact very greatly add to their security. To defend Malta against Italian shore-based aircraft by guns was virtually impossible'.

Chatfield refused to accept the 24-gun scheme, and insisted that an issue of such importance to the navy be referred upwards to the CID. To prepare for this the JDC was instructed to review the matter once again, and to make recommendations on a variety of assumptions. After further study the JDC responded, in March 1938, by recommending 24 guns as an 'immediate' requirement, 48 as 'desirable', if the prohibition on large expenditure were to be lifted, and as many as 104, if only purely military considerations were to be taken into account.[41] The Chiefs took this up once more at their meeting on 27 April,[42] but, right at the outset, General Lord Gort, who had succeeded Deverell as CIGS, pointed to the new difficulties caused by the Cabinet's February decision that £70 million was to be cut from the army's re-armament programmes. Part of this sum was to be found by delaying the proposed modernisation of Malta's coastal guns, and by retaining the approved 24-gun AA scheme.[43]

The dispute finally reached the CID in July 1938.[44] Sir Robert Vansittart, on behalf of the Foreign Office, strongly supported Chatfield's claim that 48 guns were immediately required, but even the latter was forced to acknowledge that the War Office could not in the immediate future provide any more than the 24 which had been approved many years earlier. The only improvement that could be hoped for was that these 24 guns would, in due course, be either new 3.7-inch or adapted naval 4.5-inch guns that were being manufactured for the ADGB. The CID concluded by giving approval for 48 guns, but only as an ultimate, 'desirable', objective, for which no target was set. Moreover, this approval did not overturn the Cabinet's decision in November 1937 that all new gun production was to go to the ADGB.

The Naval Staff, however, were not prepared to let the matter rest there for long. The opportunity to re-open the issue presented itself after the Munich crisis when the Cabinet, in November 1938, authorised the Admiralty to make new proposals about Malta's AA defences.[45] The first result of this was an urgent report from the JDC stressing that, despite the July authorisation for 24 guns, the dockyard, in January 1939, was still protected by only 12 3-inch guns.[46] Their replacement by eight 3.7-inch guns was scheduled for July, but the remaining 16 4.5-inch guns were not expected until December. Sounding a note of alarm, the JDC urgently recommended the completion of the approved 24-gun scheme while they considered a more ambitious and appropriate programme. This warning had the intended effect. The CID, on 26 January 1939, recommended to the Cabinet a relaxation of the ADGB priority ruling, and endorsed the War Office proposal to send to Malta immediately eight 3.7-inch and four 3-inch guns to complete the 24-gun scheme.[47]

Even more than in the case of AA guns the debate about the provision of fighter aircraft at Malta cannot be understood without recognising the overriding demands of home defence. Space will not permit discussion of the successive expansion schemes that the Air Staff presented to the government in the late 1930s, but in all of them overseas needs were subordinated to the attempt to maintain some sort of parity with the *Luftwaffe*. The only advantage that Malta eventually derived from this process was the priority given to the development of fighters and radar.[48]

The CAS had sent two squadrons to Malta in the 1935 emergency, but did not expect them to last long if Italy attacked the island. In addition, as we have seen, the 1937 Mediterranean Appreciation made no provision for fighter aircraft at Malta. The Air Staff, nevertheless, successfully campaigned for the two new aerodromes at Takali and Luqa, a prerequisite for air operations and better dispersal. Moreover, at a JDC meeting held on 1 April 1938, attended by Professor Watson Watt, AVM Peirse unveiled the potentialities of radio direction-finding (RDF) (i.e. radar), and said that the Air Ministry had decided to send an experimental mobile set to Malta.[49] This offered a much better prospect of adequate early warning of air attack than the acoustic mirror, an experimental version of which had earlier been built at Malta.[50] After a delay, caused by the Munich crisis, the first radar unit was established in Malta in January 1939.

After Munich Admiral Pound, while C-in-C Mediterranean, had made a strong plea for both fighter and bomber squadrons to be based at Malta,[51] but, after examining the matter in February 1939, the Air Staff concluded:

> In view of the incomplete state of our fighter defences at home, and of the limited value of one fighter squadron to deal with the

very heavy potential scale of air attack on Malta, the provision of such a unit cannot in present circumstances be regarded as justifiable.[52]

Malta, therefore, had no fighter defences when the JDC was given revised terms of reference by the Chiefs of Staff in February 1939. In their new European Appreciation, after confirming that light forces would in any event be based at Malta, they recommended:

> *Malta*: The scale of air defence, including fighter aircraft, be reviewed, and that one fighter squadron be provided as early as possible. The object of this review would be to decide whether the repair and docking facilities of the base could be made adequately secure for the Mediterranean Fleet to use in time of war with Italy.[53]

It is clear from this that the question the JDC were required to investigate was not whether Malta as a whole was to be defended, but whether it was possible to make the dockyard sufficiently secure to allow Main Fleet usage. With this broad instruction the Air Staff first carried out a detailed analysis of the likely scale of Italian air attack on the dockyard,[54] while the General Staff assessed the losses which 100 heavy and 48 light AA guns might inflict on this attacking force. The Air Staff assumed that a force of 276 bombers, representing 80 per cent of the Italian metropolitan bomber strength, might initially be employed, and this force, the Air Staff calculated, could deliver 600 tons of bombs on the opening day of the attack, and 200 tons daily thereafter. A weight of attack of this magnitude would, in their view, inevitably put the dockyard out of action for many months. The General Staff predicted that 100 heavy and 48 light AA guns around the dockyard area could destroy up to 50 per cent of the low-flying aircraft attacking the floating dock, but only approximately 12 per cent of the high-flying bombers. Overall, they concluded, the guns might account for 20 per cent of the attacking force on the first day of the attack. With some reluctance, therefore, the General Staff endorsed the Air Staff assessment.[55]

A third paper was then presented by Group Captain Slessor, the Director of Plans (DOP) on the Air Staff.[56] This examined the enemy losses that might be inflicted by a force of four fighter squadrons. He considered that, initially, these squadrons might destroy between 15 and 20 aircraft per raid, but, taking the view that RAF losses could not be made good by reinforcements, 'the defence in the air must be expected to be on a diminishing scale after the first engagements have been fought'. The Naval Staff predictably rejected these assessments, arguing that the presumed Italian loss rate would soon lead to a reduction in the weight of attack. In their view the outlay of £8 million, the cost of one battleship, was an acceptable one to secure the full use of the Malta dockyard.

The JDC discussed the whole problem once again at two meetings, both of which were attended by Sir Henry Tizard, Chairman of the Committee for the Scientific Survey of Air Defence.[57] In that capacity he had been closely involved in the development of Fighter Command's radar-based defence organisation in Britain, and no one was better qualified to assess the conflicting views expressed by the Naval and Air Staffs. After listening to all the arguments he thought that both views were exaggerated, but, while conceding that Malta was an ideal location for radar defences, concluded that 'it would not be possible, whatever the defences provided, to prevent bombs being dropped on the vital area'. Nevertheless, he tempered this negative view by giving his support to the Air Staff's long-held belief that counter-attacking enemy airfields in Sicily and southern Italy from French airfields in Tunisia would be the best way to reduce the weight of attack on Malta to manageable proportions. Since the JDC was unable to reach an agreed recommendation, the CID was presented with alternative proposals.[58] The first, Scale A, was the already approved, but incomplete, structure of 48 heavy and 16 light AA guns, and one fighter squadron. The alternative, Scale B, provided for 112 heavy and 60 light AA guns, and four fighter squadrons. Whichever of these was accepted, the JDC also strongly recommended that the establishment of a bomber force in Tunisia be investigated.

The whole matter went before the CID on 27 July[59] and, after another lengthy debate, Scale B was finally adopted. Sir John Simon, the Chancellor, thought 'it would be a deplorable thing if we abandoned our ancient stronghold in the Mediterranean'. Lord Halifax, the Foreign Secretary, 'agreed and said the political effect of deserting Malta would be disastrous', and Sir Thomas Inskip, now Dominions Secretary, said 'it would be tragic to leave Malta as it was'. These statements make clear that senior Ministers, unequipped to answer a technical question on which their military advisers could not agree, asked themselves whether Malta was important enough to justify a major effort to defend it. They answered this in the affirmative by authorising Scale B and did so not only to improve the prospect of Malta's use by the fleet, but also because prestige and honour demanded that every effort be made to defend a long-held and valuable part of the Empire. The significance of this decision can be measured by the observation that, when Scale B was completed in early 1941, the heavy-gun density over the Grand Harbour was greater than it was over London at any time during the war.[60]

Nevertheless, this apparent naval victory was understood by all to be no more than approval for a defence establishment that could not be achieved for a considerable time. The harsh choices required of the authorities were revealed only one week later when the Deputy Chiefs of Staff recommended that eight 3.7-inch and eight Bofors AA guns intended for Malta be diverted to Alexandria and Aden, respectively.[61] Admiral Pound, now the First Sea Lord, argued that, since there was no early possibility of raising Malta's defences to the agreed Scale B level, the Mediterranean Fleet would need to be based at Alexandria. Consequently, it was more urgent to increase the AA defences at that port. Chatfield accepted this, pointing out that risks should not be taken at the 'operational base'.[62]

A similar lack of resources prevented any early implementation of the proposal to establish a bomber force in Tunisia to attack Sicily. The CAS had supported this idea in principle at the July CID meeting, but when asked if the preliminary work could be carried out, he warned that it was a question of resources and that 'he could not advocate taking personnel now from their present duties to begin the establishment of the necessary organisation'. Consequently, although the French welcomed the proposal, nothing could be done.

There matters stood when Britain declared war on Germany on 3 September 1939. Despite the CID's July decision that Malta should have substantially increased defences, only 12 more heavy AA guns had reached the island by the end of August, raising the total to 24, and no fighters were based there. Nevertheless, although the provision of the full scale authorised was now made even more difficult by the opening of the war with Germany, an important principle had been re-affirmed. As we have seen, the Cabinet in 1935 ruled that all steps must be taken to defend Malta and this decision was confirmed at the CID meeting in July 1939. However weak the island's defences might be the government was determined that Malta should be defended not just for its potential military value but for reasons of honour and prestige.

In the event, Mussolini, in September 1939, decided to remain neutral, and thus allowed a breathing space in which some further strengthening of Malta's defences might be possible.

5

Final Preparations for War

MILITARY DEVELOPMENTS

The military measures that were undertaken in the final nine months before the first bombs fell on Malta on 11 June 1940 must be viewed in the context of wider Anglo-French strategy during this period.[1] By 1 September 1939 the Mediterranean Fleet had concentrated at Alexandria, leaving only seven submarines and 12 MTBs at Malta, and the Mediterranean had been closed to merchant shipping.[2] This state of readiness was, however, soon relaxed, as it became clear that Mussolini intended, for the moment at least, to remain neutral. Merchant shipping through the Mediterranean was resumed on 5 September, and at the first meeting of the Supreme War Council at Abbeville on 12 September Chamberlain and Daladier quickly agreed on the necessity to avoid any action that might provoke Italian hostility.[3]

In the months that followed, the Mediterranean Fleet was gradually dispersed to more active war zones until Admiral Cunningham, on 1 November, transferred his flag ashore at Malta. By that time he commanded only four light cruisers, one flotilla leader, four Australian destroyers of First World War vintage, three submarines retained for anti-submarine training, and the old aircraft carrier HMS *Argus,* which was used for deck landing training by the FAA. Malta became once more, therefore, the base for the, admittedly emaciated, Mediterranean Fleet and remained so until the following May.[4]

This relative, if somewhat uneasy, calm in the Mediterranean persuaded the Deputy Chiefs of Staff (DCOS) Committee in November to suggest that, since the Foreign Office took the view that Italy 'was moving in the right direction', some relaxation of precautions in the Mediterranean might be permitted.[5] The ODC then examined the position in each of the relevant colonies, including Malta, and some relaxation of precautions was eventually agreed. Nevertheless, it was stipulated that 'a sufficient degree of readiness should be maintained . . . so that, in the event of a change in the attitude of Italy, there would be no long delay in restoring full precautionary measures'. The Admiralty advised that the Mediterranean fleet could be rebuilt to full strength within three weeks.[6]

In December the Chiefs of Staff set out for the War Cabinet their proposed policy in the Middle East.[7] Rather surprisingly, given the earlier debates about Mediterranean strategy, they still adhered to the view that 'our interests in the Middle East, important as they are, are not as important as the security of France and Britain, or of Singapore'. They proposed, in consequence, that there should only be 'administrative development' in the Middle East, and that additional forces should only be despatched to the theatre 'when the situation admits and our resources permit'. In particular,

> with regard to air forces, we cannot at present afford to reinforce Egypt at the expense of Home Defence and the Western Front, even to the extent of providing adequate forces to meet Italian attack . . . Some time must elapse before this situation changes.

This policy document was considered in January 1940 by the recently established Military Co-ordination Committee (MCC), chaired by Admiral Chatfield, and recommended to the War Cabinet with the comment that the security of the Western Front and Singapore 'must at all times be assured'.[8] Although Malta was not mentioned, this decision clearly ruled out the formation of a fighter squadron there.

The period of wishful thinking about Mussolini's intentions came to an end in March 1940. On 18 March Hitler and Mussolini held a meeting at the Brenner Pass, the German record of which reveals that Mussolini told Hitler that Italy would be ready in three or four months.[9] However, it was not, as Hinsley observes, any knowledge of what was said at this meeting that provoked alarm, but rather the steadily mounting evidence, from intercepted signals, diplomatic sources and photo-reconnaissance, of large Italian troop reinforcements in Libya, the mobilisation of army reserves and, later, naval and air force concentrations in southern Italy and Sicily.[10]

By the end of March Cunningham was sufficiently concerned by the burgeoning evidence of Italian preparations to request reinforcements, and the Admiralty responded on 27 March by ordering a renewed concentration in the eastern Mediterranean.[11] On 30 April the War Cabinet authorised precautionary measures to be taken, including the manning of defences at Malta, and on 3 May Cunningham sailed for Alexandria where he hoisted his flag in HMS *Malaya*.[12] On this occasion only four submarines remained at Malta to provide any offensive capability. On 16 May the Mediterranean was, once again, closed to merchant shipping and by the end of the month only the date of Mussolini's intervention in the war was still a matter of doubt. On 4

June the Admiralty judged the danger period to lie between 10 and 20 June, and Cunningham, wisely in the event, assumed the earliest of these dates.[13]

We may now turn to examine a little more closely what use was made of this nine-month breathing space to bring the defences of Malta to a more efficient state. Since it provided both the infantry and the artillery to protect the island against invasion or air attack it will be appropriate to begin by looking at the army's reinforcements. The Governor's first anxiety was the weakness of his infantry force. Although it had been agreed in March 1938 after the Mediterranean Review that the garrison strength at Malta should be increased to 'Higher Colonial Establishment' levels, Leslie Hore-Belisha, the Secretary of State for War, admitted in January 1939 that lack of funds had prevented this being done.[14] In June 1939 the Governor reminded the Colonial Office that, in 1937, he had told the then CIGS, General Deverell, that unless the garrison were strengthened, 'I could not be responsible for the defence of Malta.'[15] Subsequently, a fourth British battalion had been sent to the island, but the Governor went on: 'Since then I have heard what is the plan of attack of the Italians and I have asked for a fifth battalion.' When this request was denied by the War Office, the Governor made plans to recruit four local defence companies for the KOMR in order to release regular troops for more urgent duties.[16]

The manning of the garrison had provoked much discussion about raising a regular battalion of infantry in Malta – the KOMR was a territorial, volunteer unit – but, following a visit to the island in April 1938 by Hore-Belisha, the decision was reached that it would be more useful to expand the regular RMA by an additional establishment of 43 officers and 1,000 other ranks.[17] This would relieve the pressure on the Royal Artillery, which would otherwise be required in increasing numbers to man the planned AA defences. The recruitment of Maltese, who could live at home, would also reduce expenditure on barracks. After the War Office had made a significant increase in Maltese rates of pay, recruiting began in November 1938 and there were over 1,000 applicants for the first 200 places.[18] In June 1939 the Governor was able to report that the first Maltese AA battery had been formed and that a second would be operational in August.[19] The overall result of these measures was that, when Italy declared war, Maltese citizens provided no less than 44 per cent of the military strength of the garrison.[20]

As we saw in the previous chapter, the protracted dispute about Malta's AA establishment had belatedly led, on 27 July 1939, to the CID decision to authorise Scale B of 112 heavy and 60 light AA guns, although it was understood that it would take many months, perhaps years, before the full number could be provided. We have also noted that, only one week later, the CID accepted a recommendation from the DCOS Committee that, in order to provide some AA defences at Alexandria and Aden, eight 3.7-inch and eight Bofors AA guns intended for Malta should instead go to those ports. When the war with Germany began such was the shortage of AA guns, particularly in Britain for the Home Defence programme, that the monthly allocation of new production was entrusted to the DCOS Committee.[21] In September 1939, when setting priorities for the rest of that year, the DCOS provisionally allocated eight 4.5-inch guns for Malta, subject to re-examination when the guns actually became available.[22] However, in November, when discussion turned to the allocation of guns for 1940, General Massy, on behalf of the War Office, asked the DCOS Committee whether it was still the intention to provide Scale B at Malta. In reply, Admiral Phillips 'urged most strongly that the approved scale of defences should not be watered down in any way by reason of the fact that there did not appear to be any imminent threat to Malta'.[23] His colleagues accepted this view, and the COS endorsed this recommendation in January of the following year.[24]

Admiral Chatfield then circulated a paper on the whole matter to the MCC, since the additional cost of raising the defences from Scale A to Scale B was no less than £7½ million. He also recorded a warning from the Treasury that, if orders were now to be placed for the additional guns for Malta, this would inevitably delay the production of much-needed 25-pounder field guns for the army. In the discussion at the MCC on 8 February 1940 it was Churchill, once again First Lord of the Admiralty, who recommended:

> Scale A should be completed as the immediate aim and Scale B should be accepted, with a very low priority, as the ultimate objective. It might prove from experience, before Scale B was provided, that some different form of defence would be more effective. It would be unwise, therefore, to order additional anti-aircraft guns for eventual provision at Malta if, by so doing, the provision of 25-pounders was delayed.

The other Committee members accepted this recommendation, which reflected Churchill's hopes that rockets, aerial mines, radar and the proximity fuze would improve AA capabilities.[25]

When, in April 1940, the DCOS were asked to allocate more guns to the Middle East in the light of 'the deterioration in our relations with Italy', they took the decision that, since 'the provision of an adequate scale of defence at Malta was out of the question in the near future', and the Mediterranean Fleet would therefore be based at Alexandria, the 24 guns which they were able to find should go there rather than to

Malta.[26] Nevertheless, between September 1939 and June 1940 Malta received, despite continuing shortages in Britain, an additional eight 4.5-inch, two 3.7-inch and eight Bofors guns. The total of 34 heavy and eight light AA guns on the island in June 1940 clearly fell short of the Scale A requirement set by the MCC. The question arises, therefore, whether this deficiency can be regarded as evidence that Malta's needs had been unfairly neglected by the authorities. In order to answer this question correctly the position at Malta should be considered in the context of the AA defences at other major ports.

Table 1 shows the number of guns approved, and the number installed, at several important port areas on 1 February 1940. What is immediately clear is that Malta's gun establishment was not far short of the position at major ports in Britain, and was stronger than at any other overseas port. Moreover, the 34-gun installation around Valletta was consistent with the latest Home Defence Committee recommendations.[27]

In the light of these figures Malta cannot be considered to have been harshly treated. It should also be noted that 18 of the 34 heavy guns in place were modern 3.7-inch or 4.5-inch weapons that were much more effective than the older 3-inch guns. Nevertheless, this was, in the Admiralty's view, quite inadequate. Nothing less than Scale B would permit the retention of the fleet at Malta, and since this Scale had, in February, been given 'very low priority', the limited number of additional guns that became available in April were, understandably in the light of the above figures, diverted to the Fleet's poorly defended operational base at Alexandria.

In late April, as evidence of Mussolini's hostile intentions grew, the Chiefs of Staff considered a Foreign Office recommendation that the

TABLE 1
HEAVY ANTI-AIRCRAFT GUNS ON 1 FEBRUARY 1940

Port	Authorised	Issued	% complete
Scapa Flow	88	40	45
Forth area	96	52	54
Tyne area	120	40	33
Portsmouth	56	40	71
All UK ports	696	292	42
Malta: Scale A	48	34	71
Malta: Scale B	112	34	31
Alexandria	48	12	25
Singapore	72	32	44
All overseas ports	410	124	30

Source: PRO CAB 83/4, MC Memoranda (40) 13, 'AA Equipments', 10 January 1940, and (40) 21, 'Production of Heavy and Light Guns', 7 February 1940, Appendix A.

defences of Gibraltar and Malta be strengthened to deter Italy. In response they ordered several measures, including the despatch of an additional battalion of infantry to Gibraltar. They took the view, however, that 'there is nothing practicable we can do to increase the power of resistance of Malta'.[28] They believed that Italy would be more effectively deterred by the threat of air attack on northern Italy.[29] A fortnight later, nevertheless, the War Cabinet Defence Committee reversed this decision. After receiving a warning from General Dobbie about the prospect of airborne assault on Malta the Committee, on 16 May, ordered a fifth battalion to the island from Gibraltar. With this reinforcement it was hoped that the garrison could hold out until relieved, although, in the absence of fighters, heavy air attack was feared.[30]

However, if the evidence suggests that the War Office, out of its stretched resources, had made some allocation of men and material to Malta, the same cannot be said of the Air Ministry. When Italy declared war on 10 June 1940 neither the General Reconnaissance squadron, nor the fighter squadron, both long promised, had arrived. In the preceding chapter it has been seen that the CID, in July 1939, authorised four fighter squadrons for Malta, although the Air Staff made it clear that they did not expect to be able to form any of these before 1940. At the end of June 1939 Group Captain Slessor, who had presented the Air Staff's case to the JDC enquiry, visited Malta and discussed the provision of the intended fighter squadron with the AOC. On his return he suggested that consideration be given to advancing the date of this squadron's formation from March 1940 to December 1939. This would not make the fleet base usable, but 'its moral effect would be valuable ... and it would no doubt give a good account of itself'.[31]

However, no action was taken on this suggestion before the outbreak of war with Germany. At the DCOS meeting in November that reviewed the provision of Scale B at Malta, AVM Peirse expressed the opinion that 'a fighter squadron should be allocated to Malta as soon as possible', and this was the committee's recommendation to the Chiefs of Staff. Moreover, when the Chiefs of Staff reviewed this recommendation in the following January they repeated it to the MCC.[32] Despite these recommendations, nothing was done, and this can only be explained by the agreed policy of avoiding actions that might antagonise Italy and the decision in December that no aircraft could be spared for the Middle East. In March 1940 Air Commodore Maynard, the AOC in Malta, wrote to the Air Ministry asking about its plans for the fighter squadron, protesting that the CID's decisions were being ignored. It was not until 16 May that he received a reply from Air Commodore Coryton, Director of Overseas Operations at the Air Ministry, which said that the Air Staff was 'simply unable to provide any [fighters] for Malta, as from a wide point of view, unless we can make Malta useable, we should not, in fact, waste our meagre resources'. Coryton went on to say: 'I think the experience of the last two weeks has amply proved the Air Ministry view to be the correct one.'[33] During those two weeks Fighter Command's limited fighter force was being drawn into the battle in France.

At meetings of the Chiefs of Staff and the Defence Committee on 25 May Admiral Pound urged the necessity for some Hurricane fighters to protect the reinforced Mediterranean Fleet at Alexandria, 'particularly in view of the threat of attack by German bombers'.[34] Simultaneously, new plans were being hurriedly made in case France should surrender,[35] and these even envisaged the possibility that, faced with heavy air attack, the Mediterranean Fleet might need to withdraw through the Suez Canal to Aden. The Joint Intelligence Committee (JIC) considered that the Fleet at Alexandria was likely to be Italy's first objective.[36] Despite these urgent requests from Admiral Pound, ACM Newall, the CAS, replied that, although 50 Hurricanes were being 'tropicalised', and six were ready, 'he would feel bound to oppose any further weakening of fighter strength in this country'. In the event, in early June, six Hurricanes were flown via France, Tunis and Malta to Egypt. The Middle East Air Officer Commanding-in-Chief (AOC-in-C), Air Chief Marshal (ACM) Sir Arthur Longmore, wanted to hold these aircraft in Malta, but was overruled by the Air Ministry. These aircraft had been sent out to meet the Admiralty's request for stronger air cover at Alexandria. As it happened, one Hurricane, delayed at Tunis for repairs, was eventually held at Malta.[37]

By that time Maynard had decided to take the matter into his own hands. Twelve FAA Sea Gladiators had been left at Kalafrana in packing cases when the aircraft carrier, HMS *Glorious*, sailed for Norwegian waters. He obtained Admiral Cunningham's permission to assemble six of these, while the other six were used for spare parts. A number of staff officers and several other pilots at Malta were quickly trained to fly these fighters.[38] Although these biplane aircraft were being replaced in the RAF by Hurricanes and Spitfires, they formed the only squadrons in the Middle East for some time to come, and were a match for most of the Italian fighters. At Malta it was numbers and trained fighter pilots that were lacking. Luqa, the all-weather airfield, became operational on 28 June 1940 and, in addition, the first radar established in March was supplemented by a second in July, while a third, low-level set was installed in December.[39] Without the pre-war provision of this basic infrastructure it is difficult to see how any air defence of Malta could have been mounted in the following years.

The circumstances and the decisions that led to the absence of Hurricane fighter aircraft in June 1940 have been set out above. But was this also the result of a view held by the Air Staff that the air defence of the island was impossible? Their 1939 opinion that the dockyard at Malta could not be made secure against air attack, at least not by such aircraft as could be operated from the island's limited airfields, was fully investigated at the JDC enquiry. Their arguments then repeated views expressed before and during the Abyssinian crisis. War experience was to show that the Air Staff in 1939 underestimated the growing power of radar-controlled modern fighter aircraft, and overestimated the scale of attack that the Italian air force would direct against Malta. In his memoirs Slessor later acknowledged the pre-war misjudgements about fighter defence capability when he wrote:

> It had always been an article of faith with the Air Staff that the counter-offensive was the most important element in our own defence. I think it must be admitted that we overstressed that doctrine to the extent of seriously underrating the efficacy of fighter defence.[40]

Nevertheless, partly for political reasons, the CID authorised the eventual provision of four fighter squadrons for Malta, and the first of these was planned for April 1940, although some thought was given to the possible acceleration of this to December 1939.

The Air Historical Branch's (AHB) post-war history of this period ascribes the absence of Hurricane aircraft to the Air Ministry's fears that their loss was inevitable and would be a waste of meagre resources:

> It is reasonable to conclude that the Air Ministry was largely, if not entirely, responsible for the deferment of the scheme, and that they considered it was, at the time, their only course of action.... They did not change this policy until the Malta fighter force had shown its capabilities.[41]

This interpretation, however, takes no account of the Anglo-French policy of conciliating Italy, the January 1940 decision that no aircraft could be spared for the Middle East, and, more importantly, the May decision that the protection of the vulnerable Mediterranean Fleet at Alexandria must have first claim on such Hurricanes as might be made available. This ordering of priorities was not in question in London, so that when, at the last minute, six Hurricanes were despatched to the Mediterranean the Air Ministry rightly overruled Longmore's wish to retain them at Malta.

Many years earlier during the 1932 Coast Defence Enquiry the RAF's claim to take prime responsibility for ports defence foundered on the admission that the required aircraft could not be guaranteed to be present at the critical moment. The positioning of aircraft, they conceded would, in the final analysis, be determined, not by the Air Staff, but by 'the War Cabinet or other supreme controlling body'.[42] This is what happened in May 1940. The Mediterranean Fleet, assembled at a poorly defended port within range of large Italian air forces, was the critical factor in the looming war with Italy. Serious losses were likely to give Italy control of the eastern Mediterranean and endanger Britain's hold on Egypt. The air defence of an empty dockyard at Malta was clearly less important and its defence against air attack or invasion had to be left, at least until more resources were available, to the permanent military garrison.

This is not to say that Coryton and other officers at the Air Ministry did not continue to be pessimistic about the contribution that one Hurricane squadron might make to the defence of Malta, but rather that this was not at that time the decisive factor that the AHB suggest. As was the case with the island's AA gun defences, weak air defence in June 1940 was primarily the result of inadequate resources, and the prior claims of strategically more important locations.

We may conclude this section by quoting the response of the DCOS Committee to a report by Lieutenant-General Sir William Dobbie, who had succeeded General Sir Charles Bonham-Carter as Acting-Governor of Malta in May 1940. Although the fifth battalion of infantry had arrived, Dobbie had written to the War Office about Malta's continuing weaknesses, to which the DCOS replied on 29 May that 'owing to the urgent commitments at home, and the threat of invasion, it would not be possible to meet any of the requests for additional defences for Malta'.[43] In purely material terms, only limited improvements in the island's defences had been effected in the nine months before June 1940. Consequently, it was increasingly clear that the ability of the Maltese civilian population to withstand air attack might determine whether Malta could offer an effective operational base.

SEEKING MALTESE SUPPORT

We may turn now to a brief review of the internal situation in the island on the eve of the Italian declaration of war. The object of this review is to consider the effectiveness of the measures taken, both in Whitehall and in the Governor's Palace in Valletta, to enlist Maltese support for the impending conflict with Italy, for without the active co-operation of the majority of the civil population it was doubtful whether Malta could be used as a military base, and its abandonment might then be inevitable. To do so, we must retrace our steps to April 1936 when General Sir Charles Bonham-Carter succeeded General Sir David Campbell as Governor of Malta.[44] At that time, as we have seen in

Chapter 3, British prestige and influence had fallen to a low level. The Italian conquest of Abyssinia in the summer of that year, in the face of British-led League opposition, the enforced absence of the Mediterranean Fleet and the persistent rumours that Britain intended to abandon Malta gave further encouragement to pro-Italian sentiment on the island that had been gathering momentum since the suspension of the 1921 Constitution in 1933.

In this unsettled atmosphere the new Governor's first task was, in the words of a Maltese writer, 'to dismantle what Italian influences had been built and this to be justified in the eyes of the people'.[45] This required a combination of measures that, on the one hand, would curtail Italian influence, and, on the other, accelerate the Anglicisation process that had begun in 1933 when Maltese and English had been declared the two official languages of Malta. On the restrictive side, the surveillance operations of the Defence Security Officer were stepped up. Evidence from such sources led, in February 1937, to the dismissal of two senior Maltese civil servants, although the matter was first referred to the Cabinet, which endorsed the proposed action.[46] The Governor also wished to remove the Maltese Chief Justice, Sir Arturo Mercieca, who made no secret of his pro-Italian sympathies, but Ormsby-Gore, the Colonial Secretary, declined to accept this recommendation, reminding the Governor that 'Parliament was sensitive about the independence of the judiciary'.[47] The 1935–36 Press Ordinances were invoked to control *Malta*, Enrico Mizzi's Italian-language newspaper, and, in June 1939, the Governor appealed to the Archbishop to restrain anti-British articles appearing in the Catholic newspaper, *Lehen is-Sewwa*.[48] Ciano recorded the cumulative effect of measures of this kind in his diary on 22 December 1937 when Mizzi visited Rome. After Ciano had taken Mizzi to see Mussolini he wrote:

> A very pessimistic picture of the situation in Malta. The British policy of denationalization is being intensified – time is against us. Large-scale British military preparations. Mizzi is convinced that Great Britain is preparing to have her revenge in a second round as soon as possible.[49]

The anglicisation process took many forms, but it was the activities of the Governor himself that were arguably the most effective in promoting the recovery of British influence in the island. From the outset he was assiduous in cultivating contacts with Maltese at all levels, and he was particularly anxious to remove restrictions on the entry of Maltese citizens into the British armed services. The Governor made a point of addressing all of his own officers upon their arrival in the island, insisting that the Maltese be treated as equals and as loyal citizens.[50]

Two other matters bearing on the probable reaction of the Maltese people to a war with Italy require brief attention. These are, first, the preparations to protect the civilian population against the anticipated air attacks, and, second, the development of the constitutional position. The density of the population in the communities around the dockyard and the Valletta harbours made it likely that there would be heavy casualties unless effective civil defence arrangements were made. This problem was exacerbated because, in the immediate pre-war period, it was widely assumed, in Britain as well as in Malta, that poison gas would be used. It was by then well established that the Italian air force had dropped gas bombs during their Abyssinian campaign, and it seemed reasonable to assume similar tactics in an attack on Malta.

After the Abyssinian crisis an extensive civil defence organisation had been established on lines being developed in Britain, and district councils were charged with co-ordinating local defence arrangements.[51] Plans were drawn up to evacuate families from the harbour communities, and to provide emergency food and medical supplies. The extensive passages and storage rooms in the old fortifications of Valletta and the disused railway tunnel running between Valletta and the suburb of Floriana were adapted as deep shelters, and further tunnelling in the soft Malta limestone was commenced in Senglea, the heavily populated suburb to the south-east of the Grand Harbour.[52] By the time war came to Malta a civil defence structure had been put in place, although more tunnelling became an urgent priority as it became clear that the Italian air force would use high explosives rather than gas.

The Governor's other challenge was to respond in some way to the widespread demand for the re-establishment of representative government. Since the dismissal of the Nationalist Administration in 1933 the Governor and his officials had administered the island under the supervision of the Colonial Office. In September 1936 a new Constitution was proclaimed. This provided for an Executive Council of five *ex-officio* members and not less than three nominated, unofficial members, but it was strictly an advisory body and the Governor could act without its consent. In December 1936 the Governor told Ormsby-Gore that this council was 'working well',[53] but a year later he reported a strong and growing demand from all the political parties in Malta for an elected administration.[54] Lord Strickland, the pro-British former Prime Minister, pressed this view as hard as any.

After representations by the Governor, and lengthy consideration in London,[55] what became known as the 'MacDonald Constitution' was announced in February 1939. This still gave the Governor the casting vote over an Executive Council of 20 members, but ten of these were to be directly elected. In the subsequent elections held in July, Strickland's Constitutional Party, no doubt to the relief of the Colonial Office, won six seats, the Nationalist Party three, and the Labour Party one. This limited form of representative government clearly went some way to meet the demands of the Maltese political parties, all of which contested the elections, and it provided the means by which Maltese opinions and interests could be expressed through elected representatives. Further than this the British government would not go, conscious not only of the turmoil of the early 1930s, but also of the looming crisis in Europe. Nevertheless, this Constitution persisted throughout the war, and Malta was not at any time subjected to martial law.

One less happy consequence of the approaching war with Italy was the detention in 1940 of about 60 Maltese citizens under the provisions of the Malta Defence Regulations, which came into force on 4 September 1939.[56] Among these were Enrico Mizzi, the Leader of the Nationalist Party, and the Chief Justice, Sir Arturo Mercieca. It is not our purpose here to weigh the rights and wrongs of such actions, but it should be said that many of those so detained shared the repeatedly stated view of Enrico Mizzi that attachment to Italian culture and language, and even admiration for the Italian state and its leader, was not inconsistent with loyalty to the Crown.[57] As Stewart Perowne, who knew many of them, wrote after the war, 'These men were not criminals, nor spies. . . . They were honest men with the courage of their convictions; and it was those convictions that convicted them.'[58]

These detentions were almost the last steps taken before the outbreak of war to put the island in a condition to withstand what was likely to be the second great siege in Malta's history. Since the irresolution and embarrassment of the Abyssinian crisis the British authorities had taken a firmer grip on their position in Malta. Measures had been taken, through an able and perceptive Governor, to reduce Italian influence, and a pervasive process of Anglicisation operated to increase support for British policies and objectives. Although the success of these measures could only finally be judged after war had come to Malta, the British government would have found reassuring evidence of the efficacy of its policies in Strickland's 1939 election victory, the ease with which the Maltese military units were expanded, and the relatively small number who were placed in detention in 1940.

6

The Threat of Invasion

THE ITALIAN DECISION NOT TO INVADE MALTA IN JUNE 1940

As we have seen, the Italian government had attempted over many years to undermine the military value of the British naval base at Valletta by seeking to weaken Maltese acceptance of British colonial rule. From a strategic point of view, concern about the proximity of such a powerful enemy base, together with other British and French Mediterranean possessions, was expressed in a major policy statement that Mussolini delivered to the Fascist Grand Council on 4 February 1939. In this statement, which Ciano referred to as 'The March to the Sea' speech,[1] Mussolini argued that Italy found herself imprisoned in the Mediterranean, and went on to say: 'The bars of this prison are Corsica, Tunis, Malta, Cyprus. The sentinels of this prison are Gibraltar and Suez. . . .The task of Italian policy . . . is to first of all break the bars of this prison.'[2]

In February 1939 such statements might be dismissed as empty rhetoric but, 12 months later, as Mussolini approached his decision to engage in a war parallel with Germany's, decisions were also required on the strategy required to break the bars of Italy's prison. Since overall grand strategy, like the choice between war and 'non-belligerency', was the prerogative of the dictator, an examination of the decisions affecting Malta must begin with a brief summary of the evolution of overall Italian policy in the months leading up to the declaration of war on 10 June 1940.[3]

Following Ribbentrop's successful visit to Rome on 10–11 March 1940, the two dictators met at the Brenner Pass on 18 March. At this meeting Mussolini declared his intention to intervene in the war on Germany's side in 'three to four months'.[4] He then translated this political commitment into an outline strategic directive which he set out in a memorandum of 31 March addressed to the King, Marshal Badoglio, the Chief of the armed services, and the three service Chiefs of Staff.[5]

After a general review of the war situation, Mussolini went on to analyse Italy's position. He repeated his 1939 statement about the bars to Italy's prison, and declared that Italy could not remain neutral without being reduced to 'the level of a Switzerland multiplied by ten'. The question, therefore, was not whether Italy should, or should not, enter the war, but when and how. More time was required to allow further military preparations, and 'because Italy could not conduct a long war'. He then outlined, briefly and vaguely, his conception of the overall war plan upon which the armed services should base their own studies and plans. Italy was to remain on the defensive on all its land frontiers, except for operations against British and French Somaliland to protect Eritrea. The role of the air force was to assist the army and the navy, while the latter's task was 'offensive everywhere (*su tutta la linea*) in the Mediterranean and elsewhere'.

Marshal Badoglio summoned a meeting of the service Chiefs of Staff on 9 April to consider this directive. All of them, having earlier been led to believe that Italy would not become involved in a war before 1943, complained about their lack of readiness, Pricolo, the air force commander, saying that there were 'too many illusions being entertained' about the prospects for Italian operations in the Mediterranean.[6] The naval chief, Cavagnari, was especially gloomy, and he predicted that 'one [enemy] fleet will place itself at Gibraltar and the other at Suez, and we shall asphyxiate inside'. He subsequently committed his doubts to paper in a memorandum addressed to Badoglio on 11 April. Against the 'two huge fleets' of the British and French, already fully mobilised, a naval encounter could only lead to losses which Italy, unlike her enemies, could not replace. He also ruled out any combined operations against strategic objectives, although Malta was not specifically mentioned in this context.[7]

This pessimistic analysis, and Badoglio's own warnings, had no effect on Mussolini who was more impressed by German successes in Norway in April. On 12 April the Italian fleet was mobilised, reinforcements were ordered to Libya, and the air force brought to a state of readiness. By 13 May, according to Ciano, Mussolini declared that 'within a month I shall declare war. I shall attack France and Great Britain in the air and on the sea'.[8] In his memoirs, Badoglio described the scene at the Palazzo Venezia on 26 May when Mussolini told him and Marshal Balbo of his resolve to declare war. Badoglio recorded that he drew attention to the continued deficiency in Italy's military preparations, and ended by saying, 'It is suicide.'[9]

Nevertheless, Mussolini's mind was at last made up, and, on the same day, he summoned a meeting of the Chiefs of Staff. He declared that any day after 5 June would be suitable for Italian intervention in the war, and confirmed *le direttive politico-strategiche* set out in his memorandum of 31 March. On the land frontiers 'nothing spectacular' could be done, although there was a possibility of action against

Yugoslavia. He then went on to say: 'Our forces will be directed against England, that is against her positions and naval forces in port and at sea in the Mediterranean. As I foresaw on 26 May 1939, an air and sea attack on all fronts.'[10]

To consider these new instructions Badoglio once again called a meeting of the Chiefs of Staff on 30 May. When he forwarded the minutes of this meeting to Mussolini he recommended that the whole month of June was necessary to complete preparations. With regard to naval operations he declared that 'if it is possible to assign an objective to the Navy it is that of keeping watch in the Mediterranean with submarines', while Cavagnari summarised his directives as 'defensive to left and right: hold control of the Sicilian Channel'.[11] Pricolo, the air force chief, had meanwhile misinterpreted Mussolini's Delphic reference to Jugoslavia and had deployed his forces for an attack in that direction. On 3 June Badoglio informed him that such an attack was not then contemplated, with the result that these squadrons were hurriedly redeployed to southern Italy and to Sicily for a war against France and Britain. Only on 5 June, however, was Pricolo instructed to prepare for an air assault on Malta, and the final orders were not given until war was declared five days later.[12]

On 8 June Badoglio convened a further meeting of the service Chiefs.[13] Apart from the preparations for an air bombardment, no other action against Malta was envisaged. When Graziani, the Chief of the Army Staff, raised the question of an invasion of the island, Cavagnari rejected this, citing the island's strong defences, 'bristling with weapons of all kinds'. He subsequently supported this decision with a memorandum of 18 June, which is examined later. It was, therefore, left to the air force to neutralise Malta by air attack alone.

Before we look more closely at the reasons that persuaded Cavagnari not to risk an invasion of Malta, several points should be made about overall Italian war aims. No one in Rome in 1940, not even Mussolini, as he made clear in his 31 March directive, considered Italy capable of fighting a long war against first-class opposition. Moreover, such military preparations as had been authorised were, in early 1940, still far from completion. For example, the navy did not expect its full strength of six battleships, including the two new 35,000-ton *Littorios*, to be ready for action before the late summer of that year. On the other hand, Mussolini saw, in the impending defeat of France and Britain, the opportunity, described later by Ciano as 'a chance which comes only once in five thousand years',[14] to achieve his long-held aim of establishing a Mediterranean-centred Italian empire. But the achievement of these objectives required, in his mind, a real, if limited, Italian participation in the war in order that her claims might be successfully pressed at the resulting peace conference. As Mussolini put it to Badoglio at their strained meeting on 26 May: 'I assure you the war will be over in September, and that I need a few thousand dead so as to be able to attend the peace conference as a belligerent.'[15] In the event, the military chiefs, with whatever reservations, accepted Mussolini's assurances that the necessary Italian involvement in the war would be brief, and that her objectives would be achieved at the peace table rather than by prolonged fighting. In these circumstances, an aerial bombardment of Malta made sense; an invasion did not.[16] Santoro later described the prevailing view in Rome as the *calamitosa illusione della guerra breve*.[17]

Moreover, Cavagnari was fully aware that an invasion of Malta had been considered in only the most general terms and that no detailed inter-service plan existed. From the moment when, in 1935, Mussolini decided to invade Abyssinia Italian naval planning had to take account of the British base at Malta. As early as 30 August 1935 an Italian planning document listed the primary targets to be attacked in Malta, placing at the top the 60,000-ton floating dock that had been towed out to the island in 1925.[18] In the following year, as the threat of oil sanctions grew, an outline strategy for war against Britain and France was drawn up. In this document the advantages of occupying Malta were enumerated and the conclusion was reached that this was only likely to succeed if it were attempted right at the outset of any conflict. If, on the other hand, invasion were ruled out air action, '*le più intense e frequenti*', would be essential to neutralise the base.[19]

Further studies reinforced these conclusions. In early July the naval plans department issued a general directive, DG 1, relating to an Italo-German war with Britain and France. This envisaged the occupation of both Albania and Malta.[20] Later in the same year, '*Documento Zero*' considered the occupation of Malta to be essential, and not impossible to carry out. A more elaborate analysis was contained in the study DG 10/A2, which focused on the problem of transporting an expeditionary force to North Africa.[21] It judged that Anglo-French forces based at Malta and Bizerta could make Italian convoys to North Africa impossible, and, once again, the conclusion was reached that this problem could only be solved by the occupation of Malta. Neutralisation by air attack would not give the same results since enemy forces on the island could always be reinforced from more distant bases. However, this study did not examine how an invasion of Malta might be carried out, other than to say that this would require *preparazione e la sorpresa*.

The next major examination of the Malta problem was a naval study entitled 'Project for the Invasion of Malta in the Spring of 1940', which set out in greater detail a plan to seize Malta.[22] The key assumption made in this study was that Italian air and naval forces could only hope to establish a *temporary* local control of Maltese waters before superior British and French forces arrived from Alexandria and Oran. It was essential, therefore, to land in one wave an overwhelming force, at least twice the size of the defending garrison. Since the British defences were grossly over-estimated – for example, 15,000 infantry, 100 armoured vehicles and over 80 coastal guns, when the true figures were, respectively, about 5,000, none (excluding infantry Bren gun carriers) and 26 – the required attacking force was put at 40,000 men. The Italian navy had no specialised landing or beaching ships, but it was planned to adapt a number of light coastal steamers which would all be run aground on selected beaches in the northern part of Malta. This large force, quickly disembarked with only light weapons, would then be expected to overwhelm the defending troops holding positions on the Victoria Lines. This was a defensive line, fortified in the nineteenth century, which ran along an escarpment that divides the island of Malta into two (see Map 1). The entire available Italian fleet was to provide gun support on the landing day, but the principal supporting role was assigned to the air force. No fewer than 500 aircraft were required to provide heavy and continuous attacks on all military targets for a period of at least five days prior to the assault. On X-Day itself, gas bombs were to be dropped and 600 paratroops landed in the southern part of the island to create a diversion.

An intriguing aspect of this analysis is the gross over-estimation of Malta's defences. In discussing the reasons for this Gabriele cites several pre-war Italian intelligence reports, which indicated that as many as 280 aircraft might be available at Malta, and suggested that the Italian naval staff were simply, and prudently, making a 'worst-case' assumption.[23] The steady expansion of military airfields in Malta, especially the all-weather airfield at Luqa, would have been noted by the Italian authorities, while the frequent presence of disembarked carrier aircraft was a reminder of the ease with which air reinforcements might arrive, particularly from French North Africa.

In his overall analysis of this early 1940 plan Gabriele remarks on the elements of *fantasia* which it contained, 'especially if account is taken of the lack of preparation, both general and specific, which characterised the Italian armed forces at that time'.[24] The Italian army had no troops trained for an amphibious opposed landing, the navy lacked any specialised landing craft, and, as was noted earlier, the air force was, until early June, deployed for an attack on Yugoslavia. Knowing all this, Cavagnari had no hesitation in rejecting, at the Chiefs of Staff meeting on 5 June, Graziani's suggested seizure of Malta.

Nevertheless, in order to meet Badoglio's request that the problem be given further study, the naval staff produced a revised analysis, entitled 'Project of 18 June 1940: The Attack on Malta'.[25] This concentrated more specifically on the naval aspects of the plan, simply demanding the greatest possible support from low-flying aircraft and paratroops. The invading force was, in this study, reduced to only 20,000 troops, although the earlier over-estimates of the defending garrison were retained. This study concluded by asserting that 'the exceptional difficulty of the attack and the forces which would need to be committed to it would only be justified if Malta represented a decisive objective'. However, in the planners' view, given that the British no longer regarded Malta as a major operational base, the threat posed by the island was 'of secondary importance'. Consequently, aerial attack and naval blockade would suffice, and the study concluded by declaring: 'Malta will fall into our hands as a consequence of final victory, won by concentrating all our energies on those theatres containing decisive objectives.' What Gabriele calls 'this muddled analysis' was, perhaps, designed simply to justify the decision which Cavagnari had already announced on 5 June, and it contributed little to the earlier analyses of a possible invasion of Malta.

As to whether an invasion attempt in June 1940 would have been successful, several writers have assumed that the island could have been seized with little difficulty. Jellison, for example, believed that 'when the Duce finally decided to join the conflict, he could have seized Malta before lunch if he had chosen to do so'.[26] More convincing is Gabriele, who, after a full review of the evidence, reached the conclusion that an attempt to invade Malta in June 1940 would probably have failed.[27] Even though the defending garrison was significantly weaker than the Italian naval planners had assumed, the transport of a force of between 20,000 and 40,000 troops from the nearest Sicilian ports could not have been completed during a short summer night. But even if the force reached Malta undetected and undamaged, an early morning landing on the relatively small number of suitable beaches, from ships not designed for rapid disembarkation, against five battalions of regular infantry dug in on higher ground, conjures up images of Gallipoli and Dieppe. Close air support by air forces trained for such a role might have made a difference, as they did in Crete, but such units did not exist in the Italian air force. In the complete absence of any detailed inter-service planning a hastily launched *coup de main* attempt in June 1940 with improvised forces would almost certainly have failed.

But why, despite the many studies that concluded that only occupation could eliminate the threat posed by Malta, were practical plans to do this not ready to be implemented when Italy declared war in June 1940? A full answer to this question lies beyond the scope of this study. Knox, in a recent detailed study seeking to explain why the Italian armed forces were so ineffective in the war, argues that Italian failings can only be properly explained by 'deficiencies in military culture that prevented the armed forces from imagining, much less preparing for modern war'.²⁸ On this view, a co-ordinated inter-service plan to seize Malta, and the provision and organisation of the means to carry it out, lay beyond Italian military capabilities.

PRE-WAR BRITISH ASSESSMENTS OF ITALIAN INTENTIONS

The threat posed by Malta to Italy's control of the central Mediterranean, and to its supply route to Libya, caused as much concern in London as in Rome. It was natural, therefore, that the British Chiefs of Staff should employ every means to discover what Italian intentions with regard to Malta might be, and, in particular, whether an invasion was planned. By 1939, as Hinsley makes clear, GC&CS had broken most of the Italian cyphers, including those of the three services.²⁹ One product of this may have been an Italian naval document dated 25 June 1939 and entitled 'Conduct of the War in the Mediterranean', an English translation of which is included in the records of the Admiralty's Naval Intelligence Division (NID) in the Public Record Office.³⁰ Its provenance is not at all clear. Hinsley states that the NID had been given a copy by the French government in August 1939, and he describes it as 'purporting to be an Italian Admiralty directive'. However, the text has, in one place, the phrase, 'indecypherable sentence', which suggests the possibility that the document was directly acquired, deciphered and translated by GC&CS, which had had an Italian section since the Abyssinian crisis of 1935–36. Whatever its origin, the document, which is entitled 'General Instructions to the Naval Commands (Bases)', is a lengthy one, and the opening pages describe the expected strength and disposition of the opposing naval forces in the Mediterranean. It then lists 'the principal objectives to be undertaken by Group No.1 [i.e. Italy and her allies] in the least possible time after the outbreak of hostilities'. Our interest lies in the eighth of these objectives, which was 'isolating and neutralising Malta'. This is repeated later in the text when the laying of minefields in the Malta channel is referred to. The only invasion attempts mentioned are those to capture Corfu and other Greek Ionian Islands, and a plan to land forces in Palestine to support an attack on the Suez canal.

Attached to the copy in the PRO is a covering note of 30 August 1939, on the eve of the German attack on Poland, from Rear-Admiral Godfrey, the Director of Naval Intelligence (DNI), to Admirals Pound, the CNS, and Phillips, the DCNS. This noted that the most significant sections of the document had been marked in red ink, and that a copy was being sent to Cunningham at Alexandria by destroyer. The question is whether this was a genuine document. It is not specifically referred to by Gabriele, Mallett or Knox, who have all studied the Italian naval archives in detail. However, the document appears to lay down only general principles, and it concludes with a reference to other plans which 'are exclusively in the principal instructions'. It is equally uncertain, in the absence of comment or relevant minutes in the NID records, whether the Admiralty regarded this document as genuine. Hinsley's post-war description of it may suggest that it was regarded by the NID at the time with a degree of scepticism, although this is not the implication of Godfrey's covering note.

Whatever value the Admiralty may have attached to this document in 1939, it was not until April 1940, when Italian restlessness was becoming more evident, that attention focused once again on Italian military intentions. Consequently, when General Dobbie requested an additional infantry battalion to meet a possible airborne assault, a fifth battalion was sent in mid-May.[31] Dobbie's reference to the possibility of an airborne attack may simply have been prompted by the German employment of such units in the Low Countries, or by other general considerations. Nevertheless, there remains the possibility that, since an airborne landing was in fact an element of the Italian spring 1940 study, the Governor may have gained some knowledge of this.

Other intelligence, however, did not point to an imminent invasion for which large-scale preparations would have been necessary. It was not until 7 June that the Middle East Intelligence Centre (MEIC) reported the arrival of 122 modern Italian bombers in Sicily, the response to Badoglio's order to Pricolo of 5 June.[32] Moreover, the arrival of these aircraft did not necessarily indicate an invasion attempt. For this, large numbers of landing or beaching craft would also need to be assembled in Sicilian ports, and, to watch for these, two PR Spitfires, sent from England, took photographs over much of southern Italy between 28 May and 15 June.[33] No doubt these were supplemented by reconnaissance flights from Malta. Equally important, the continuing flow of normal trading traffic between Malta and Sicily would have allowed virtually continuous observation of Italian harbours where any build-up of potential invasion craft could hardly have escaped notice. An invasion attempt would also have required a substantial infantry force to be assembled in Sicily, and, once again, there was no evidence of such a build-up. Decrypts revealed on 7 June the arrival of 17,000 additional Italian troops in Libya, but no comparable movements to Sicily were indicated.[34]

The JIC in London assessed all of the available intelligence, much of it negative, in a report to the Chiefs of Staff on 24 May. They correctly concluded that 'we consider that all the indications point to the fact that Signor Mussolini has made up his mind to enter the war on the side of Germany'.[35] Five days later, in a paper that examined possible Italian courses of action, the JIC judged the most likely Italian objective to be an attack on the British and French fleets. With regard to Malta they wrote: 'The object of an Italian attack on Malta would be to neutralise its value as a naval base and to achieve a spectacular success. . . . Sudden attack by air-borne troops is highly probable.'[36]

By early June Italy's intention to declare war could no longer be in doubt, not least because, as the Daily Situation Report of 10 June noted: 'Ciano continues the curious policy of giving us full information.'[37] The probable date of Italy's declaration of war was placed by the Admiralty between 10 and 20 June, and Cunningham's first anti-submarine sweep was carried out at 4 a.m. on 10 June. Later that evening a submarine was attacked south of Crete. By that date Dobbie in Malta might have anticipated early and heavy air attack, possibly using gas as well as high-explosive bombs. On the other hand, an immediate seaborne assault must have seemed unlikely since there was no evidence of the necessary ships and landing craft, while an airborne attack by itself would have been too weak to be effective. Nevertheless, it was prudent to assume that initial air attacks might be a prelude to a subsequent invasion attempt, as, indeed, the Italian naval study of spring 1940 had envisaged.

On the eve, therefore, of Mussolini's declaration of war the available intelligence suggested that it was more likely that Malta would suffer heavy air bombardment than an invasion. If, however, these attacks were as heavy and as damaging as the pre-war Air Staff estimates thought likely, the island's defences might soon be so reduced in effectiveness that an invasion could be more easily mounted. There was the further possibility that, as a result of bombing alone, the strategic value of the base would be fatally undermined by a collapse of morale among the civilian population.

THE RISK OF INTERNAL COLLAPSE

It is beyond the scope of this study to examine the profound social and political impact on a traditional, close-knit and largely defenceless community of a persistent air onslaught, particularly one carried out by a country which had long professed friendship. Our interest here lies, as in earlier chapters, in the official concern that such attack might so demoralise the population that Malta would be rendered useless as a military base. This section briefly examines the measures that the Malta government took to meet this situation, and the reaction of the Maltese population.[38]

Concern about the possibility of internal unrest was expressed to the War Office by Colonel Ede soon after the first air raids. He warned then that 'if Fighters are not sent [Maltese reaction] will, in my opinion, take the form of a dangerous mass demand for surrender, if we are not able to give reasonable protection to the population'.[39] The seriousness with which this warning was treated is shown by a hand-written notation on Ede's telegram, dated 16 June, which recorded that the Air Staff were urgently considering the despatch of six Hurricanes to Malta. These were in fact sent, via France, on 18 June, and Maynard was authorised to retain four. Fears of a collapse were raised again by the Governor when he wrote to General Dill, the CIGS, in early July. After recording that, despite the 'great upheaval of the normal life of the place and a great exodus of population from some parts to others . . . so far the morale of the people has been surprisingly good', he then expressed his concern about the possible effects of intensified air attack:

> At best we would be handicapped by an interruption of essential services for which we rely on the Maltese, at worst we might be faced with an angry and actively hostile population, who might force us to throw our hand in. . . . Again I do not know how far, in such circumstances, one could rely on the Maltese troops.[40]

The first day's bombing on 11 June, on which eight separate raids between 7 a.m. and 7.25 p.m. caused the death of 11 civilians and 12 military personnel, led to a mass exodus from the crowded harbour communities of Senglea, Cospicua and Vittoriosa.[41] All work in Valletta and the dockyard ceased, and the pre-war evacuation plans drawn up by the authorities were largely ignored. Families who had no relatives or friends in the country sought refuge where they could. Nevertheless, emergency plans, dependent on large numbers of Maltese volunteers, had been prepared and these were at once put into effect. The police force was augmented by over 2,000 special constables to help maintain public order, the Air Raid Precautions rescue organisation was mobilised, and a 'Home Guard', to counter the threat of airborne landings, was recruited from those owning sporting guns.[42] Assistant district commissioners were appointed, and local protection officers assigned to each community to deal with the problems caused by the large displacement of people. Local community leaders, such as parish priests, teachers and doctors played a leading part in this emergency work. The teachers were particularly important, and the Governor wrote in early June to Dr Laferla, the Director of Education, saying, 'we're counting on you and your teachers to run things'.[43]

The evidence of contemporary witnesses is that, after the initial panic and confusion, many people began to adapt to bombing attacks, which, although persistent, were not as heavy and destructive as they were later to become. Moreover, there was no use of gas, as many had feared. The Government ordered public employees back to work, shops were required to re-open, revised bus schedules introduced, and cinemas and other public places re-opened. More significantly, after two or three weeks an increasing number of people who had fled during the first days of the war began to return to their homes.[44]

The Governor took a number of other immediate steps. The local Italian community was interned and eventually repatriated to Italy. Detention orders, some of which had already been issued to several Maltese citizens before war was declared, were extended. Among those detained were the Chief Justice, Sir Arturo Mercieca,[45] and the leader of the Nationalist Party, Enrico Mizzi. These measures received wide publicity.[46]

But perhaps the most powerful influence in the early days of the war was the personal example set by the Governor, Lieutenant-General Sir William Dobbie. Although he had only arrived in Malta on 28 April to succeed the ailing Bonham-Carter, he soon became a well-known figure in the island as he visited the defence positions and sought to meet as many people as possible. A tall and imposing figure, his deeply held religious convictions made an immediate appeal to the Maltese, and, soon after his arrival, he began to make regular broadcasts on the local Rediffusion relay service. Many contemporaries have paid tribute to his qualities, and Admiral Cunningham's is typical: 'An Ironside of a man, his profound faith in the justice of our cause and the certainty of Divine assistance made a great impression upon the highly religious Maltese.'[47]

However, the main task facing the authorities was that of providing adequate protection for the civilian population to minimise the effects of bombing attack. In a long report of 20 June 1939 the then Governor, Sir Charles Bonham-Carter, set out plans for a large deep shelter programme, and urged that a start be made on a tunnelling project beneath Senglea, one of the harbour communities.[48] Given the large population, and the absence of any really safe areas to which people could be evacuated, he took the view that the provision of shelters was the only responsible long-term solution to the problem of civilian protection. These proposals were approved by the ODC on 12 July 1939, and the sum of £250,000 was subsequently authorised.[49] The Senglea project was begun later that year and consulting engineers, in April 1940, put forward a three-year, £300,000 scheme for the whole island. But it was only shortly before the outbreak of the Italian war that a senior dockyard engineer, Mr Mavity, was recalled from leave in England to establish and manage a Shelter Construction Department within the Malta administration.[50]

It was fortunate that in and around Valletta there was already underground shelter for significant numbers in the tunnels beneath the historic bastions, in the disused railway tunnel between Valletta and Floriana, and in several underground garages. In the dockyard itself the Admiralty had excavated shelters capable of accommodating as many as 1,000 workmen in the surrounding cliffs. Nevertheless, particularly after the slow return of many people from outlying villages to the Three Cities area, there was a growing demand for additional deep-rock shelters. Similar anxiety about the deep shelter situation was expressed in London. On 19 September the War Office advised the Colonial Office of its concern that 'unless adequate shelters are provided they feel that the effect on the Maltese may be such as to embarrass the efforts of the defending troops'. They asked for information about the progress of deep shelter construction.

The reply from the Governor, which was not sent until 13 December, was rather disconcerting. He advised that all existing deep-shelter work had been discontinued when Italy declared war so that resources could be applied to the digging of covered slit trenches and the provision of blast and splinter-proof shelters.[51] These may have had some value for people caught in the open during an air raid, but they soon became filled with water and rubbish, and Dobbie later admitted that they 'no longer command public confidence'. It appears, however, from a letter to the Admiralty by the Vice-Admiral Malta (VAM), Admiral Ford, that the need to resume rock shelter construction had already been recognised as early as October, since Ford reported then that he had seconded several of the dockyard's senior engineers and numerous men to assist Mavity with the shelter construction scheme.[52]

There was much criticism at the time, and later, about the Malta government's failure to provide adequate deep-shelter accommodation before the war, and of the slow pace of later tunnelling work. Some of the later criticism is misplaced. Jellison, for example, writing in 1984, cites the very limited amounts spent by the Malta government on civil defence as evidence of the government's neglect of its responsibilities.[53] But this misses the point that the Malta government, *with the Governor's backing*, refused to spend local tax revenues on what they perceived to be an imperial responsibility. Jellison quotes a local Maltese allocation of a mere £322 for shelter work in 1940, although the ODC in London had, as noted above, allocated a total of £250,000 for such work in 1939. By November 1941, the amount spent had risen to over £600,000.[54]

It seems fair to say, nevertheless, that, partly for the reasons already discussed, not enough was done before the war to provide more shelter accommodation, and that progress to rectify this during wartime conditions was then inevitably slow. In order to speed up shelter accommodation encouragement was given for private construction, often excavated under the bastion walls, and in the course of the subsequent two years a large number of these were completed in the most exposed areas. It was fortunate for Malta that the heaviest German raids did not develop until early 1942 by which time the deep-shelter programme was much further advanced. To this, and to the movement of many people away from the principal target areas, was due the fact that throughout the whole war, when it is estimated that at least 15,000 tons of bombs were dropped on the island, no more than 1,486 of the civilian population lost their lives. During the period from June 1940 to May 1941 civilian casualties were 282 killed and a further 282 seriously wounded.[55] Comparable figures in England during the 1940–41 'Blitz' were, respectively, 43,000 and 139,000.[56]

The Governor's other overriding problem was that of ensuring adequate supplies of food and other necessities for a densely populated island heavily dependent upon imports. As early as February 1939 the ODC had recommended that essential stocks be built up to a six-month consumption level,[57] and in early June 1940, on the eve of war, the reserves of certain key items were:

8 months supply: wheat, flour, and edible oil
6 months supply: coal, coffee
5 months supply: soap, sugar, fats, kerosene[58]

However, before the arrival of the first supply convoy at the end of August, stocks of many of these items, other than coal and wheat, had fallen to a two-month level. Vice-Admiral Ford consequently recommended that reserves be raised to an eight-month level by sailing convoys every two months.[59] Although the position was 'fairly satisfactory', he warned that 'in view of shipping delays early action is imperative to start building up these reserves, which are an essential part of fortress defences'.[60] These recommendations were accepted by the Chiefs of Staff on 23 August.[61]

In mid-September the Governor advised Lord Lloyd, the Colonial Secretary, that although Malta's monthly requirements stood at 40,000 tons, twice that much would need to be delivered if the eight-month reserve target were to be reached. Lloyd brought this matter before the War Cabinet in September, but first warned the Prime Minister, in a note of 11 September, that the proposals 'would throw a very great burden on the Mediterranean Fleet and it seems, therefore, to be a question of major policy whether arrangements are still to proceed with that end in view'.[62] The upshot was that, when Lloyd put the matter to the War Cabinet on 19 September, the Minister of Shipping said 'he

THE THREAT OF INVASION

would do his best to meet these new demands', and the War Cabinet accordingly approved the Governor's proposals.[63] However, reserves had only reached a seven-month level before the beginning of the intensive *Luftwaffe* attacks in mid-January 1941 brought a temporary halt to Malta convoys.[64]

A system of rationing was not immediately introduced in June 1940. It was argued that the Maltese would not welcome this, and that it would be administratively difficult, not least because most of the shopkeepers were illiterate. Instead, the authorities simply reduced the amounts of certain items released to the wholesalers, a practice that inevitably led to hoarding, price inflation and a growing 'black market'. This prompted one of the Maltese nobles, Marquis Barbaro, to institute an unofficial rationing system in the north of the island, and, in February 1941, the Governor appointed Barbaro as Food Distribution Officer with the task of establishing an island-wide scheme. This came into force on 7 April, and initially applied to only four items, sugar, coffee, soap and matches.[65]

The evidence of contemporary records and eyewitnesses is that, despite the casualties and the inevitable fear and confusion of the early weeks of the bombing, many Maltese soon adapted to the dangers of attack and to the dislocation of normal life which resulted.[66] When Vice-Admiral Ford called for 400 volunteers from the dockyard workforce to man a dockyard defence battery of AA guns, 5,000 offered their services.[67] Many Maltese, before conscription was introduced in February 1941, joined the KOMR and the RMA, or enlisted in the British services in Malta, while 1,700 enrolled in the Home Guard.[68] Even larger numbers were absorbed into the civil defence organisation, which was almost entirely Maltese. The Governor's early action in detaining a limited number of known, or suspected, Italian sympathisers, and the publicity which surrounded these arrests, served to remind others who may have still harboured similar views of the powers which the Governor held by virtue of the Malta Defence Regulations.

This brief survey of conditions in Malta during the first six months of the Mediterranean war suggests that the fears of an internal collapse expressed by General Dobbie to the War Office in early July were, even then, wide of the mark. The process of civilian adjustment was, doubtless, helped by the steady reduction in enemy air attacks, but, in addition, the Maltese people, like those living in other heavily bombed European cities, demonstrated an unexpected resilience and tolerance in the face of moderate air attack. That is not to say that there were not complaints, particularly about inadequate shelter protection, which were voiced in the Council of Government and in the columns of *The Times of Malta*. But these were often fully justified and did not indicate a wider loss of confidence in the government.

By the close of 1940, therefore, the authorities in Malta and London could reasonably assume that, while the majority of the civilian population could do little more than endure and adapt as best they could to Italian air attack, Maltese support for the Colonial Government was strong enough to encourage the belief that the island would not suffer an internal collapse that might prevent the island's use for offensive purposes.

7

The Initial Onslaught

THE EVOLUTION OF A STRATEGY FOR MALTA

Before examining the discussions and decisions which followed the Italian declaration of war and the French surrender, it will be convenient, first, to consider briefly the assertion that plans were made in London to offer Malta to Mussolini in the summer of 1940 as an inducement to maintain his neutrality and to influence Hitler to offer Britain reasonable peace terms. Mark Arnold-Forster has written that, at the end of May 1940, Halifax and Chamberlain had developed 'precise' plans that 'involved offering Malta and other British colonies to Mussolini . . . in return for his interceding with Hitler to obtain peace terms for Britain'.[1] This assertion is based on the official record of War Cabinet discussions between 26 and 28 May, and contemporary diary entries, including those of Halifax and Chamberlain.[2] These key discussions were prompted by a flying visit to London, on Sunday 26 May, by the French Prime Minister, Paul Reynaud, who urged that Mussolini be offered specific territorial concessions in order to remain neutral and to intercede with Hitler. He assumed that Mussolini would require the 'demilitarisation of Malta', and he stressed, then and later, that 'geographical precision' was essential.

After Reynaud's departure, and during the following two days, Halifax argued persistently, and almost to the point of resignation, that the government should support the French in their proposed approach to Mussolini. 'If we found that we could obtain terms', he said, 'which did not postulate the destruction of our independence we should be foolish if we did not accept them.' However, he quite specifically rejected Reynaud's insistence that precise territorial concessions be offered. Chamberlain at first sided with Halifax, but largely to avoid giving the French a pretext for negotiating a separate peace with Hitler. Attlee and Greenwood were opposed to making any approach to Mussolini, while Sinclair, invited to join the later meetings as leader of the Liberal Party, thought that 'the suggestion that we were prepared to barter away pieces of British territory would have a deplorable effect'.

Everyone assumed that, if Mussolini could be bought off by territorial concessions, Malta was likely to be one of his demands. Churchill argued that not only would any approach to Mussolini be rejected with contempt, but also that acceptable terms were unlikely to be offered. Moreover, should an approach to Mussolini become known, British determination to resist might be fatally undermined. He added that any such approach

> ... implied that if we were prepared to give Germany back her colonies and to make certain concessions in the Mediterranean, it was possible for us to get out of our present difficulties. He thought that no such option was open to us.

We need not follow the course of these protracted discussions because, although no formal vote was taken on the matter, Halifax received no support and Churchill, on 28 May, sent a telegram to Reynaud declining to join in an approach to Mussolini. The subsequent French offer of territorial concessions was simply ignored by the Italian dictator. Nowhere in the course of these incompletely recorded discussions is there any evidence to support Arnold-Forster's assertion. Halifax made no mention of Malta or any other territory, and it can only be a matter of speculation whether, if Mussolini had in fact demanded Malta as the price of his intercession with Hitler, Halifax would have suggested such a surrender. It seems clear that neither Churchill nor any other member of the War Cabinet would have accepted this.[3]

Churchill's appointment as Prime Minister was to have a major impact on the purely military considerations affecting Malta, as we shall see in the following chapters. The public quickly became aware of the nature of his leadership through the series of speeches that have become famous, but the effect on his staff was equally profound. Two comments will serve to illustrate this. Lieutenant-General Sir Ian Jacob, a senior member of the Defence Secretariat in 1940, later wrote: 'His pugnacious spirit demanded constant action. The enemy must be assailed continuously: the Germans must be made to "bleed and burn".' Lord Bridges, then Cabinet Secretary, expressed a similar view:

> But, for all the calm and confidence which Churchill radiated, within a very few days of his becoming Prime Minister, the whole machinery of government was working at a pace, and with an intensity of purpose, quite unlike anything that had gone before.[4]

Malta and its defenders were to be major beneficiaries of Churchill's energy and determination in the following years.

We may now turn to the consideration of the strategy to defeat Italy and Malta's part in such plans. In previous chapters we have examined the formulation of the Anglo-French plan of action. Within weeks these painstakingly elaborated plans were invalidated by the collapse of France. In retrospect, one may be surprised that it was not until 18 May that the Chiefs of Staff first considered 'British Strategy in a Certain Eventuality', the euphemism for French surrender, since the circumstances which might entice Mussolini to enter the conflict were those which were likely to deprive Britain of French support.[5] Belatedly, plans to meet this new 'eventuality' were hurriedly prepared and considered by the War Cabinet on 27 May.[6] The primary focus of this initial reassessment was, necessarily, on the defence of Britain against the air attack that, unless defeated, was likely to be a prelude to invasion. However, overseas interests were not wholly ignored. Germany and Italy, it was assumed, 'will strive to overthrow our position in Egypt and the Middle East'. Naval control of the western Mediterranean would be lost, leaving Italy free to concentrate her attack on Malta, Gibraltar and Egypt. With regard to Malta the Appreciation went on to say:

> Malta has six months' food reserve for the population and garrison, but anti-aircraft guns and ammunition are short, and the island is not likely to withstand more than one serious seaborne assault, nor could it be used as a naval base.[7]

The pessimistic tenor of this element of the COS's thinking did not, however, commend itself to the Prime Minister, who, on 28 May, sent to the Chiefs, through General Ismay, his personal Chief of Staff, one of the earliest of his many minutes about Malta and the Middle East. He criticised what he took to be a purely defensive strategy outlined by Admiral Cunningham, and urged that 'the Fleet at Alexandria should sally forth and run some risks'.[8] Cunningham naturally resented this 'prodding', and made clear in a signal of 6 June that 'it is intended that a strong force, including battleships, should proceed westward at first, countering Italian action on Malta or in other directions'.[9] This was, in fact, the action that he took on the morning of 11 June.

However, within days of the Italian intervention the Admiralty produced something of a bombshell, one of the implications of which was that Malta might be left defenceless. On 17 June the CNS, Admiral Pound, circulated to his fellow Chiefs a one-page proposal that, if the French surrendered, the Mediterranean Fleet should be withdrawn to Gibraltar.[10] Two reasons were advanced for this proposal. First, the Fleet at Alexandria, exposed to potentially heavy air attack, and lacking proper repair facilities, would be a 'wasting asset'. Second, the

Mediterranean battleships would be needed at Gibraltar to protect the Atlantic trade routes against German surface raiders soon, perhaps, to be operating from French Atlantic ports. On the previous evening Pound signalled to Cunningham to warn him of this possibility. The latter, while agreeing that such a move was feasible, replied, on 17 June, that it would mean the loss of Malta and, probably, of Egypt too. Concerned that this may have sounded 'somewhat acquiescent', he followed this up by a further signal on the next day in which he expressed the opinion that 'the effects of this withdrawal would mean such a landslide in territory and prestige that I earnestly hoped such a decision would never have to be taken'.[11]

By then Churchill had learned of this proposal and he minuted to the First Lord, A. V. Alexander, on 17 June: 'It is of the utmost importance that the Fleet at Alexandria should remain to cover Egypt from an Italian invasion, which would otherwise destroy prematurely all our position in the East.'[12] He reiterated this view at a meeting that evening with Alexander, Pound and the Vice-Chief of the Naval Staff (VCNS), Admiral Phillips, and in a later minute to Pound on 15 July Churchill referred to the fact that he had earlier 'vetoed the proposal to evacuate the Eastern Mediterranean'.[13] The COS referred Pound's original paper to the Joint Planning Staff (JPS), who came to the same conclusion as the Prime Minister.[14] There the matter ended, and, on 3 July, the COS advised the Middle East C-in-Cs of their intention to retain the Fleet in the eastern Mediterranean as long as possible.[15]

This quick dismissal of Pound's proposal, not merely by Churchill but by his service colleagues too, suggests that, on this key element of strategy, Pound was out of tune with his fellow Chiefs. The two signals sent by Cunningham make clear the implications, not merely for Malta, but for the entire British position in the Middle East, of Pound's proposal to withdraw the Fleet to Gibraltar. Roskill believed that it was these signals that influenced Churchill, but it is clear that Churchill's minute to Alexander preceded the receipt of these signals at the Admiralty.[16] Although the protection of trade routes was a clear and urgent Admiralty responsibility, it remains surprising that Pound did not appear, in this matter, to appreciate the implications of his plan for Middle East strategy in general, particularly in view of his long service in the Mediterranean.

The rejection of the proposal to withdraw the Mediterranean Fleet to Gibraltar at least served to clear the air, and the signal of 3 July from the Chiefs of Staff to the Middle East commanders set out their initial instructions. Although tactical offensive opportunities were to be sought and exploited, the overall stance was bound to be a defensive one, as had been envisaged even in the Anglo-French plan. The subsequent loss of French support, soon to be replaced, after the naval action at Mers-el-Kebir, by her possible hostility, dictated the defensive character of early Mediterranean strategy. Within this overall strategic plan policy at Malta must also be initially defensive in character, and the measures which were taken in this regard are examined in the following section. But there was clearly no point in attempting a costly and, after the French surrender, a doubly difficult defence of the island if forces based there could not make a contribution which would justify the cost. What then became clear was that, despite all the pre-war attention given to the *defence* of Malta, there had been very little detailed planning regarding potential offensive operations. When the JPS in late August presented a lengthy report on 'Future Strategy', the paragraph on Malta stated that 'the situation . . . is a difficult one', but then simply enumerated the advantages to be gained from the retention of the island. They concluded by writing: 'We, therefore, consider that the air defences of Malta should be increased.'[17]

The three services had different ideas about Malta's uses. For the Admiralty, now deprived of French naval bases, Malta was the only port upon which forces could be based to regain some measure of control of the central Mediterranean and interrupt Italian supply convoys to her Libyan forces. Despite the early loss of the floating dock, and mounting damage to dockyard installations, Valletta continued to offer a well-equipped and viable naval base from which surface and submarine forces might be operated. On a longer view, the Admiralty continued to be beguiled by the prospect that, if only the Mediterranean Fleet could be re-established at Malta, there would be no need to keep two separate fleets at the ends of the middle sea. But, as Cunningham had stressed in his 23 May signal, any Malta-based forces would require accurate and timely intelligence if they were to intercept Italian convoys to Libya.

An aerial reconnaissance capability was for the Air Staff, too, a major potential advantage offered by Malta. Offensive air force operations, whether directed at Libyan convoys or at targets in Italy or in North Africa, demanded current photographs, and these could only be secured by Malta-based aircraft. Malta squadrons might also deliver attacks on such targets although the weight of such attack was necessarily constrained by the island's limited airfield capacity. In late June Air Commodore Maynard, the Malta AOC, had acquired a small strike force of Swordfish torpedo bombers. 830 Squadron of the FAA, which had been serving with the French fleet at Toulon, was ordered to Malta by Cunningham where it came under Maynard's command.[18] However, the request of ACM Longmore, the Middle East Air Officer Commanding-in-Chief (AOC-in-C), for an RAF squadron of Beaufort torpedo bombers was denied. As the Air Staff saw it, the most valuable advantage of Malta in the summer and autumn of 1940 was as a staging post for medium bomber reinforcements for Egypt. After the loss of French landing grounds, fighters would need to be shipped around the Cape, or, after September, fly across the Takoradi–Khartoum air route, while Wellington medium bombers could, with extra fuel tanks, fly non-stop from Britain to Egypt. But Blenheims, which were to be the mainstay of the Middle East bomber force, would need to refuel at Malta, and this was convenient for Wellingtons as well. In consequence, the Air Staff were anxious, given the urgent need for Middle East air reinforcements in the autumn of 1940, that this essential capability was not jeopardised by the plans of the other services.[19]

The War Office viewed Malta's potential value in a somewhat longer perspective. When the offensive stage of Mediterranean strategy was reached, Malta would provide an indispensable base for an invasion of Sicily and the Italian mainland. Meanwhile, it might serve as a base for the operations for which Churchill had established the Combined Operations Command in mid-July. An attack on Pantelleria, 100 miles to the west of Malta in the narrow seas between Cape Bon and the western tip of Sicily, was one of Admiral Sir Roger Keyes's early plans to implement his instructions.[20]

These initially unco-ordinated conceptions of Malta's potential uses were brought into sharper focus by two enquiries in mid-August. A month earlier Churchill had established a new Ministerial Middle East Committee, under Eden's chairmanship, to 'consult together upon the conduct of the war in the Middle East'.[21] At a meeting of this committee on 12 August, Lord Lloyd, the Colonial Secretary, wanted to know 'if it was contemplated that Malta would be developed as a base for offensive operations'.[22] Other committee members, including General Wavell, who was then in London for talks, expressed the view that a bombing offensive on Italy would relieve Italian pressure on Egypt. The Air Staff quickly rejected this suggestion as 'not practicable in present circumstances'.[23] Not only were bombing resources being concentrated on the primary target, Germany, with the reinforcement of Egypt as a secondary aim, but the use of Malta to achieve this secondary objective might be put at risk if bombing raids from Malta were to provoke heavy retaliation. The COS endorsed this analysis at their meeting on 23 August, at which Admiral Phillips, for the Admiralty, stressed the need to establish 'fighter and reconnaissance aircraft and anti-aircraft defences before increasing the bomber strength'.[24]

At the same time Admiral Cunningham outlined in a signal of 22 August his own proposals regarding Malta.[25] After complaining about the lack of a co-ordinated approach to the problem, he went on to propose that every effort should be made to complete the defences of Malta by April 1941, prior to which 'offensive action from Malta should be restricted to attacks on sea targets and to reconnaissance'. If this were done, he expected that he would then be able to base there a force of cruisers and destroyers, and a flotilla of submarines. The other services might then develop their own offensive operations from the island. This proposal, together with a detailed War Office analysis of the AA position at Malta, provoked a wide-ranging discussion at a COS meeting on 26 August, the upshot of which was an agreement to install, by April 1941, the 172 AA guns envisaged in the 1939 Scale B plan.[26] However, although there was rather vague talk of eventually being able to operate six fighter and six bomber squadrons from Malta, the provision of the Scale B fighter garrison of four fighter squadrons could only take place 'as soon as circumstances permit'. With the Battle of Britain raging over their heads the COS could hardly reach any other conclusion.

It was always to be expected, however, especially in the early defensive stage of the Italian war, that enemy initiatives might compel an adjustment to, or a more radical re-shaping of, existing plans. Two such events occurred in the autumn of 1940, one long anticipated and the other less so, but offering unexpected opportunities. On 13 September, upon strict orders from Mussolini, Marshal Graziani began his advance into Egypt. This underlined the urgent need, on the one hand, to accelerate as far as possible the trickle of reinforcements to the Middle East commanders, and, on the other, to interrupt Italian supplies to Libya. The latter objective was made more pressing by the loss of the Sidi Barrani airfields that made it more difficult to strike at the main eastern port of Benghazi from Egypt.

Up to this point the British submarine campaign against the Italian convoys had been singularly ineffective. By the end of August only three Italian merchant ships had been sunk by submarines while five British boats had been lost.[27] There were several reasons for this. The most damaging was a change, on 17 July, in the Italian naval cyphers, which, unlike the new air force and army cyphers, were never broken by GC&CS.[28] Moreover, this loss of previously plentiful intelligence about Italian shipping movements could not be made good by visual air or submarine reconnaissance. The few Sunderlands at Cunningham's disposal, whether flying from Malta or Alexandria, were too vulnerable for operations close to Italian ports, and the first three Marylands did not arrive at Malta until 6 September.[29]

Equally important, the heavy losses suffered by Cunningham's initial fleet of 17 large submarines led to the withdrawal of the remaining boats from waters adjacent to enemy harbours and coasts. As Cunningham wrote to Pound in August, 'it is not a question of sending them where they will be useful, but where they will be safe'.[30] Although these heavy losses are usually attributed to such factors as the large size of the boats and the clarity of the waters, it is possible that the Italian navy, which had no operational asdic equipment at the beginning of the war,[31] knew about their patrol areas from direction-finding (D/F) bearings and decyphered signals. The interrogation in early 1944 of Commander Cianchi, who had been Head of the Italian Naval Cryptographic Department, confirmed that the Royal Navy's operational cyphers had been broken before the war.[32]

All these developments demanded an urgent reappraisal of strategy and operations, and, at a COS meeting on 9 October, Pound, after consulting Cunningham, put forward revised proposals about the use of Malta. Since it was only from Malta that Italian traffic could be intercepted, he planned to accelerate the establishment there of a cruiser and destroyer force. For this there were two prerequisites. First, there must be an equivalent acceleration in the build-up of the island's air and AA defences, and, second, there was a need for improved air reconnaissance, in the continued absence of which the Admiralty were still not sure which routes the Italian convoys were taking.[33] The COS agreed that the existing reconnaissance capability be augmented by the despatch of a further six Marylands, while, a little later, the Sunderlands of 228 Squadron were transferred from Alexandria to the flying boat base at Kalafrana. The Defence Committee endorsed these revised plans on 15 October and reached the following decision: 'When the defence of Malta had been strengthened light forces should be based there, and that visits of increasing length should also be paid by heavy ships to Malta, depending on the results of experience in the early stages.'[34]

A further acceleration in the offensive use of Malta was occasioned two weeks later by the Italian invasion of Greece. This possibility had long been expected in London, but it was only in September that evidence began to emerge of Italian army and air force reinforcement of their forces in Albania.[35] Although the immediate British objective was to secure Crete to obtain the use of the fleet anchorage at Suda Bay and an advanced airfield, air assistance was also requested by the Greek government. Part of the response to this appeal was a proposal by ACM Sir Charles Portal, who had several days earlier succeeded Newall as CAS, that bombing attacks be launched from Malta against Rome and other Italian cities, details of which he outlined to the Defence Committee on the evening of the Italian invasion.[36]

For some time Wellington reinforcements for Egypt had been staged through Malta. From this flow of aircraft Portal decided to detain 12 as a makeshift force to bomb Italian targets, and plans were hurriedly made to send 200 airmen, stores and bombs to Malta by cruiser. When this was done it was hoped that as many as 24 Wellingtons might temporarily operate from Malta before going on to Egypt. As a result, in mid-December, 148 Squadron was formed at Luqa and by the end of the year had carried out attacks on Taranto, Brindisi and Bari, as well as on North African targets. Perhaps the most notable of these was an attack on 8 December on the airfield at Castel Benito, near Tripoli, during which 29 aircraft were destroyed or damaged.[37]

By December, therefore, plans to develop Malta for offensive purposes had evolved, partly as an integral element of British strategic planning for the Middle East, and partly in response to enemy initiatives. What was accomplished in these first six months will be considered at the end of this chapter, but, first, it will be necessary to review the concurrent improvements made in Malta's defences during the same period.

STRENGTHENING MALTA'S DEFENCES UNDER ENEMY ATTACK

In the second volume of his history of the war Churchill wrote: 'In July 1940 I began, as the telegrams and minutes show, to concern myself increasingly about the Middle East.'[38] Not the least of his preoccupations was to build up the defences of Malta so that the island could be used for offensive purposes. Numerous minutes in the succeeding months attested to his continuing concern about this and two of these were sent on 12 July. In the first, addressed to the Chiefs of Staff, he asked: 'A plan should be prepared to reinforce the air defences of Malta in the strongest manner with AA guns of various types and with aeroplanes. . . . Let me have it in three days.'[39] The second, directed to the Admiralty, suggested that the new aircraft carrier, HMS *Illustrious*, be employed to 'take a good lot of Hurricanes to Malta' where they could be flown by the Gladiator pilots.[40]

Even before receiving the Prime Minister's minute, the Chiefs had been considering how to reinforce Malta in the light of a 4 July report from General Dobbie, the Acting Governor, and his naval and air force commanders.[41] At a series of meetings between 9 and 23 July, urged on by Churchill's minute, they hammered out what became the pattern of future reinforcements. The initial problem of finding the required resources had not diminished; indeed, the claims on AA gun and aircraft production had risen faster than output. In the case of AA guns, for example, the CIGS on 13 July reported that the ADGB programme had a deficiency of 1,021 heavy and 1,429 light AA guns.[42] The fighter aircraft position was even worse as a result of the need to replace losses incurred in the air battles over France. In the face of these more insistent claims all the CAS felt able to offer for Malta's defence was a further flight of Hurricanes, 12 aircraft in all, to supplement an earlier batch of five flown out across France in mid-June. Of these only three were now serviceable. To provide some protection for their airfields, the CIGS promised to send 20 heavy and 16 light AA guns, numbers subsequently reduced to 12 and eight, respectively, when Maynard decided to operate his aircraft from only two airfields. The COS warned, however, that additional guns might not be forthcoming for some time.[43]

But however grave the misgivings may have been about depriving Britain's defences of even this limited amount of equipment at such a critical time, the principal difficulty now was that of transporting to the island, not just the guns and aircraft, but also the personnel, the ammunition and the stores to maintain them in action. In mid-July Pound and Cunningham weighed the risks of escorting a merchant ship to Malta, and found them too great. As Pound explained to his fellow Chiefs on 15 July: 'The chances of the ship getting through were very slight and the heavy forces escorting the vessel would also be dangerously exposed to air bombardment.'[44]

Pound's decision did not meet with the Prime Minister's approval. In a minute of the same date, Churchill wrote: 'The immense delay involved in passing these ships around the Cape cannot be accepted', pointing out that the passage from Alexandria to Malta was, if anything, even more hazardous than the western route.[45] Pound, however, refused to change his mind and, as a result, this first shipment of guns and stores was despatched via the Cape. It was not until the end of August, during a major reinforcement of Cunningham's fleet under the operational code name 'Hats', that two merchant ships and an oil tanker were escorted to Malta from Alexandria, although one of the merchant ships was heavily damaged in an air attack *en route*. During the same operation the battleship HMS *Valiant*, and two cruisers, HMS *Coventry* and HMS *Calcutta*, delivered eight 3.7-inch and ten Bofors, together with related equipment.[46] The first through convoy from Gibraltar to Egypt did not sail until the end of November, when, despite the alarms and excitement of Vice-Admiral Somerville's clash with the Italian Fleet south of Cape Spartivento, two fast merchant ships delivered additional guns and supplies to Malta, while two cruisers took 1,400 airmen on to Alexandria.[47]

Fighter aircraft, too, could be, and were, sent to Malta by ship. However, in the July discussions in the COS Committee, Pound, prompted by Churchill's minute, proposed that the 12 Hurricanes offered by Newall be flown to the island from the old training aircraft carrier, HMS *Argus*, from a point south of Sardinia. This was successfully carried out on 2 August, and the requisite ground crews were transported from Gibraltar by submarine.[48] But that this method was not without its hazards was shown in November when, of a further reinforcing flight of 12 Hurricanes, eight ran out of fuel before reaching Malta and were lost.[49] Newall was unable to promise any more before 1941, but, on 10 October, he undertook to send out the ground crews and equipment to service four Hurricane squadrons. This was important because it had now become clear to all that, although squadron aircraft could be moved with relative ease, they could not become operational without their extensive, and far from mobile, ground organisation. Churchill later described the RAF as the 'least mobile of the services'.[50]

Given this limited air reinforcement, the weight of the defensive improvement fell on the AA gun establishment. After their decision on 26 August to complete the Scale B gun programme by April 1941, the COS in the following months approved plans, the execution of which was expedited at times by the use of warships to carry heavy guns to Malta. A monthly allocation of 12 heavy and eight light AA guns was approved, and the Chiefs gave instructions on 22 October that 24 heavy and 24 light AA guns be sent in December out of current production.[51] By the end of the year only 18 heavy guns remained to be provided.

As if the transportation of all these men and their weapons was not already a sufficiently daunting task, concern grew in September that the garrison needed to be strengthened to enable it to resist an invasion attempt. In May, as we have seen, a fifth infantry battalion was sent to Malta amid fears that an airborne attack might be launched, but this lightly armed force, together with the KOMR, was the only barrier to an Italian assault. Once more, it was Churchill, at a COS meeting on 14 September, who set enquiries in motion by suggesting that a further two infantry battalions were needed in Malta.[52] The timing of this latest intervention is interesting, not least because this was the week when an attempt to invade Britain was thought most likely. Indeed, on the following day, the Prime Minister spent the morning at the underground operations room of 11 Group, Fighter Command, observing the air battle that he judged to be 'the crux of the Battle of Britain'.[53] In the same week, Marshal Graziani had at last crossed the Egyptian frontier with substantial forces, while, 600 miles to the north, there was growing evidence of an Italian build-up in Albania. With Italian forces clearly committed to these two widely separated theatres it must have seemed most improbable that even Mussolini would order a third significant operation against Malta. Churchill's concern to strengthen Malta as quickly as possible is best explained by his anxiety that, if the German plans to invade Britain were frustrated, powerful forces might then be diverted towards the Middle East.[54]

General Dobbie was consulted and he naturally seized the opportunity to explain why he needed at least two additional battalions.[55] His reference to a battalion frontage of 15 miles caught Churchill's military eye and provoked a further minute of 21 September. He thought that, although four battalions were probably needed, the Governor would have to make do with two, but 'we must find two good ones'.[56] Dill, the CIGS, doubtless more concerned about Graziani's advance to Sidi Barrani, and anticipating a possible further move against Wavell's main position at Mersa Matruh, suggested to Dobbie that a battery of 25-pounders might be more useful than a second battalion, and this was agreed. To make up for this infantry shortfall the existing five battalions on the island were brought up to strength by drafts amounting to a total of 750 officers and men who had been awaiting passage from Alexandria.[57]

If Dill hoped that these arrangements would satisfy the Prime Minister he was soon shown to be mistaken. On 6 October Churchill minuted:

> Whenever the Fleet is moving from Alexandria to the Central Mediterranean reinforcements should be carried in to Malta, which I consider to be in grievous danger at the present time. . . . Pray let me have proposals on these lines, and make sure that at least one battalion goes to Malta on the next occasion.[58]

A few days later, as noted in the previous section, Pound recommended the acceleration of the agreed programme for the reinforcement of Malta to allow for the stationing of light naval forces there, and General Dobbie, in a further Appreciation of 9 October, asked for an additional three battalions, a second battery of 25-pounders, and an anti-tank detachment.[59] The Defence Committee, with yet another Churchill minute before them that began 'First in urgency is the reinforcement of Malta . . .'[60] weighed all these matters on 15 October, and it was agreed that Dobbie should receive an additional battalion from Egypt, and two batteries of 25-pounders. It was further agreed that a mixed troop of infantry and light tanks also be despatched.[61] The Italian invasion of Greece on 28 October diverted the attention of the Prime Minister and the COS to the needs of this new theatre of operations, and one immediate result was the diversion to Crete of the battalion that Wavell had planned to send to Malta.

By these various decisions and expedients forces were scraped together in the first six months of Malta's war to strengthen the infantry garrison and to raise the AA defences towards the levels agreed the year before. Much less satisfactory was the slow progress in increasing the island's fighter defence. The exigencies of the Battle of Britain, soon to be followed by the need to support Wavell, and, later, the Greeks, meant that Maynard in Malta had to make do with just one of the four Hurricane squadrons he had been led to expect. His only comfort was the promise of the requisite ground crews for the missing squadrons. Despite early fears about the threat posed by the Italian air force, and the even greater potential damage that might have been inflicted by the Italian navy, none of the merchant ships that had made the passage to or from Malta in 1940 was sunk. By the end of 1940, therefore, there was some reason to believe that the objective of making Malta safe enough to harbour a valuable offensive strike force was within reach.

THE ACHIEVEMENTS OF THE FIRST SIX MONTHS

It will be convenient to end this chapter by asking how much had been achieved by the end of 1940. That there was a role of any kind to be developed was due entirely to the Italian decision not to launch an immediate invasion, and it soon became clear that the Italian plan, initially at least, was to make Malta unusable by persistent air attack. After the confusion about deployment in early June, the *Regia Aeronautica* transferred to Sicilian bases its 2nd Air Squadron. This comprised 137 S.79 bombers and 69 fighters of which only 26 were monoplane MC 200s.[62] However, only 35 bombers were employed on the initial raids on Malta, and it was not until after the French surrender on 24 June that orders were given to 'sterilise' the island. By concentrating on the three airfields and the dockyard a certain amount of damage was done in the following weeks and the important floating dock was sunk. Nevertheless, the frequency and weight of attack steadily diminished. There were several reasons for this. As the Admiralty had anticipated in 1939, the Italian air forces in Sicily were soon diverted to other tasks. For example, during the naval clash between the two battle fleets on 8 July large numbers of aircraft were deployed to attack the British force, although some of them indiscriminately bombed both fleets. A more serious depletion of the Sicilian force came about after Mussolini's invasion of Greece on 28 October. The 2nd Air Squadron also suffered mounting losses and damage as Malta's air defences steadily grew in numbers and skill. Between June and December 1940 Santoro recorded 35 aircraft lost, and no fewer than 205 damaged, of which he attributed 147 to AA fire.[63] These were significant losses in relation to the initial establishment of this force. Finally, Santoro admitted that the Italian bomber pilots, continually directed to the same, apparently demolished and abandoned, targets were not prepared to undertake unnecessary risks.[64]

The pattern of the Italian air offensive in the first six months is illustrated by the figures shown in Table 2.[65]

TABLE 2
NUMBER OF AIR RAID ALERTS IN 1940

June	July	August	September	October	November	December
53	51	22	25	10	32	18

Source: P. Vella, *Malta: Blitzed but not Beaten* (Progress Press, Valletta, 1958), p. 249.

Santoro later argued that this offensive had achieved the aim of preventing the establishment of offensive British forces at Malta, but he accepted that by the end of the year the island's defences were stronger since the Italian air force and navy had been unable to prevent the arrival of reinforcements.[66] He speculated whether a heavier initial attack might have prevented the reinforcement of the island, but in the light of later events concluded that this was unlikely. However, in his analysis of this period Gabriele was critical of the limited weight of attack, pointing out that too little use was made of the Ju 87 dive-bombers that Germany had supplied to the Italian air force, before they, too, were transferred to the Greek front.[67]

In these first six months the test of war suggested that the Air Staff's pre-war doubts about Malta had been ill judged, and the Admiralty's view more prescient. Despite a defence establishment which, at the start of hostilities, had not reached the 1939 Scale A level, much less the four squadrons and 172 guns of Scale B, no invasion had been attempted, no 'knock-out blow' delivered, and no decisive permanent damage done. On the contrary, quite apart from the effects of the steady accretion of gun and air resources, war experience had taught such lessons as the effective use of radar, the repair of damaged runways, and improved gunnery techniques, such as the 'box barrage'.

Nevertheless, stronger defences were but one of the pre-conditions for offensive operations. Target intelligence was also a *sine qua non* for successful attack on Italian shipping or land targets, and here, although the need had belatedly been recognised, much less progress had been made. There were two main reasons for this failure. First, the loss of naval Sigint was an unexpected blow. As Hinsley put it: 'These reverses came as a great shock to intelligence authorities long accustomed to receiving a steady supply of Italian Sigint.'[68] Second, the loss of this source of information about Italian activities could not be made good by other sources. In particular, Cunningham's air reconnaissance resources were quite inadequate, as he often complained. The few Sunderlands at Alexandria and Malta were ill suited for this work, while the three Marylands at Malta were too few in number, despite their invaluable contribution to the attack on the Italian fleet at Taranto. Furthermore, there was until early 1941 only one trained photographic interpretation officer in the entire theatre.[69] Without adequate intelligence the limited offensive forces available, that is, the dozen Swordfish of 830 Squadron and four T-class submarines transferred to Malta from the North Sea in September,[70] could achieve little against the Italian convoys to Libya. The result was that between June and December 1940 297,475 tons of supplies were shipped to North Africa with only 2 per cent lost.[71]

In this and the following chapters, where an attempt is made to evaluate the impact of Malta-based forces on the fighting in North

Africa, it will be appropriate to consider the various stages of the 'battle of the convoys' from the Italian viewpoint. In the first six months of the Mediterranean war the safe arrival of almost 300,000 tons of supplies in Libya owed nothing to pre-war naval planning. Indeed, at the outbreak of the war the Italian *Supermarina* had decided that the provision of supplies to North Africa was not one of its principal tasks. Despite the estimate in the Navy's DG 10/A2 study of 1938 that the armed forces there and the civilian population would require 113,000 tons of supplies every month,[72] the provision of these amounts was considered impossible in the face of overwhelming Anglo-French naval superiority. Consequently, in Cavagnari's Directive *Di. N.A. n. 0 (zero)* of 29 May 1940, 'protecting our communications with the Islands, Libya and Albania' was placed ninth among the Navy's ten principal objectives.[73] It was only at the Chiefs of Staff meeting on 5 June, during which Cavagnari had resisted the suggestion that an attempt be made to seize Malta, that the problem of North African supplies claimed urgent attention. Badoglio then offered the assistance of requisitioned civil aircraft and endorsed the naval proposal to use minelaying submarines and some merchant ships sailing overnight from western Sicily. 'In this way', he concluded, 'we might hope to supply Libya.'[74]

The North African forces had been expected to be self-sufficient with supplies stockpiled before the war, but such was the state of Italian resources and planning that within three days of the declaration of war urgent demands for additional supplies began to reach *Supermarina*, compelling the navy to improvise almost overnight a convoy system.[75] Apart from the lack of planning, the Italian navy and merchant marine were ill equipped for such a task. Mussolini's precipitate entry into the war on 10 June led to the immediate loss or capture of 212 Italian merchant ships aggregating 1,216,637 tons, over a third of Italy's merchant fleet.[76] Although these captures were partially offset by the addition of 56 German ships of 203,512 tons, the magnitude of this initial loss, mostly of the larger and faster units in the fleet, can be seen in the fact that new construction during 1940–43 amounted to only 305,733 tons.[77] The navy had built no specialised vessels to escort these convoys, and so fleet destroyers and lighter patrol boats, without Asdic or radar to give warning of attack by surface ships, submarines or aircraft, were pressed into service. The escort problem was also exacerbated by the development of 'mini-convoys' of one or two ships, each requiring escort, rather than the 'grand convoys' of 5–20 ships envisaged in the 1938 study.[78] The reasons for this, and the question of Libyan port capacity, will be considered in a later chapter.

Nevertheless, a convoy system was organised and the naval battle off Cape Calabria of 8 July followed the successful arrival of a convoy of five merchant ships carrying 72 medium tanks, 232 other vehicles and

16,165 tons of supplies and fuel.[79] The further development of this early system was then seriously undermined by Mussolini's unexpected invasion of Greece in late October 1940. Quite apart from the diversion of valuable supplies to this new front, the additional convoy commitment, increased later after the Axis capture of Greece and Yugoslavia, eventually overshadowed the Libyan requirement. As Giorgerini has recorded, the eastern theatre required, in total, 3,116 convoys, involving 19,379,786 tons of shipping, compared with 993 of 9,245,171 tons for North Africa.[80] Naval escort capabilities were similarly over-stretched by the Greek adventure.

The safe arrival of virtually all of the supplies sent to North Africa in the first six months of the Mediterranean war was due, therefore, not to careful pre-war planning and subsequent execution, but to the fact that the convoys faced very little opposition. Even the British submarine force that was later to prove so effective achieved negligible results in this period. In the event, these very Italian convoy successes simply served to increase the magnitude of their losses when Wavell's offensive of 7 December swept the Italian army out of Egypt and Cyrenaica and brought Germany into the Mediterranean war.

8

The German Intervention in the Mediterranean in 1941

NEW STRATEGIES IN THE MEDITERRANEAN

Since the initiative lay with Hitler and British strategy was largely compelled to counter anticipated German moves, we may start by considering the implications for Malta of his Mediterranean strategy.[1] In his Directive No. 18 of 12 November 1940 Hitler laid down the main lines for the future conduct of the war.[2] Much of this Directive was devoted to Operation 'Felix', the plan to capture Gibraltar, and to the possible renewal of Operation 'Sea-Lion', the invasion of England, in the spring of 1941. With regard to the Balkans preparations were to be made for a possible occupation of the Greek mainland north of the Aegean, largely to protect the Rumanian oilfields. As for Russia, Hitler's overriding objective for 1941, 'further directives will follow on this subject'. North Africa was covered in a brief paragraph that simply stated that one armoured division was to be held in readiness for North African operations, and that 'German ships in Italian ports . . . will be converted to carry the largest possible forces either to Libya or to North-west Africa'. The air force was instructed to develop plans for attacks on Alexandria and the Suez Canal, but 'the employment of German forces will be considered, if at all, only after the Italians have reached Mersa Matruh'. Malta was not mentioned. These plans were developed further on 10 December when, on the day after Wavell began his attack on the Italian forces in Egypt, Hitler issued instructions for the transfer of *Fliegerkorps X*, a balanced force of approximately 350 aircraft, from Norway to southern Italy. This force was made available, for a limited period only, to attack British shipping in the Sicilian Narrows. At that point, however, Hitler had no plans to send a military force to Libya.[3]

But, far from advancing to Mersa Matruh, Graziani's forces had, by early 1941, been expelled from Egypt and were being pushed back across Cyrenaica. Fearful that complete Italian defeat in North Africa might lead to the fall of Mussolini, Hitler, at a conference on 9 January, decided to send to Libya a blocking force. Directive No. 22 of 11 January set out his overall instructions.[4] *Fliegerkorps X*, advance squadrons of which had already severely damaged HMS *Illustrious* in the 'Excess' convoy on the previous day, was given the primary task of attacking British shipping and sea communications. Its secondary task was to support the Italian forces in Libya by attacking British bases on the African coast from airfields in Libya.

Reconsideration of these plans was forced by the unexpectedly rapid British advance in Cyrenaica, coupled with a pessimistic report that Hitler received on 1 February from General von Funck, the commander of the 5th Light Division that was intended as the blocking force. Funck thought that at least one full armoured division would be required to halt the British advance, but doubted whether this could arrive in time. Nevertheless, on 3 February Hitler re-affirmed his intention to support Mussolini and ordered that the despatch of 5th Light Division, strengthened by an armoured regiment, be expedited.[5] Moreover, since a full armoured division was to be sent later, Hitler appointed General Rommel to command what was subsequently to be called the *Deutsches Afrika Korps* (*DAK*). After agreeing with the Italian *Comando Supremo* in Rome on 10 February that the whole of Tripolitania was to be defended, Rommel arrived at Tripoli on 12 February, one day after the first German troops had disembarked.[6] The despatch of this enlarged German force required an enormous shipping programme that continued from February until May.[7] Although the Italian navy was responsible for the escort of these convoys at sea, *Fliegerkorps X* was charged with providing air cover and given the additional task of putting Malta out of action as a naval and air base. However, no invasion attempt was envisaged at this stage for reasons discussed later in this chapter.

Hitler's Directives and other German records make quite clear the fundamentally defensive purpose of these decisions. It was not the retention of Libya that was important in itself, but the need to support and maintain the alliance of Mussolini's Italy that determined Hitler's decision to order the *DAK* to Africa. However, since planning for 'Barbarossa', the attack on Russia ordered in Directive No. 21 of 18 December,[8] was already taking shape, the army was reluctant to release even one armoured division for Libya. On 27 January General Halder, the German Army Chief of Staff, observed that 'we cannot cut any further into resources for "Barbarossa"'.[9] In March, during a visit to Germany, Rommel was told by Field Marshal von Brauchitsch, the C-in-C of the army, that 'there was no intention of striking a decisive blow in Africa in the near future, and that for the present I could expect no reinforcements'.[10]

1. Four Fairey Flycatchers over the Grand Harbour, Valletta, 1931. In the harbour can be seen HMS *Glorious*, the floating dock (beneath the aircraft) and the floating crane. (IWM. HU. 65202)

2. The submarine base at Manoel Island, Valletta. Seven U-class submarines can be seen. (IWM. A. 6929)

3. Three hurricanes at Hal Far airfield. (IWM. CM. 1356)

4. Excavating a private shelter in the soft Malta limestone. (IWM. GM. 177)

5. German air attack on the damaged HMS *Illustrious* in Grand Harbour, Valletta, January 1941. (IWM. MH. 4625)

6. Bofors position looking over the Grand Harbour towards Senglea. (IWM. GM. 946)

7. Wellington medium bomber at Luqa airfield. (IWM. CM. 1358)

8. Fleet Air Arm Albacore torpedo bomber in a dispersal bay. (IWM. A. 16116)

9. German air attack on SS *Talabot* while unloading in Grand Harbour, Valletta, March 1942. (IWM. HU. 3611)

10. Bomb damage in Valletta. Much of Valletta is built of limestone blocks, limiting fire risk. (IWM. GM. 563)

11. The Governor, General Sir William Dobbie, with Sir Walter Monckton and Air Marshal Sir Arthur Tedder, at Malta, April 1942. Alongside his visitors the Governor's physical condition after two years on the island is all too evident. (IMW. CM. 2794)

12. The Prime Minister in Malta, November 1943. (IWM. GM. 3996)

This new phase of the war in North Africa would almost certainly have had a different beginning if Hitler had been able to read the signals that were passing between London and Cairo in the early months of 1941. As early as 10 January Churchill warned Wavell that 'nothing must hamper capture of Tobruk, but thereafter all operations in Libya are subordinated to helping Greece'.[11] When, after the capture of Benghazi and O'Connor's crushing victory at Beda Fomm on 7 February, Wavell enquired, with a marked lack of enthusiasm, whether he was to push on to Tripoli, he was told, on 12 February, that the capture of Benghazi 'confirms our previous directive, namely, that your major effort must now be to aid Greece and/or Turkey. This rules out any serious effort against Tripoli'.[12] Had Hitler become aware of this British decision to go on to the defensive in Cyrenaica, it seems unlikely that the 15th Panzer Division, better employed in Russia, would have been ordered to reinforce the 5th Light Division. The latter, strengthened by an armoured regiment, should have been quite capable of maintaining a defensive front in Tripolitania. Rommel's corps command would not then have been created and a stalemate would most likely have developed.

What persuaded the British government to adopt the same defensive posture in Libya as Hitler had already ordered was also the result of a strategic miscalculation, but one with more severe consequences. Inevitably, the attempt to predict German intentions was a major preoccupation of the British War Cabinet and its intelligence advisers during this period.[13] The conclusions reached in early 1941 were reflected in the lengthy Appreciation that the Prime Minister presented to the Chiefs of Staff on 6 January 1941.[14] The Prime Minister was convinced that an attack on Greece, or possibly Turkey, was likely, since the build-up of German forces in Rumania had, since October 1940, been revealed by intercepted German air force Enigma traffic and by other intelligence sources. However, it was the misunderstanding in London of the *purpose* of the expected invasion of Greece that wrong-footed British strategy. As Hinsley put it:

> But while it was an immense advance to be able to chart in detail Germany's preparations for the attacks on Greece and Crete, Whitehall still failed to discern that the strategic purpose underlying these attacks was to safeguard the southern flank of Germany's invasion of Russia.[15]

Hinsley called this 'the major failure of intelligence at the strategic level at this time'. The British presumed that the impending attack on Greece was an element of a wider plan to drive Britain out of the Middle East and to secure the area's oil reserves, a strategy that had been consistently, but unsuccessfully, urged on Hitler by Admiral Raeder, the German Chief of the Naval Staff (CNS).[16] This was the conclusion reached by the British Chiefs of Staff on 5 November 1940,[17] just one day after Hitler had rejected such a plan to drive south through Turkey towards Syria and the Suez Canal.[18] It was in this state of misunderstanding that the War Cabinet, accepting after some hesitation the advice of Eden, Dill and Wavell, supported by Field Marshal Smuts, took the decision on 7 March 1941 to halt the Libyan offensive and to transfer large elements of the Army of the Nile to Greece.[19]

The mistaken judgements on both sides about their opponent's intentions might still have resulted in stalemate in North Africa had it not been for two further miscalculations at the operational level. On the German side, the intention that the *DAK* be employed simply to stiffen Italian resistance to a further British advance was negated by Rommel's natural inclination to act aggressively, even before the arrival of his Panzer division. His probing attacks, nevertheless, would probably have been contained had Wavell, on his side, not misjudged the probable weight and timing of a German advance. Consequently, when this developed on 31 March the weakened British defences were quickly brushed aside, and by the end of April the whole of Cyrenaica had been lost. By the end of the same month the British and Commonwealth forces sent to Greece had been evacuated.

It is with the implications for Malta of these decisions and their consequences that we are concerned in this chapter. Slowly, two conclusions emerged. First, contrary to the initial intentions of both sides, it became clear that North Africa, far from being a relative backwater in which limited forces would stand on the defensive, was likely to become the scene of significant fighting. Second, since the growing Axis forces there could only be supplied by sea, Malta's geographical position made it inevitable that the island would become a part of the wider North African conflict as long as it remained in British hands. Whether or not Malta-based forces could effectively interfere with Rommel's supply convoys might then have a strong influence on, and possibly even determine, the outcome of the North African fighting.

EARLY ATTEMPTS TO STOP ROMMEL'S SUPPLY CONVOYS

Rommel's advance into Cyrenaica in early April 1941 brought the gaze of the British authorities back to the central Mediterranean. There was no dispute that the gravity of the situation demanded urgent measures, prominent among which were ideas and proposals designed to stop, or at least, restrict Rommel's supplies from Italy. But how this was to be accomplished led to a series of sharp disagreements between the Prime Minister, generally supported by Admiral Pound, and Admiral Cunningham.

The first area of disagreement between the Prime Minister and Cunningham concerned the offensive contribution to be made by the RAF to the task of stopping Rommel's convoys. Cunningham had long been critical of the weakness of the RAF in the Middle East. In March 1941, for example, he wrote to Pound, saying that he thought the Chiefs of Staff 'are badly misinformed about the number of fighter squadrons here',[20] and he had also unsuccessfully urged the establishment of a coastal command in the Mediterranean to provide better air support to the Mediterranean Fleet. When the April crisis broke he expressed the view, in a lengthy signal to the Admiralty, that the RAF were not doing enough.[21] This provoked a minute from Churchill to Pound and the First Lord, Alexander, which began: 'I am distressed at the C-in-C Mediterranean's signal . . . which reaches the very easy conclusion that, in spite of the numerous difficulties about Malta, the Air Force must do it.' He went on to argue that the RAF, with restricted bases in Malta, was 'not strong enough to do the work', and concluded by asserting: 'It is the duty of the Navy, assisted by the Air, to cut the communications between Italy and Tripoli.'[22]

In order to make his view of the priorities quite clear the Prime Minister issued a Directive on 14 April in which he repeated that it was

> . . . the prime duty of the British Mediterranean Fleet . . . to stop all sea-borne traffic between Italy and Africa. . . . Every convoy which gets through must be considered a serious naval failure. The reputation of the Royal Navy is engaged in stopping this traffic.[23]

Naval units were, therefore, to be based at Malta and the principal role of the RAF on the island became the protection of these forces. Fighters, consequently, were to have priority in aerodrome use over bombers, a change in air policy that is discussed further below. Undeterred by this statement, Cunningham continued to complain that the 'the Air Ministry are trying to lay their responsibilities on Navy's shoulders and are not helping us out here on Naval side as they should'.[24] He instanced the decision, recently made, not to send to Malta the long-promised Beaufort torpedo bomber squadron.[25]

Cunningham was right to point to the limited offensive air capability at Malta. In March the Wellington squadron had been withdrawn, after it had suffered serious losses on the ground, leaving only the Swordfish of 830 Squadron.[26] These slow and vulnerable aircraft could only be operated at night, and the first new Air-to-Surface Vessel (ASV) radars were not fitted to this squadron until July.²⁷ In addition, the morale of this squadron, which had operated from Malta since June 1940, had also reached a low point,²⁸ and it was overdue for relief. A replacement squadron of Beauforts had been tentatively promised as early as January, but its arrival had been postponed, first by engine problems and later by incomplete training. Churchill pressed the matter again at a Chiefs of Staff meeting on 4 April, but the proposed despatch of this squadron was finally cancelled on 15 April.²⁹ Instead, two weeks later, Portal advised the Chiefs of Staff that he had decided to send, 'as an experiment', six Blenheim aircraft which had been specially trained in low-level anti-shipping bomb attack.³⁰ More than this Portal felt unable to do since it was accepted that Malta's overriding air requirement was for defensive fighters.

There was no argument about the need to strengthen Cunningham's submarine forces, not only at Malta but also at Alexandria and Gibraltar. The first U-class submarines had arrived at Malta in January and Pound quickly promised to send a further eight boats to the Mediterranean.³¹ As a result the number of submarines at Malta rose to eight by early May. The achievements of this enlarged 10th Flotilla were initially, however, disappointing for various reasons. The U-class submarines, designed for coastal operations, had a surface speed of only ten knots, carried a limited number of torpedoes and had a restricted range. In addition, it took the recently arrived captains some time to 'get their eye in'. At first even Wanklyn, according to his Commanding Officer (CO), Commander Simpson, 'was actually making me wonder whether such a poor shot could be kept in command'.³² It was only on Wanklyn's fifth patrol that his string of remarkable successes began.

Consequently, if more losses were to be inflicted on the enemy convoys, this was only likely to be brought about by stationing surface ships at Malta. The Prime Minister's Directive of 14 April was accepted by Cunningham as sound in principle, but subject to numerous difficulties in execution, as he explained in various signals. First, Malta would require further supplies of fuel oil to sustain destroyers or heavier units steaming at high speed. This would place an additional strain on the Malta convoy system, and it was not until the 'Tiger' convoy in early May that Cunningham was able to send in two tankers with 24,000 tons of fuel oil.³³ A second difficulty was that the waters around and within Valletta's harbours had become heavily mined, and that Vice-Admiral Ford at times had no operational sweepers to clear a safe passage. The two oil tankers were only able to enter Valletta after a channel had been cleared by exploding depth charges.³⁴

A more general problem was that of locating enemy convoys, for which Malta still had very limited capability. The remaining Sunderlands had been sent away in March with the Wellingtons, and there were at times only three or four serviceable Marylands for long-distance reconnaissance work. Any convoy that was spotted from the air could only be attacked by surface ships at night, due to the daytime dive-bomber risk, but the first ASV aircraft did not reach Malta until July. There was, consequently, a large element of luck involved in finding and engaging a reported convoy, which had plenty of time to take evasive action after it had been spotted by aircraft.

All of these practical difficulties, however, stemmed from the larger problem that the *Luftwaffe* retained air control over Malta and the surrounding waters. In 1940 Cunningham had agreed that, when Malta's defences had been raised to the approved 1939 standard of four fighter squadrons and 172 AA guns, Malta might then be safe to use as a naval base. By early April 1941 the AA gun establishment was almost complete, but there was still only one hard-pressed squadron of Mark I Hurricanes. Moreover, the enemy now was *Fliegerkorps X* not the *Regia Aeronautica*. After Churchill had directed that fighter defences be given priority over bombers, Portal and Maynard made plans to establish a second, and even a third, fighter squadron out of the large number of aircraft due to be delivered in April and May.[35] Cunningham reluctantly accepted that two squadrons with 150 per cent reserves of aircraft and 100 per cent of pilots might suffice.

Before this, however, Cunningham's hand had been forced. On 11 April four destroyers from the 14th Flotilla arrived at Malta, and this was the direct result of intercepted enemy signals. Hinsley and others have fully described the contribution made by decyphered Italian and German air force signals to this phase of the Middle East war, and this is considered more fully in Chapter 9.[36] For our purpose here it will be sufficient to note that, on 2 April, GC&CS sent the following signal to Cairo on a recently established direct link: 'Advanced elements of German fifteenth armoured division moving second April from Trapani to Palermo. Probably going to Tripoli.'[37] On 7 April the Admiralty, in a direct communication to Cunningham at Alexandria, repeated to Vice-Admiral Ford at Malta, amplified this information: 'Advanced element of German fifteenth armoured division embarking at Palermo on or after 9th April probably for Tripoli.'[38] Churchill quickly passed this information to the Chiefs of Staff on the same day and Cunningham was at once requested to send surface forces to Malta to intercept this convoy.[39] Cunningham replied on 8 April to the effect that four destroyers of the 14th Flotilla had been ordered to Malta, but that he had decided not to send a cruiser because of the air threat.[40] After the arrival of these destroyers on 11 April air reconnaissance was stepped up, but the difficulties entailed in a night interception 200 miles from Malta were revealed by the fact that on the nights of 11 and 12 April the target convoys were not discovered. This frustrating news provoked in London an angry minute from the Prime Minister to the First Sea Lord: 'This is a serious *NAVAL* failure. Another deadly convoy has got through. We have the right to ask why did not the Navy stop them. It is the duty of the Navy to stop them.'[41] Fortunately, a third convoy, referred to as the *'Tarigo* convoy', was successfully intercepted on the night of 16/17 April, and the five merchant ships and their three escorts were all sunk, for the loss of one British destroyer. Upon the First Lord's note about this success Churchill, only partly mollified, wrote: 'Yes: brilliantly redeemed. But what about the next?'[42]

Encouraged by this successful interception, the Admiralty ordered a further six destroyers of the 5th Flotilla to Malta from Home waters to replace the remaining three of the 14th Flotilla. To support these, Cunningham, on 22 April, also despatched the cruiser HMS *Gloucester*. Nevertheless, he firmly opposed Pound's further suggestion that he also send a battleship to Malta until the air defences were strengthened.[43] This was fortunate because *Fliegerkorps X*, stung by the loss of the *Tarigo* convoy on 17 April, increased the weight of attack on Malta, and *Gloucester*, together with two destroyers, was forced to return to Gibraltar. Although the 5th Flotilla subsequently returned to Valletta the surface ships achieved only limited successes before they were all withdrawn in late May to support the evacuation from Crete.

The limited results achieved by surface units operating from Malta did not surprise the VCNS, Admiral Phillips. At a Chiefs of Staff meeting on 12 April he had warned that such forces could harry the enemy's line of communications but could not stop the traffic.[44] Cunningham later added his weight to this view when he telegraphed to the Admiralty on 26 April: 'I feel we should be blind to facts if we imagine that six destroyers or for that matter sixteen can be quite sure of intercepting Libyan convoys unless they have proper air support to enable them to work by day.'[45] Malta's contribution to the sinking of Axis merchant ships in the early months of 1941, as a percentage of the losses in the central Mediterranean, is summarised in Table 3. The construction of this table and of similar ones in later chapters is explained in the Appendix following Chapter 12.

These statistics relating to Malta's offensive against the Italian convoys largely speak for themselves. The RAF, for reasons discussed below, achieved little but the 10th Flotilla submarines began the series of successes that was to prove the most persistent in the following years. The surface force in April and May demonstrated the devastating effect of naval gunfire, but the provision and maintenance of such a force at Malta presented many difficulties.

Although the rising level of successes was encouraging, the impact on the Axis supply traffic in this period was limited, as is shown by the

TABLE 3
PROPORTION OF AXIS SHIPS SUNK BY MALTA FORCES, JANUARY–MAY 1941

(number and tonnage of ships sunk)

	Submarine	Ship	Aircraft	Shared	Malta total	C. Med. total	Malta (%)
January	(3) 12,323	–	(1) 3,950	–	(4) 16,273	(6) 19,381	84
February	(1) 2,365	–	(1) 4,920	–	(2) 7,285	(3) 15,574	47
March	(4) 10,122	–	–	–	(4) 10,122	(7) 16,669	61
April	(2) 7,902	(6) 17,709	–	(1) 1,524	(9) 27,135	(12) 35,095	77
May	(5) 31,939	–	(1) 3,313	–	(6) 35,252	(15) 68,781	51
Total	(15) 64,651	(6) 17,709	(3) 12,183	(1) 1,524	(25) 96,067	(43) 155,500	62

Source: See Appendix.

TABLE 4
AXIS SUPPLIES LANDED AND PERCENTAGES LOST, JANUARY–MAY 1941

(amounts in tons)

	General cargo	% lost	Fuel	% lost	Total sent	Total arrived	% lost
January	46,187	3	2,897	6	50,505	49,084	3
February	68,501	1	10,682	8	80,357	79,183	2
March	88,694	9	4,059	0	101,800	92,753	9
April	57,796	6	23,676	13	88,597	81,472	8
May	49,304	11	20,027	0	75,367	69,331	8

Source: See Appendix.

figures in Table 4. These are taken from official Italian naval records as explained in the Appendix. During this period the transfer of the *DAK* to North Africa had been achieved with negligible losses.[46] Giorgerini, noting the arrival in the December–May period of 93.1 per cent of the supplies convoyed, regarded this as an Italian naval success, but he has also commented on the change that took place in April.[47]

Various factors contributed to these indifferent results. Some, such as the need for better reconnaissance, for ship and airborne radar, more modern anti-ship aircraft, and a stronger submarine force, were to be corrected in the months ahead. To Cunningham, however, the naval operations conducted in April and May with only limited success demonstrated quite clearly that Malta still lacked adequate air defences. The risks to surface vessels posed by Axis air control were too great. Beyond this, moreover, was the greater risk that any marked increase in the effectiveness of British forces based in Malta might provoke an invasion. In order to see how the British government assessed, and responded to, these twin dangers to the island's security, we must retrace our steps to the early weeks of 1941.

THE DEFENCE OF MALTA AGAINST GERMAN ATTACK

In this section the problem of defending Malta is considered in the light of three critical decisions taken by the authorities in London in the early months of 1941. The first decision concerned the despatch of additional troops to Malta to guard against the renewed risk of invasion; the second altered the methods used to send aircraft reinforcements to the island; and the third led to a radical overhaul of the RAF Command in Malta, including the appointment of a new AOC to succeed AVM Maynard.

Before considering these decisions, however, it will be helpful to review briefly the development of Axis plans and operations as they affected Malta. Hitler's Directive No. 22 of 11 January 1941 gave *Fliegerkorps X* the primary task of attacking British naval forces and sea communications in the central Mediterranean. The attacks on HMS *Illustrious* at sea and in Valletta harbour were early evidence of this objective. Its secondary task was the support of Italian forces in the desert, a requirement that grew after the transfer of Rommel's force to Libya in February. Although Malta was not specifically mentioned in this Directive, *Fliegerkorps X* began an intensive bombing campaign on Malta's airfields, docks and military installations, the course of which is illustrated in Table 5.[48]

However, if by the end of March it might have appeared that the objective of neutralising Malta by air attack had been achieved, April showed this to be an illusion. The return of surface ships, leading to the destruction of the *Tarigo* convoy, the growing submarine successes and the increased flow of fighter aircraft to the island supported the conclusion reached by an Italian analysis in June that the German air campaign, despite its greater weight, had been no more successful than the earlier Italian one.[49]

TABLE 5
NUMBER OF BOMBING AND STRAFING ATTACKS ON MALTA, JANUARY–MAY 1941

	January	February	March	April	May
Bombers	285	158	236	383	403
Fighters	30	138	158	72	80

Source: M. Gabriele, 'L'offensiva su Malta (1941), in R. Rainero and A. Biagini (eds), *Cinquant'anni dopo l'entrata dell'Italia nella 2a guerra modiale. Aspetti e problema, L'Italia in guerra: il 2o anno–1941* (Gaeta, Rome, 1992), p. 440.

The German intention of neutralising Malta by air attack obviated, it seemed, the need to plan an invasion. Nevertheless, the occupation of Malta continued to be studied by the German High Command. Admiral Raeder, in particular, repeatedly urged the need to seize the island, developing a plan for an airborne attack employing two German divisions.[50] General Warlimont, Head of the Home Defence Planning Section L, recorded in his memoirs that, after a discussion with Hitler on 3 February 1941, Section L studied the problem of invading Malta 'and considered that the prospects were good'.[51] Somewhat later, after the Balkan campaign had begun, Warlimont recalled that, when the Section was asked whether it was more important to capture Malta or Crete, 'all officers of the section, whether from the Army, Navy or Air Force, together with myself, voted unanimously for the capture of Malta since this seemed to be the only way to secure permanently the sea-route to North Africa'.[52] The Naval Staff also urged this course but, on 22 February, they were advised that the occupation of Malta was now deferred until the autumn of 1941, after the conclusion of the war in the east.[53] When Admiral Raeder raised the matter with Hitler once again on 18 March the latter supported his earlier decision by quoting Göring's argument that an air landing on Malta would be made particularly difficult by the close network of stone walls on the island.[54] The subsequent diversion of the German airborne forces to Crete and the losses they suffered there removed any immediate threat to Malta. Throughout this period the Italian authorities, led by *Supermarina*, had also considered the possibility of invading Malta, but reached the conclusion in May that an attack on a scale likely to be successful would need equipment not then available, and a period of preparation and training that would take until the end of the year to complete.[55]

The course and outcome of this debate could not have been known to British Intelligence, which, on the contrary, began to receive, in the early weeks of 1941, growing reports of the arrival of German military units in Italy. On 18 January the Director of Naval Intelligence advised Malta of reports from the US naval attaché in Rome that '50,000 German and Italian troops including motorised units now in Sicily will invade Tunisia' and asked if there was any evidence of such a force.[56] Vice-Admiral Ford replied that photo-reconnaissance had found only the usual numbers of ships at Palermo and Messina, but conceded that others might be assembling at Naples.[57]

The CIGS passed on to the Governor these rumours about German armoured forces in Sicily, but added that 'the volume of these reports is greater than their reliability'. The Governor thought the terrain of Malta made the island an unlikely destination for armoured units, and expressed confidence in the ability of the garrison to resist an attack.[58] However, a more anxious warning on 30 January about a possible airborne attack, derived from a 'Rome source described as authentic',[59] caused the Governor, on 5 February, to request an additional infantry battalion. General Dill read the Governor's telegram to his fellow Chiefs at their meeting on 6 February, and reminded them that a sixth battalion for Malta, which it had been agreed to send in the previous November, had been diverted to Crete when Italy had invaded Greece.[60] The Chiefs of Staff recommended sending one additional battalion but, when the matter was discussed later the same day, the Prime Minister thought that two were required. He minuted that 'it seems a pity to let the baker's cart go with only one loaf, when the journey is so expensive and the load available, and it might as easily carry two'.[61] When asked if a machine gun battalion would be of more value, the Governor replied that 'it was not so much a question of fire power as man power'.[62] The two additional battalions arrived at Malta by cruiser on 21 February.

The threat of invasion was raised again after the successful German airborne capture of Crete in late May. On 5 June General Dobbie sent a long signal to the War Office in which he analysed the garrison's ability to resist an airborne attack on the Cretan model. Apart from the overriding need for more fighter aircraft, which is discussed later, he requested two further infantry battalions, together with additional AA, anti-tank and field artillery units. The Prime Minister, in a signal of 6 June, immediately replied that, although 'it does not seem that an attack on Malta is likely within the next two or three weeks', the War Office was dealing with his requests. He concluded by affirming: 'You may be sure we regard Malta as one of the master-keys of the British Empire. We are sure that you are the man to hold it, and we will do everything in human power to give you the means.'[63]

The scale of the Governor's request, requiring the transport of almost 6,000 men and much equipment, caused the planning staff considerable difficulty, but eventually a six-ship convoy from the UK, together with a troopship, was arranged to take place during a moonless period in mid-July. The overall result of the two invasion alarms in January and June was that the defensive capability of the Malta garrison had been much improved. This was to have its effect on Axis calculations in 1942.

Whatever the uncertainties about a possible invasion, there could be no doubt about the German intention to eliminate Malta as an effective British base by sustained and heavy air attack. Although elements of *Fliegerkorps X* were diverted to bases in North Africa and the Dodecanese, a powerful force remained in Sicily to attack Malta. Air raids developed in scale and variety after the first raid on 16 January, and increasingly urgent appeals for help began to reach the authorities in London.[64] On February 16 AVM Maynard, who had available only one fighter squadron of Mark I Hurricanes, warned Portal of 'a systematic attempt to neutralise our small fighter effort', and he requested, in particular, reinforcement with Mark II Hurricanes to match the performance of the ME 109s which had just made their appearance over the island.[65] Later that month Vice-Admiral Ford told Cunningham that there were only eight Hurricanes left and that 'many pilots are war weary'.[66] A formal request for fighter reinforcement was made by the Governor in a signal to the CAS of 7 March. He emphasised that the problem could not be solved by more AA guns but only 'by a fighter force adequate in numbers and performance'.[67]

This stark warning of the deteriorating situation in Malta brought into question the prevailing method of supplying fighters to Malta. In January the merchant ship *Essex* had brought 12 crated Mark I Hurricanes to Malta as part of the 'Excess' convoy, and Cunningham had supplemented the Hurricanes by increasing to a total of 12 the Fulmar fighters disembarked from the damaged *Illustrious*.[68] The consequences for Malta of the arrival in Sicily of *Fliegerkorps X* were debated in the Defence Committee on 20 January, and, on the following day, the Prime Minister minuted: 'The first duty of the AOC-in-C is none the less to sustain the resistance of Malta by a proper flow of fighter reinforcements.'[69] To meet this injunction ACM Longmore in Cairo had, out of the flow of fighter aircraft reaching Egypt along the Takoradi route, despatched reinforcements, six at a time, to Malta from airfields in North Africa.

On 8 March Portal replied to Dobbie's telegram by saying that every effort was being made to increase the supply of fighters, including some Mark II Hurricanes, but that the main obstacle was 'transportation difficulties'.[70] The Prime Minister then intervened with a minute of 9 March. He suggested that the old aircraft carrier, HMS *Argus*, which was then loading with more Hurricanes should deliver these to Malta through the Mediterranean, rather than take them to Takoradi, which would add another fortnight to the delivery time. 'It would be a fine thing', he added, 'to reinforce Malta direct.'[71] Admiral Pound, however, was opposed to this suggestion, arguing at a Chiefs of Staff meeting on 11 March that the navy's remaining carriers, vulnerable to dive-bomber attack in the Mediterranean, were needed to protect Atlantic convoys from the German battle cruisers.[72]

The Naval Staff continued to procrastinate and Churchill finally lost patience. On 27 March he summoned a meeting of the Defence Committee to review the lack of progress. 'Despite the urgent appeals of the Governor of Malta,' he charged, 'all kinds of objections had been raised,' and he went on to list some of them. Pound, supported by Alexander, the First Lord, denied that the Admiralty had ignored the problem and repeated that they had been told that their first priority was the Battle of the Atlantic. They could not fight this battle 'if their forces were liable at any moment to be snatched away for other operations'. Portal, naturally, supported the Prime Minister and so, too, did Attlee and Beaverbrook. It was decided, therefore, that a carrier operation (Operation 'Winch') be undertaken at the earliest opportunity.[73] That, nevertheless, this decision rankled with Pound is revealed in his letter of the following day to Cunningham. After saying that he was reluctant to divert HMS *Ark Royal* for this operation, he added: 'I do feel that the Navy has more than played their part, as we have put a great many more [aircraft into the Middle East] than have gone there by any other means.'[74]

Nevertheless, the Prime Minister judged that the next critical phase of the war was to be fought in the Mediterranean. It was imperative, therefore, that available British resources be transferred to the active theatre of operations in increasing numbers and with the utmost speed. On 30 April Churchill issued an 'Action This Day' Directive to the Chiefs of Staff.[75] This ordered that 'an operation similar to TIGER must be planned for the Air', and directed that all four of the navy's aircraft carriers be employed to deliver up to 130 Hurricanes to Malta. Hence, Operation 'Winch' was but the first of a series of carrier-borne operations that, between April and June, delivered no fewer than 224 fighters to Malta, of which 109 remained on the island, while the remainder flew on to Egypt.[76]

By early May, however, it seemed that this reinforcement programme had come too late, and that the situation in Malta had reached breaking point. Despite the measures put in hand as a result of the Prime Minister's pressure on the Admiralty, the position at Malta continued to deteriorate alarmingly. On 16 May the Governor wrote: 'Air superiority . . . has completely passed into enemy's hands.'[77] He added that the morale of one squadron had almost been destroyed. The official historians pass quickly over this May crisis in Malta, and make no reference to the decision to relieve Maynard as AOC, or the reasons for that decision. Moreover, the continued retention of personal service records means that the published records permit only a general reconstruction of the problem and its solution.

April had been a month of disaster for British arms in the Mediterranean. Cyrenaica and Greece had been lost, and, in both London and Cairo, the two German offensives had all the appearance of a converging attack whose objective was Egypt. This grave danger led Churchill to insist on the acceleration of the carrier aircraft operations mentioned above. At Malta, however, many of the newly arrived Hurricanes were lost within a few days, either in the air or on the ground, and concern about the effectiveness of the air defence of the island was growing. On 15 May Vice-Admiral Ford telegraphed to Cunningham and Pound that 'I am getting extremely perturbed with the state of our air defences'. He attributed this to inferior aircraft, inexperienced pilots, and 'reasons which I will send to the C-in-C Mediterranean in writing'.[78] This additional memorandum is not in the PRO files, but its contents are, surely, reflected in the personal letter which, three days later, Cunningham wrote to Pound. In this he observed:

> There is something badly wrong in Malta with the ground arrangements. By this time they should have had all their aircraft protected somehow from this ground straffing [sic] but I fear little has been done. The fighter pilots themselves are most discontented about it.[79]

The Governor, however, had already grasped the nettle. On 8 May, after reviewing the situation with Maynard, he wrote at length to Portal later that day. He repeated points made earlier, such as the need for more Mark II Hurricanes, the replacement of exhausted pilots by others with greater combat experience, and the requirement for a strengthened ground organisation. But the main problem, as he saw it, was the 'shortage of efficient personnel on Maynard's staff. . . . The consequence is that Maynard has had to devote himself to small details, and has had his burdens greatly increased.'[80] He went on to urge that there be 'a very generous increase in the number of really first class staff officers'. As regards Maynard himself Dobbie had nothing but praise. 'He has done extremely well. He has made bricks without straw, but unless he gets the sort of help I have indicated he will be unable to compete.'[81] Portal acted quickly, and AVM Hugh Lloyd later wrote in his invaluable memoirs that he found himself in Malta 145 hours after receiving the first call from the Air Ministry. More significantly, he was told by Portal himself before he left: 'You will be on the Island for six months as a minimum and nine months as a maximum as by that time you will be worn out.'[82] Maynard had been there for more than one year.

There is nowhere any suggestion in these papers that there was any other reason for Maynard's replacement than exhaustion exacerbated by inadequate staff support. That he had not lost the confidence of the Prime Minister or of Portal, as did Wavell and Longmore, is indicated by Churchill's reply to Dobbie's telegram of 17 May: 'Everyone here appreciates splendid work Maynard has done working up from the very beginning, but it is felt that a change would be better now. Maynard will be well looked after here.'[83] The only criticism that might be levelled against Maynard was implied by Maynard himself. When Churchill asked Portal about the problems in Malta, he was told about 'certain deficiencies in the higher control which have only just come to light'.[84] It may be that, had Maynard been quicker to explain his growing difficulties to Portal, and pressed his needs with greater insistence, remedial action might have been taken at an earlier stage. The actual changes which accompanied Lloyd's appointment on 1 June will be examined in the next chapter, but their beneficial effect was revealed by the Governor in a letter to the CIGS of 2 June: 'We have had some drastic RAF changes here and these have done much good and will do more.'[85]

9

Malta's Contribution to 'Crusader'

THE BUILD-UP OF MALTA'S OFFENSIVE POWER

In the preceding chapter attention was focused on Malta's increasingly precarious position in the spring and early summer of 1941 under the weight of German air attack. Soon after AVM Lloyd arrived in Malta in late May, bearing Portal's instructions, 'Your main task at Malta is to sink Axis shipping sailing from Europe to Africa',[1] he learned of the departure of *Fliegerkorps X* from Sicily. The campaigns in Greece and Crete, and the need to support Rommel in Cyrenaica, had already reduced the number of German aircraft in Sicily, but, in early June, Enigma decrypts revealed that the remainder had flown to bases in Greece and North Africa.[2]

Apart from the departure of the *Luftwaffe* from Sicily, Lloyd had other advantages not enjoyed by Maynard, his predecessor. He had, a mere two weeks earlier, been Senior Air Staff Officer (SASO) at No. 2 Group, Bomber Command, which flew a force of Blenheim aircraft engaged on anti-shipping attacks. He brought with him not only this clearly relevant experience, but also the unqualified support of the CAS. When Portal had received the Governor's letter of 8 May about the critical air situation in Malta, he immediately minuted to his staff: 'I regard Malta as the station which, above all others, anywhere, should have priority in personnel and material.'[3] The speed with which Lloyd, accompanied by several other experienced senior officers, was transferred to Malta is sufficient evidence of Portal's concern.

The numerous problems that Lloyd discovered upon his arrival are well described in the opening chapters of his book, and attention here will be concentrated on three of his principal difficulties. He was the beneficiary of a growing number of fighter and bomber aircraft of various types, and there was a pressing need to give them better protection on the ground. The answer was dispersal. 'In Britain,' he wrote, 'there was a craze for dispersal.'[4] The shortage of labour in Malta and the limited supply of mechanical equipment made this a slow process, but Lloyd at once put the work in hand. As a result, he was able to report as early as 20 June that, although the construction of blast-proof pens would take many more months, no aircraft were held on the airfields.[5]

His second difficulty was that of servicing and repairing his growing air force. It needs to be emphasised again that, in the eyes of the Air Staff, Malta's role as a staging post for aircraft reinforcements to the Middle East was only slightly less important than its offensive function. In the first ten months of 1941, 326 bombers and 106 fighters passed through Malta, all requiring refuelling and servicing. By comparison, the Takoradi route handled a total of 1,141 aircraft of all types during the same period.[6] To service his growing air force, as well as the transit traffic, Lloyd reported that he had a total of 1,630 airmen, fewer than required at a single Bomber Command station in England.[7] More men arrived in the following months, but the shortage of spares, proper tools and maintenance equipment meant that it was difficult to maintain high serviceability levels. Average serviceability in July, for example, was 30 out of 84 Hurricanes, and 5 out of 21 Blenheims.

A third problem facing Lloyd was the need to provide a more effective control system for the growing force of fighters. Several senior controllers came out with him at the end of May, and on 3 June a new underground fighter operations room became operational.[8] The exposed radar stations were given better protection, and gaps in the coverage of the main stations filled by the use of army gun-laying radar equipment.[9] Further improvements in fighter control and interception only became possible in 1942 with the installation of more advanced radar.

In July 1941 ACM Sir Edgar Ludlow-Hewitt, former C-in-C of Bomber Command, and then Inspector General of the RAF, made a tour of inspection of the Mediterranean theatre. On 21 July he wrote to Portal from the Palace at Valletta: 'This place I find in much better form than I expected. Lloyd has and is working wonders. Everybody here is singing his praises, and he has certainly got a move on.' He was able to recommend that, as a result of Lloyd's dispersal arrangements, as many as nine squadrons could in future be based at Malta, a significant increase over the five that had previously been considered the maximum. He also urged the despatch of Beaufort torpedo bombers, which had a much greater range than the Swordfish, and whose torpedoes he considered more effective than the 250 lb bombs carried by the Blenheims.[10]

By August Lloyd's fighter forces had grown significantly. He now commanded three squadrons of Hurricanes with a total of 75 aircraft, mostly Mark IIs, together with eight long-range Beaufighters. But, although the organisation of an effective air defence system was clearly essential, it was the development of Malta's offensive forces that was Lloyd's main task (see Map 2). By August he had available a growing force of Blenheims, Wellingtons and Swordfish, together with ten Marylands for reconnaissance.[11] These aircraft enabled Lloyd to develop a three-pronged offensive strategy. The Wellingtons carried out night attacks, mainly on embarkation ports in Italy and on the arrival ports in North Africa, but also on other targets as required. Torpedo-carrying Swordfish of 830 Squadron, later reinforced by the Albacores of 828 Squadron with a longer range, attacked shipping, again usually at night, and also laid mines off Italian ports.[12] These attacks were assisted, after July, by the introduction of short-range ASV in some of the Swordfish, while, in September, three Wellingtons, equipped with a long-range ASV radar, were flown out from England. These soon became invaluable in directing aircraft, and, later, the ships of Force K on to distant targets.[13]

Lloyd's third weapon was two squadrons of Blenheims trained to deliver attacks against ships at masthead height, and used, alternatively, against ground targets in Sicily and North Africa.[14] The loss rate in these squadrons, particularly after the Axis convoys were provided with stronger AA defences, soon gave cause for concern. In August AM Tedder, who had succeeded Longmore as AOC-in-C Middle East, had warned the Air Ministry that day attacks on heavily defended convoys 'were likely to involve heavy casualties'. However, his proposal to divert more effort to the bombing of ports received the reply from the VCAS, Freeman, that 'I expect Lloyd to employ these forces with greatest determination against enemy lines of communication.'[15]

Continued severe Blenheim losses forced a reconsideration of the matter. On 1 October Portal addressed a personal letter to Tedder expressing his own concern about mounting Blenheim losses.[16] After noting that 18 Blenheim crews had been lost in the previous three months, he told Tedder that a replacement squadron was being sent out and urged that he adopt a policy of rotating Blenheim squadrons through Malta for relatively short periods. Lloyd, who had received a copy of this letter, replied on 13 October, rebutting the 'impression that I have used my Blenheims constantly in low level attacks on heavily escorted merchant ships'. On the contrary, he had been so worried about Blenheim losses that he had written to Tedder as early as 18 August warning that such attacks were, in his view, 'sheer murder'. This had only brought a 'sharp rebuke from C-in-C Mediterranean [i.e. Admiral Cunningham] that the statement was too strong'.[17] The only available alternatives were the longer range torpedo-carrying Beauforts, but although these had on several occasions, as we have seen, been promised to Maynard, as well as to Lloyd, none appeared in Malta before 1942.

MAP 2
RADIUS OF ACTION OF AIRCRAFT FROM MALTA, 1942

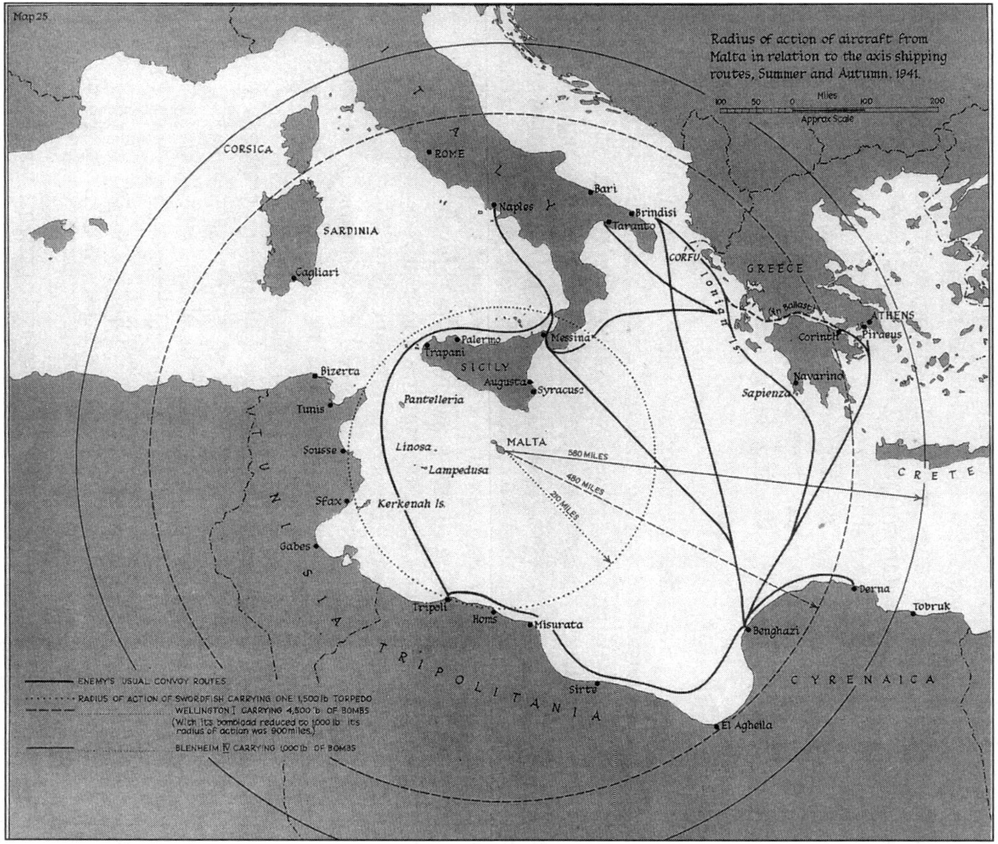

Source: The Mediterranean and Middle East, Vol. III, p. 179, Map 25.

It was with these growing resources, operated in conditions of great difficulty, that Lloyd set about his task of sinking Axis shipping. The expansion of his force is shown in Table 6, which has been compiled from daily returns made to the Air Ministry.[18] This RAF table does not include the FAA Swordfish and Albacores, of which up to 25 became available to Lloyd during this period. It also ignores temporary reinforcements, such as long-range Beaufighters, which were sent in connection with special operations.

Whereas the records show that the Air Staff had, in the summer and autumn of 1941, made a major effort to augment Malta's offensive capability, this cannot be said with the same confidence about the Admiralty's response. Cunningham's problems after the losses sustained by his fleet during the evacuations from Greece and Crete were undoubtedly acute. The Syrian campaign and the supply of Tobruk took a further toll on his diminished resources, and he often lacked the destroyer screen to enable him to take his battleships to sea. With regard to his ability to interfere with the Libyan supply convoys he wrote to Pound in early June, after the losses incurred in the Cretan campaign, to express the view that the attack on these convoys must, for the time being, be left to aircraft and submarines.[19]

Pound in London fully endorsed these views. He sent as many submarines to the Mediterranean as could be spared, writing in September that 'you either have or will have every available submarine'.[20] However, following the withdrawal of the 5th Destroyer Flotilla in May to help defend Crete, there were no longer any surface ships at Malta and the absence of such a force was to cause an increasingly sharp disagreement with the Prime Minister in the ensuing months. On 19 June Pound told Cunningham that the demands of the Atlantic U-boat campaign were such that he was unable to send him any destroyer reinforcements.[21] These convictions coloured Pound's reply to a minute addressed by the Prime Minster to the Chiefs of Staff on 30 June, which read:

TABLE 6
AIRCRAFT SERVICEABLE WITHIN 14 DAYS, JUNE–DECEMBER 1941

	Hurricanes	Wellingtons	Blenheims	Marylands
1 June	24	1	8	6
1 September	76	22	15	7
1 December	75	33	28	11
28 December	102	24	26	9

Source: PRO AIR 8/506.

Although we take a heavy toll, very large enemy reinforcements are crossing to Africa continually. The Navy seem unable to do anything. The Air Force only stop perhaps a fifth. You are no doubt impressed with the full gravity of the situation.[22]

On behalf of the Chiefs of Staff, who were, indeed, 'fully impressed with the gravity of the situation', Pound replied that the navy and the RAF had sunk a total of 52 ships in May and June, and judged this a 'creditable effort' deserving of praise rather than censure.[23] Attached to his reply was a four-page 'Note by Naval Staff', which, after drawing attention to the dangers faced by ships without air cover, concluded that convoy attacks could only be carried out by submarines and aircraft. The Note conceded that such attacks were 'intermittent and do not achieve complete stoppage of the supply line'. The Prime Minister's comment on this reply can no longer be read; it is difficult to believe that it was not critical.[24]

The Prime Minister returned to this matter in mid-August. After learning from General Ismay that the Axis had landed 265,000 tons of supplies in July and a further 194,000 tons in the first 20 days of August,[25] the Prime Minister addressed a lengthy minute to Pound on 22 August.[26] This began: 'Will you please consider the sending of a flotilla, and, if possible, a cruiser or two, to Malta, as soon as possible.' The minute went on to deplore the Admiralty's lack of action and charged that 'we have lost sight of our purpose . . . in which the Admiralty was so forward and strong'. Upon receiving intelligence about other Axis convoys the Prime Minister was provoked to minute the CNS on 24 August:

What action will C-in-C Mediterranean take on this information? Surely he cannot put up with this kind of thing. . . . Is he going simply to leave these ships to the chance of a submarine without making any effort by his surface forces to intercept them? Please ask specifically what if anything he is going to do. We are still at war.[27]

Pound at once signalled to Cunningham asking whether he could provide a surface force for Malta. On 24 August Cunningham replied that he had been thinking of such a force, and agreed that 'it can and should be done and it is only the question of how to provide the destroyers that has delayed my taking any action'.[28] Nevertheless, he added, such a force would only have a deterrent and delaying effect and was unlikely to cause the enemy much damage. He concluded by writing that, in any case, he could spare no ships until after 30 September.

Pound incorporated this reply in a lengthy memorandum that he forwarded to the Prime Minister on the same day. In this he made two principal points. First, the limited force that might be found could not be expected to achieve very much, since the Italian navy could always 'bring a much more powerful force against them at any moment'. Second, in view of the reduced number of the navy's fleet destroyers and cruisers, of which he gave detailed figures, he questioned whether the diversion of any of these to Malta could be justified. The whole matter was then debated at a Chiefs of Staff Meeting, at which the Prime Minister presided, on 25 August.[29] There Pound went even further by asserting that 'a force of the kind which Admiral Cunningham could afford to employ at Malta would be faced with an almost impossible task'. The minutes of the meeting do not make clear whether the Prime Minister took issue with this statement, but the negative tone of Pound's report and comments must surely have irritated him, to say the least. In his history of the war he later wrote: 'The policy was accepted, though time was needed to bring it into force.'[30] That this was not Pound's understanding of the decision reached is shown by his letter to Cunningham of 3 September. 'I am extremely doubtful,' he wrote, 'whether a weak force of two 6-inch cruisers and four destroyers would be able to achieve anything commensurate with their loss.' He thought it best to see what the additional submarines and Blenheims might achieve before putting a surface force at Malta.[31]

The Prime Minister, characteristically, would not let the matter rest. On 5 October, as Auchinleck's 'Crusader' attack drew closer, yet another minute was despatched to the First Sea Lord: 'Is there no possibility of helping the Air Force on the Tripoli blockade with some surface craft, including a cruiser or two? We seem to leave it all to the Air Force and Submarines.'[32]

Pound responded by reiterating the difficulties of finding the ships to make up a surface force at Malta, and again voiced his doubts about the results they might achieve. On this reply Churchill wrote: ' . . . Cunningham seems to be lying low since Crete. Is he going to play any part in Crusader?'[33] Within a week Pound had changed his mind. On 11 October he signalled to Cunningham to advise that two 6-inch cruisers were being sent to him to help stop the African convoys.[34] That his hand had finally been forced is revealed in the personal letter he sent to Cunningham on the same day. 'It is with great reluctance,' he wrote, 'that we are sending *Aurora* and *Penelope* to Malta.' He still expected only limited results, but went on to write that 'should "Crusader" fail . . . then I think there would have been lasting criticism because we had not made any attempt to cut the communications to Africa by surface forces'.[35] The question whether more decisive results might have been achieved had surface ships been sent earlier is considered later.

THE ATTACK ON ROMMEL'S SUPPLIES IN THE SECOND HALF OF 1941

Before examining the British attack on the Libyan supply route, it may be helpful to give some account of the North African supply problem in the autumn of 1941 as seen from Rome. In Chapter 7 consideration has been given to the initial difficulties that stemmed from the unforeseen establishment of a convoy system to the Libyan ports. The Italian official histories and Italian historians, such as Giorgerini and Gabriele, as well as several British historians, notably Knox, have devoted considerable attention to the supply problem and a complex picture emerges.

The principal underlying problem was the limited industrial potential of the Italian economy. This was measured in 1938 at an index figure of 46 compared with a figure of 181 for the British economy. Moreover, unlike other belligerents after the war began, Italy never increased above about 23 per cent the percentage of GNP devoted to military production.[36] Consequently, armaments production was always limited in quantity quite apart from questions of quality. This limited military output was then spread too thinly over too many fronts. Not only were resources urgently needed in Libya diverted to Albania and Greece, but Mussolini also insisted on sending 200 bombers to participate in the Battle of Britain.[37] Inevitably, therefore, the volume of Italian equipment and supplies for North Africa was always limited and intermittent, while the quantity of German supplies allocated to the Mediterranean war was subordinated in 1941 and 1942 to the overriding needs of the Russian front.

The speedy and efficient transfer of such goods as became available was then subject to the capacity of the loading ports in Italy and the unloading ports in North Africa. The naval study of 1938 referred to earlier expected that, in peacetime conditions, the loading ports in Italy would be able to handle 24 ships at a time and the unloading ports 19, although it was expected that war conditions might considerably reduce these figures. Nevertheless, in practice actual unloading capacity in North Africa was very variable, as shown by the fact that in June 1941 125,000 tons of supplies were successfully unloaded, and as much as 150,000 tons in April 1942. These figures make clear that port capacity was not always the limiting factor that Van Creveld has alleged.[38] This point is considered further in Chapter 11.

Giorgerini has drawn attention to two other considerations.[39] First, very few cargo ships sailed to North Africa fully laden. He has estimated the average cargo at only 1,200–1,500 tons compared with average capacity of 5,500 tons. Second, the Italian navy abandoned pre-war plans to sail heavily escorted 'grand' convoys and adopted a system of 'mini-convoys'. The 993 convoys in the period from June 1940 until January 1943 consisted on average of 1.9 ships with 2.2 escorts. The same quantity of goods could, Giorgerini calculated, have been shipped in 400 'grand' convoys. He attributed the actual convoy practice to various factors such as the wish to limit the risk of loss by distributing valuable supplies among several ships and convoys, and by the urgent demands for supplies before a full cargo load had been assembled at an embarkation port. Nevertheless, as British experience confirmed, risks were increased by the use of smaller convoys and Giorgerini pointed out that the 49 'grand' convoys that were sailed suffered a lower rate of loss than the smaller ones.

A further factor was the steady erosion of available shipping and naval escorts. The initial loss of the best third of the Italian merchant fleet, the growing demands of the Albanian and Greek theatres, and the mounting war losses and damage that far outstripped new construction all took their toll, although Admiral Raeder complained to Hitler that the Italians were trying to preserve their fleet for post-war service.[40] The escort position was also deteriorating, and the need for escorts for North African convoys rose from 25–30 in 1940 to 45 by mid-1941. By then the Italian navy had lost 20 destroyers, while many others were undergoing repair. As Admiral Cocchia put it, the tasks facing the destroyer force grew daily as its numbers diminished.[41]

Underlying all these separate elements of the supply problem was what Knox has described as Italy's 'logistical ineffectiveness. . . . Its logistical base was wholly inadequate to the demands of war.'[42] He has pointed out that no fewer than five government departments were involved in supplying North Africa, and that the army and navy maintained separate offices at each arrival port. Co-ordination was so poor that the Italian Chiefs of Staff devoted much time at their meetings to the movements of individual ships.[43] Giorgerini has also noted that the capacity of the North African ports was considerably higher when they were in British hands.[44] What this necessarily brief survey of a complex problem makes clear is that the carrying capacity of the Italian logistical system and the supply of the Axis forces in North Africa were seriously hampered by resource inadequacies and by administrative inefficiencies. Consequently, any sustained attack on this supply system was likely to lead to losses and delays that could jeopardise Axis operations.

Against this picture of a vulnerable supply route we may now turn to consider the development of British operations against it. Essential to an understanding of what Malta forces were able to achieve in the last half of 1941 is a brief account of the Intelligence breakthrough in the summer of 1941.⁴⁵ A growing volume of decrypted material was one of the benefits that followed the arrival of the German air force in the Mediterranean theatre. The 'Red' and 'Light Blue' versions of the *Luftwaffe's* Enigma-encoded signals were quickly and regularly read by GC&CS.⁴⁶ The departure of *Fliegerkorps X* to Greece in early June reduced somewhat the volume of German traffic, but this was more than offset by GC&CS's breaking of an Italian naval medium-grade machine code, which is referred to by Hinsley as C38m. Ironically, this had been introduced, at German insistence, to provide a safer means of transmitting details of Axis convoys to Libya.⁴⁷ This cypher was first broken in June 1941, and it was thereafter read with diminishing delays and interruptions until Italy's surrender. The C38m signals gave full details of all convoy operations to the North African ports, but rarely, at this time, details of the cargoes carried.⁴⁸

The reading of C38m, the German air force traffic, and, after mid-September, some German army signals gave the British authorities an increasingly complete and current picture of Rommel's supply situation and of the difficulties he was encountering. Improved arrangements for handling this material were made in August by the establishment of a Special Liaison Unit (SLU) at Malta.⁴⁹ This enabled GC&CS to transmit the gist of the C38m signals, which could be intercepted in England, directly to Vice-Admiral Ford at Valletta, although the Admiralty rejected the further suggestion that, to save more time, these signals should be decrypted at Malta.⁵⁰

Nevertheless, aerial reconnaissance was also essential, not merely to provide 'cover' for operations prompted by Enigma decrypts, but to locate convoys that might have departed from the pre-arranged routes. The provision of such reconnaissance was not always easy. Apart from the difficulties caused by poor weather, the serviceability level of the Marylands was variable. These aircraft had recently gone out of production and their replacement, the Baltimore, was slow to arrive.⁵¹ Nevertheless, and largely due to the operational skill of the photo-reconnaisance (PR) pilots such as Warburton, Lloyd was able to record that 'if a photograph was wanted of Naples or Taranto it was as good as done, even two or three times a day'.⁵² Equally important for a successful night attack was the work of the handful of ASV-equipped Wellingtons of 69 Squadron. With their long endurance they were able to sweep the seas for enemy convoys and direct attacking forces on to them.⁵³ It was this combination of aerial reconnaissance and Ultra material that allowed Ford and Lloyd to concert their plans.

Malta-based operations in the last six months of 1941 are fully described by the official historians and need not be repeated in detail. Attention here is focused on several key aspects of these events that can be conveniently considered in two phases. The first ran from June to the end of October when only aircraft and submarines were available to carry out offensive operations. The second phase began with the first attack by the surface Force K in early November. These phases roughly correspond with the periods before and after the beginning of the 'Crusader' offensive on 18 November.

During the first phase, since the Cyrenaican ports and airfields were in Axis hands, it was only from Malta that the Italian ports and Tripoli, the principal unloading port, could be attacked. Most of this work fell to the night-flying Wellingtons. Between mid-June and mid-October 1941 Malta-based Wellingtons attacked Tripoli 72 times, flying 357 sorties.[54] This is equivalent to raids by six aircraft every other night. According to Lloyd, these aircraft flew a further 452 sorties in the four weeks before the opening of 'Crusader'. This figure may be compared with the overall total of nearly 3,000 sorties flown by British and Commonwealth air forces during the five weeks prior to 18 November.[55] The results of these Wellington raids defy precise analysis. However, on the evidence of photographs, Lloyd believed that, after intensive attacks in September, the damage at Tripoli was such that unloading could only be carried out by ships' derricks, and that the turn-round time had been multiplied by three and a half since June. The Italian official history records that by the middle of 1941 the capacity of Tripoli had been reduced by 50 per cent.[56] Similar damage and delays were the object of raids on Naples, Brindisi and Taranto, for which purpose 4,000 lb bombs were later used.

Lloyd's other offensive aircraft were employed, in the main, to attack ships at sea, although the Blenheims, and, occasionally, even the Marylands, also bombed ports. The main task of the FAA Swordfish and Albacores, however, as it had been since 830 Squadron arrived at Malta in 1940, was to launch torpedo attacks on Axis convoys. These night operations were much helped by the introduction of ASV radar, but the Swordfish, in particular, suffered from limited range. Although convoys bound for Tripoli could still be reached, an increase in the number of Axis convoys using the passage down the Greek coast to Benghazi placed a greater burden on the Blenheim squadrons (see Map 2).

During this first phase of the attack submarine dispositions were closely co-ordinated by Vice-Admiral Ford with Lloyd's air operations. Wanklyn and other commanders of the 10th Flotilla took an increasing toll of Axis shipping, although three British submarines were lost in this period and others subjected to severe depth-charge attacks. The losses suffered by Axis merchant ships, by number and tonnage, in the central Mediterranean in the summer and autumn of 1941, and Malta's contribution to them, are summarised in Table 7. These figures show that, although the 10th Flotilla submarines continued to make a steady contribution to the overall losses, including the sinking of two large passenger liners in September, the difference, compared with the first five months of 1941, was due to air operations, which accounted for more than one half of the losses.

Table 8 shows the impact of these losses on Rommel's build-up for his planned attack on Tobruk. These figures make clear that, despite a rising level of losses, the Italian navy managed to deliver, on average, more than 70,000 tons of supplies a month, an amount that is discussed later in the chapter. It was the perception in London that it was necessary, as 'Crusader' approached, to inflict even greater losses on these supply convoys that led, as we have seen, to the despatch of Force K to Malta, and this marks the beginning of the second phase of the Malta offensive. The arrival of these four ships on 21 October, quickly detected by Italian reconnaissance aircraft, had an immediate effect. Without a shot fired, convoys to Tripoli were suspended. After missing on 25 October a destroyer force carrying troops to Libya,[57] Force K achieved its first dramatic success on 7 November when seven heavily

TABLE 7
PROPORTION OF AXIS SHIPS SUNK BY MALTA FORCES, JUNE–OCTOBER 1941

(number and tonnage of ships sunk)

	Submarine	Ship	Aircraft	Shared	Malta total	C. Med. total	Malta (%)
June	(2) 5,084	–	(2) 12,249	–	(4) 17,333	(10) 29,063	60
July	(3) 12,940	–	(4) 19,467	–	(7) 32,407	(10) 36,464	89
Aug.	(3) 16,238	–	(6) 33,425	–	(9) 49,663	(11) 53,023	94
Sept.	(2) 38,982	–	(6) 25,964	(1) 5,996	(9) 70,942	(12) 79,660	89
Oct.	–	–	(7) 33,800	–	(7) 33,800	(11) 43,850	77
Total	(10) 73,244	–	(25) 124,905	(1) 5,996	(36) 204,145	(54) 242,060	84

Source: See Appendix.

TABLE 8
AXIS SUPPLIES LANDED AND PERCENTAGES LOST, JUNE–OCTOBER 1941

(amounts in tons)

	General cargo	% lost	Fuel	% lost	Total landed	Total sent	% lost
June	89,226	6	35,850	8	125,076	133,331	6
July	50,706	12	11,570	41	62,276	77,012	19
August	46,755	20	37,201	1	83,956	96,021	13
September	54,105	29	13,408	24	67,513	94,115	28
October	61,663	20	11,951	21	73,614	92,449	20

Source: See Appendix.

escorted merchant ships were sunk. Enigma decrypts made this interception possible, but it was only a radar-assisted night engagement that permitted the complete destruction of this convoy without any British damage.[58]

In the following six weeks the initial four ships of Force K were reinforced by a further two cruisers and two destroyers from Alexandria (Force B), and, in mid-December, by four more destroyers from the Home Fleet. This latter force, warned by Enigma intercepts, and directed by an ASV Wellington from Malta, sank two Italian cruisers pressed into service as emergency fuel carriers. Such measures had been made necessary by Force K's sinking of two German supply ships, the *Procida* and the *Maritza*, on 24 November. On the following day German air force signals revealed that these ships carried fuel and ammunition, the loss of which had placed German operations in North Africa in 'real danger'.[59] British records also show that the Prime Minister took a close personal interest in this action. After several discussions with Pound, he signalled directly to Admiral Cunningham on 23 November asking to be informed of the action proposed to intercept these two ships, and he prompted Pound to send a direct order to Vice-Admiral Ford at Malta to sail Force K on the following day.[60] Further fuel losses resulted from the sinking of the Italian tanker *Iridio Mantovani* on 1 December. This ship, carrying 9,000 tons of fuel, had been damaged by Blenheims from Malta, and was then sunk by Force K.[61]

Axis shipping losses caused by Malta forces in November and December 1941 within total losses in the central Mediterranean are set out in Table 9. The cargoes, including fuel, which reached North Africa and the percentages lost *en route* are set out in Table 10. This virtual

TABLE 9
PROPORTION OF AXIS SHIPS SUNK BY MALTA FORCES,
NOVEMBER–DECEMBER 1941

(number and tonnage of ships sunk)

	Submarine	Ship	Aircraft	Shared	Malta total	C. Med. total	Malta (%)
November	(1) 2,469	(10) 47,566	(3) 7,784	–	(14) 57,819	(14) 57,819	100
December	(2) 13,673	(1) 1,976	(2) 1,902	(1) 10,540	(6) 28,091	(12) 47,867	59
Total	(3) 16,142	(11) 49,542	(5) 9,686	(1) 10,540	(20) 85,910	(26) 105,686	81

Source: See Appendix.

TABLE 10
AXIS SUPPLIES LANDED AND PERCENTAGES LOST, NOVEMBER–DECEMBER 1941

(amounts in tons)

	General cargo	% lost	Fuel	% lost	Total landed	Total sent	% lost
November	27,372	58	2,471	92	29,843	79,208	62
December	31,869	20	7,223	5	39,092	47,689	18

Source: See Appendix.

halving of earlier months' deliveries, coming at the height of the 'Crusader' battles, and the particularly heavy losses of fuel in November, provoked a number of responses that will be more closely examined in the next section. One immediate step, however, was a decision by the Italian navy to provide battleship protection for its convoys, the safe arrival of which appeared essential to prevent the defeat of the Axis armies in Cyrenaica. The first of these in early December was a failure, and the second, on 12 December, was ordered by *Supermarina* to turn back after a false report that the Mediterranean Fleet was at sea. On its return British submarines damaged two merchant ships and the escorting battleship, *Vittorio Veneto*, and two other cargo ships collided.[62]

Nevertheless, the Italians tried again on 16 December with Convoy M 42 at the same time as Forces B and K, supported by further cruisers from Alexandria, were escorting HMS *Breconshire* to Malta with essential fuel oil. Luck now deserted the Royal Navy. In what became known as 'The First Battle of Sirte', although *Breconshire* was safely escorted to Malta, and the submarine *Upright* on 13 December sank two ships carrying 45 tanks, the German merchant ship *Ankara* reached Benghazi on 19 December with a vital cargo of 21 tanks. Three more ships, including the *Mongenevro* with a further 23 tanks, arrived at Tripoli on the same day. Worse still, Force K, in an attempt to attack the Tripoli-bound convoy, ran into a minefield. One cruiser and a destroyer were lost, and two other cruisers damaged. Hinsley remarked that 'it was the arrival of these supplies in north Africa which permitted Rommel to mount his successful counter-offensive of 21 January 1942'.[63] More immediately, however, the 44 new tanks, warnings of whose arrival had been discounted by General Ritchie's Intelligence Staff, enabled Rommel to inflict two defeats on 22nd Armoured Brigade on 28 and 30 December, in which 60 British tanks were destroyed for the loss of only 14 German tanks. These clashes effectively brought 'Crusader' to an end.

MALTA'S CONTRIBUTION TO 'CRUSADER'

On 5 January 1942 another Italian battleship convoy, M 43, safely escorted to Tripoli six merchant ships, carrying 144 armoured vehicles and 29,000 tons of supplies, and a further convoy, T 48, on 24 January carried 97 more armoured vehicles and 15,000 tons of supplies.[64] Substantially re-supplied, Rommel, on 21 January 1942, launched the surprise attack which soon pushed the 8th Army back to the Gazala line.

SUCCESS AND FAILURE IN THE 1941 CONVOY BATTLE

A full account of the initial success of 'Crusader' and the subsequent reversal lies beyond the scope of this study. The matters to be considered in this section relate more closely to Malta's part in these events. The customary yardstick for measuring Malta's contribution to 'Crusader' is the number of ships sunk by Malta-based forces during the period between June and December 1941. These statistics have been summarised in the previous section, but, taken in isolation, they do not fully reflect the overall value of retaining the Malta base. In the first place, throughout the 'Crusader' offensive, and, indeed, throughout the entire Mediterranean war, Malta provided an indispensable staging post for Middle East air reinforcements. Some figures relating to this role have been presented above. Had Malta not been available for this purpose the build-up of the Desert Air Force to support the 8th Army would almost certainly have been delayed. A concentration on the shipping losses also leaves out of account the effects of the almost continuous bombing offensive carried out, principally, by Wellingtons flying from Luqa. As noted earlier, raids on Tripoli were carried out on average every other night and the Italian naval history estimates that these reduced port capacity at Tripoli, which with Cyrenaica in Axis hands could only be reached from Malta, by about 50 per cent. Malta-based attacks on Sicilian and Italian ports, especially Naples, caused further unquantifiable losses and delays.

A further drawback of placing too much dependence on the shipping losses alone is that this measure tends to ignore the essential time factor. After all, in the early autumn of 1941 both sides were in a race to build their supplies to levels thought necessary to support their respective plans. In this race Rommel appeared, because of his shorter lines of communication, to have a clear advantage. Consequently, *delaying* the arrival of supplies was second only in importance to their destruction. This was particularly evident in the critical month of December when the restricted amounts that arrived were due not so much to losses at sea, but to the reduced cargoes despatched. An alternative way of assessing the losses and delays caused by Malta forces is to compare the

TABLE 11
AXIS SUPPLIES LANDED IN NORTH AFRICA, JUNE–DECEMBER 1941

June	July	August	September	October	November	December
125,076	62,276	83,956	67,513	73,614	29,843	39,092

Source: See Appendix.

volume of supplies that actually arrived in North Africa with the Axis requirements. The pattern of late 1941 tonnages landed, including fuel, is shown in Table 11.

Establishing a figure for Rommel's requirements in this period is more problematic. The 1938 naval study estimated an overall monthly requirement, including civilian needs, of 113,000 tons, while in a memorandum of May 1941 the Italian army cited a figure of 140,000 tons, of which 20,000 tons were civilian needs.[65] Van Creveld quoted a military requirement of 10,000 tons a month for a motorised division and assumed a total of 70,000 tons a month for a seven-division force. At times he seemed to include the air and naval needs in these figures, but they appear to exclude the needs of the base and supply organisation. He also ignored the steady expansion of the Axis army to a total of ten divisions.[66] Playfair wrote that 70,000 tons a month was not sufficient, and quoted Mussolini as arguing to Hitler that 120,000 tons were required each month.[67] Bragadin assumed a total of 70,000 tons as the overall requirement in early 1941.[68] Precision is not possible or necessary, but it seems reasonable to assume that Rommel in this period needed between 70,000 and 100,000 tons a month to allow him to accumulate the reserves for his planned attack on Tobruk.

On this broad assumption, only in June did deliveries exceed requirements, after which they fell during the July–October period to the lower end of the scale of his needs. This helps to explain why Rommel's planned attack on Tobruk was first postponed until October, and then to November. Nevertheless, although Malta operations, coupled with Rommel's other supply constraints, caused a vital delay, Sigint made clear that a German attack on Tobruk was likely in late November.[69] It was the prospect that Auchinleck would then confront a German force with more or less adequate reserves that moved the Prime Minister to insist on the stationing of Force K at Malta in an attempt to reduce the Axis build-up. The results, as we have noted, were dramatic. As soon as Force K was detected after its arrival on 21 October, convoy sailings were halted, so that, as a result of delays and losses, only 27,000 tons of general supplies and negligible amounts of fuel reached North Africa in November. Later that month, having been fought to a standstill by Ritchie in the desert, Rommel and General Bastico appealed for substantial reinforcements. However, on 5 December, Colonel Montezemolo, Head of the Operational Staff of *Comando Supremo*, brought the news that only the most essential supplies could be delivered in December.[70] After a series of acrimonious arguments with the Italian Generals Cavallero and Bastico, Rommel insisted on withdrawing from Cyrenaica and successfully disengaged all of his forces, other than the garrisons trapped on the Egyptian frontier.

There can be no doubt but that it was the supply shortfall in November, which was entirely the result of forces operating from Malta, and the expectation that this would continue in December, that compelled Rommel to abandon Cyrenaica and opened up the possibility of his complete defeat. This, it is suggested, is a fair measure of Malta's contribution to the 'Crusader' offensive. Giorgerini, whose overall conclusions about Malta's influence on the Mediterranean war are more fully considered later, conceded that Malta presented its greatest threat in the last three months of 1941. Moreover, he reached this conclusion purely on the strength of shipping losses without taking any account of the other benefits that Britain derived from the retention of the island. He accepted that 'had the war been over in the first fortnight of December 1941 we could affirm that Malta played a vital role in precluding or defeating the Italian traffic'.[71] As he quickly observed, however, Malta's offensive power abruptly ceased on 19 December with the effective loss of Force K, and the Mediterranean war went on for a further two years. Gabriele reached the similar conclusion that it was in the June–December period that Malta posed the greatest threat to the convoy supply route.[72] Even Van Creveld, whose thesis is that inadequate port capacity and road transport were Rommel's two principal difficulties in the North African campaigns, maintained that what he calls 'the aero-naval struggle' was not decisive 'except, perhaps, in November–December 1941'.[73]

The reasons why Malta's anti-convoy operations of the last two months of 1941 were not sufficient to bring complete victory now need to be briefly considered. In the first place, luck turned against the British forces in mid-December. Although two tank-carrying ships were sunk, the German supply ship *Ankara* reached Benghazi on 19 December with 21 tanks three days before its capture by British forces. However, Force K was within 20 miles of intercepting the *Mongenevro*, which carried a further 23 tanks, when it ran into the minefield which crippled it.[74] Churchill, in his history, quoted the German Staff comment on this night's events:

> The sinking of the *Neptune* [leading Force K] may be of decisive importance for holding Tripolitania. Without this the British

force would probably have destroyed the Italian convoy. There is no doubt that the loss of these supplies at the peak of the crisis would have had the severest consequences.[75]

By that time other factors were beginning to reduce Malta's effectiveness. As we have seen, Rommel was able to receive substantial supplies in January 1942 with minimal losses. Why was this? Four principal reasons, taken together, largely explain, as Playfair put it, 'what caused the pendulum to swing back in favour of the Axis in a surprisingly short time'.[76] Pedestrian though it may seem, bad weather had a powerful impact on operations. Bragadin wrote that 'a violent storm developed over the Mediterranean and lasted the entire first three weeks of December'.[77] Lloyd has given a graphic account of the problems caused by heavy rain on Malta's much-repaired airfields, and flying conditions were often dangerous.[78] Coincident with the onset of bad weather was the re-appearance of the *Luftwaffe* in Sicily. As early as 13 September Hitler had ordered *Fliegerkorps X*, based in Greece, to suspend attacks on the Suez Canal in order to provide better protection to the Libyan convoys.[79] By October, however, he had decided that further air forces should be diverted from the Russian front to the Mediterranean and orders for this were issued in November. On 2 December his Directive No. 38 confirmed the transfer of *Fliegerkorps II*, together with the headquarters staff of *Luftflotte 2*, to Sicily. The same Directive appointed Field Marshal Kesselring as C-in-C South with instructions to regain control of the area between Sicily and North Africa, and, 'in particular, to keep Malta in subjection'.[80] The squadrons of *Fliegerkorps II* began to assemble on the Sicilian airfields in early December, and from the middle of the month Malta began to experience an increasing weight of attack that was to reach a new climax in April 1942.

A third factor was the virtual elimination of the Mediterranean Fleet as a force that could restrict the operations of the Italian fleet. Admiral Raeder had resisted earlier suggestions that U-boats be sent to the Mediterranean but, at a conference on 17 September, Hitler ordered the despatch of an initial force of six boats to the area. Further boats were then sent so that, by 12 December, Raeder was able to report that 36 boats were in, or *en route* to, the Mediterranean.[81] German U-boat successes were few, but critical. They included the aircraft carrier HMS *Ark Royal*, the battleship HMS *Barham*, and the light cruiser HMS *Galatea*. On 19 December Force K was crippled, and, on the same night, Italian frogmen sank Cunningham's two remaining battleships, HMS *Valiant* and HMS *Queen Elizabeth*, at their moorings in Alexandria harbour. Following the declaration of war by Japan on 7 December there was no prospect that these Mediterranean losses could be made good.

The fourth reason for the decline of Malta's effectiveness was the decision by the Italian navy to employ virtually the whole of their fleet, including battleships, to protect their convoys, a decision made possible by the transfer by Germany of 90,000 tons of fuel oil.[82] This Italian decision was made before the loss of the British battle fleet became known, but their subsequent operations were aided by the fact that the only surface opposition came from a dwindling number of British light cruisers. By then, too, the air threat from Malta was restricted by the weather and by the attacks of *Fliegerkorps II* on Malta's airfields.

Could more have been done? This question is prompted by the thought that Rommel appeared so close to defeat in December 1941 that a further small increase in his losses might have proved decisive. Bennett, for example, arguing that Rommel only just prevailed after losing 20 per cent of his supplies, believed that a greater effort could have ensured his defeat. It is also his view that the navy did as much as could have been expected, but that 'it does now seem as if the RAF could have done more'.[83] The evidence presented in this chapter does not support this judgement about the relative contributions of the navy and the RAF. What reduced Rommel's supplies in November and December 1941 from the required monthly total of about 70,000 tons to the 30,000–40,000 ton range was the arrival and subsequent operations of Force K. It was this halving of supplies reaching North Africa that, in December, forced Rommel to abandon Cyrenaica. Both Pound and Cunningham misjudged what might be achieved by a relatively small surface force at Malta, and it was only in October that Pound bowed to the Prime Minister's pressure to establish such a force. It is tempting to speculate that, if the Prime Minister had had his way when he first raised this matter of surface forces in August, the shipping losses that were inflicted in November and December might have occurred in September or October before Axis counter-measures could have taken effect. If this had happened, Rommel's ability to withstand 'Crusader' might have been considerably impaired.

Nevertheless, the Admiralty had correctly warned that it was impossible to sink every ship and some were bound to get through. Consequently, although the supply losses inflicted on the Axis armies during the 'Crusader' battles were grave, they were ultimately not sufficient to ensure British victory. The reason why a seriously weakened Axis army was able to hold off the 8th Army lies in the relative fighting abilities of the opposing armies. Field Marshal Lord Carver later wrote that the 8th Army during the 'Crusader' campaign suffered from 'inherent deficiencies in organization, training and command which meant that the army's full power was never fully developed'.[84] As John Ferris has observed in his study of the contribution of Sigint to 'Crusader', superior Intelligence can be regarded as a 'force multiplier', but its value depends on the force to be multiplied. He concluded that during 'Crusader' the 'British Army was good at Intelligence, but not operations'.[85] Much the same can be said of the shortage of supplies caused by Malta operations. These were, especially in November and December, serious enough to compel Rommel to withdraw from Cyrenaica, but supply losses, short of a total blockade that prevented any supplies at all arriving, could not of themselves bring defeat. That could only be achieved on the battlefield by an army able to match the fighting abilities of Rommel's force. Malta's forces had brought Rommel to his knees, but the 8th Army could not administer the *coup de grâce*.

10

The 1942 Siege of Malta

THE DISPUTE ABOUT THE STRATEGIC VALUE OF MALTA IN EARLY 1942

In early January 1942, as British forces stood facing Rommel at El Agheila, no doubts had yet surfaced about the wisdom of holding Malta. When the Chiefs of Staff, on 9 January, discussed a Middle East Appreciation, it was agreed that Operation 'Acrobat', the planned advance to Tripoli, should be carried out despite the growing diversion of forces to the Far East.[1] Such an advance would provide additional security for Malta, and this was important since the threat to the island was increasing. The arrival at Valletta on 19 January of three merchant ships carrying 21,000 tons of supplies, and successful voyages by the naval supply ships HMS *Breconshire* and HMS *Glengyle*, encouraged the view that, despite the recently arrived German air forces in Sicily, the island could be supplied from the east. However, the success of these operations was attributed in large part to the protection provided by long-range Beaufighters operating from airfields around Benghazi. All these plans and assumptions were overturned by Rommel's counter-attack on 21 January, which had, by the end of the month, forced the 8th Army back to the Gazala line west of Tobruk. Axis forces, once again, occupied the port of Benghazi and the surrounding airfields.

The relevance of these airfields to Malta's security was soon demonstrated. When a further supply convoy of three supply ships sailed from Alexandria on 12 February two were sunk by air attack, while the third, heavily damaged, was forced to seek refuge at Tobruk. Without airfields in Cyrenaica the RAF was powerless to provide adequate air cover for the final stage of the passage to the island. The Governor quickly reacted to this loss by signalling, on 18 February, details of the worsening supply position.[2] The Prime Minister read this telegram and, at his request, General Sir Alan Brooke, who had succeeded Dill as CIGS in December 1941, brought the matter before the Chiefs of Staff on 24 February.[3] Brooke pointed out that the situation at Malta was 'becoming acute'. Although the island was thought to need 30,000 tons of supplies each month, a bare minimum of 15,000 tons was essential if the fortress was to hold out.

As a result, the JPS was instructed to prepare an Appreciation showing:

> ... the relative strategic importance of Malta, in comparison with the effort and cost of maintaining it, with particular reference to the latest date by which the offensive in the Western Desert must be launched in order to permit the maintenance of Malta during the summer.

It was unfortunate for the debate that followed that the JPS did not carry out these instructions. They did not weigh the strategic importance of Malta relative to other objectives with which its defence might conflict, notably the need to make proper preparation for a resumed offensive in the desert. Instead, the Chiefs of Staff approved a telegram that began: 'Our view is that Malta is of such importance both as air staging point and as impediment to enemy reinforcement route that the most drastic steps are justifiable to sustain it.'[4] They concluded by signalling: 'We must aim to be so placed in Cyrenaica by April dark period that we can pass substantial convoy to Malta.'

Despite these anxious references to Malta, it nevertheless seems clear from the overall tenor of these discussions that the principal reason for urging an early offensive was the opportunity to defeat Rommel and advance to Tripoli. The view in London at that time was that Auchinleck, despite his January defeat, retained a superiority of forces that might evaporate if he delayed. The overall objective continued to be the clearance of North Africa. The worry about Malta was growing but it was not, at this point, the main reason for urging an early offensive.

Although other signals discussed below intervened, it will be helpful to consider first Auchinleck's reply of 4 March to this London telegram.[5] In his response he stressed two points. First, his assessment of comparative tank strengths led him to conclude that 'the resumption [of the offensive] with the objective of recapturing Benghazi before April dark period is likely to lead to failure'. Second, he argued, 'the reoccupation of Cyrenaica is not a complete answer to the problem of supply to Malta'. German air forces in Sicily had become so strong that they could prevent the unloading of any ships which might get through to Malta. This assessment of where the real danger to Malta lay was soon proved to be more accurate than London's.

Coincident with this exchange of telegrams the Prime Minister had also signalled to Auchinleck on 26 February asking about his intentions.[6] He suggested that Auchinleck had a current superiority in ground and air forces, but feared that Rommel might be reinforced more rapidly. He added that 'the supply of Malta is causing us increased anxiety'. Once more, it was unfortunate that a detailed new Appreciation by Auchinleck was despatched on 27 February before he had the opportunity to gauge the growing concern about Malta that had recently emerged in London. As a result, his central conclusion, that no offensive offering a reasonable prospect of success could be launched before mid-June at the earliest, caused dismay and anger in London from which his standing with the Prime Minister never fully recovered.[7]

The C-in-C's Appreciation rested, first, on the territorial considerations that reflected his military responsibilities, and, second, on his experiences during and after 'Crusader'. Iraq and Persia had been added to the Middle East Command on 12 January and the weakness of this northern flank troubled Auchinleck. His concern was heightened when the War Office advised him on 17 February that the seasoned 70th Division was to go east, to be followed, probably, by the 9th Australian Division and a further division from Iraq.[8] Three days later he expressed this concern to the Chiefs of Staff, and warned that these withdrawals had compelled him to revise his plans.[9] He assumed he had the support of the CIGS for this, since the latter had written on 17 February 'your plans for regaining Cyrenaica may have to be abandoned in favour of the defence of the Egyptian frontier'.[10]

It was these broad considerations that led Auchinleck to the following conclusion in his 27 February Appreciation: 'It is clear that we cannot have reasonable numerical superiority before 1st June and that to launch major offensive before then would be to risk defeat in detail and possibly endanger safety of Egypt.' While recognising the peril in which the island stood, the most he felt able to offer was the possibility of a limited offensive to regain the Derna–Mechili landing grounds, but this could not be allowed to put the principal offensive at risk.[11]

As soon as he received this Appreciation the Prime Minister dictated an angry draft reply that reflected 'the thoughts which had come into his mind on reading it'. Although this was replaced by a more restrained version drafted by the Chiefs of Staff, it provides evidence of the growing gulf between Auchinleck's cautious calculations and the Prime Minister's impatience for action.[12] In his draft the Prime Minister pointed out that a delay until June 'will seal the fate of Malta', and after much forceful argument he concluded:

> No one is going to stand your remaining in deep peace while Malta is being starved out, while the Russians are fighting like mad and while we are suffering continued disasters in Burma and India at the hands of the Japanese. . . . It is imperative that our

forces everywhere shall come to grips with the enemy and force him to consume lives, munitions, tanks, and aircraft around the whole circle of his fighting front.

One reason for this outburst was surely the loss of Singapore on 14 February, or, rather, the manner of its surrender. He was later to call this 'the worst disaster and largest capitulation in British history',[13] and in his draft telegram he wrote, 'I was looking to the 8th Army . . . to repair the shame of Singapore.'

The Prime Minister's draft signal set the agenda for a debate in the Defence Committee on 2 March.[14] By that time the Prime Minister's anger had abated, and it was helpful that Oliver Lyttleton, recently returned from Cairo where he had been Resident Minister of State, was able to answer some of the questions about relative tank strength that puzzled the Committee. Nevertheless, the Minutes of the meeting suggest that the Committee, which had not then received Auchinleck's signal of 4 March, did not accept that an early attempt to recover the Cyrenaican airfields in order to assist the passage of convoys to Malta would risk defeat in the desert. A second telegram was therefore despatched which stated: 'We are greatly disturbed by your review of the situation. The dominant factor in the Mediterranean and Middle East situation at the present time is Malta.' The practical advantages offered by the island were again cited, and the telegram went on to question Auchinleck's assessment of the tank position, calculations that the Committee considered 'heavily biased in favour of the enemy'. Their signal concluded:

> To sum up, we consider that an attempt to drive the Germans out of Cyrenaica in the next few weeks is not only imperative for the safety of Malta but holds out the only hope of fighting a battle while the enemy is still comparatively weak and short of resources of all kinds.[15]

To this signal Auchinleck replied on 5 March. He was, he protested, 'fully aware of the urgency of securing Western Cyrenaica, both to assist in running convoys into Malta, and for the broader reasons given in your telegram', and he rejected the charge of over-estimating the enemy's growing tank strength. He then posed the question 'whether or not, in the effort to save [Malta], we are to jeopardise our whole position in the Middle East'. His own view was clear. A premature offensive was likely to result in the piecemeal destruction of his new armoured forces, and this would endanger Egypt.[16]

Since agreement could clearly not be reached by an exchange of crossed telegrams, the Prime Minister invited Auchinleck to return to

London. When the General declined to do so, Sir Stafford Cripps, *en route* to India, was instructed to break his journey at Cairo for a few days, and Lieutenant-General Nye, the Vice-Chief of the Imperial General Staff (VCIGS), was also sent out to review the situation with the Middle East C-in-Cs. To Churchill's intense annoyance, both were persuaded that an April offensive was too risky, and, with marked reluctance, the Defence Committee on 26 March accepted a mid-May date for the attack.[17] When this decision was taken it was believed that Malta's immediate supply problem had been eased by the arrival on 23 March of HMS *Breconshire* and two merchant ships. Three days later, however, as Auchinleck had feared, all three were sunk by air attack after discharging only 5,000 tons of the 26,000 tons of supplies they carried.[18]

In late March and April the position at Malta steadily worsened. Heavy German air attack led to the cancellation of the April convoy, and, at a long Defence Committee meeting on 22 April, Churchill himself concluded that the intended May convoy would also need to be cancelled.[19] Everything therefore depended on the success of two June convoys since food supplies in the island were expected to be exhausted by the end of that month. Auchinleck's proposed mid-May offensive, offering the prospect of the recovery of the Cyrenaican airfields, was regarded as essential to the safe arrival of these two convoys.

At this critical juncture Auchinleck telegraphed once more. On 6 May he advised that, by 1 June, he expected that Rommel would have 360 German and 160 Italian tanks compared with the 8th Army's 460, with reserves of 100. By 15 June, however, he anticipated that he would have 600, plus reserves of 140. These would give him the superiority of 3 to 2, which he was now prepared to accept given the arrival of the new American 'Grant' tanks and 6-pounder anti-tank guns. These calculations led him to propose a postponement of his offensive until mid-June, at the earliest.[20]

The Prime Minister referred this bombshell directly to the War Cabinet, which considered the matter on 8 May. During a long debate much emphasis was laid on the plight of Malta. Brooke thought it 'strange' that the C-in-C had not taken into account the possibility of an offensive by Rommel, for which Enigma decrypts were providing growing indications. He, nevertheless, thought Auchinleck should not be ordered to attack in May, but told to carry out an attack to provide support for the June convoy. The majority of the Cabinet, however, judged that the advantages of the proposed postponement were more than offset by its disadvantages. 'In this connection great importance was attached to the position at Malta.' The Prime Minister summed up by stating that 'battles were not won by arithmetical calculations', and he drafted a reply which was sent on 8 May.[21] In this the Prime Minister told Auchinleck that the War Cabinet had considered his proposal 'with particular regard to Malta, the loss of which would be a disaster of first magnitude to the British Empire, and probably fatal in the long run to the defence of the Nile Valley'. Their conclusion was that 'you would be right to attack the enemy and fight a major battle, and the sooner the better'.[22]

Two days later, on Sunday 10 May, an emergency meeting of the War Cabinet was hastily summoned to consider a telegram from Auchinleck refusing to accept the decision of 8 May.[23] As Brooke put it in his diary, 'he had again stuck his toes in and was refusing to attack till a later date. . . . He entirely failed to realize the importance of Malta and overestimated the danger to Egypt in the event of his being defeated.'[24] Auchinleck's signal reiterated the dangers of a premature advance with inadequate forces, and argued that even a successful attack would take some months to recover the Cyrenaican airfields. His view about Malta was that, since air attack had eliminated its offensive capability, 'its fall (much though this would be deplored) would [not] necessarily be fatal to security of Egypt for a very long period if at all'.[25]

Major-General Kennedy, Director of Military Operations at the War Office, later called Auchinleck's view about Malta an 'incredible misconception', and judged that this had lost him the confidence of both the Cabinet and the Chiefs of Staff.[26] At the Sunday Cabinet meeting Brooke rejected Auchinleck's analysis, paragraph by paragraph. He pointed out that Malta had only recently 'fallen into disrepair', and that 'with an improvement in the situation, Malta might regain its position'. He emphasised again the island's staging post function, and said that the C-in-C had over-stressed the danger to Egypt and under-stressed the value of Malta. More significant, however, was his first point that 'it would be a disaster to sacrifice the garrison in the fortress'. Brooke, when he spoke, was not to know that the RAF, that very morning, reinforced by no fewer than 62 Spitfires flown in from HMS *Eagle* and USS *Wasp* on the previous day, had engaged in a fierce air battle over Malta that marked the recovery of air supremacy over the island. The Chiefs were now agreed that 'the security of Malta was vital'. After a long discussion the Cabinet concluded that 'the supreme importance of Malta had not been adequately appreciated in General Auchinleck's telegram, and that a battle should be fought to save it'. Instructions to this effect were immediately despatched, and, after an uneasy delay, were accepted by Auchinleck on 19 May.[27]

Although the renewal of the fighting was brought about by Rommel rather than by the decision of the War Cabinet, nevertheless the authorities in London had in May decided to permit no further delay. Although they persuaded themselves that a possible defeat at Gazala would not necessarily entail the loss of Egypt, they acknowledged that Rommel's forces had been considerably strengthened. Why then was

Auchinleck not given the extra time he thought essential if defeat were to be avoided? Two new factors appear to have swayed the Cabinet in May. First, conditions in Malta had worsened considerably since March. The limited amount of supplies unloaded in that month, and the decision to cancel both the April and May convoys, made the success of the two planned for June vital to the island's survival. The second factor that appears to have influenced the Cabinet and the Chiefs of Staff was the greater prestige value that now attached to the defence of the fortress. The plight of the garrison and the civilian population, and the efforts to defend them, had been given great publicity around the world. Moreover, on 16 April the unusual award of the George Cross had been announced. Malta had, in consequence, become as potent a symbol of Britain's determination to stand and fight as Stalingrad was later to be for the Russian people. The ignominy of Singapore was not to be repeated.

THE STRUGGLE TO RETAIN MALTA'S STRATEGIC VALUE

There was general agreement that there were three principal ways in which the bases on the island could contribute to overall objectives. The first was the use of Malta's airfields to re-fuel aircraft flying on to the Middle East, or beyond; the second, the interruption of the flow of Axis supplies to North Africa; and the third, the engagement and erosion of enemy forces which might otherwise be employed in other theatres. The degree to which these three objectives were achieved in the worsening conditions of early 1942 is considered in this section.

Figures cited in Chapter 9 show that, during the first ten months of 1941, 326 bombers and 106 fighters passed through Malta *en route* to the Middle East.[28] The corresponding figures for the 11 months from November 1941 to September 1942 were 385 bombers, but only 48 fighters, since no fewer than 323 were held at Malta.[29] The entry of Japan into the war in December 1941, and the subsequent invasions of Malaya and Burma, made even more important the speedy flow of aircraft to Egypt, whence they could be flown on, or shipped by aircraft carrier, to India, Ceylon or further east. In a paper which examined the 'Relation of Strategy in the Middle East and India', the JPC wrote: '[Malta] is at present vital as a staging post for medium bombers proceeding to the Middle East and India . . . and our only means of sending light bombers.'[30] A month later they added that this need had been given greater urgency by the deterioration of the naval position in the Indian Ocean, which could only be repaired by shore-based aircraft.[31]

This new requirement was added to the existing objective of strengthening the Desert Air Force to support Auchinleck's new offensive. At the same time, however, Malta's airfields, and the main transit airfield at Luqa in particular, were being subjected to an increasing weight of air attack. After 20 March, when Kesselring launched a full-scale attack on the island, Luqa and the surrounding taxiways were struck almost every day, often several times. Yet at the War Cabinet meeting on 10 May Portal was able to advise that 300 aircraft had flown through Malta during 1942. Of these, no fewer than 163 had passed through in the previous month during the worst of the bombing.[32] Nonetheless, on 1 July, during a Chiefs of Staff discussion about whether to suspend transit flights through Malta in order to conserve fuel supplies, Portal reported that the use of the Takoradi route would only cause aircraft a one-week delay in reaching Egypt.[33] Later that month, Portal agreed that transit flights through Malta should be temporarily suspended.[34] This makes it clear that, by that time, Malta was an advantageous, rather than an essential, link in the Middle East reinforcement route.

It was to prove much more difficult to sustain Malta's offensive threat to Rommel's supplies in the early months of 1942 as the second German 'blitz' gathered strength. This is demonstrated by Table 12, which shows the supplies landed in North Africa and the losses suffered. During January several 'battleship convoys' delivered sufficient tanks and other supplies to enable Rommel to launch his successful counter-attack on 21 January. Average deliveries dropped during the next two months before rising to a new peak in April. Rommel was, consequently, well supplied for the offensive that he launched at Gazala on 26 May.

The proportion of Axis merchant ship losses, by number and tonnage, attributed to Malta-based forces in this five-month period is shown in Table 13. Immediately noticeable is the absence of any losses caused by surface warships. In late 1941 the striking results achieved were the result of the addition of the cruisers and destroyers of Force K to the operations of aircraft and submarines. Despite the losses and

TABLE 12
AXIS SUPPLIES LANDED AND PERCENTAGES LOST, JANUARY–MAY 1942

(amounts in tons)

	General cargo	% lost	Fuel	% lost	Total landed	Total sent	% lost
January	43,328	0	22,842	0	66,170	66,214	0
February	34,507	1	24,458	0	58,965	59,468	1
March	32,483	21	15,105	8	47,588	57,541	17
April	102,358	1	48,031	1	150,389	151,578	1
May	67,858	8	18,581	3	86,439	91,188	7

Source: See Appendix.

TABLE 13
PROPORTION OF AXIS SHIPS SUNK BY MALTA FORCES, JANUARY–MAY 1942

(number and tonnage of ships sunk)

	Submarine	Ship	Aircraft	Shared	Malta total	C. Med. total	Malta (%)
January	(1) 3,252	–	(1) 5,741	–	(2) 8,993	(5) 32,520	28
February	(3) 15,024	–	–	(2) 10,257	(5) 25,281	(6) 29,451	88
March	(2) 10,228	–	(3) 13,104	(1) 1,778	(6) 25,110	(10) 45,396	55
April	(2) 9,743	–	–	–	(2) 9,743	(5) 14,366	68
May	–	–	–	–	–	(3) 7,130	0
Total	(8) 38,247	0	(4) 18,845	(3) 12,035	(15) 69,127	(29) 128,863	54

Source: See Appendix.

damage suffered in December, Force K, composed of one or two light cruisers and several destroyers, continued to be based at Malta, and Cunningham took steps to increase the stocks of oil fuel and 5.25-inch ammunition there. These ships frequently sailed to protect the *Breconshire* and the *Glengyle* on their solo passages to Malta, as well as the merchant ship convoys in January and February. Force K also played a vital part in the Second Battle of Sirte, which developed around the March convoy.[35] By that time the growing destruction in the Grand Harbour, the mining of the harbour approaches, the exhaustion of fuel stocks after the loss of the *Breconshire*, and the greater air threat to surface ships led to the decision that all remaining ships that could be made seaworthy should leave Malta. HMS *Penelope* was the last to leave on 9 April, but four destroyers were sunk or left disabled in the Grand Harbour. No offensive surface units of the fleet returned to Valletta until November. Attempts to intercept Axis supply convoys from Alexandria proved unsuccessful and costly. On 10 March a force of cruisers and destroyers was sailed to attack a northbound convoy, but no ships were sighted and Admiral Vian's flagship, HMS *Naiad*, was sunk by U 565 on the return to Alexandria. Two months later, on 11 May, a similar attempted interception led to the loss, under a concentrated bombing attack, of three of the four destroyers sent out.[36]

Effective naval action from Malta was, after the elimination of Force K, restricted to the patrols of the submarines of Captain Simpson's 10th Flotilla, supported from time to time by transit submarines carrying supplies and personnel from Gibraltar and Alexandria. The continuing effectiveness of these patrols is shown in the loss figures shown above. Malta's submarines also sank six enemy submarines and the Italian cruiser *Banda Nere*.[37] These operations, too, became progressively more hazardous. Between January and March 1942 four British submarines were lost, and three more in the following two months, including Wanklyn's *Upholder* and Tomkinson's *Urge*.[38] It was, however, the growing dangers at Malta that led to the decision on 26 April, after one of the heaviest air raids on Valletta, to withdraw the remaining boats of the 10th Flotilla to Alexandria. Bombing attacks on the submarine base in Lazaretto Creek in March damaged several boats, and forced others to remain submerged during air raids.[39] More seriously, German E-boats and aircraft had laid many more mines in and around Malta's harbours, and these caused the loss of *Olympus* and, it was assumed, of *Urge* in early May. The diminishing number of minesweepers could not clear these expanding minefields, and it was this circumstance which finally persuaded Simpson to order withdrawal to Alexandria on 26 April.[40]

The departure of all offensive naval units from Malta placed the burden of attacking Axis convoys on the RAF. However, the figures quoted above show that these operations, too, gradually petered out as the growing weight of German bombing destroyed or damaged aircraft, airfields and maintenance facilities. The British estimate of the weight, in tons, of bombs dropped in early 1942 is shown in Table 14.[41]

In the early part of the year Lloyd continued to direct his bomber force against targets in Italy, Sicily and North Africa, but, by mid-February, he was forced to send away his remaining Blenheims. On the night of 2/3 March, Wellingtons of 37 Squadron made a highly successful attack on Palermo Harbour, sinking three fully laden merchant ships and damaging many others. A week later, however, after losing five aircraft on the ground, the remaining Wellingtons were also withdrawn.[42] The dwindling number of serviceable torpedo-bombers continued to attack Axis convoys, but with little success. The one or two aircraft available for each attack often encountered strong air and gun defences, and, despite many damage claims, few ships were sunk.[43]

Attempts were made to compensate for the decline of Malta operations by sorties from North African airfields where the Naval Co-operation 201 Group had been built up to 16 squadrons. The loss of the Benghazi airfields, however, forced these squadrons out of range of the principal sea route to Tripoli, and, apart from the sinking of the 13,000-ton cargo ship *Victoria* on 23 January, few ships were sunk by air attack.

TABLE 14
BOMB TONNAGE DROPPED ON MALTA, 1942

January	*February*	*March*	*April*	*May*
669	1,020	2,170	6,700	520

Source: General I. Playfair *et al.*, *The Mediterranean and Middle East*, 6 vols (Her Majesty's Stationery Office, London, 1954–73), vol. III, pp. 162–88.

By the early summer of 1942, therefore, Malta's contribution to the interruption of Rommel's supply lines had virtually ceased. Moreover, it had become clear that offensive operations must take second place to the air defence of the island. This air battle would, nevertheless, meet Churchill's demand that the enemy be engaged and worn down.[44] Two decisions decided its outcome. On the British side, the crucial decision was the replacement of the out-classed Hurricane IIs by cannon-armed Spitfire Vs, the first to be released from Fighter Command. After much hesitation, Portal ordered their despatch to Malta in early February 1942, minuting to the DCAS: 'We must gamble on the Spitfire being a success.'[45] The first batches sent by HMS *Eagle* proved too small to provide effective defence, and Spitfire serviceability was hampered by a lack of spares and repair facilities. It was only after a second large delivery of 62 aircraft by the US carrier USS *Wasp*, and HMS *Eagle*, on 9 May that Lloyd was able to deploy a force which could match the German and Italian raiders. On 20 May Portal told the Prime Minister that, in the ten days to 18 May, 64 enemy aircraft had been reported destroyed, 45 probably destroyed and 74 damaged. Air superiority, he claimed, had been recovered.[46] Post-war analysis concluded that 40 Axis aircraft were destroyed in May for the loss of 25 RAF fighters.[47]

The critical decision by the Axis was the postponement of the planned invasion of Malta, 'Operation C3' to the Italians, 'Herkules' to the Germans. A full study of these plans, and the reasons for their postponement and eventual abandonment, has been made by Gabriele, most recently in a 1993 article, and can only be briefly summarised here.[48] The initial decision to begin planning for an invasion of Malta was taken by Cavallero as early as October 1941 but preparations, which required German help, proceeded slowly. However, in February 1942, Admiral Raeder, supported by Kesselring, persuaded a doubtful Hitler that the seizure of the island was essential to safeguard supplies to North Africa. Although preparations then gathered momentum it was thought, particularly by the Italian *Supermarina*, that an attempted *coup de main* in mid-April, when Malta appeared to be defenceless, posed too great a risk since preparations were far from complete. At a conference at the end of April Hitler and Mussolini agreed that 'C3' should be undertaken in mid-July after Rommel's planned capture of Tobruk. Preparations therefore continued but in mid-May Kesselring, judging that Malta had been effectively neutralised, transferred some of his Sicilian squadrons to North Africa to support Rommel's offensive, while the German High Command ordered others to the Russian front.[49] It was, consequently, against a dwindling *Luftwaffe* force in Sicily that the RAF on 10 May began the process of recovering air superiority in Malta's skies. To take the story of 'C3' to its conclusion, the agreed plan to return to the attack on Malta after the capture of

Tobruk was overturned in June by Rommel, who, against the strong protests of Kesselring, persuaded both Hitler and Mussolini that the supplies captured at Tobruk and the evident disarray of the British forces gave him the opportunity to advance to Cairo.

Hitler has received most of the blame for the failure to carry out 'C3'. He has been charged with a limited interest in the Mediterranean theatre, the significance of which he failed to appreciate, a distrust of wholehearted Italian support, and lingering doubts about the feasibility of a second airborne assault on an island much better defended than Crete had been. General Warlimont, Deputy Head of the *Oberkommando der Wehrmacht* (OKW) Operations Staff, later wrote that Hitler had always been opposed to 'Herkules' and on 21 May told his staff that preparations were to continue only 'psychologically'.[50] Gabriele has also drawn attention to Hitler's refusal on 15 June of a request by Mussolini for the 40,000 tons of oil fuel without which the Italian navy could not support the landings.[51] These decisions preceded the capture of Tobruk and Rommel's request to advance into Egypt. On the other hand, Santoni and Mattesini in their study of the German involvement in the Mediterranean war have pointed to the slowness of Italian preparations, due in part to Cavallero's indecisiveness. This meant that a *coup de main* attempt could not be launched in April–May at what appeared to be Malta's weakest moment.[52]

The preceding analysis makes clear that, by the early summer of 1942, Malta was able to make little offensive contribution to the war in the Mediterranean. No submarines or surface ships, and very few aircraft, operated from Malta against Axis supply convoys, and the task of intercepting these convoys was assumed by forces based in North Africa. Even its staging post function, as Portal subsequently made clear, was an advantage rather than a necessity. Malta's only continuing contribution was that of tying down aircraft that might otherwise have operated against the 8th Army.

THE RELIEF OF GENERAL DOBBIE

Although the heavy bombing of Malta eased in late April and the threat of invasion, for the moment at least, passed, it seemed, nevertheless, that civil unrest brought about by the fear of starvation might force the island's surrender. In such desperate circumstances firm, inspiring leadership was essential to the maintenance of morale and it was believed in London that the Governor, Lieutenant-General Sir William Dobbie, was providing such leadership. It consequently came as a great shock to the Prime Minister and his colleagues to receive from the Middle East Defence Committee on 20 April a telegram that recommended:

> That General Dobbie should be relieved as soon as possible on grounds that he is a tired man, has lost grip of situation, and is no longer capable of affording higher direction and control which is vital (repeat) vital to present situation.[53]

Churchill later wrote of Dobbie that he was 'a Cromwellian figure at the key point. But the long strain had worn him down. I received this news with very deep regret, and I did not at first accept what I was told.'[54]

At that time Dobbie was almost 63 years old, and he had been Acting Governor, then Governor, of Malta since May 1940, shortly before the Italian attack. After two years of increasing strain, Dobbie was certainly in poor health by April 1942. Like all Malta residents he had lost much weight, and the low-calorie ration diet undermined strength and energy.[55] Upon his return to England a month later he collapsed and had a serious operation.[56] His telegrams to the War and Colonial Offices in the early months of 1942 make clear his growing concern about the plight of the Maltese people, a responsibility not borne by the other service commanders.

He carried awkwardly divided responsibilities. As Governor of the Colony he was answerable to the Colonial Secretary, Viscount Cranborne, but he was also the C-in-C of the garrison, and in this respect he reported directly to the War Office. As the garrison grew in numbers, direct command of the troops was delegated to a General Officer Commanding (GOC), reporting to the Governor, but the naval and air force commanders reported to their respective C-in-Cs in Cairo. Whatever merits this chain of command may have had before the war, it was unlikely to prove workable in the conditions prevailing in April 1942. Not only was the Governor answerable to two Secretaries of State, but there was no single person charged with the co-ordinated defence of the island.

What seems to have led to some loss of confidence in Dobbie was the fate of the March convoy. As noted earlier, two cargo vessels, *Talabot* and *Pampas*, and the tanker *Breconshire*, reached Malta on the morning of 23 March, but were then subjected to fierce, continual air attack. All were sunk in harbour on 26 March after only 5,000 tons of their combined cargoes of 26,000 tons had been unloaded. AVM Lloyd was incensed by the failure to unload these ships in the three days and nights before they were sunk. Inexplicably, he maintained in his 1949 memoirs that only 807 tons had been unloaded from these ships and much of that by his airmen. In fact, 5,000 tons were landed at the time, and a further 2,500 tons recovered by subsequent salvage operations. Moreover, Lloyd was present at a meeting on 13 April 1942 at which the 5,000-ton figure was mentioned.[57] He nevertheless complained strongly to Tedder about this failure, saying 'he had pressed without effect that sailors, soldiers, airmen and civilians should be forced to unload throughout 24 hours'. Tedder passed this on to Portal.[58]

Although Lloyd mentions no names, it seems clear that much of his anger, whether justified or not, was directed at Vice-Admiral Leatham and the dockyard staff. But he also appears to have held Dobbie responsible for not compelling the civilian stevedores to work throughout the raids, and it seems, too, that he made these views known to the Governor. Whether he was aware, then or later, that eight Maltese stevedores had been killed while unloading one of these ships during an air raid is not clear.[59] Tedder records that, several days later, he received a private letter from Dobbie requesting the relief of Lloyd, on the grounds that 'he was a difficult person to absorb into a team'.[60] Tedder declined to do so. It was these matters which persuaded him to visit Malta with Sir Walter Monckton, the Acting Minister of State at Cairo, and they were there for two days on 12–13 April.

Upon their return to Cairo Monckton and Tedder discussed the position with their colleagues and this led to the telegram quoted at the beginning of this section. They also took advantage of Sir Stafford Cripps's return from India via Cairo to brief him so that he could give a verbal account to the Defence Committee of the reasons for their recommendation. The Prime Minister brought the matter before the Defence Committee on 22 April, and, after hearing from Cripps, said that he had reluctantly accepted the recommendation of the CIGS that Dobbie be relieved.[61]

There was then an unexpected development. Cranborne, who had professed to being bewildered, and rather angry, at the unexpected recommendation that Dobbie be relieved, received a telegram from the Governor complaining that Mabel Strickland, Lord Strickland's daughter and the editor of *The Times of Malta*, had organised a 'back-stairs intrigue' to have him removed, and had enlisted the support of Lord Mountbatten. He had invited her to explain her position and she had admitted 'she was urging a change of Governorship owing to alleged lack of co-ordination, which was responsible for disaster to the last convoy'.[62] When shown this telegram the Prime Minister immediately cabled Dobbie that Richard Casey, the newly appointed Minister of State in the Middle East, would stop at Malta on his way to Cairo. When Monckton, irritated that Casey's visit implied distrust of his own judgement, urged quick action, he was brusquely told: 'Governor has complained of Strickland intrigue. Matter is one of high importance.'[63]

Casey spent 2–3 May in Malta and discussed the situation with the Governor and the service commanders. 'I found', he later wrote, 'rather a bad state of affairs, with cross-currents of mistrust and bad feeling in several directions.'[64] Before leaving for Cairo he sent a long telegram to the Prime Minister:

> I have no doubt that Dobbie should be replaced by Gort as soon as possible. . . . The team here are not working together and the main reason is that Dobbie is no longer capable of vigorous leadership. He has little grasp of the situation or power of decision and lacks the knowledge and drive which would enable him to guide and, where necessary, impose his will on the forceful commanders under him.[65]

The Prime Minster accepted this clear-cut recommendation, and General Lord Gort arrived on the night of 7 May. He was sworn in as Governor during an air raid at Kalafrana, and had a private conversation with Dobbie before the latter, with his family, left on the return flight to Gibraltar.[66]

Since, however, it was the 'Strickland intrigue' that had brought Casey to Malta, he must have enquired into this. There is no evidence that he met Mabel Strickland, but he would, no doubt, have learnt of her views from Lloyd, who was a friend of hers. Indeed, her allegation that the defence of the island lacked co-ordination clearly reflected Lloyd's opinion. However, in 1996 her biographer, Joan Alexander, added a further serious allegation. She wrote that Mabel Strickland feared that General Dobbie intended to surrender Malta after he had told her that 'if it were God's will he would have no objection to painting a white cross over Luqa airport'.[67] Melita Strickland, the wife of Mabel's cousin Roger, who was then Leader of the elected majority in the Council of Government, made a similar allegation in an interview with Jellison in the early 1980s.[68] Although Mabel Strickland, on the basis of Lloyd's assessment, may well have felt that the Governor was no longer capable of providing firm leadership, it is difficult to accept literally the charge that he intended to surrender the island. The telegrams Dobbie sent to London and Cairo show a determination to hold out, even after the decision on 23 April to cancel the May convoys.[69] Moreover, as a purely practical matter, any unauthorised attempt by Dobbie to surrender the island would have been immediately disowned by the War Cabinet and by the service commanders in Malta. There is no reason to look beyond Casey's assessment of the situation.

What made the difficult organisational structure unworkable in the 1942 crisis was undoubtedly Dobbie's declining health. Although Cranborne described the Governor's cable of 20 April as 'a most sensible and balanced exposition, which shows no trace of any loss of grip at the helm',[70] Casey must have been struck by Dobbie's physical and mental lassitude brought about by an inadequate diet during a period of prolonged strain (see Photograph 11). Casey later wrote that, while he was in Malta, 'it became clear that the situation was critical, and that General Dobbie might break at any time; he had reached the limit of his endurance after long and gallant service'.[71] It was this, rather than any 'Strickland intrigue', which gave a reluctant Prime Minister no choice but to order his relief.

11

Malta's Contribution to the Recovery of North Africa

RE-BUILDING MALTA'S OFFENSIVE CAPABILITY

A correct assessment of Malta's contribution to the North African campaigns of late 1942 and early 1943 must take account of the difficulties that confronted the authorities on the island after the heavy air attacks in March and April 1942. Although the RAF had, by the end of May, regained local air superiority, it was to be several months before the island's offensive power could be restored. There were two principal reasons for this. First, the island continued to be short of food for the civil and military population, and of fuel and military supplies to maintain its defensive and offensive capabilities. Second, the need to protect successive relief convoys at times diverted resources from offensive operations, and at the beginning of the 'Torch' campaign this had unfortunate consequences. The limitations imposed by these factors, and the consequent choices forced upon the authorities in London, Valletta and Cairo, provide the strategic framework within which Maltese offensive operations were only slowly re-established.

The virtual failure of the two June convoys, 'Harpoon' and 'Vigorous', which delivered only 15,000 tons of supplies, meant that the state of siege was intensified. The severe rationing imposed in May could not be relaxed, and, on 26 June, two officials of the Ministry of Food, recently returned from Malta, told the Chiefs of Staff of conditions on the island. The rations provided only 2,600 calories per day, compared with a normal requirement of 3,500 calories. Moreover, remaining stocks of food would be exhausted by mid-August.[1] The danger of starvation-induced surrender had prompted the Prime Minister, on 16 June, to order plans for a further relief convoy:

> It will be necessary to make another attempt to run a convoy to Malta. . . . The fate of the island is at stake, and if the effort to relieve it is worth making it is worth making on a great scale. . . .

Lord Gort must be able to tell [the Maltese people] that 'The Navy will never abandon Malta.'[2]

However, the need to provide a powerful naval escort for the Russian convoy, PQ17, in July meant the postponement of Operation 'Pedestal' to August, almost the last possible moment before food supplies would be exhausted.

A second consequence of the failure of the June convoys was a severe shortage of aviation fuel. One of the losses in the 'Harpoon' convoy from Gibraltar was the tanker *Kentucky*. This ship was damaged by air attack and then, to AVM Lloyd's dismay, sunk by its escorting destroyers, despite being under fighter protection from Malta. He later wrote: 'The Axis might have sunk that ship but we ought never to have done so.'[3] In late June the Governor reported on the petrol situation and, a week later, requested a policy decision as to the operational allocation of the remaining stocks.[4] Portal had earlier told his fellow Chiefs that he favoured the suspension of transit flights through Malta, but wished to consult the Middle East Commanders first.[5] They, bearing the full weight of Rommel's first attempt to breach the Alamein position, were reluctant to see any relaxation of the attacks on Axis supply convoys, or reduction in the flow of air reinforcements to the Middle East. Consequently, it was not until 30 July that the Chiefs of Staff agreed a policy. They then laid down that 'strikes from Malta must be reduced to an absolute minimum, e.g. extremely good chances at close ranges. Transits except for Beauforts will cease.'[6] Explaining this decision, Portal said, 'the Middle East required guidance in this matter since they were inclined very naturally to view the situation in the light of the present battle in Egypt, possibly even at the expense of Malta'.[7] The Mediterranean Fleet's hurried departure from Alexandria on 28 June suggested that the loss of Egypt was now feared, and, in such circumstances, the security of Malta was unlikely to be Cairo's most pressing concern.

By early August all other operations from Malta were subordinated to the planning of the 'Pedestal' convoy. Additional Spitfires and Beaufighters were flown in from England, together with Beauforts and torpedo-carrying Wellingtons from Egypt. The 10th Submarine Flotilla, whose re-establishment at Malta is described later, was also deployed to protect the convoy from any sortie by heavy Italian ships. Despite these measures, the arrival of only five ships of this convoy, carrying 32,000 tons of supplies and 15,000 tons of fuels, provided only temporary relief. One reason for this was that, five days after the convoy's arrival, the Chiefs of Staff, learning of Rommel's planned offensive at the end of August, issued a Directive ordering that, 'for the next ten days or so, supreme importance should be attached to [strike] operations and that considerations of economy in petrol would not justify limiting these operations'.⁸ The initial period of ten days was extended by a further ten days on 31 August, after Rommel launched his attack on Alam Halfa ridge.

Inevitably, therefore, by the end of August aviation petrol supplies were once more depleted. Portal, who, on 28 August, had already ordered the cessation of fighter sweeps over Sicily, circulated a note about the petrol situation that led to a series of discussions throughout September and October.⁹ Instructions were given on 25 September that aviation fuel consumption be restricted further to 150 tons per week.¹⁰ A measure of the dilemma facing the authorities was their decision on 21 October that the fast minelayer, HMS *Welshman*, on a passage to Malta during November, should carry 300 tons of food rather than petrol.¹¹

Meanwhile, the Governor sent back to London Mr Rowntree, the Deputy Director of Communal Feeding in Malta. Introducing him to the Chiefs of Staff on 28 September, Sir George Gater said that the Colonial Office 'were distressed to find that the food situation was more serious than had been expected'. Rowntree explained the effects of the prevailing rationing system, pointing out that an increase of about one-third in calorific value was required to prevent serious medical problems. A substantial convoy in the November dark period was essential.¹² This could not have come at a more awkward time. In the west, the Admiralty was assembling the largest available force to carry out Operation 'Torch', the Allied landings in Morocco and Algeria. D-day for this was 8 November. In the east, the breakthrough at El Alamein came on 4 November, and there was then much pressure on Montgomery to capture the Martuba airfields, 450 miles further west, so that the RAF could provide air cover for an eastern convoy. A further complication was that the rapid German reaction to the 'Torch' landings, discussed later, put pressure on the Malta authorities to intervene more actively. All these interlocking considerations meant that the convoy from the east, Operation 'Stoneage', did not sail until 16 November. A further five ships on 5 December – Operation 'Portcullis' – were followed by a succession of other vessels later in the month. It was only at the end of December 1942 that the siege of Malta could be said to have ended.¹³ This brief survey of conditions in Malta in the last six months of 1942 serves to show how difficult it was to re-establish and sustain offensive operations at a time when the 8th Army was in most need of its help, and the 'Torch' plans were being made and implemented.

ASSISTING THE 8TH ARMY

Many factors combined to bring about the repulse of Rommel's attack on Alam Halfa ridge on 2 September 1942 and his defeat at El Alamein two months later. The relative weight to be attached to these has been debated since these battles took place but there is general agreement that Rommel's increasing supply shortages contributed to his defeat. However, before considering the direct contribution made by Malta-based forces to these shortages it is important to pay due regard to two other less direct advantages that the 8th Army obtained from continued British possession of Malta.

First, the Axis air attacks on Malta and on the June and August relief convoys led to the diversion of many German and Italian aircraft from the desert. This was particularly valuable when, in the two weeks before Montgomery's offensive planned for 23 October, Kesselring transferred over 600 aircraft from North Africa and Crete to attempt a last neutralisation of Malta. Not only did this fail to reduce Malta's attacks on Axis shipping,[14] but the German fighters transferred from North Africa did not return until 26 October. In addition, throughout the summer of 1942 air attack on the 8th Army was also reduced by the employment of many German bombers on convoy escort work. On 2 September Kesselring gave orders that 'the main object of all operations in all circumstances is to be the escort of convoys'.[15]

A second consequence of the continued threat posed by Malta, particularly after mid-August, was the Italian decision to route all but the fastest cargo ships to Benghazi and Tobruk on an extended passage through the Corinth Canal and down the east coast of Greece (see Map 3). However, while leaving these ships exposed to Malta attack in the first part of their passage, this considerably extended route pushed them towards the stronger British air and submarine forces operating from secure eastern bases. Had Malta by then been in Italian hands, the direct sea crossing to Benghazi would have been quicker and less vulnerable to attack from the east.

To turn now to Malta's direct impact on Axis supply difficulties we may look first at the official Italian naval figures for total tonnage shipped to North Africa in this period and the losses suffered *en route* (see Table 15). The monthly amounts actually required by Rommel's forces to prepare for, and conduct, operations are no easier to establish for this period than for his earlier North African campaigns. Rommel himself later quoted various figures in his criticisms of the Italian supply system. In one place in his account he cited a 'real requirement of 60,000 tons, a figure which was never in fact attained'. In the run-up to El Alamein: 'I demanded as a minimum the shipment of 30,000 tons in September and 35,000 tons during October.'[16] A study by the German naval staff in October put Rommel's minimum monthly requirements at 40,000 tons and concluded that 60,000 tons were needed to carry out all the Panzer Army's tasks.[17] It seems reasonable to assume, therefore, that approxi-mately 60,000 tons per month were needed to support active operations.

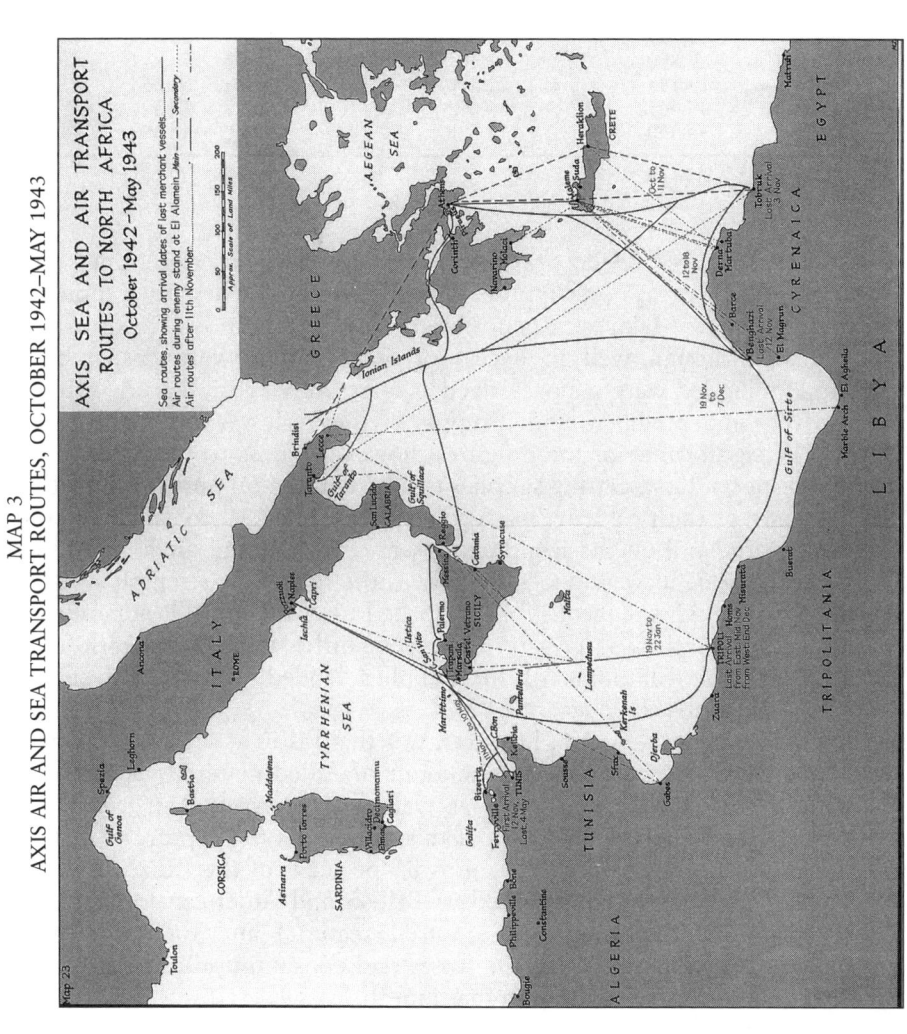

MAP 3
AXIS AIR AND SEA TRANSPORT ROUTES, OCTOBER 1942–MAY 1943

Source: *The Mediterranean and Middle East*, Vol. IV, p. 193, Map 23.

TABLE 15
AXIS SUPPLIES LANDED AND PERCENTAGES LOST, JUNE–OCTOBER 1942

(amounts in tons)

	General cargo	% lost	Fuel	% lost	Total sent	Total arrived	% lost
June	26,759	23	5,568	17	41,519	32,327	22
July	67,590	5	23,901	11	97,794	91,491	6
August	29,155	25	22,500	41	77,134	51,655	33
September	46,465	18	31,061	23	96,903	77,526	20
October	34,390	41	12,308	52	83,695	46,698	44

Source: See Appendix.

These figures reveal that, after very low deliveries in June, due largely to a shortage of shipping space, the volume of delivered supplies in July, when Malta was neutralised, rose significantly. However, in August, although well in excess of 60,000 tons were despatched, supplies landed were almost halved as losses at sea rose sharply. After a recovery in September, landed supplies fell even lower in October.

The significance of these figures, however, needs to be qualified in two respects. First, getting supplies to a North African port was only the first part of the problem. The growing weight of Allied air attack on these ports, and on the lengthening sea, road, rail and air links to the forward areas, increased significantly as the RAF, now strengthened by the first USAAF squadrons, re-established itself on airfields adjacent to its supply and repair bases. Consequently, increasing, although unquantifiable, amounts of the supplies landed were destroyed or damaged in Africa.

A compensating factor, however, was that losses at sea and in North Africa were offset by the large amount of Allied material captured at Tobruk and at Mersa Matruh, as well as at overrun British dumps. Perhaps the most valuable part of this booty was the capture of 2,000 lorries. As Rommel observed, up to 85 per cent of the Panzer Army's supply columns were composed of British and American lorries.[18] In broad terms, therefore, the captured material and the large July shipments compensated for the losses and consumption caused by the heavy, inconclusive fighting in that month.

In the early part of August, as a result of the large July deliveries, Enigma decrypts revealed that Rommel's infantry and tank forces had been considerably strengthened. In addition, by the end of the month the Axis air forces in North Africa had also been raised to a total of 310 German and 460 Italian aircraft.[19] Although these reinforcements, many of which had arrived by air without lorries and heavy weapons, began to reduce his reserve stocks Rommel, nevertheless, proposed, in an

Appreciation signalled to OKW on 15 August and read two days later in Cairo, to renew his offensive on the Alamein position during the next full moon period on 26 August.[20] Crucially, however, because he had been unable to accumulate reserves, his plan was conditional on the shipment of 4,000 men, 1,250 vehicles and 60 guns still waiting in Italy, and on the steady flow of petrol, ammunition and provisions thereafter. To meet this latter condition Cavallero promised a series of convoys, but between 27 and 30 August five supply ships were sunk, as discussed further below. These losses first caused Rommel to postpone his attack until the night of 30 August, and then to limit his objectives.[21] He, nevertheless, decided to attack then despite having fuel for only 4½ days' fighting, relying on the promise that further ships would be sailed and on Kesselring's assurance that 500 cubic metres of petrol would be flown in each day.[22]

The Panzer Army's advance was, however, soon brought to a halt by minefields, heavy air attack and a strong gun defence on Alam Halfa ridge. These operations consumed much petrol and Kesselring's promised emergency fuel supply did not reach the forward area. On 1 September the German Quartermaster's War Diary recorded: 'Troops screaming for fuel; they have only 0.5 Consumption Units left.'[23] On the following day Rommel received news of the loss or delay of two more tankers but by then he had already decided to go over to the defensive, due, he signalled OKW, to the sinking of the tanker *San Andrea*, and the non-arrival of another, the *Abruzzi*.[24] The only ship to arrive during the battle was the *Gualdi* with 830 tons of fuel.

Throughout this six-day battle a continuous stream of Enigma intercepts gave Montgomery a running commentary on Rommel's mounting supply difficulties. They also enable us to understand the effect of supply losses on Rommel's decisions and operations. On 30 August the German Quartermaster in Rome, noting Malta's 'new lease of life', warned that if there were further sinkings the supply position 'would become still more strained'. The arrival of the *Picci Fassio* and the *Abruzzi* was regarded on 31 August as being of 'decisive importance', but two days later signals reported the loss of the former and the damage to the *Abruzzi* that led to its failure to arrive during the battle. Early on 2 September a further signal told Montgomery that 'Panzer Army is temporarily going over to the defensive today second owing to lack of fuel'. Finally, an intercept of 6 September confirmed Rommel's decision 'to go over to the defensive utilising the extensive British minefields'.[25]

In a report to OKW on 11 September Rommel reported the loss of only 36 German and 11 Italian tanks, and stated that his attack 'was broken off because the supplies of fuel and ammunition promised by *Comando Supremo* did not arrive'. However, in a subsequent report to

Hitler, he gave the supply problem as only the third of the factors that forced his withdrawal, after strong British defences and air superiority, and he repeated this in his memoirs.[26] Kesselring, writing from memory in 1946, denied that fuel shortages in the battlefield area compelled Rommel to withdraw, pointing out that he was engaged in 'more or less mobile defensive operations until 6 September' for which he had sufficient petrol. He did acknowledge, nevertheless, that the petrol flown in from Crete did not reach the front line forces.[27]

It would be wrong to conclude that supply shortages *caused* Rommel's defeat at Alam Halfa. Enigma intercepts having denied him the advantage of surprise Rommel was then halted by strong British defences that he might have overcome only with air superiority. The lack of this made withdrawal unavoidable. Nevertheless, what the August attack on his supplies achieved was the removal of any possibility that he might re-group and attack again, as he had successfully done at Gazala in May. Rommel still had a strong tank force and a well-supplied second thrust on a different axis might have been successful. The supply position ruled this out.

To what extent were these supply difficulties the result of direct Malta operations? The figures for Axis shipping losses in the central Mediterranean in this period, by number and tonnage, and Malta's contribution to them, are set out in Table 16. After relatively low losses in June and July sinkings rose sharply in August. This was initially the result of the renewed activity of submarines based in the eastern Mediterranean. When Admiral Harwood, the C-in-C Mediterranean, ordered the evacuation of Alexandria on 24 June the 1st Flotilla moved to Beirut. However, on 30 June its depot ship, HMS *Medway*, was sunk by U 372. With her were lost not only the necessary maintenance equipment and supplies but also the reserve stock of torpedoes. Consequently, only one small enemy ship was sunk by submarine attack in July.

TABLE 16
PROPORTION OF AXIS SHIPS SUNK BY MALTA FORCES, JUNE–OCTOBER 1942

(number and tonnage of ships sunk)

	Submarine	*Ship*	*Aircraft*	*Shared*	*Malta total*	*C. Med. total*	*Malta (%)*
June	–	–	(2) 14,580	–	(2) 14,580	(6) 26,102	56
July	–	–	(1) 6,339	–	(1) 6,339	(4) 10,486	60
Aug.	(2) 10,320	–	(2) 6,604	(1) 8,326	(5) 25,250	(11) 56,809	44
Sept.	(3) 11,342	–	(2) 3,498	(1) 1,148	(6) 15,988	(11) 36,272	44
Oct.	(7) 16,730	–	(1) 2,552	(2) 14,070	(10) 33,352	(13) 44,965	74
Total	(12) 38,392	–	(8) 33,573	(4) 23,544	(24) 95,509	(45) 174,634	55

Source: See Appendix.

August was a different matter. The 1st Flotilla submarines sank five ships aggregating 29,716 tons. However, two others, aggregating 10,320 tons, and one shared with the RAF, the *Rosalino Pilo* of 8,326 tons, fell to submarines re-established at Malta. Malta's Beauforts sank two others, including the 5,077-ton tanker *San Andrea*.[28]

The Axis shipping losses between 17 August and 6 September best illustrate the contribution Malta made to Rommel's supply difficulties before and during Alam Halfa. In that period 12 ships, totalling 47,443 tons, were sunk, of which Malta forces accounted for six, totalling 27,511 tons (58 per cent). Among these were two oil tankers, the *San Andrea* of 5,077 tons and the *Picci Fassio* of 2,261 tons In addition to these outright losses, another tanker, the *Pozarica* of 7,751 tons, and the supply ship *Manara*, of 7,720 tons, were beached on Corfu and Leucas, respectively, after attacks by Beauforts from Malta. Finally, Malta-based Wellingtons damaged and diverted the small tanker *Abruzzi* of 680 tons, the non-arrival of which also influenced Rommel's decision to withdraw. In total, therefore, Malta forces in this critical three-week period deprived Rommel of the supplies carried in 43,662 tons of shipping. This must be accounted a major contribution to his supply difficulties when he was trying to breach the Alam Halfa defences.

The pattern of Axis shipping losses in August was repeated in the next two months. 'In the period from 6th September to 23rd October', Rommel later wrote, 'the battle of supplies was waged with new violence. At the end of the period it had been finally lost by us and won by the British – by a wide margin.'[29] The effect of these ship and cargo losses was followed closely by Montgomery's Intelligence staff through the large number of Enigma intercepts. Hinsley has pointed out that in June 1942 intercepted Enigma signals rose to a peak level of 4,000 per month and that GC&CS read virtually every enemy signal sent during this period.[30] What they revealed was an inability to accumulate the reserves demanded by Rommel before he went on sick leave on 23 September. Indeed, the oil position steadily deteriorated. On 1 October, for example, reserves of fuel were reported to be 10½ Consumption Units (CUs), compared with a target of 30 CUs. They had fallen to 8½ CUs by 6 October, and the Quartermaster's Report of 19 October, the last before Montgomery's offensive began, disclosed petrol stocks of no more than 5½ CUs. This was largely the result of an attack on the tanker *Panuco*, which carried fuel equal to 3½ CUs. On 18–19 October Malta-based Wellingtons damaged her and caused her to be towed to Taranto for repairs.[31] On 20 October the Panzer Army reported that, by 25 October, fuel stocks would fall to only 3½ CUs and warned that 'it did not possess the operational freedom of movement' essential to meet the expected 8th Army attack.[32]

At a conference at Taormina on 22 October, the day before Montgomery's attack, Cavallero reported that the tanker *Proserpina* had set out with fuel, and that another, the *Luisiana*, would follow. Both these ships were sunk in the opening days of the Alamein battle, the latter by Malta-based Wellingtons. Rommel later wrote: 'I received the shattering news that the tanker *Louisiana* [*sic*], which had been sent as a replacement for the *Proserpina*, had been sunk by aerial torpedo. Now we were really up against it.'[33] Five other supply ships were sunk by Egyptian-based aircraft in the opening phase of the Alamein battle, compelling Rommel to depend increasingly on air supplies.[34] On 28 October Kesselring ordered a maximum effort to deliver fuel 'by day and night down to the last crew and last aircraft'.[35] This deterioration in the fuel position was due almost entirely to the fact that, as shown in Table 15, only 12,000 tons of fuel arrived in North Africa in October, only one half of what had been despatched.

The effect of these supply losses was that Rommel was compelled to fight a largely static battle with limited scope for manoeuvre. The Panzer Army Daily Report of 26 October, noting the loss of the *Proserpina*, stated: 'It is, therefore, impossible at the moment to carry out the mobile operations with the Panzer and motorised divisions which are so urgently necessary.' When, later that day, Rommel ordered the 21st Panzer division to move north, he realised that fuel shortages would prevent its return south if another attack came there. Even a general withdrawal was ruled out, he decided, because this might lead to mobile warfare for which fuel was lacking.[36]

Malta's contribution to these supply shortages, before and during the Alamein battle, is made clear in the statistics quoted above. Ten of the 13 ships sunk in October fell to Malta forces. Seven of these were the victims of 10th Flotilla submarines but the attack on the tanker *Panuco*, and the sinking of the tanker *Luisiana*, were the work of Malta's Wellingtons. Earlier, as a result of aviation petrol shortages in Malta, the Beauforts of 39 Squadron had been flown to Egypt to reinforce the attack on Tobruk-bound convoys sailing from Greece and Crete. It was these aircraft, and others operating from Egyptian airfields, that accounted for most of the sinkings off Tobruk during the Alamein fighting.[37]

Without losing sight of the indirect benefits flowing from British retention of Malta, how, in the light of the preceding analysis, should Malta's direct contribution to the autumn battles in Egypt be assessed? Giorgerini has alleged that in this period the shift of the battle front and the principal Axis supply route to the east meant that most of the shipping losses were caused by British eastern forces rather than by those based at Malta.[38] Knox has echoed this view, writing: 'Once Rommel drove on Egypt in the summer of 1942 Malta was largely out of the picture.'[39] Neither of these conclusions is supported by an examination of the shipping losses. Mattesini, on the other hand, to support his view that the 'Pedestal' convoy was a strategic British success, compiled a table showing that 72 per cent of the Italian shipping losses in the August–November 1942 period were due to Malta-based forces.[40] The analysis presented in this section makes clear that the statements of Giorgerini and Knox are incorrect. Although Malta's contribution was not as emphatic as in the autumn of 1941 the 75,000 tons of Axis shipping sunk, equal to 51 per cent of the shipping losses, and the further ships damaged by Malta-based forces in the August–October period must be considered a major contribution to the attack on Rommel's supply convoys.

But were losses at sea, however caused, the main reason for Rommel's supply difficulties? Van Creveld has argued that 'the importance usually attributed to the "battle of the convoys" is grossly exaggerated'.[41] In his view Rommel's supply difficulties stemmed largely from inadequate port capacity and, above all, from the shortage of lorries. As noted earlier, port capacity in North Africa was highly variable and Tobruk, although captured intact, could only handle at most 30,000 tons carried in smaller ships. Nevertheless, 91,000 tons were unloaded in July and 77,000 tons in September, and the Axis clearly expected the ports to be able to handle the larger amounts despatched (see Table 15).[42] Overall port capacity, therefore, principally at Tobruk and Benghazi, was, despite the disruption caused by continual bombing, sufficient to meet the 60,000-ton monthly requirement assumed to be necessary. It was losses at sea that prevented this figure being reached in the critical months of August and October, not insufficient unloading capacity.

Delivering supplies to the forward area was undoubtedly a growing problem as distances lengthened and air attacks intensified. Coastal shipping and rail facilities eased the problem to a degree but the main burden of delivery fell upon Rommel's poorly maintained fleet of Axis and captured Allied lorries. However, there are no statistics to show that losses incurred in delivering supplies were greater than those at sea, or any evidence that the Axis supply authorities thought their principal difficulty was that of getting supplies to forward areas. On the contrary, the thousands of Enigma intercepts, which were not available when Van Creveld wrote, show greater concern with the bulk losses at sea and the consequent inability to accumulate the necessary reserves.[43] The Axis assessment of where the main difficulty lay was made clear by the constant employment of aircraft to protect convoys and, above all, by Kesselring's decision in October to withdraw aircraft from North Africa, where they were needed to protect ports and supply columns, to mount a final offensive against Malta. These decisions are inexplicable if the crux of the supply problem was thought to lie in North Africa. Van Creveld's dismissal of the significance of sea losses and his emphasis on ports and lorries is, therefore, unconvincing. Certainly, the Axis supply chain was a weak one but the Enigma intercepts, despite the numerous references to transport problems in North Africa, make quite clear that it was the bulk losses at sea that, by limiting the overall amount of supplies, had a more powerful effect on Rommel's decisions and operations

A final question to be considered is the degree to which supply problems, however caused, influenced the outcome of these battles. Most of the senior German officers involved in the North African campaigns have commented on the weak supply position relative to the abundance of material enjoyed by Montgomery. General Warlimont, for example, who visited Rommel at the end of July, later wrote that neither military skill nor courage 'could make up for the catastrophic situation brought about by the failure of the overseas supply lines'.[44] However, only those engaged in the fighting could weigh the impact of supply shortages against other factors. It is too much to expect Rommel to attribute his defeat to his request, agreed by Hitler and Mussolini, to advance into Egypt, overturning the agreed strategy of pausing to allow the capture of Malta. This was, in his view, a calculated risk, 'a plan with a chance of success – a try on'.[45] However, more weight may be attached to his views about the relative importance of external factors beyond his control. Although he was unaware of the Enigma intercepts, Rommel's considered view was that 'in every battle to come the strength of the Anglo-American air force was to be the deciding factor'. Supply difficulties were, in his mind, a powerful but secondary factor, but he recognised Malta's contribution to these difficulties when he wrote: 'Malta has the lives of many thousands of German and Italian soldiers on its conscience.'[46]

This section has sought to assess, as far as possible in concrete, statistical terms, the extent of the assistance Montgomery gained from the possession of Malta during the autumn battles. The analysis supports the conclusion that Malta's influence, although not decisive, was a powerful one. Had Malta then been in Italian hands a better-supplied Axis force in North Africa might have fought the 8th Army to a standstill and might possibly have justified Rommel's calculated risk.

MALTA'S ROLE IN THE TUNISIAN CAMPAIGN

Given Malta's powerful participation in the Egyptian battles it is puzzling that in the last three weeks of November, under Malta's nose, a significant Axis force was established in Tunisia without the loss of a single soldier or ton of supplies. Why did this happen?

After President Roosevelt had on 30 July 1942 committed US forces to the invasion of French North Africa joint Anglo-American planning began.⁴⁷ However, a troubling aspect of the final plan was that the most easterly landing would be made at Algiers, 400 miles from Tunis, rather than at Bône, 200 miles closer, as General Eisenhower, the 'Torch' Supreme Commander, had initially wished. The distance between Algiers and the Tunisian ports of Bizerta and Tunis might have not been so critical if the initial appreciation of the British JIC, that the reaction of the Axis to the landings would be a limited one, had proved correct. As Hinsley. has observed: 'This turned out to be an under-estimate in every respect.'⁴⁸ Nevertheless, since such help as the Axis powers decided to give was bound to flow into the two main ports of Tunis and Bizerta, the planners were clear about the need to attack this vital supply route from Malta and other bases.⁴⁹ In October, the JIC remained sanguine about the level of Axis intervention even after D-day had been postponed to 8 November. Hinsley has noted that 'final plans . . . made little provision against the intervention of German troops', and 'hardly any steps were taken to include Malta's air strike forces in the general strategic plan'.⁵⁰

It was not until the COS meeting on 29 September that the subject of 'Malta – Offensive Operations in Conjunction with Operation TORCH' first appeared on the agenda.⁵¹ Admiral Pound had already, on 19 September, warned Admiral Harwood, the C-in-C Mediterranean, 'it will be essential to prevent or delay enemy reinforcements reaching Tunisia before we do. To this end operations will be necessary from Malta on the greatest scale possible.'⁵² But when, ten days later, he asked his fellow Chiefs what operations from Malta were planned, he was no doubt surprised to hear from General Brooke that Malta's role had been 'shelved when it had been decided to limit the extent of the initial landings'. Rather belatedly, however, the Chiefs of Staff instructed the JPS to examine what Malta could do to assist 'Torch'.

It was against a background of growing concern about Malta itself that on 7 and 8 October the Chiefs of Staff discussed the JPC report on Malta's possible contribution to 'Torch'.⁵³ The RAF contribution, they reported, was necessarily limited by the acute shortage of aviation petrol. Eight hundred tons was being held back to provide air cover for the arrival and unloading of the 'Stoneage' convoy and for limited 'Torch' assistance, but more extensive operations must await the fuel to be brought in the convoy. Only then could the RAF freely attack ports and bases in Sicily and Tunisia, and ships and aircraft travelling between them. As far as naval action was concerned, it had already been agreed that the principal task of the submarines of the 10th Flotilla at Malta, strengthened by boats from the 1st and 8th Flotillas, was a defensive one. It was to prevent any attempt by the Italian fleet to attack the Allied invasion fleets. For this purpose, its boats would be disposed to cover the Italian naval ports and the passages to the western

Mediterranean, but would not be deployed off the Tunisian ports.[54] As for the establishment of a surface force at Malta, this could only come from the east since no 'Torch' units would be available until D + 20. The eastern convoy with naval escort was expected to reach Malta about D-Day, but Pound conceded that, if this convoy were postponed as a result of the slow progress of the El Alamein offensive, it might be possible to send a small force to Malta ahead of the convoy, so long as air cover could be provided.

However, what was unexpected in the JPC review was its analysis of a request from General Eisenhower's HQ that a Malta military force be made ready to seize the small port of Sousse, 80 miles south of Tunis. The evolution of this request into Operation 'Breastplate' merited only a footnote in the official history,[55] but deserves some recognition. Out of the Malta garrison of 14 battalions, the JPC considered that a brigade group of three battalions, supported by field and AA artillery, was the most that could be made available. However, this force would have very little transport, and could bring only limited supplies with it. It could not then be re-supplied from Malta until the convoy arrived, and could not be supplied from 'Torch' before D + 35. More significantly, the physical condition of the troops was so poor that an opposed landing, or extended operations, were precluded. The JPC concluded that, although plans for such a force should be prepared, the operation would not be justified unless 'it would tip the balance'. The Chiefs of Staff accepted this recommendation and advised Eisenhower accordingly.

The JPC analysis thus made clear that Malta's air and naval forces could only make a significant contribution to 'Torch' if, before D-Day, the island had been re-supplied and its forces were ready for action. However, earlier hopes that the 'Stoneage' convoy would arrive before the 'Torch' landings were fading. Despite the Prime Minister's persistent complaints about the delay,[56] Montgomery did not launch his offensive at El Alamein until 23 October. It then met stubborn opposition, and hopes of a quick breakthrough, followed by the early capture of the Cyrenaican airfields, evaporated. Consequently, the ships of the Malta relief convoy had not left the eastern Mediterranean when the landings in North Africa began on 8 November. Although these were accomplished with less difficulty than some had feared, concern quickly grew about the rapidity and strength of the Axis reaction.

The German and Italian High Commands had, in early November, become aware of the assembly near Gibraltar of a large Allied merchant fleet but there was no agreement about its purpose or objective.[57] When he heard of the landings in the early hours of 8 November Hitler immediately decided that this new Allied offensive should be resisted and within the next 48 hours Kesselring, who was initially given command of all German forces, had flown over a growing force of aircraft and troops to seize the principal airfields. The first convoy, carrying tanks, lorries and other heavy equipment, sailed on 12 November and before the end of the month 40 ships had arrived in 25 separate convoys without suffering any losses. In these first three weeks 25,000 men and 34,000 tons of supplies had been transported to Tunisia by air and sea, including a full German Panzer division.[58]

The Chiefs of Staff reviewed these unwelcome developments on 11 November.[59] By then, the delayed breakthrough at Alamein had been made, and the Chiefs were hopeful that, within the week, the Malta convoy might set sail. An urgent signal was, therefore, sent to Cairo:

> It is important that Malta should take maximum air action against German forces in Tunisia at once. Extent to which they can afford to use up their fuel depends on date of arrival of convoy from your end. Please give us earliest date to which it would be safe for Malta to work.[60]

This underlined the dilemma that had now arisen. Should more of the limited petrol available in Malta be used to assist 'Torch' operations, running the risk that insufficient might then remain to protect the arrival and unloading of the convoy? The C-in-Cs replied that the convoy might be able to set out on 15 November, provided that some of the Cyrenaican airfields had by then been captured. The Chiefs of Staff were minded to leave it to the Governor to decide how much of the dwindling petrol stocks should be used on 'Torch' support, but the Prime Minister rejected this. 'We cannot', he minuted, 'divest ourselves of responsibility for the convoy from the east to Malta. . . . This is no time to throw away four fast heavily-laden ships.' It would be better, he advised, to wait a few more days until the Derna airfields were secured.[61] The convoy finally left Alexandria on 16 November and the four supply ships reached Malta safely four days later.

The arrival of the Malta convoy on 20 November permitted the belated implementation of plans to interrupt the growing flow of men and equipment to Tunisia. This did not mean, however, that the parallel flow of supplies to Rommel's army in Libya could now be ignored. Twice before, a British advance to the borders of Tripolitania had been thrown back by Rommel as a result of a sudden German reinforcement, and no one was prepared to assume that he could not do this a third time if supplies were successfully run into Tripoli. It was Malta's responsibility to prevent this since Tripoli had again become Rommel's only port of supply, although from December he began to receive an increasing volume of his supplies via Tunisia. Submarine operations were further complicated by a command structure that made Captain

Simpson at Malta responsible to Cunningham for Tunisian operations, but to Harwood for the interception of Libyan convoys.[62]

As many as 26 submarines were, by the end of November, based at Malta under Captain Simpson's command, and, on 11 November, Cunningham directed him to re-dispose his force to attack ships on the Tunisian route.[63] There, however, they faced difficult conditions, described by Lieutenant Lumby, Captain of the submarine *P247*, as 'quite the nastiest patrol area I have ever endured'.[64] The shallow waters around Cape Bon and the Tunisian ports were heavily mined, and Italian anti-submarine measures had improved considerably. Poor winter weather and the longer hours of darkness also played a part. As a result, four British submarines were lost in the last two months of the year. Lieutenant-Commander Ben Bryant, the successful commander of *Safari*, later wrote that British submarines hit a 'bad patch' with 'far too many misses' after the 'Torch' landings.[65]

The Admiralty was slow to establish a surface force at Malta. Pound did not send a surface force ahead of the delayed convoy, as he had earlier suggested he might. On the contrary, as late as 17 November, he laid down that the protection of Malta convoys must have priority over 'Torch' support. As a result, the naval ships that had escorted 'Stoneage' at once returned to Alexandria to prepare for the next convoy.[66] On 22 November, however, the Admiralty, after noting the conflict between the supply of Malta and 'Torch', asked Cunningham and Harwood to signal their plans for a surface force. Cunningham replied that he intended to establish such a force at Bône as soon as reasonable air cover could be provided at that port, but Harwood said that he preferred to employ all his surface units to protect the next convoy. Nevertheless, he could, if required, send a force of three cruisers and four fleet destroyers, which could sail on 25 November. This he was then ordered to do after the Prime Minister had pressed the matter at a Defence Committee meeting on 23 November.[67] Force K was therefore re-established at Malta on 27 November, while Force Q, of a further three cruisers and two destroyers, was formed at Bône three days later when satisfactory air cover had been arranged.

By that time, however, Kesselring had established air superiority over the Sicilian Channel so that surface forces could only operate safely at night. On the night of 1/2 December Force Q, directed by an ASV Wellington from Malta, sank a convoy of four supply ships and a naval escort, and, on the following night, Force K, with FAA assistance, sank a naval ship rescuing survivors from another convoy. Kesselring promptly suspended night crossings and ordered the laying of an extensive mine barrier to the west of Bizerta. These measures severely hampered the operations of the two surface forces. Not for the first time the Prime Minister thought the Admiralty were being too cautious, minuting to the First Sea Lord on 6 December: 'The first duty of the Navy for the next ten days is to stop the reinforcement of Tunisia. This duty should be discharged even at a heavy cost.'[68] Pound replied on 9 December that if Cunningham attempted to attack by day without air cover, 'two convoys might be stopped at cost of the whole of Force Q. There are no ships for another.'[69]

Given the limited effectiveness of naval operations much depended upon air attack, but the RAF, too, faced difficulties. Nevertheless, despite the impression given by Hinsley, the air authorities had given some thought to what could be done from Malta. On 16 October Tedder offered to transfer from Malta to North Africa a squadron of Beauforts and escorting Beaufighters for anti-shipping strikes, and, three days later, the Air Ministry suggested various diversionary operations to support the 'Torch' landings, subject to the availability of fuel.[70] In the event, in the first critical days after the landings, air operations were restricted by the shortage of fuel. In addition, the composition of the force at Malta was determined by the need to protect the convoy from air and sea attack. It was these defensive squadrons that were strengthened in early November, and there was room for only six bomber Wellingtons.[71] It was only after the arrival of the convoy that Portal could issue instructions calling for 'the air forces at Malta to assist to the utmost in the battle for Tunisia'.[72]

This could not be done overnight. Space was still limited and, in order to make room for a Wellington bomber force that eventually increased to 36 aircraft, the Beauforts of 39 Squadron, which could not be risked by day against the strong single-engined fighter force that Kesselring had now established, had to be sent away again. The night-flying Albacores of 821 Squadron were also ordered in, but did not arrive until 29 November. Apart, therefore, from daylight sweeps by Beaufighters and Spitfires, Malta's air forces in December concentrated on night bombing of Tunis and Bizerta.[73] The effectiveness of these operations was, in Tedder's view, hampered by the absence of any air co-ordinating authority, and it was not until mid-February 1943 that he himself was appointed to command all air forces in the Mediterranean theatre.[74]

It is these circumstances at Malta that provide the answer to Hinsley's question why the Allied air forces were so slow to attack the Axis build-up in Tunisia.[75] It was not so much a lack of planning, or a failure to appreciate the dangers that flowed from the Axis reinforcements pouring into Tunisia, but rather the inability of the forces at Malta to take any significant action until the relief convoy had been unloaded. The delay of 12 days before the arrival of 'Stoneage' gave Kesselring enough time to establish a force strong enough to block Anderson's weak thrust for the Tunisian ports. It is ironic that Malta's forces, one of whose principal tasks was to deny oil supplies to the Axis forces, were incapacitated at a critical moment by a similar deficiency.

Although Kesselring and the Italian navy had, in November, taken full advantage of the Allied pre-occupation with the landings and Malta's fuel shortages, the problem of maintaining supplies to a growing Axis force in Tunisia as well as the retreating Libyan army was considerable. The loss of so many of the largest and fastest merchant ships, eased only partially by the seizure of French ships, forced the use of smaller vessels, supplemented by a growing fleet of ferries of various types, auxiliary sailing ships and other light coastal craft. Naval ships, whose numbers were also much reduced, were used to transport troops and urgently needed supplies. One result was that average cargoes on the Tunisian route were only 3,400 tons compared to 4,100 tons on the Libyan route. At first sight the short sea crossing from western Sicily to Tunisia appeared to offer a secure passage, especially after mine barriers had been laid to endanger surface and submarine attack. But Allied counter-mining within the channel and the lack of sea room for evasive action made the convoys easier to identify and attack. More importantly, since two-thirds of the supplies were loaded at Naples these ships were vulnerable to attack in their initial passage to Palermo or Messina. By the end of the Tunisian campaign 154 of the 344 ships employed on the *rotta della morte* had been sunk and a further 138 damaged.[76]

Space will permit only a largely statistical account of Malta's contribution to the Tunisian campaign.[77] The supplies delivered to the two fronts in this period are set out in Table 17.

The rapid expansion of the Axis forces in North Africa to approximately 350,000 men led to an inevitable escalation of supply requirements. By February 1942 General Von Arnim, the commander of the German 5th Army, and Rommel put their combined operational needs at 150,000 tons a month. An absolute minimum of 69,000 tons was needed for subsistence alone. *Comando Supremo*, however, protested that it could ship only 80,000 tons a month, of which it expected to lose about a quarter at sea. The figures in Table 17 show that the Italian estimate was more realistic. Although in November the Italian navy had landed almost 100,000 tons of supplies in Tunisia and Libya, supplies unloaded in December fell to 66,000 tons. In January, when losses were held to 21 per cent, 70,000 tons got through, but again fell to the 60,000 mark in February after 23 per cent losses. In March a loss rate of 36 per cent held landed supplies to no more than 49,000 tons and this was halved again in the last full month of fighting.

TABLE 17
AXIS SUPPLIES LANDED AND PERCENTAGES LOST, NOVEMBER 1942–MAY 1943
(amounts in tons)

	General cargo	% lost	Fuel	% lost	Total sent	Total arrived	% lost
			Supplies to Libya				
November	42,005	9	21,731	46	85,970	63,376	26
December	6,151	19	2,058	74	12,981	6,151	53
			Supplies to Tunisia				
November	22,392	0	11,947	0	34,339	34,339	0
December	45,781	25	14,838	38	84,804	60,619	29
January	44,613	25	25,580	13	88,933	70,193	21
February	45,240	13	14,798	42	77,781	60,038	23
March	32,727	40	16,634	27	77,193	49,361	36
April	18,571	40	10,052	43	48,703	28,623	41
May	2,736	80	623	35	14,416	3,359	77

Source: See Appendix.

In addition to these losses at sea, growing amounts of supplies were destroyed after arrival as the air offensive against the docks and the lines of communication slowly gathered momentum. When General Warlimont visited Von Arnim in early February the latter explained that supply shortages made his 5th Army unfit for large offensive operations, and Warlimont, on his return to Germany, reported that the Axis position was a 'house of cards' as a result of the supply position.[78] Thus when Rommel and Von Arnim launched their offensives on 14 February their forces had only 3½ CUs of fuel and 1½–2 issues of ammunition.[79]

Malta's contribution to the attack on the Tunisian supply route was, as before, a multifaceted one. Much of the photo-reconnaissance of Tunisia, Sicily and Naples was carried out by 69 Squadron at Malta before a new PR unit was sent to Algeria. Malta's ASV Wellingtons and Albacores tracked Axis ships attempting a night crossing, directing surface, submarine and air units to the attack. Spitfire and Beaufighter squadrons struck at the almost continuous flow of Axis transport aircraft carrying troops to Tunisia and at their airfields in Sicily. Finally, a reinforced Wellington squadron attacked the harbour facilities at Tunis and Bizerta with results that cannot be accurately identified.[80]

It was well understood, nevertheless, that Malta's main task was to sink, damage or delay Axis supply ships. The overall number and tonnage of ships of more than 500 tons sunk during the Tunisian

TABLE 18
PROPORTION OF AXIS SHIPS SUNK BY MALTA FORCES,
NOVEMBER 1942–13 MAY 1943

(number and tonnage of ships sunk)

	Submarine	Ship	Aircraft	Shared	Malta total	C. Med. total	Malta (%)
Nov.	(4) 6,517	–	(3) 6,437	(2) 14,110	(9) 27,064	(17) 54,584	50
Dec.	(9) 32,342	–	(10) 28,180	(1) 2,875	(20) 63,397	(31) 87,271	73
Jan.	(9) 20,695	(1) 4,537	(2) 6,907	(1) 6,107	(13) 38,246	(26) 87,098	44
Feb.	(11) 37,939	–	(4) 25,982	–	(15) 63,921	(20) 77,641	82
March	(13) 33,582	–	(3) 19,093	–	(16) 52,675	(34) 102,247	52
April	(7) 20,219	(1) 575	(1) 2,943	(2) 7,021	(11) 30,758	(29) 104,250	30
May	(1) 763	(1) 3,566	–	–	(2) 4,329	(16) 49,821	9
Total	(54) 152,057	(3) 8,678	(23) 89,542	(6) 30,113	(86) 280,390	(173) 562,912	50

Source: See Appendix.

campaign, and Malta's contribution to these losses, is shown in Table 18. Despite the problems discussed earlier Malta's forces accounted for nine ships in November, including the 10,534-ton tanker *Giulio Giordani*, and more than doubled this number in December. The bad weather of January partly explains the reduced results in that month before the tonnage figures rose again in February. From then on the growing Allied air forces in Algeria and Libya, which eventually comprised more than 3,000 aircraft, played the dominant role in the mounting losses inflicted on the convoy traffic.

An increasing number of ships were sunk in port. Of the 254 ships lost during this campaign 154 were sunk in various harbours, of which 118 were destroyed in the ten weeks from March until mid-May.[81] Nevertheless, Malta forces sank 29 ships, totalling 87,000 tons, between March and 13 May 1942.

Over the six-month campaign as a whole Malta's air and naval forces accounted for 86 ships, aggregating 280,000 tons, representing 50 per cent of the total tonnage destroyed. These figures compare with Malta-caused losses of 81 ships aggregating 390,000 tons in the whole of 1941 and 48 ships aggregating 160,000 tons in the first ten months of 1942. When considering these figures it should be borne in mind that Malta forces also accounted for many smaller vessels, including ferries and naval *Kriegtransporter* vessels that the Axis used increasingly to transport supplies to Tunisia. Bragadin's figures reveal that of the 243 ships sunk in the Tunisian campaign only 151 were supply ships of more than 500 tons. In addition, a further 242 ships were damaged to a greater or lesser degree.[82]

Without, to repeat yet again, ignoring or discounting the less direct and less measurable benefits of Malta's possession, the shipping figures set out above are the best objective measure of Malta's contribution to the final campaign in North Africa. It is a contribution that has not received due recognition in the official British histories because no attempt has been made there to identify separately the losses attributable to Malta-based forces. Even Spooner, who devotes his book to Malta's operations, does not attempt to measure Malta's contribution in this way.[83] On the Italian side Giorgerini has simply stated that by that stage of the war the odds against the Axis were so great that it did not matter which side held Malta and he offers no analysis of the losses resulting from Malta operations. In his view the fundamental problem facing the Axis by 1943 was an underlying relative shortage of war material and supplies and the progressive erosion of the means to get what was available to its destination. There can be no doubt but that in the course of Tunisian campaign the growing material inferiority of the Axis became even more evident. Nevertheless, had all or most of the supplies that were despatched to Tunisia arrived, as they did in November 1942, Axis resistance might have been considerably extended.

What the analysis presented here shows is that, after a slow start due very largely to a lack of fuel, 280,000 tons of shipping were sunk by forces operating from Malta between November 1942 and May 1943, equal to 50 per cent of the ships sunk. The supplies lost on these ships substantially weakened Von Arnim's fighting strength and helped to bring about the defeat that Warlimont had feared.

The surrender of the Axis armies in Tunisia on 12 May 1943 brought to a successful conclusion the long campaign in North Africa, Malta's contribution to which has been the subject of the second part of this study. From that point Malta's offensive capability, strengthened by an increasing flow of supplies from east and west, was re-directed to the invasion of Sicily, which had been agreed, after much debate, at the Casablanca Conference in January.[84] Thus Malta, if only for geographical reasons, became the forward HQ for Operation 'Husky', launched on 10 July 1943. For this purpose her harbours were crammed with assault vessels and supporting naval ships. No fewer than 35 squadrons of aircraft were assembled, three of them Spitfire squadrons of the USAAF flying from a new airfield on Gozo, built from fields in 17 days.[85]

The capture of Sicily was followed by the Allied invasion of Italy itself, and on 8 September 1943 Italy surrendered. By one of those fortunate accidents of history this was the day, celebrated in Malta, and especially in the heavily damaged Grand Harbour community of Senglea, as the feast day of our Lady of the Nativity, on which the Great

Siege of 1565 ended. Malta's endurance of her second Great Siege was fittingly marked on 10–11 September by the arrival in her waters of the main units of the Italian fleet. As Admiral Cunningham, after receiving the Italian fleet surrender, proudly signalled to the Admiralty: 'Be pleased to inform their Lordships that the Italian battle fleet now lies at anchor under the guns of the fortress of Malta.'[86]

12

Conclusion

In the first part of this study reasons have been sought to explain the condition of Malta's defences when Italy declared war in June 1940. Had the island been written off as indefensible, as continues to be alleged? Even if not, had the authorities neglected to provide adequate defences? How weak were Malta's defences when war broke out, and why were they not stronger? To answer these questions fully it has been considered necessary to follow the twists and turns of events throughout the inter-war period. In this span of 20 years British military policy and planning was shaped by profound and often unexpected changes in national relationships, not the least of which were the circumstances that led to the enmity of two countries that had been allies in the First World War. Economic conditions were also uncertain. After a gradual recovery from the destruction and dislocation of the Great War, the British and European economies were thrown into a new crisis by the Wall Street 'crash' of 1929. Recovery demanded, by the economic tenets of the time, severe reductions in public expenditure from which defence spending was not exempt. These were also years in which technical developments in the military sphere raised questions to which past experience could offer no reliable answers. Prominent among these was the growing power of military aircraft, particularly the bomber, and it was not until late in the inter-war period that the means to counter the bomber threat began to emerge.

It is in the context of these unpredictably changing political, economic and technical conditions that the defensive needs of Malta were considered and decided. Malta's requirements could not be considered in isolation, or as a priority, but the voluminous records in the government archives make clear that the modernisation of the island's defences attracted continual attention. Certainly, it was not a failure to consider the defensive deficiencies, or to make plans to remove them, that explain their condition in 1940. Rather, explanations must be sought in the interplay of many diverse factors, and the strategic choices that followed from them.

The modernisation of Malta's pre-war defence system has been considered in three phases, each characterised by special features that affected the progress of improvements. The first was the decade of the 1920s and the others the two halves of the 1930s. It was in the first period that Malta's role in relation to the Far East became established and its function as the base from which the Main Fleet would, if necessary, move east was determined. There was at that time no question, certainly in military minds, of any retreat from Empire. Against the provision of shrinking resources to meet expanding commitments the Chiefs of Staff constantly complained, but no thought was given to cutting those commitments. On the contrary, the massive expenditure at Singapore marked a resolve to defend the most distant and vulnerable part of the Empire; the need to defend Malta was taken for granted. However, the pace of modernisation in this period was slow for a variety of reasons but what above all delayed the implementation of defence plans in the 1920s was the hope for continued international peace based on an expanding world economy.

It was this hope that was shattered in the early years of the next decade as the effects of the Wall Street crash of 1929 worked their way through the international economic structure. In such circumstances there was little hope that any significant amounts could be spared for Malta's defences. Moreover, the island's low claim to resources was reinforced by the belief, not shared by all, that Italy's continued friendship could be relied upon. In November 1933, therefore, when the first modest re-armament programme was being debated, it was decided that no defences against Italian attack need be prepared. Despite this ruling the military planners sought ways to continue the modernisation of Malta's defences and first Portal and then Harris for the RAF argued strenuously that as many as five squadrons were needed as part of Malta's defences with more airfields to accommodate them.

At the end of this second phase the Abyssinian crisis of 1935–36 removed the convenient assumption of Italian friendship and exposed the risks that had been run at Malta. The Cabinet then formally declared that every effort was to be made to defend Malta and this was agreed without significant debate once the Chiefs of Staff had recommended it. No Minister or other official argued the case for the abandonment of the island notwithstanding the departure of the Fleet, and the principle thus established was never subsequently challenged in the pre-war years. That this decision was so easily made without any dissent is important for a correct understanding of the decisions concerning Malta made in the remaining third period before Italy's declaration of war in June 1940. Although the Admiralty decided to improve the facilities at Alexandria the notion of 'writing off' Malta simply did not arise. In the years between the end of the Abyssinian crisis in June 1936 and June 1940 what the Chiefs of Staff and their planners wrestled with was not whether to defend Malta but what use could be made of the air and naval bases there in the event of a conflict with Italy, and how resources were to be found to allow such use.

The struggle to strengthen Malta's defences in the late thirties has been considered in Chapter 4 but two points bear repeating here. The absence of any modern fighter aircraft at Malta when Italy declared war has been taken to prove that the Air Staff considered that Malta was 'indefensible', an allegation still being published. This is a misunderstanding of the RAF's position and derives from a failure to distinguish between the general defence of the island against invasion and the more specific task of providing sufficient air cover for the naval dockyard to permit its use by the Mediterranean Fleet. In the case of Malta the Air Staff were certainly confronted with a difficult problem. Despite Fighter Command's encouraging developments in eight-gun fighters and an effective radar system the RAF's generally held belief until 1940 was that the bomber, Italian as well as British, would get through to achieve its strategic objective. Malta's location and size exacerbated the problem of defending against such a threat. Nevertheless, the Air Staff developed a defensive plan that was clearly explained by AVM Ludlow-Hewitt as early as 1934 and repeated at the CID investigation in 1939. Since Malta could not accommodate an air force large enough to resist by itself a large-scale Italian attack a counter-attacking force based in neighbouring French territory, the availability of which was taken for granted, became an essential element in the defence plan. Such counter-attacks would reduce the weight of attack on Malta to a level that could be contained by local air and gun defences. In this way the RAF intended to play a part in the overall defence of Malta against possible invasion in order to secure its use at least for light forces.

However, the Air Staff, despite their proposed contribution to the general defence of the island, remained doubtful about the RAF's ability to make the naval dockyard sufficiently safe for its use as a main base by the Mediterranean Fleet. It was this question, not whether Malta as a whole could be defended, but whether the dockyard could be made safe by a much larger defence establishment, that is Scale B, that the JDC was instructed to examine in 1939. On this question the services could not reach agreement, and later events were to show that both sides were partially correct in their forecasts. The Admiralty rightly anticipated that Italian air attacks would be intermittent and would peter out as their losses rose. On the other hand the Air Staff correctly saw that, even with a Scale B level of AA guns and modern fighters, heavy air attacks, albeit German rather than Italian, would make the dockyard unusable. Nevertheless, in 1939 Ministers voted for the provision of Scale B partly in the hope that this might increase the operational value of the island, but also convinced in any event that prestige and honour demanded that every effort be made to defend an imperial possession and protect its people.

This brings us to the second point that requires re-emphasis. The implementation of whatever decisions were taken about Malta's defences was governed by the fundamental shortage of resources, especially fighter aircraft, trained pilots and modern AA guns, coupled with the inevitable subordination of Malta's claims to those of Home Defence. Time and again plans to strengthen Malta's defences were deferred or watered down not because they were not agreed to be necessary, but because other claims, initially at Singapore and later in Britain, came first. This is the key to a proper understanding of the state of Malta's defences in 1940. Although Scale B was approved in July 1939, everyone realised that it could not be implemented for several years. Consequently, as time ran out and the Admiralty pointed out that half measures would not provide the security required, such few guns, aircraft and pilots as could be spared from Home Defence followed the Mediterranean Fleet to its war station at Alexandria. To provide larger defences for an empty dockyard at Valletta when Alexandria had even fewer defences made no sense.

What is surprising, therefore, is not that Malta's defences were inadequate to allow the Mediterranean Fleet's use of its principal dockyard, but that they were as strong as they were. Despite the low priority given to Malta's needs an AA establishment of only 12 obsolescent 3-inch guns in early 1939 was increased a year later to 34 heavy AA guns, of which 18 were modern 4.5-inch or 3.7-inch, and eight light guns. This scale of AA defences compared favourably with that at other major UK and overseas ports. Although none of the remaining 9.2-inch guns had been placed on 35° mountings, the coastal artillery had been significantly modernised. It was provided with the latest ammunition, improved lights, range finding and communications equipment and was in much better condition to engage a bombarding force. The infantry garrison had been raised to war establishment by drafts and in May 1940 a fifth battalion arrived. In addition, growing numbers of Maltese had been recruited into the KOMR and the RMA to augment the garrison and to man both the coastal and AA guns. Finally, although the long-agreed fighter squadron had still not been formed, three airfields, including the main all-weather runway at Luqa, were ready, and the first mobile radar had been installed with another two on their way. Without the long-term provision of these costly facilities the RAF could not so quickly have operated a fighter force at Malta when the aircraft became available. In the light of these facts the claim that Malta was written off as indefensible simply collapses.

CONCLUSION

Why this allegation was made and continues in circulation is due in part to Roskill's brief comments quoted in the Introduction. When writing the official naval history in the 1950s, Roskill was anxious to press on the authorities the avoidable risks that had been taken in the pre-war years. Perhaps under this influence what he wrote about Malta in the official history was, at best, misleading, and the statement in the later one-volume history simply incorrect. Later writers, such as Ian Cameron, who had no access to official papers, misquoted Roskill, and Gabriele, quoting Cameron, then attributes to the Chiefs of Staff the statement: *'Nulla può essere fatto per difendere Malta'* (Nothing can be done to defend Malta).[1] Those later writers who have repeated this version of the position, despite having access to the relevant records, have simply ignored them.

The truth is that Malta was in 1940 somewhat better prepared than might reasonably have been expected given the dire shortage of war material and trained men, and this was due in no small part to Maltese co-operation. Throughout the first part of this study attention has been directed to the need to retain Maltese support for British policies and aims without which military operations might have proved impossible. Given the pro-Italian sympathies of the Nationalist Party and the suspension of the 1921 Constitution, this was not an easy task. Largely, however, due to the sensible policies pursued between 1936 and 1940 by the Governor, Sir Charles Bonham-Carter, and to the re-establishment of some measure of self-government and firmer measures to counter pro-Italian influence, the risk of internal disruption slowly faded. By June 1940 thousands of Maltese had voluntarily joined the armed services and civil defence units and fewer than 60 were taken into detention.

After Italy's declaration of war and the first bombing attacks on Malta, there can be no doubt about the scale of the attempt to derive maximum advantage from the bases on the island. For this Churchill was largely responsible. At the very beginning of his premiership Cabinet records show his determination not to surrender Malta or any other British territory in an attempt to win Italian neutrality. A month later, even as the French collapse and the loss of her powerful Mediterranean fleet loomed, he rejected Pound's proposal to withdraw the British Mediterranean Fleet from Alexandria. As the shape of the Mediterranean war unfolded, his many minutes about Malta show his determination that as powerful a force as possible be established there to defend the island and to harass Italy. His 'prodding' of the Chiefs of Staff and area commanders was not always welcome, and at times resisted. He failed to persuade Pound and Cunningham to establish Force K at Malta in the summer of 1941 and it has been suggested in Chapter 9 that the earlier establishment of this force might have increased the pressure on Rommel's supply position during the 'Crusader' offensive. In mid-December 1941 Rommel stood close to total defeat.

In 1942 Churchill, angered by the manner of Singapore's surrender, fiercely opposed Auchinleck's plan to delay his next offensive, fearful that Malta, recently awarded the George Cross for its heroic resistance, might then be lost, and it was he who ordered the massive 'Pedestal' relief convoy in August 1942. These are but a few examples, more fully described in the previous chapters, of Churchill's determination that, on the one hand, Malta and its people were entitled to British protection, and, on the other, that the island had a valuable part to play in the defeat of the Axis. Without such powerful advocacy it is possible that Malta might have been lost.

Exactly what Malta's role was to be in a Mediterranean war had been the subject of continual debate in the pre-war period, but events showed that the most realistic forecast was that it would make an ideal base for light forces. Before weighing what those forces achieved, it is important to recognise that Malta's most likely contribution was seen in terms of an 'irritant' or, more frequently, as a 'thorn in the enemy's side', not as a war-winning asset. The location and size of the island imposed strict limitations on the size of the air and naval forces that could be based there, and these could only assist the main forces based in Egypt and the eastern Mediterranean by attacking Italian supply routes and by 'fixing', in Bonham-Carter's phrase, some enemy forces. It would only have been expected to play a broader role had it been possible to base units of the Main Fleet there.

What was actually achieved and what contribution Malta made to the war in North Africa has been examined in detail in the second part of this study. We may first review what may be called Malta's non-offensive functions. Easily discounted, and often scarcely recognised, is Malta's dual air force role as a staging post for aircraft *en route* to the Middle and Far East, and as a reconnaissance base. Some figures have been quoted to show the steady flow of transit aircraft through Malta, but the reconnaissance effort cannot be so easily summarised. 69 Squadron at Malta eventually comprised a collection of high-flying PR Spitfires and, later, a few Mosquitoes, one or two Beaufighters, a number of long-range Marylands and Baltimores, and several ASV-equipped Wellingtons. These aircraft, as numbers and experience grew, gathered invaluable intelligence about enemy dispositions and movements, directed submarines and surface ships on to distant targets, and, not least, provided the essential 'cover' for information already known from Enigma intercepts. These advantages, particularly in the first 18 months of the war, deserve greater recognition than has usually been accorded them. Eventually more aircraft reached Egypt by the

CONCLUSION

Takoradi transit route and long-range reconnaissance aircraft were subsequently based in Egypt and later in Tunisia, but throughout the war in the Mediterranean the staging and reconnaissance capabilities of Malta were of great value.

An additional non-offensive function was that of 'fixing' or, in Churchill's phrase, 'consuming' some of the enemy's forces to deflect pressure from British and American forces in North Africa. Quite apart from the losses suffered by the Italian air force in attacking Malta, some figures for which have been quoted, the *Luftwaffe* also lost considerable numbers during the two winter periods when substantial forces were withdrawn from the Russian front to bases in Sicily. For example, in the period from December 1941 to November 1942 the Germans admitted the loss of 249 aircraft and damage to another 60. Another compilation for just fighter-caused losses between June 1940 and October 1942 shows 863 Axis aircraft destroyed, 316 probably destroyed and 814 damaged. Unspecified additional losses were caused by AA fire.[2] Whatever the actual figures, and they are difficult to determine with precision, losses on this scale undoubtedly reduced the forces that otherwise would have been deployed against the Allied armies in North Africa. Perhaps the best illustration of the diversion caused by Malta is Hitler's order to Kesselring to neutralise the island in October 1942 when Montgomery was making his final dispositions for his offensive at Alamein on 23 October. This final blitz was called off after a week due to unacceptable losses, and on several other occasions Kesselring reported that his aircrews were exhausted.

Taking all these non-offensive functions together and giving them their proper weight, it may be estimated that they constituted as much as one half of the overall advantage that Britain gained from the retention of Malta's air and naval bases. The other half of Malta's value, and the one that has attracted more attention, was the contribution of its forces to the destruction, damage or delay of the supplies flowing continually from Italy to North Africa. Italian and some British historians have made clear the many factors that made the supply of the Axis forces in North Africa a difficult problem quite apart from the risk of losses at sea. These range from the limited productive capacity of the poorly organised Italian war economy, the dispersion of available war material to new fronts in the Balkans and Russia, the steady erosion of the Italian merchant fleet and its escorts that could only partially be replaced by new building, the extemporised and inefficient mini-convoy system that the Italian navy adopted, the limited capacity and poor management of the unloading ports, and the shortage of lorries and efficient repair and maintenance facilities in North Africa. It was a supply chain with many weak links.

It was the flow of material along this vulnerable supply route that Malta's forces attacked, first at the loading ports in Italy, then along the sea passage, and finally at the unloading ports and supply dumps in North Africa. The contribution of RAF Malta to the loss of supplies caused by bombing and strafing attacks at both ends of the sea crossing cannot be measured with precision. AVM Lloyd continually flew his bombers and torpedo-bombers as weather, blitz conditions and serviceability permitted and there can be no doubt in general terms of the cumulative value of this offensive. The Wellington raid on Palermo on the night of 2/3 March 1942, during which three supply ships were sunk and dozens of others damaged, is just one striking example of this continual air assault on the Axis supply chain.[3]

Nevertheless, it is the attack on the Axis trans-Mediterranean shipping that constitutes Malta's most measurable contribution to the depletion of Axis supplies in North Africa. Throughout this study official British and Italian records have been used to identify those Axis merchant ships sunk or damaged by forces operating from Malta. The overall results of this analysis are summarised in Table 19. It should be emphasised that this method of calculating Malta's contribution to Axis supply losses understates that contribution in several ways. It measures only Malta's share of shipping tonnage sunk and these loss figures can only be generally related to the supply losses shown. More detailed tables in earlier chapters show the proportionately higher fuel losses resulting from Enigma-directed targeting. More importantly, these figures take no account of those ships and cargoes that were damaged and failed to reach North Africa, those that were delayed or returned to harbour because they were threatened by attack, and those that were sunk or damaged by other forces while sailing on a longer route to stay out of range of Malta. Bearing these qualifications in mind, Malta's overall 58 per cent share of Axis shipping losses is a conservative and objective measure of Malta's contribution to Axis supply shortages.

TABLE 19
AXIS SUPPLY AND SHIPPING LOSSES IN THE CENTRAL MEDITERRANEAN, 1940–43

Period	Supplies lost (%)	Total ships sunk (tons)	Sunk by Malta forces (tons)	Malta share (%)
1. June–Dec. 1940	2.3	101,150	20,713	21
2. Jan.–June 1941	6.2	184,563	113,400	61
3. July–Dec. 1941	26.8	318,683	272,722	86
4. Jan.–June 1942	5.9	154,965	83,707	54
5. July–Dec. 1942	24.7	290,387	171,390	59
6. Jan.–May 1943	31.1	421,057	189,929	45
Totals	16.3	1,470,805	851,861	58

Source: See Appendix.

CONCLUSION

It is the failure to analyse in detail the results of Malta's attacks on Axis convoys, coupled with the almost total disregard of the island's non-offensive advantages, that undermines the assessments of Malta's value made by Van Creveld and Barnett. Without undertaking such an analysis Van Creveld concluded that losses at sea, to which the figures above demonstrate that Malta made the major contribution, were of less importance than logistical bottlenecks in North Africa. This interpretation, however, conflicts with the Enigma evidence, which shows that bulk losses at sea repeatedly caused greater concern to the Axis authorities. Moreover, it fails to explain the constant diversion of Axis aircraft to suppress Malta and to protect convoys at the expense of air support in North Africa. Barnett's judgement, based on Van Creveld's interpretation, that the damage caused by Malta's forces did not justify the 'grievous losses' incurred in sustaining the island, is even less convincing since he made no attempt to analyse and measure either the damage caused or the costs incurred. The evidence examined in the second part of this study, of which the results of Malta's attacks on Axis convoys are summarised in Table 19, shows that the assessments of Van Creveld and Barnett cannot be accepted.

Equally, however, the evidence will not support the views of Macintyre and others that Malta's attack on the convoys was the *decisive* factor in causing Axis defeat in the North African campaign. There were several periods when, under fierce air attack, Malta's contribution was limited to the non-offensive tasks described above. Giorgerini has correctly observed that 84 per cent of the total supplies sent to North Africa arrived and even in the worst periods of 1942 and early 1943 roughly two-thirds of the supplies arrived. It was only in the last quarter of 1941 that Malta's forces came close to stopping supplies altogether. To achieve a complete blockade was beyond the capabilities of what was always a small force so long as the Italian authorities persisted.

The analysis presented in this study shows that no one factor was decisive in the strict sense that it determined the outcome. In a prolonged see-saw conflict the balance of advantage repeatedly swung from one side to the other and Allied victory was only achieved when resources that the Axis could not match were brought to bear together with sufficient fighting skill to make the material superiority count. However, it follows that where the relative advantages were so evenly distributed the addition or removal of one element of the equation could tip the balance to one side or the other. It is no coincidence that Rommel's two successful campaigns in early 1941 and early 1942 were carried out when Malta was neutralised by *Luftwaffe* attack and supplies flowed freely, and that British successes were achieved in periods of greater Malta pressure on the stream of Axis supplies.

Weighing the relative importance of factors as diverse as supplies, Intelligence and air power can only be subjective but there is no reason to question Rommel's considered assessment. While reticent about his own strategic miscalculations, he judged that, among the external factors outside his control, supply shortages ranked only second to Allied air power in causing his defeat.

The conclusion that most satisfactorily explains the evidence examined in the second part of this study is that Malta's destruction of roughly 60 per cent of the Axis ships lost and of the supplies they carried, when added to the equally valuable if less quantifiable non-offensive benefits that the British derived from the use of the island's naval and air bases, was of major importance to the winning of the war in North Africa. This contribution surpassed what might reasonably have been expected in June 1940 and fully justified the pre-war defence planning and the subsequent decisions by the Chiefs of Staff, urged on by Churchill, that every effort be made to defend the island and to develop its military value. In their assessment of the influence of Enigma intercepts on the Mediterranean war, Hinsley suggested that, without that contribution, the conquest of North Africa might have been set back by at least a year.[4] It is not unreasonable to conclude that the absence of Malta's contribution might have had similar consequences.

Appendix: Axis Supply and Shipping Losses

SUPPLY LOSSES

The various tables showing the volume and composition of the supplies despatched to and landed in North Africa are drawn from the official Italian naval history, *La Marina Italiana nella seconda guerra mondiale, Vol. I, Dati Statistici* (USMM, Rome, 1950–72), Table liv, pp. 124–27.

SHIPPING LOSSES

In 1955 the Air Historical Branch (AHB) of the Air Ministry undertook a detailed analysis of Axis shipping losses in the Mediterranean during the Second World War. The results are contained in the AIR 20/9598 file at the Public Record Office at Kew under the title 'Enemy Shipping Losses in the Mediterranean, 10 June 1940 to 2 May 1945'. This analysis was compiled from existing Italian and German records, the information contained in vol. III of *Lloyd's War Losses: The Second World War*, and the records of the Admiralty and Air Ministry. The file contains numerous summaries but its main purpose was to establish what caused the loss of 3,082 merchant ships with an aggregate tonnage of 4,147,523 tons. In the great majority of cases the location and general cause of loss – that is, whether by aircraft, surface ship, submarine or mine – can be accurately established, but as the Introduction to the analysis notes, 'a number of cases are susceptible to more than one interpretation'. Moreover, 646 ships, aggregating 243,656 tons, were lost for unknown causes. In some instances the ship, submarine or squadron responsible for a particular loss is noted, but none of the summaries sought to identify separately those losses incurred in supplying the Axis armies in North Africa, or losses caused by forces operating from Malta. A recently published analysis of submarine operations, J. Rohwer's *Allied Submarine Attacks of World War Two: European Theatre of Operations 1939–1945* (Greenhill Books, London, 1997), drawing on the latest research, has permitted one or two adjustments to the AHB record. Additional information about specific attacks is given in many of the books cited in this study, for example, those by Poolman, Gillman and Wingate, which describe air and naval operations from Malta.

From these various, not always consistent, sources the tables of Axis shipping losses presented in this study have been compiled. They analyse the contribution of air and naval forces operating from Malta to the sinking of the 394 Axis merchant ships of more than 500 tons in the central Mediterranean between June 1940 and May 1943. Of this number 210 were sunk by forces operating from Malta. The 'central Mediterranean' for this purpose is taken to be the general area extending from Sardinia to the west, Crete and the west coast of Greece to the east, the Bay of Naples to the north, and the North African coast to the south. Several ships sunk by submarines operating from Malta outside this area, for example in the Adriatic or off the French coast, have been ignored.

In virtually every case the identity of the submarine, surface ship or aircraft responsible, sometimes on a shared basis, for each sinking is known. In most cases, too, it is clear whether or not the attacker was 'operating from Malta'. This definition includes aircraft and surface ships based at Malta, if only for a limited period, and also the submarines of the U-class. Most of the larger submarines of the O, P, R, S, and T classes were officially based at Alexandria, Gibraltar or later at Algiers. However, on their patrols into the central Mediterranean they usually called at Malta to rest their crews, re-fuel, re-charge their batteries and re-load with torpedoes. In these cases they came under the operational orders of Captain Simpson after his arrival at Malta in January 1941. This was particularly true at the time of the 'Torch' landings at the end of 1942 when Simpson controlled as many as 26 submarines of all classes. Where it is clear from the operational detail that a particular sinking was caused by a submarine operating from, although not formally based at, Malta, these losses have been included in the Malta figures. On the other hand, the ships sunk by mines laid by HMS *Rorqual*, although included in the central Mediterranean totals where appropriate, have not been counted in the Malta figures. This mine-laying submarine, although based at Alexandria, and later at Algiers, was a frequent visitor to Malta since the island had the only mine depot in the Mediterranean. Its mines, laid in various locations accounted for numerous Axis ships, including the German tank carrier *Ankara*, in February 1943.

The nature of the underlying records does not permit complete accuracy or certainty, but it is considered that the tables presented in this study provide a conservative estimate of the Axis shipping losses in the central Mediterranean that can be attributed to forces operating from Malta.

Notes

Introduction

1. A. Levine, *The War against Rommel's Supply Lines 1942–1943* (Praeger, Westport, CT, 1999), p. 6.
2. C. Jellison, *Beseiged: The World War II Ordeal of Malta 1940–1942* (University Press of New England, Hanover, NH, 1984), p. 22.
3. D. Macintyre, *The Battle for the Mediterranean* (Batsford, London, 1964), p. 16.
4. M. van Creveld, *Supplying War: Logistics from Wallenstein to Patton* (Cambridge University Press, Cambridge, 1977), pp. 181–201.
5. C. Barnett, *Engage the Enemy More Closely: The Royal Navy in the Second World War* (Penguin, London, 2000), p. 525.
6. M'A. Bragadin, *The Italian Navy in World War II* (United States Naval Institute, Annapolis, MD, 1977), p. 20; G. Giorgerini, *La battaglia dei convogli in Mediterraneo* (Mursia, Milan, 1977), p. 78.
7. N. Gibbs, *Rearmament Policy*, vol. I (1976) of *Grand Strategy*, 6 vols (Her Majesty's Stationery Office, London, 1954), pp. 187–222.
8. Major-General I. Playfair *et al.*, *The Mediterranean and Middle East*, 6 vols (Her Majesty's Stationery Office, London, 1954–73).
9. S. Roskill, *The War at Sea*, 3 vols (Her Majesty's Stationery Office, London, 1954–61), vol. I, p. 77; idem, *The Navy at War 1939–1945* (Collins, London, 1960), p. 101.
10. D. Rollo, *The Guns and Gunners of Malta* (Mondial Publishers, Malta, 1999).
11. T. Spooner, *Supreme Gallantry; Malta's Role in the Allied Victory* (John Murray, London, 1996).
12. F. Hinsley *et al.*, *British Intelligence in the Second World War*, 5 vols (Her Majesty's Stationery Office, London, 1979–90).
13. G. Schreiber *et al.*, *Germany and the Second World War*, vols III and VI (Clarendon Press, Oxford, 1995, 2001).
14. B. Liddell Hart (ed.), *The Rommel Papers* (Collins, London, 1955), p. 289.
15. Ufficio Storico della Marina Militare (hereafter USMM), *La Marina Italiana nella Seconda Guerra Mondiale*, 19 vols (Rome, 1950–72).

1: The Base at Malta in the 1920s

(Note: The prefix PRO denotes a document held at the Public Record Office, Kew.)
1. See P. Halpern, *A Naval History of World War I* (UCL Press, London, 1995), pp. 6–7; P. Kennedy, *The Rise and Fall of British Naval Mastery* (Fontana, London, 1991), p. 268.
2. PRO ADM 116/3195, M.0472/22, 'Strategical Review of the Naval Situation after Washington, as Affecting the Peace Distribution of the Fleet', 24 February 1922.
3. S. Roskill, *Naval Policy between the Wars*, 2 vols (Collins, London, 1968, 1981), vol. I, p. 536.
4. PRO CAB 3/5, CID Memorandum 119-C, 'Naval Situation in the Far East', 31 October 1919.
5. *Treaty between the British Empire, France, Italy, Japan and the United States of America*

for the Limitation of Naval Armaments, Cmd. 2036 (His Majesty's Stationery Office, London, 1924).
6. PRO CAB 23/26, Cabinet 50(21), 16 June 1921.
7. PRO CAB 8/53, ODC Memorandum 537-M, 'Some General Principles of Imperial Defence', 12 March 1928.
8. PRO ADM 167/67, Board Minute 1760, 'Redistribution of the Fleet', 13 December 1923.
9. PRO CAB 4/12, CID Memorandum 557-B, 'Diversion of British Shipping in Time of War', 5 January 1925.
10. PRO ADM 116/3195, Director of Plans Minute, 24 February 1922.
11. PRO ADM 116/3195, Plans Division Memorandum, 'Redistribution of the Fleet', 23 October 1923.
12. PRO ADM 116/3195, 'Remarks by the C-in-C Mediterranean', 20 June 1923.
13. PRO ADM 116/3195, Plans Division Memorandum, 'Redistribution of the Fleet', 23 October 1923.
14. PRO CAB 23/47, Cabinet 18(24), 5 March 1924.
15. PRO CAB 2/4, CID 199th Meeting, 2 April 1925.
16. PRO CAB 23/50, Cabinet 24(25), 6 May 1925.
17. PRO CAB 2/4, CID 199th Meeting, 2 April 1925.
18. PRO ADM 116/3125, 'War Memorandum (Eastern)', Appendix B, 29 August 1924.
19. Ibid.
20. Admiral Keyes's report on Exercise 'MU', carried out in August 1925, is reprinted in P. Halpern (ed.), *The Keyes Papers, Vol. II, 1919–1938* (Navy Records Society, London, 1980), pp. 152–55.
21. PRO ADM 116/3195, Memorandum by Director of Operations Division, 1 September 1923.
22. PRO CAB 36/1, JDC 1st Meeting, 24 March 1920.
23. The Minutes and Memoranda of the JDC and DOP are in CAB 36/1–13 and 36/21, respectively; the Minutes of the ODC are in CAB 7/9–15 and the Memoranda in CAB 8/1–56.
24. PRO CAB 4/15, CID Memorandum 700-B, 'Summary of Defence Policy', Appendix F, 15 June 1926.
25. PRO CAB 36/6, JDC Memorandum 66, 'Coast Defence: Forms of Attack and Forms of Defence', 23 November 1927.
26. PRO CAB 11/190, 'Malta Defence Scheme 1935'.
27. PRO CAB 36/6, JDC Memorandum 59, 'Order of Priority for Installation of Armament', 9 May 1927, and JDC Memorandum 77, 'Classification of Defended Ports Abroad', 25 June 1928.
28. PRO CAB 36/1, JDC 8th Meeting, 16 February 1926.
29. Sir Maurice Dean, *The Royal Air Force and Two World Wars* (Cassell, London, 1979), p. 40.
30. PRO CAB 53/1, COS 35th Meeting, 6 July 1926.
31. PRO CAB 24/307, CP 332 (29), 'The Fuller Employment of Air Power in Imperial Defence', Section VI, 'Air Forces in Coast Defence', November 1929.
32. PRO ADM 116/2654, 'Berthing Arrangements at Malta 1928–30'.
33. PRO WO 32/2409, 'KOMR: Re-organisation on a Territorial Basis, 1929–34'.
34. PRO WO 32/10211, 'Royal Malta Artillery–Improvement of Terms and Conditions of Service, 1925–28'.
35. A detailed account of Malta's gun defences is given in Rollo, *The Guns*.
36. The early history of the RAF in Malta is described in J. Hamlin, *Military Aviation in Malta G.C. 1915–1993* (GMS Enterprises, Peterborough, 1994).
37. PRO CAB 8/53, ODC Memorandum 513-M, 'Malta: Vulnerability to Air Attack', 18 February 1926.
38. PRO CAB 8/9, Air Staff Memorandum ODC-147, 'Vulnerability of Malta to Air Attack', 23 February 1925.
39. PRO CAB 7/9, ODC 267th Meeting, 15 December 1925.
40. PRO CAB 36/21, DOP(M) 11, 'Malta: Scales of Seafront and Anti-Aircraft Defence', 29 May 1928.
41. PRO CAB 36/21, DOP(M) 12, 'Air Defence of Malta', 14 June 1928.

NOTES

42. PRO CAB 36/21, DOP(M) 16, 'Malta: Defence against Seaborne Land Attack', [n.d. *c.* July 1928].
43. PRO CAB 16/67, CID Memorandum 866-B, 'Report of the Anti-Aircraft Research Sub-Committee', 24 March 1928.
44. PRO CAB 16/67, War Office Memorandum, 'Anti-Aircraft Gunnery Equipment', 21 February 1927.
45. PRO WO 32/4121, 'Malta: Employment of RAF. Appreciation by Air Officer Commanding', 21 February 1936.
46. PRO CAB 4/15, CID Memorandum 701-B, 'A Review of Imperial Defence, 1926', 22 June 1926.
47. See W. Hancock, *Survey of British Commonwealth Affairs, Vol. I, Problems of Nationality* (Oxford University Press, London, 1937), pp. 406–28; also H. Frendo, *Party Politics in a Fortress Colony: The Maltese Experience* (Midsea Publications, Valletta, 1991), pp. 183–218.
48. Quoted in Frendo, *Party Politics*, p. 100.
49. L. S. Amery, *My Political Life, Vol. II, War and Peace 1914–1929* (Hutchinson, London, 1953), p. 196.
50. A. Cassels, *Mussolini's Early Diplomacy* (Princeton University Press, Princeton, NJ, 1970), p. 86.
51. Major-General Sir Kenneth Strong, *Intelligence at the Top: The Recollections of an Intelligence Officer* (Cassell, London, 1968), pp. 11–13.
52. PRO CO 158/441/22110, Lt.-Gov. to Colonial Office, 19 April 1927.

2: *The Failure to Strengthen Malta's Defences, 1930–35*

1. PRO CAB 53/12, COS Memorandum 41, 'Review of Imperial Defence, 1926', 22 June 1926.
2. PRO CAB 53/21, COS Memorandum 247, 'Review of Imperial Defence, 1930', 29 July 1930.
3. M. Smith, *British Air Strategy between the Wars* (Clarendon Press, Oxford, 1984), p. 336.
4. PRO CAB 36/7, JDC Memorandum 104, 'The Defence of Ports at Home and Abroad', 3 May 1929.
5. PRO CAB 53/1, COS 35th Meeting, 6 July 1926.
6. PRO CAB 7/9, ODC 263rd Meeting, 21 July 1924.
7. PRO CAB 53/17, COS Memorandum 182, 'Summary of the Reports Received by the War Office on the Coast Defence Trials Held at Malta and Portsmouth, 1928', 3 January 1929; see also Rollo, *The Guns*, pp. 160–63.
8. PRO CAB 36/7, JDC Memorandum 133, War Office Minute, 10 April 1931.
9. PRO CAB 2/5, CID 239th Meeting, 13 December 1928.
10. PRO CAB 16/105, CID Memorandum 370-C, 'Coast Defence. Report of Sub-Committee', 24 May 1932.
11. PRO CAB 16/105, Memorandum CD-9, 15 February 1932.
12. PRO CAB 16/105, CID Memorandum 370-C, 24 May 1932, para. 28.
13. PRO CAB 16/105, CID Memorandum 370-C, 24 May 1932, para. 54(b).
14. Marshal of the Royal Air Force Sir John Slessor, *The Central Blue: Recollections and Reflections* (Cassell, London, 1956), p. 74.
15. PRO CAB 36/1, JDC 23rd Meeting, 18 October 1932.
16. B. Bond (ed.), *Chief of Staff: The Diaries of Lieutenant-General Sir Henry Pownall, Vol. I, 1933–40* (Leo Cooper, London, 1972), pp. 15–16.
17. PRO CAB 36/1, JDC 24th Meeting, 2 February 1933; details in Rollo, *The Guns*, pp. 164–6.
18. PRO CAB 36/21, DOP 2nd Meeting, 19 July 1928.
19. PRO CAB 36/3, JDC 25th Meeting, 27 April 1933.
20. M. Postan, D. Hay and J. Scott, *Design and Development of Weapons: Studies in Government and Industrial Organisation* (Her Majesty's Stationery Office, London, 1964), p. 355.
21. B. Liddell Hart, *The Defence of Britain* (Faber and Faber, London, 1939), pp. 166–7.

22. PRO ADM 116/3473, Fisher to Admiralty, 20 June 1933; Admiralty to Fisher, 3 October 1933.
23. PRO AIR 8/138, 'RAF Confidential Intelligence Summaries 1931-5', pp. 233-42.
24. PRO CAB 53/22, COS Memorandum 274, 'The Air Threat to our Sea Communications in the Mediterranean', Appendix C, 8 July 1931.
25. PRO CAB 16/105, Memorandum CD-10, 'Effectiveness of Modern Anti-Aircraft Fire', 29 February 1932.
26. PRO CAB 36/6, JDC Memorandum 66, 'Coast Defence. Forms of Attack and Forms of Defence', 23 November 1927.
27. PRO CAB 53/22, COS Memorandum 274, 'The Air Threat to Our Sea Communications in the Mediterranean', 8 July 1931.
28. PRO CAB 53/4, COS 109th Meeting, 11 April 1933.
29. PRO CAB 36/3, JDC 24th and 25th Meetings, 2 February and 27 April 1933.
30. See Admiral Chatfield's letter of 1 June 1933 to Admiral Dreyer in the Chatfield Papers, National Maritime Museum, CHT/4/4.
31. PRO CAB 53/23, COS Memorandum 305, 'The Situation in the Far East', 31 March 1933.
32. PRO CAB 53/4, COS 108th Meeting, 27 March 1933.
33. PRO CAB 2/5, CID 258th Meeting, 6 April 1933; CAB 23/75, Cabinet 27(33), 12 April 1933.
34. PRO CAB 36/3, JDC 25th Meeting, 27 April 1933.
35. PRO CAB 53/4, COS 110th Meeting, 2 May 1933.
36. Bond, *Pownall*, p. 15.
37. PRO ADM 116/3473, Fisher to Admiralty, 20 June 1933.
38. Chatfield Papers, National Maritime Museum, CHT/4/5, Fisher letter to Chatfield, 21 July 1933.
39. PRO ADM 116/3473, Admiralty to Fisher, 3 October 1933.
40. PRO CAB 36/7, JDC Memorandum 166, 'Defence of Ports at Home and Abroad, Malta', 4 July 1933.
41. PRO CAB 36/3, JDC 26th Meeting, 28 July 1933.
42. PRO CAB 53/23, COS Memorandum 310, 'A Review of Imperial Defence, 1933', 12 October 1933.
43. PRO CAB 2/6, CID 261st Meeting, 9 November 1933.
44. Ibid.
45. PRO CAB 53/23, COS Memorandum 307, 'The Foreign Policy of His Majesty's Government in the United Kingdom', 19 May 1933.
46. Ibid.
47. Ibid.
48. See A. Goldman, 'Sir Robert Vansittart's Search for Italian Co-operation against Hitler 1933-36', *Journal of Contemporary History*, 9, 3 (July 1974), pp. 93–130.
49. PRO CAB 4/20, CID Memorandum 1034-B, 'The Military Tendencies of Italy', 2 February 1931; see also PRO WO 190/108, 'Military Appreciation of the Situation in Europe, March 1931', 31 March 1931.
50. PRO CAB 4/20, CID Memorandum 310, 'A Review of Imperial Defence, 1933', 12 October 1933.
51. Ibid.
52. PRO CAB 2/6, CID 261st Meeting, 9 November 1933.
53. PRO CAB 21/434, Attachment to Hankey letter to McDonald, 9 November 1933.
54. PRO CAB 2/6, CID 261st Meeting, 9 November 1933.
55. PRO CAB 16/109, DRC 14, 'Report of Defence Requirements Sub-Committee', 28 February 1934.
56. Ibid., para. 14.
57. PRO CAB 36/8, JDC Memorandum 176, 'Malta: Interim Air Force Requirements', 31 January 1934.
58. PRO CAB 36/8, JDC Memorandum 180, 'Air Staff Memorandum', 30 April 1934.
59. PRO CAB 27/504, CP 205(34), 'Defence Requirements Report', 27 July 1934.
60. PRO CAB 27/504, CP 193(34), 'Interim Report by Committee Dealing with Air Defence', 16 July 1934.

NOTES

61. PRO CAB 23/79, Cabinet 31(34), 31 July 1934.
62. PRO CAB 36/8, JDC Memorandum 184, 'Malta', 1 October 1934, para. 33; see also Rollo, *The Guns*, p. 166, for details of the gun modernisation programme, estimated to cost £725,000 over the six years, 1934/35–1939/40.
63. PRO CAB 36/8, JDC Memorandum 184, 'Malta', para. 11.
64. PRO CAB 2/6, CID 266th Meeting, 22 November 1934.
65. PRO T 161/1459/S39650/1, Air Ministry letter to Treasury, 28 January 1935, and Treasury reply of 26 February 1935.
66. PRO CAB 27/507, Disarmament Conference Committee, 50th Meeting, 25 June 1934.
67. Admiral of the Fleet Lord Chatfield, *It Might Happen Again, Vol. II, The Navy and Defence* (Heinemann, London, 1947), p. 7. (This second volume was written in 1940, but not published until 1947.)
68. PRO CAB 53/4, COS Memorandum 372, 'Review of Imperial Defence, 1935', Appendix 3, 29 April 1935.

3: Malta in the Abyssinian Crisis, 1935–36

1. Chatfield wrote to Admiral Dreyer on 16 September 1935, 'It is a disaster that our statesmen have got us into this quarrel with Italy.' Chatfield Papers, National Maritime Museum, CHT/4/4.
2. PRO CAB 53/5, COS 146th Meeting, 5 July 1935.
3. Admiral Keyes had applied the 'mad dog' description to Mussolini as early as 1923. See his letter to Admiral Beatty of 7 September 1923 in Halpern, *Keyes, Vol. II*, p. 95.
4. PRO CAB 53/25, COS Memorandum 388, 'Military Implications of the Application of Article 16 of the covenant of the League of Nations. Interim Memorandum', 2 August 1935.
5. PRO CAB 23/82, CP 159(35), 6 August 1935.
6. Earl of Avon, *The Eden Memoirs: Facing the Dictators* (Cassell, London, 1962), p. 253.
7. Sir Samuel Hoare (Viscount Templewood), *Nine Troubled Years* (Collins, London, 1954), p. 164.
8. PRO CAB 53/25, COS Memorandum 392, 'Italo-Abyssinian Dispute', 9 August 1935.
9. PRO ADM 116/3038, Fisher to Admiralty, 20 August and 16 September 1935.
10. PRO CAB 53/25, COS Memorandum 392, 'Italo-Abyssinian Dispute', 9 August 1935.
11. PRO CAB 53/25, COS Memorandum 390(JP), 'Italo-Abyssinian Dispute', 9 August 1935.
12. PRO FO 371/19197, J3863, Minute by Sir V. Wellesley to Secretary of State, 20 August 1935.
13. PRO T 161/1459/S.39650/1, Bridges to Air Ministry, 2 August 1935.
14. PRO AIR 9/35, Enclosure 27, 'Memorandum on the Operational Necessity for an Additional Aerodrome at Malta' [n.d. September 1935].
15. PRO T 161/1459/S.39650/1, Note of a Meeting, 12 August 1935.
16. PRO AIR 9/68, Air Staff Memorandum, 'Italy Appreciation: France as Ally', 10 September 1935.
17. PRO AIR 9/68, Air Staff Memorandum, 'Appreciation of the Air Measures Required in the Event of a Single-handed War against Italy' [n.d. September 1935].
18. PRO AIR 9/68, Air Staff Memorandum, 'Appreciation of War with Italy', 12 August 1935.
19. PRO FO 371/19197, J3862, Copy of Admiralty to Fisher, 21 August 1935.
20. PRO CAB 23/82, Cabinet 42(35), 22 August 1935.
21. PRO FO 371/19197, J3861, Hoare letter to Cunliffe-Lister, 17 August 1935.
22. PRO CAB 16/136, DPRC 5th Meeting, 23 August 1935.
23. PRO ADM 116/3049, 'Summary of events in connection with Italo-Abyssinian Dispute from Naval point of view', 24 August 1935.
24. Chatfield letter to Admiral Fisher, 25 August 1935, Chatfield Papers, National Maritime Museum, CHT/4/5.
25. PRO CAB 16/138, Memorandum DPR 15, 'Naval Strategical Situation in the Mediterranean', 3 September 1935.
26. PRO ADM 116/3038, Fisher to Admiralty, 1 September 1935.
27. PRO AIR 8/188, Ellington to Cunliffe-Lister, 4 September 1935.
28. PRO CAB 53/25, COS Memorandum 394(JP), 'Italo-Abyssinian Dispute', 4 September 1935.

29. PRO CAB 53/5, COS 149th Meeting, 6 September 1935.
30. PRO CAB 53/25, COS Memorandum 395, 'Possibilities Arising out of the Application of Sanctions', 9 September 1935.
31. PRO CAB 16/136, DPRC 7th Meeting, 11 September 1935.
32. PRO CAB 16/138, Memorandum DPR 18, 'Garrison of Malta', 9 September 1935.
33. PRO CAB 16/136, DPRC 7th Meeting, 11 September 1935.
34. PRO CAB 53/5, COS 150th Meeting, 13 September 1935.
35. PRO CAB 53/5, COS 158th Meeting, 9 December 1935.
36. PRO FO 850/2, Y775/G, 'Security of Documents at H.M. Embassy, Rome', 20 February 1937.
37. Sir Geoffrey Thompson, *Front Line Diplomat* (Hutchinson, London, 1959), p. 104.
38. Italian military and naval planning in this period is discussed in R. Mallett, *The Italian Navy and Fascist Expansionism 1935–1940* (Frank Cass, London, 1998), pp. 21–37. The Minutes of the 13 August meeting of the Italian Chiefs of Staff are re-printed in his Appendix 2, pp. 205–17.
39. Chatfield letter to Vansittart, 21 January 1938, Chatfield Papers, National Maritime Museum, CHT/3/1.
40. Quoted in G. Baer, *The Coming of the Italian–Ethiopian War* (Harvard University Press, Cambridge, MA, 1967), p. 255.
41. Hinsley, *British Intelligence*, vol. I, p. 52.
42. Clarke's papers at the PRO are in HW 3/1-38.
43. PRO HW 3/1, Enclosure 35, 17 August 1935.
44. Ibid., Enclosure 40, 29 June 1936.
45. Clarke's copies of some of Alastair Denniston's papers are in PRO HW 3/32.
46. Fisher to Chatfield, 29 August 1935, Chatfield Papers, National Maritime Museum, CHT/4/4.
47. Hinsley, *British Intelligence*, vol. I, p. 51.
48. Ibid., vol. I, pp. 26, 28.
49. PRO AIR 8/138, 'Confidential Intelligence Summary No.14', September 1935.
50. Hinsley, *British Intelligence*, vol. I, p. 200.
51. *Documents on British Foreign Policy, 1919–1939*, 2nd Series, vol. XIV (Her Majesty's Stationery Office, London, 1976), Nos 620 and 630, 23 September 1935.
52. G. Ciano, *Ciano's Diary 1937–1938* (Methuen, London, 1952), p. 47.
53. PRO CO 158/484/89001/3, Campbell to Shuckburgh, 20 August 1935.
54. T. Jones, *A Diary with Letters 1931–1950* (Oxford University Press, London, 1954), p. 159.
55. For detailed accounts see Hancock, *Problems*, pp. 406–28, and Frendo, *Party Politics*, pp. 210–12.
56. PRO CO 158/489/89152, Defence Security Officer Memorandum, 'The General Situation', 2 September 1935, enclosed with Luke Despatch to Colonial Office, 4 September 1935.
57. Ibid., Luke to Colonial Office, 6 August 1935.
58. Ibid., Luke to Colonial Office, 4 September 1935.
59. Admiral French to Chatfield, 3 September 1935, Chatfield Papers, National Maritime Museum, CHT/3/1.
60. Admiral Fisher to Chatfield, 29 August 1935, Chatfield Papers, National Maritime Museum, CHT/4/5.
61. PRO CO 158/490/89152/6, Chamberlain to Colonial Office, 18 October 1935.
62. PRO CAB 16/138, Memorandum DPR 22, 'Evacuation of Wives and Families of Service Ranks and Ratings', 14 September 1935. (The writer of this study, aged one year, was one of these children.)
63. PRO CAB 16/136, DPRC 8th Meeting, 17 September 1935.
64. PRO FO 371/19537, R5551, 'Ordinance No. XXXI of 1935', 14 September 1935.
65. See N. West, *MI6: British Secret Intelligence Service Operations 1909–1945* (Weidenfeld & Nicolson, London, 1983), p. 20.
66. PRO FO 371/19537, R5616, Minute on McDonald telegram to Luke, 19 September 1935.
67. PRO CO 158/491/89001/3, Enclosure 110, Dawe to Ede, 10 July 1936.

NOTES

68. Ibid., Enclosure 128, Governor to Colonial Office, 30 October 1936, enclosing transcript of a conversation between the Italian Consul General and Professor Mallia
69. PRO FO 371/19535, R363/G, Governor to Colonial Office, 5 April 1935.
70. PRO CO 158/491/89001/3, Defence Security Officer Report, 31 March 1936, enclosed with Luke Despatch to Colonial Office of same date.
71. PRO CO 883/10, Enclosure 23, Governor to Colonial Office, 8 July 1936.
72. PRO CO 158/484/89001/3, Enclosure to Governor's Despatch to Colonial Office, 27 May 1935.
73. H. Smith and A. Koster, *Lord Strickland, Servant of the Crown* (Progress Press, Valletta, 1986), vol. II, p. 544.

4: Prelude to War, 1936–39

1. *Parliamentary Debates*, 5th Series, vol. 313, cols 973, 1205, 17–18 June 1936.
2. PRO CAB 53/28, COS Memorandum 477, 'Problems Facing His Majesty's Government in the Mediterranean as a Result of the Italo-League Dispute', 18 June 1936.
3. PRO CAB 53/28, COS Memorandum 506, 'Eastern Mediterranean: Understanding with Turkey and Greece', 29 July 1936.
4. PRO CAB 16/112, DRC 37, 'The Third Report of the Defence Requirements Committee', 21 November 1935.
5. *Statement Relating to Defence*, Cmd. 5107 (His Majesty's Stationery Office, London, March 1936).
6. PRO CAB 36/9, JDC Memorandum 280, 'Report of the Governor of Malta', 11 September 1936.
7. PRO CAB 2/6, CID 288th Meeting, 11 February 1937.
8. Gibbs, *Rearmament Policy*, p. 386.
9. PRO CAB 16/181 contains the minutes of the meetings of the Defence Plans (Policy) Committee.
10. PRO CAB 4/26, CID Memorandum 1332-B, 'Probability of War with Italy', 15 June 1937.
11. PRO CAB 63/52, Hankey to Chamberlain, 3 July 1937.
12. PRO CAB 63/51, Hankey to Baldwin, 8 June 1936.
13. PRO CAB 2/6, CID 295th and 296th Meetings, 1 and 5 July 1937.
14. PRO CAB 53/29, COS Memorandum 514(JP), 'Cyprus: Potentialities as a Naval, Military and Air Base', 16 October 1936.
15. PRO CAB 53/7, COS 200th Meeting, 5 March 1937.
16. PRO CAB 53/30, COS Memorandum 560, 'Review of Imperial Defence', 22 February 1937.
17. PRO PREM 1/276, fol. 381, Perth to Vansittart, 2 July 1937.
18. See P. Beesly, *Very Special Intelligence: The Story of the Admiralty's Operational Intelligence Centre* (Hamish Hamilton, London, 1977), pp. 36–7.
19. PRO CAB 53/32, COS Memorandum 603(JP), 'Mediterranean and Middle East Appreciation; Interim Report', 24 July 1937.
20. PRO CAB 53/35, COS Memorandum 655(JP), 'Mediterranean, Middle East and North East Africa', para. 71, and Appendix VI, 'Defence of Malta', 22 January 1938.
21. Ibid.
22. Ibid.
23. PRO CAB 2/6, CID 296th Meeting, 5 July 1937.
24. PRO CAB 53/45, COS Memorandum 843, 'European Appreciation 1939–40', 20 February 1939. For a detailed review of this period see L. Pratt, *East of Malta, West of Suez: Britain's Mediterranean Crisis 1936–1939* (Cambridge University Press, Cambridge, 1975), pp. 161–90.
25. PRO CAB 53/45, CID 348th Meeting, 24 February 1939.
26. PRO PREM 1/345, Churchill to Chamberlain, 27 March 1939.
27. PRO CAB 16/209, SAC 1st Meeting, 1 March 1939.
28. PRO CAB 16/209, SAC Memorandum 13, 'Interim Report: European Appreciation', 13 April 1939.
29. PRO CAB 53/11, COS 309th Meeting, 19 July 1939. See also Gibbs, *Rearmament Policy*, p. 673.

MALTA AND BRITISH STRATEGIC POLICY, 1925–43

30. PRO CAB 2/9, CID 368th Meeting, 24 July 1939.
31. PRO T 161/1459/S39650/1, Treasury letter to Air Ministry, 10 September 1935.
32. PRO CAB 2/6, CID 281st and 293rd Meetings, 30 July 1936 and 29 April 1937.
33. PRO T 161/1459/S39650/1, 'Malta: Provision of Aerodromes, 1936–42'.
34. PRO CAB 36/9, JDC Memorandum 280, 'Report of the Governor of Malta', 16 October 1936.
35. Details in Rollo, *The Guns*, pp. 166–79.
36. Ibid.
37. PRO CAB 2/7, CID 301st Meeting, 18 November 1937, noting decision of 8 November 1937.
38. PRO CAB 36/9, JDC Memorandum 300, 'Order of Priority for Installation of Armament', 22 January 1937.
39. PRO CAB 53/7, COS 203rd Meeting, 20 April 1937.
40. PRO CAB 53/8, COS 221st Meeting, 4 November 1937.
41. PRO CAB 36/10, JDC Memorandum 378, 'Defended Ports Abroad: Anti-Aircraft Defences', 21 March 1938.
42. PRO CAB 53/9, COS 237th Meeting, 27 April 1938.
43. PRO CAB 16/183A, DP(P) Memorandum 25, 'Defence Expenditure in Future Years: The War Office Programme', 28 April 1938.
44. PRO CAB 2/7, CID 331st Meeting, 27 July 1938.
45. PRO CAB 23/96, Cabinet 53 (38), 7 November 1938.
46. PRO CAB 36/11, JDC Memorandum 445, 'Defended Ports Abroad: Anti-Aircraft Defences', 16 January 1939.
47. PRO CAB 2/8, CID 345th Meeting, 26 January 1939.
48. For detailed accounts see Gibbs, *Rearmament Policy*, pp. 565–89, and Smith, *Air Strategy*, pp. 173–226.
49. PRO CAB 36/4, JDC 53rd Meeting, 1 April 1938.
50. PRO WO 32/2415, 'Malta: Acoustic Mirror Warning System: Trials, 1935–1938'.
51. PRO ADM 116/3900, Med. 011961/031/8, C-in-C Mediterranean to Admiralty, 23 December 1938.
52. PRO CAB 5/9, CP 31(39), Memorandum by Secretary of State for Air, 'Anti-Aircraft Defences, Gibraltar, Malta and Aden', 1 February 1939, annexed to CID 491-C, 14 February 1939.
53. PRO CAB 53/45, COS Memorandum 843, 'European Appreciation 1939–40', 20 February 1939.
54. PRO CAB 36/11, JDC Memorandum 473, 'The Air Defence of Malta', 29 March 1939.
55. PRO CAB 36/11, JDC Memorandum 487, 'Defended Ports Abroad: Anti-Aircraft Defences', 17 May 1939.
56. PRO CAB 36/12, JDC Memorandum 493, 'The Air Defence of Malta', 25 May 1939.
57. PRO CAB 36/4-5, JDC 63rd and 67th Meetings, 27 February and 9 June 1939.
58. PRO CAB 5/9, CID Memorandum 506-C, 'The Air Defence of Malta', 20 July 1939.
59. PRO CAB 2/9, CID 370th Meeting, 27 July 1939.
60. See Rollo, *The Guns*, pp. 225, 261.
61. PRO CAB 5/9, CID Memorandum 508-C, 'Anti-Aircraft Defences of Alexandria and Aden', 27 July 1939.
62. PRO CAB 2/9, CID 373rd Meeting, 3 August 1939.

5: *Final Preparations for War*

1. For this period see M. Budden, 'British Policy towards Fascist Italy in the Early Stages of the Second World War' (PhD Thesis, King's College, University of London, 1999).
2. PRO ADM 186/800, *Naval Staff History: Mediterranean*, vol. I, p. 7.
3. PRO CAB 99/3, Supreme War Council, 1st Meeting, 12 September 1939.
4. PRO ADM 186/800, *Mediterranean*, vol. I, p. 11.
5. PRO CAB 82/1, DCOS (39) 16th Meeting, 28 November 1939.
6. PRO CAB 83/4, MC Memorandum (40) 40, 'Defence Measures in the Colonies', 2 February 1940.

NOTES

7. PRO CAB 80/6, COS Memorandum (39) 146, 'Review of Military Policy in the Middle East', 5 December 1939.
8. PRO CAB 83/4, MC Memorandum (40) 8, 'Military Policy in the Middle East', 13 January 1940.
9. *Documents on German Foreign Policy 1918–1945* (hereafter *DGFP*) (Her Majesty's Stationery Office, London, 1956), Series D, vol. IX, no. 1, 17 [*sic*] March 1940.
10. Hinsley, *British Intelligence*, vol. I, pp. 199–205.
11. PRO ADM 186/800, *Mediterranean*, vol. I, p. 13.
12. PRO CAB 65/6, War Cabinet (40) 80th Meeting, 30 April 1940.
13. Hinsley, *British Intelligence*, vol. I, p. 205.
14. PRO CAB 2/8, CID 345th Meeting, 26 January 1939.
15. PRO CO 158/528/89328, Governor to Colonial Office, 28 June 1939.
16. PRO WO 32/2411, Governor to War Office, 5 May 1939.
17. PRO CO 158/520/89404, Governor to Colonial Office, 29 August 1938; see also R. Minney, *The Private Papers of Hore-Belisha* (Collins, London, 1960), especially Chapter XII, 'Visit to Malta and Mussolini', pp. 107–21.
18. PRO CO 158/520/89404, Governor to Colonial Office, 22 November 1938.
19. PRO CO 158/528/89328, Governor to Colonial Office, 28 June 1939.
20. PRO CAB 79/5, General Dobbie to General Dill, 4 July 1940, annexed to minutes of COS (40) 214th Meeting, 9 July 1940.
21. Britain's AA defences are described by General Sir Frederick Pile in his *ACK-ACK: Britain's Defences against Air Attack During the Second World War* (Harrap, London, 1949), pp. 105–20.
22. PRO CAB 82/1, DCOS (39) 6th Meeting, 19 September 1939.
23. PRO CAB 82/1, DCOS (39) 13th Meeting, 7 November 1939.
24. PRO CAB 79/3, COS (40) 15th Meeting, 25 January 1940.
25. PRO CAB 83/8, MC (40) 9th Meeting, 8 February 1940.
26. PRO CAB 82/2, DCOS (40) 15th Meeting, 3 April 1940.
27. PRO CAB 83/4, MC Memoranda (40) 13, 'AA Equipments', 10 January 1940, and (40) 21, 'Production of Heavy and Light Guns', 7 February 1940, Appendix A.
28. Ian Cameron misquoted this statement as 'Nothing can be done to defend Malta', in his *Red Duster, White Ensign: The Story of Malta and the Malta Convoys* (Bantam Books, London, 1983), p. 1; this error was repeated in M. Gabriele, *Operazione C3: Malta* (USMM, Rome, 1965), p. 25.
29. PRO CAB 66/7, COS Memorandum (40) 312, 'Measures to Deter Italy from Entering the War against the Allies', 28 April 1940.
30. PRO CAB 69/11, Defence Committee (Operations) (40) 3rd Meeting, 16 May 1940; PRO CAB 80/11, COS Memorandum (40) 351, 'Allied Military Action in the Event of War with Italy', 13 May 1940.
31. PRO AIR 9/108, Slessor Report, 'Priority of Formation of Fighter Squadrons Overseas: Malta and Singapore', 31 July 1939.
32. PRO CAB 79/3, COS (40) 15th Meeting, 25 January 1940.
33. Ministry of Defence, Air Historical Branch (hereafter AHB) Narrative, *The Middle East Campaigns, Vol. XI, Malta*, pp. 11–12 (n.d.).
34. PRO CAB 79/4, COS (40) 149th Meeting, 25 May 1940, and PRO CAB 69/1, Defence Committee (Operations) (40) 8th Meeting, 25 May 1940.
35. PRO CAB 66/7, WP (40) 168, 'British Strategy in a Certain Eventuality', 25 May 1940.
36. PRO CAB 80/12, COS Memorandum (40) 407(JIC), 'Possible Military Courses Open to Italy', 29 May 1940.
37. AHB Narrative, *Malta*, p. 13.
38. See C. Shores and B. Cull with N. Malizia, *Malta: The Hurricane Years 1940–1941* (Grub Street, London, 1987), pp. 5–7; Admiral of the Fleet Viscount Cunningham, *A Sailor's Odyssey* (Hutchinson, London, 1951), p. 236; J. Sadkovich, *The Italian Navy in World War II* (Greenwood Press, Westport, CT, 1994), p. 70. Sadkovich insists that 'the three Gladiators of legend were actually fourteen'.
39. AHB Narrative, *Malta*, pp. 20–21.
40. Slessor, *The Central Blue*, pp. 166–7.
41. AHB Narrative, *Malta*, p. 13.

42. PRO CAB 16/105, Coast Defence Enquiry, CD 9, 'Air Staff Memorandum', 12 February 1932.
43. PRO CAB 82/2, DCOS (40) 24th Meeting, 29 May 1940.
44. For an account of his father's Governorship of Malta see V. Bonham-Carter, *In a Liberal Tradition* (Constable, London, 1960).
45. J. Attard, *Britain and Malta: The Story of an Era* (Publishers Enterprises, Valletta, 1988), p. 131.
46. PRO CO 158/501/89001/7, 'Italian Activities: Proposed Dismissal of Maltese Civil Servants', 18 January 1937; PRO CAB 23/87, Cabinet (37) 6, 3 February 1937.
47. PRO CO 158/505/89146, Ormsby-Gore to Governor, 11 February 1937.
48. PRO CO 158/528/89328, Governor to MacDonald, 7 June 1939.
49. Ciano, *Diary 1937–1938*, p. 47.
50. The text of his address is reprinted in Bonham-Carter, *Liberal Tradition*, Appendix A, pp. 247–51.
51. The duties established for the District Councils in an order issued on 14 July 1939 are reprinted in S. Perowne, *The Siege within the Walls: Malta 1940–1943* (Hodder & Stoughton, London, 1970), p. 31.
52. PRO CO 158/534/89152/13, 'Passive Defence: Deep Shelter Construction'.
53. PRO CO 158/508/89328, Governor to Ormsby-Gore, 22 December 1936.
54. PRO CO 158/513/89008/13, Governor to Ormsby-Gore, 24 December 1937.
55. Ibid., Note of Meetings, 14 and 18 March 1938.
56. PRO CO 162/80, 'Malta Defence Regulations 1939', *Malta Government Gazette*, Supplement CXIII, 4 September 1939, pp. 1813–77.
57. *The Times of Malta*, 10 May 1940, reporting Mizzi's speech in the Council of Government on 9 May 1940.
58. Perowne, *Siege*, p. 45.

6: *The Threat of Invasion*

1. M. Muggeridge (ed.), *Ciano's Diary 1939–1943* (Heinemann, London, 1947), p. 22.
2. Quoted in M. Knox, *Mussolini Unleashed 1939–1941: Politics and Strategy in Fascist Italy's Last War* (Cambridge University Press, Cambridge, 1988), p. 40.
3. This account draws heavily on the detailed examination of relevant Italian documents in Ufficio Storico della Marina Militare (USMM), *La Marina Italiana nella seconda guerra mondiale, Vol. XXI, Tomo I, L'organizzazione della marina durante il conflito: Efficienza all'apertura delle ostilità* (USMM, Rome, 1972); Gabriele, *Operazione C3*; Knox, *Mussolini*; and Mallett, *Italian Navy*.
4. *DGFP*, Series D, vol. IX, no. 1, 17 [sic] March 1940, p. 13.
5. *Documenti diplomatici Italiani* (hereafter *DDI*), Series IX, vol. III, no. 669, 31 March 1940 (Rome, 1952–53).
6. Knox, *Mussolini*, pp. 42, 91.
7. USMM, *Marina, Vol. XXI, L'organizzazione*, Appendix 6, pp. 350–52; Bragadin, *Italian Navy*, p. 6.
8. Muggeridge, *Ciano*, p. 249.
9. P. Badoglio, *Italy in the Second World War: Memories and Documents* (Oxford University Press, London, 1948), p. 15.
10. *DDI*, Series IX, vol. IV, no. 642, 29 May 1940.
11. USMM, *Marina, Vol. XXI, L'organizzazione*, p. 310. Cavagnari's Directive *Di. N.A. n. 0 (zero) concetti generali di azione nel Mediterraneo*, 29 May 1940, is re-printed in Appendix 7, pp. 353–5.
12. G. Santoro, *L'Aeronautica Italiana nella seconda guerra mondiale*, 2 vols (Edizioni esse, Milan, 1966), vol. I, pp. 233–5; Gabriele, *Operazione C3*, p. 46; Knox, *Mussolini*, p. 119.
13. USMM, *Marina, Vol. XXI, L'organizzazione*, p. 312; Knox, *Mussolini*, pp. 120–21.
14. Quoted by Sir W. Churchill in *The Second World War*, 6 vols (Cassell, London, 1949), vol. II, p. 114, who then added: 'Such chances though rare, are not necessarily good.'
15. Badoglio, *Italy*, p. 15.
16. See Knox, *Mussolini*, pp. 121–2, for an analysis of Mussolini's intentions. An alternative

view, that Mussolini intended 'to declare war, not to make it' is argued by D. Mack Smith, *Mussolini's Roman Empire* (Longman, London, 1976), p. 217.
17. Santoro, *L'Aeronautica*, vol. I, p. 252.
18. Gabriele, *Operazione C3*, p. 12.
19. Ibid., p. 14.
20. Mallett, *Italian Navy*, pp. 115–16.
21. USMM, *Marina, Vol. VI, La guerra nel Mediterraneo: La difesa del traffico coll'Africa settentrionale dal 10 giugno 1940 al 30 settembre 1941* (USMM, Rome, 1958), pp. 4–10; Gabriele, *Operazione C3*, pp. 17–20.
22. Gabriele, *Operazione C3*, pp. 34–42; the naval study is reprinted in Appendix II, pp. 303–6.
23. Gabriele, *Operazione C3*, footnote (33), p. 45; see also Mallett, *Italian Navy*, p. 182, who is more critical of pre-war Italian Intelligence capabilities.
24. Gabriele, *Operazione C3*, p. 42.
25. Ibid., pp. 55–9; this study is reprinted in Appendix III, pp. 307–10.
26. Jellison, *Besieged*, p. 18.
27. Gabriele, *Operazione C3*, p. 64; similar doubts have been expressed by Giorgerini, *Battaglia*, p. 74, and by Sadkovich, *Italian Navy*, p. 70.
28. M. Knox, *Hitler's Italian Allies: Royal Armed Forces, Fascist Regime, and the War of 1940–1943* (Cambridge University Press, Cambridge, 2000), p. 170.
29. Hinsley, *British Intelligence*, vol. I, pp. 199–200.
30. PRO ADM 223/488, Naval Intelligence Division, vol. 34, 'Italy'.
31. PRO CAB 69/1, Defence Committee (Operations) (40) 3rd Meeting, 16 May 1940.
32. Hinsley, *British Intelligence*, vol, I, p. 200.
33. Ibid., vol. I, p. 203.
34. Ibid., vol. I, p. 203.
35. PRO CAB 80/11, COS Memorandum (40) 387(JIC), 'Italian Situation', 24 May 1940.
36. PRO CAB 80/12, COS Memorandum (40) 407(JIC), 'Possible Courses Open to Italy', 29 May 1940.
37. PRO ADM 223/82, 'Italy – Daily Situation Report, 10 June 1940'.
38. A good account of civilian life in Malta during the war is found in J. Micaleff, *When Malta Stood Alone (1940–1943)* (Interprint, Valletta, 1981).
39. PRO WO 106/3062, Extract from Colonel Ede's telegram to the War Office dated 14 June 1940.
40. PRO CAB 79/5, Governor to Dill, 4 July 1940, annexed to minutes of COS (40) 214th Meeting, 9 July 1940.
41. See J. Attard, *The Battle of Malta* (Hamlyn Paperbacks, London, 1982), pp. 30–33.
42. P. Vella, *Malta: Blitzed but not Beaten* (Progress Press, Valletta, 1985), pp. 13–14.
43. Jellison, *Besieged*, p. 61.
44. Attard, *Battle of Malta*, pp. 49–51; Micaleff, *Malta*, pp. 39–41.
45. Mercieca's account of his interview with the Governor is reprinted in Perowne, *Siege*, pp. 42–5.
46. *The Times Of Malta*, 7 June 1940.
47. Cunningham, *Odyssey*, p. 236.
48. PRO CAB 8/52, ODC Memorandum 1761, 'Malta: Passive Defence Measures', 5 July 1939.
49. PRO CAB 7/15, ODC 389th Meeting, 12 July 1939.
50. PRO CAB 106/491, 'Malta. 1939–1945. Section 10: Shelters'. This is one of a series of post-war monographs, with full references, covering virtually every aspect of wartime administration in Malta.
51. PRO CO 158/534/89152/13, War Office to Colonial Office, 19 September 1940; Governor to Colonial Office, 13 December 1940.
52. Ibid., Copy of Vice-Admiral Malta signal to Admiralty, 27 October 1940.
53. Jellison, *Besieged*, p. 25.
54. PRO CAB 106/491, 'Malta. 1939–1945. Section 10: Shelters', p. 22.
55. Jellison, *Besieged*, p. 25.
56. I. Dear and M. Foot (eds), *The Oxford Companion to the Second World War* (Oxford University Press, Oxford, 1995), p. 140.

57. PRO CAB 7/15, ODC 382nd Meeting, 3 February 1939.
58. PRO CAB 106/483, 'Malta. 1939–1945. Section 2: Supply', p. 1.
59. In *Odyssey*, p. 277, Cunningham writes of two convoys every month. This appears to be a misunderstanding.
60. PRO CAB 80/6, COS Memorandum (40) 636, 'Supplies for Malta', 16 August 1940.
61. PRO CAB 79/6, COS (40) 278th Meeting, 23 August 1940.
62. PRO PREM 3/266/10A, fols 948–9, Colonial Secretary to Prime Minister, 11 September 1940.
63. PRO CAB 65/9, War Cabinet (40) 254th Meeting, 19 September 1940.
64. PRO CAB 106/483, 'Malta. 1939–1945. Section 2: Supply', p. 3.
65. PRO CAB 106/483, 'Malta. 1939–1945. Section 4: Food and Rationing', p. 11.
66. C. Boffa, *The Second Great Siege: Malta 1940–1943* (Progress Press, Valletta, 1992), p. 30.
67. Perowne, *Siege*, p. 42.
68. PRO WO 106/3062, Governor to War Office, 31 May 1940.

7: *The Initial Onslaught*

1. M. Arnold-Forster, *The World at War* (Collins, London, 1975), p. 54.
2. PRO CAB 65/13, War Cabinet Meetings WM (40) 140th, 142nd, and 145th, 26–28 May 1940; see also note 3 below.
3. For detailed analysis of these discussions see A. Roberts, *'The Holy Fox'; A Biography of Lord Halifax* (Weidenfeld & Nicolson, London, 1991), pp. 223–37; P. Bell, *A Certain Eventuality . . . Britain and the Fall of France* (Saxon House, Farnborough, 1974), pp. 37–52; D. Reynolds, 'Churchill and the British "Decision" to Fight on in 1940: Right Policy, Wrong Reason', in R. Langhorne (ed.), *Diplomacy and Intelligence during the Second World War* (Cambridge University Press, Cambridge, 1985), pp. 147–67; J. Lukacs, *Five Days in London, May 1940* (Yale University Press, New Haven, CT, 1999). For the Italian reaction see Muggeridge, *Ciano*, p. 255; *DGFP*, Series D, vol. IX, no. 340, 28 May 1940, p. 462.
4. Quotations respectively from M. Gilbert, *Winston S. Churchill, Vol. VI, Finest Hour 1939–1941* (Heinemann, London, 1983), p. 327, and Sir J. Wheeler-Bennett (ed.), *Action This Day: Working with Churchill* (Macmillan, London, 1968), p. 220.
5. PRO CAB 79/4, COS (40) 137th Meeting, 18 May 1940.
6. PRO CAB 65/13, War Cabinet (40) 141st Meeting, 27 May 1940.
7. PRO CAB 66/7, WP (40) 168, 'British Strategy in a Certain Eventuality', 25 May 1940, Appreciation annexed, para. 36.
8. PRO CAB 80/12, COS Memorandum (40) 404, 'Policy in the Mediterranean', 28 May 1940. Cunningham's signal of 23 May is annexed to COS Memorandum (40) 421(JP), 'Policy in the Mediterranean', 30 May 1940.
9. PRO ADM 186/800, *Mediterranean*, vol. I, p. 102; see also Cunningham, *Odyssey*, p. 231.
10. PRO CAB 79/5, Naval Staff Memorandum, 'Withdrawal of the Eastern Mediterranean Fleet', annexed to minutes of COS (40) 183rd Meeting, 17 June 1940.
11. Cunningham, *Odyssey*, p. 241.
12. Reprinted in Churchill, *Second World War*, vol. II, p. 563.
13. A. Marder, *From the Dardanelles to Oran: Studies of the Royal Navy in War and Peace 1915–1940* (Oxford University Press, London, 1974), p. 228, n. 1; Churchill, *Second World War*, vol. II, p. 392.
14. PRO CAB 80/13, COS Memorandum (40) 469(JP), 'Military Implications of the Withdrawal of the Eastern Mediterranean Fleet', 17 June 1940.
15. PRO CAB 80/14, COS Memorandum (40) 521, 'Military Policy in Egypt and the Middle East', 3 July 1940.
16. S. Roskill, *Churchill and the Admirals* (Collins, London, 1977), p. 151; Barnett, *Engage*, pp. 209–13; R. Brodhurst, *Churchill's Anchor: Admiral of the Fleet Sir Dudley Pound* (Leo Cooper, Barnsley, 2000), p. 156. Copies of the relevant signals are in the British Library, Cunningham Papers, Add. MS. 52566.
17. PRO CAB 80/16, COS Memorandum (40) 647(JP), 'Future Strategy', 21 August 1940.
18. Playfair, *Mediterranean*, vol. I, p. 120.

NOTES

19. PRO CAB 80/16, COS Memorandum (40) 623, 'Reinforcement of Garrisons Abroad', 12 August 1940, Appendix B.
20. Churchill, *Second World War*, vol. II, p. 120: Cunningham, *Odyssey*, pp. 290–91. Operation 'Workshop', the proposed commando assault on Pantelleria, was eventually cancelled after strong opposition from Cunningham and the Admiralty.
21. Churchill, *Second World War*, vol. II, p. 375.
22. PRO CAB 95/2, Committee on Military Policy in the Middle East, 6th Meeting, 23 July 1940.
23. PRO CAB 80/16, COS Memorandum (40) 650, 'Development of Malta as a Base for Offensive Operations', 22 August 1940.
24. PRO CAB 79/6, COS (40) 278th Meeting, 23 August 1940.
25. PRO ADM 186/800, *Mediterranean*, vol. I, pp. 112–13.
26. PRO CAB 79/6, COS (40) 280th Meeting, 26 August 1940.
27. Playfair, *Mediterranean*, vol. I, p. 164.
28. Hinsley, *British Intelligence*, vol. I, p. 210.
29. Ibid., vol. I, p. 195; Shores, *Hurricane Years*, p. 69.
30. Cunningham, *Odyssey*, p. 269.
31. See J. Greene and A. Massignani, *The Naval War in the Mediterranean 1940–1943* (Chatham Publishing, London, 1998), p. 44.
32. PRO ADM 223/803, 'Interrogation of Commander Cianchi in Feb.–April 1944 about RN Cyphers'.
33. PRO CAB 80/20, COS Memorandum (40) 810, 'Malta – Use as a Fleet Base', 8 October 1940.
34. PRO CAB 69/11, Defence Committee (Operations) (40) 34th Meeting, 15 October 1940.
35. Hinsley, *British Intelligence*, vol. I, p. 218.
36. PRO CAB 69/11, Defence Committee (Operations) (40) 37th Meeting, 28 October 1940.
37. Playfair, *Mediterranean*, vol. I, p. 266, and n. 1. The operations of 148 Squadron in Malta are described by its CO, Group Captain P. Foss, in *Climbing Turns* (Linden Hall, Yeovil, 1990), pp. 98–126.
38. Churchill, *Second World War*, vol. II, p. 374.
39. Ibid., p. 568.
40. Ibid., p. 392.
41. PRO CAB 79/5, Acting Governor to Dill, 4 July 1940. General Dobbie was not appointed Governor until 19 May 1941.
42. PRO CAB 80/14, COS Memorandum (40) 547, 'Review of AA Equipments', 13 July 1940.
43. PRO CAB 79/5, COS (40) 221st Meeting, 14 July 1940.
44. PRO CAB 79/5, COS (40) 222nd Meeting, 15 July 1940.
45. Churchill, *Second World War*, vol. II, p. 393.
46. Playfair, *Mediterranean*, vol. I, pp. 202–3.
47. Ibid., p. 299.
48. PRO CAB 79/5, COS (40) 222nd Meeting, 15 July 1940.
49. Playfair, *Mediterranean*, vol. I, p. 243.
50. Churchill, *Second World War*, vol. II, p. 384.
51. PRO CAB 79/7, COS (40) 356th Meeting, 22 October 1940.
52. PRO CAB 79/6, COS (40) 310th Meeting, 14 September 1940.
53. Churchill, *Second World War*, vol. II, pp. 293–7.
54. Ibid., p. 397.
55. PRO CAB 80/19, COS Memorandum (40) 763, 'Reinforcements for Malta', 21 September 1940, with Dobbie's telegram of 19 September 1940 attached.
56. PRO CAB 79/6, COS (40) 320th Meeting, 23 September 1940, Annex I.
57. PRO CAB 80/19, COS Memorandum (40) 789, 'Reinforcements for Malta', 30 September 1940.
58. PRO CAB 80/20, COS Memorandum (40) 805, 'Reinforcements for Malta', 6 October 1940.
59. PRO CAB 80/20, COS Memorandum (40) 814, 'Defence of Malta', 9 October 1940.
60. PRO CAB 80/20, COS Memorandum (40) 833, 'The Mediterranean', 15 October 1940.
61. PRO CAB 69/1, Defence Committee (Operations) (40) 34th Meeting, 15 October 1940.

62. Santoro, *L'Aeronautica*, vol. I, pp. 231–54.
63. Ibid., pp. 253–4.
64. Ibid., p. 239.
65. Vella, *Malta*, p. 249.
66. Santoro, *L'Aeronautica*, vol. I, p. 249.
67. Gabriele, *Operazione C3*, pp. 65–9
68. Hinsley et al., *British Intelligence*, vol. I, p. 206.
69. Ibid., p. 208.
70. J. Wingate, *The Fighting Tenth: The Tenth Submarine Flotilla and the Siege of Malta* (Leo Cooper, London, 1991), pp. 7–8.
71. USMM, *Marina, Vol. I, Dati statistici* (USMM, Rome, 1950), Table LIV, p. 124.
72. USMM, *Marina, Vol. VI, La difesa*, p. 5.
73. USMM, *Marina, Vol. XXI, L'organizazzione*, pp. 353–5.
74. Ibid., pp. 311–12.
75. Bragadin, *Italian Navy*, p. 7.
76. Giorgerini, *Battaglia*, p. 32.
77. Greene and Massignani, *Naval War*, p. 50.
78. G. Giorgerini, 'La Guerra Per mare e il problema dei convogli', in R. Rainero and A. Biagini (eds), *Cinquant'anni dopo l'entrata dell'Italia nella 2a guerra mondiale. Aspetti e problemi. L'Italia in guerra: il 2o anno-1941* (Gaeta, Rome, 1992), p. 416.
79. Greene and Massignani, *Naval War*, p. 67.
80. Giorgerini, *Battaglia*, p. 235.

8: *The German Intervention in the Mediterranean in 1941*

1. German Mediterranean strategy in this period is examined in Schreiber, *Germany*, vol. III, *passim*. An Italian account is given in M. Gabriele, 'L'offensiva su malta', in R. Rainero and A. Biagini (eds), *Cinquant'anni dopo l'entrata dell'Italia nella 2a guerra mondiale. Aspetti e problema, L'Italia in guerra: il 2o anno–1941* (Gaeta, Rome, 1992), pp. 435–50.
2. H. Trevor-Roper (ed.), *Hitler's War Directives 1939–1945* (Pan Books, London, 1966), pp. 81–7.
3. A. Martiensson (ed.), *Fuehrer Conferences on Naval Affairs 1939–1945* (Greenhill Books, London, 1990), p. 167.
4. Trevor-Roper, *Directives*, pp. 98–100.
5. Schreiber, *Germany*, vol. III, p. 655.
6. Liddell Hart, *Rommel*, pp. 98–102.
7. Schreiber, *Germany*, vol. III, pp. 658–9.
8. Trevor-Roper, *Directives*, pp. 93–8.
9. Quoted in Schreiber, *Germany*, vol. III, p. 656, n. 8.
10. Liddell Hart, *Rommel*, pp. 105–6.
11. Churchill, *Second World War*, vol. III, p. 17.
12. Ibid., vol. III, p. 58.
13. Hinsley, *British Intelligence*, vol. I, pp. 249–64.
14. Churchill, *Second World War*, vol. III, pp. 5–13.
15. Hinsley, *British Intelligence*, vol. I, p. 259.
16. See the German Naval Staff Memorandum of 14 November 1940 in Martiensson, *Conferences*, pp. 154–6; also Schreiber, *Germany*, vol. III, pp. 221–3.
17. PRO CAB 79/7, COS (40) 374th Meeting, 5 November 1940.
18. Martiensson, *Conferences*, p. 146.
19. J. Connell, *Wavell: Scholar and Soldier* (Collins, London. 1964), pp. 352–4.
20. British Library, Cunningham Papers, Add. MS. 52561, Cunningham to Pound, 11 March 1941.
21. PRO PREM 3/274/1, fol. 107, Cunningham to Admiralty, 10 April 1941.
22. Ibid., fol. 106, Prime Minister Minute M 429/1, 12 April 1941.
23. Churchill, *Second World War*, vol. III, pp. 186–8.
24. British Library, Cunningham Papers, Add. MS. 52567, Cunningham to Admiralty, 22 April 1941.

NOTES

25. PRO AIR 8/499, CAS to Longmore, 15 April 1941.
26. PRO AIR 23/5706, HQ Mediterranean to HQ Middle East, 7 March 1941.
27. See K. Poolman, *Night Strike from Malta: 830 Squadron RN and Rommel's Convoys* (Jane's Publishing Company, London, 1980), pp. 75–7.
28. C. Lamb, *War in a Stringbag* (Arrow Books, London, 1978), pp. 205–16.
29. PRO AIR 8/499, CAS to AOC-in-C Middle East, 15 April 1941.
30. PRO CAB 79/11, COS (41) 144th Meeting, 23 April 1941.
31. PRO PREM 3/274/1, fols 104–5, Pound to Cunningham, 11 April 1941.
32. Rear-Admiral G. Simpson, *Periscope View: A Professional Autobiography* (Macmillan, London, 1972), p. 126. Although Simpson commanded the U-class submarines, and directed the operations of other visiting submarines, from January 1941, the 10th Flotilla was not formally established until October when Simpson was promoted to Captain.
33. Cunningham, *Odyssey*, p. 360.
34. Ibid., p. 361.
35. PRO AIR 8/499, CAS to Maynard, 15 April 1941, and the latter's reply, 17 April 1941.
36. Hinsley, *British Intelligence*, vol. I, pp. 375–401; see also R. Bennett, *Ultra and Mediterranean Strategy 1941–1945* (Hamish Hamilton, London, 1989), pp. 47–67.
37. PRO DEFE 3/686, Enigma Signal OL 26, 2 April 1941.
38. PRO ADM 223/76, Naval Intelligence Division Papers, F 294, 7 April 1941.
39. PRO CAB 79/9, COS (41) 127th Meeting, 7 April 1941.
40. PRO ADM 223/76, Naval Intelligence Division Papers, Cunningham to Admiralty, 8 April 1941.
41. PRO PREM 3/274/1, fol. 102, Prime Minister Minute M. 435/1, 14 April 1941.
42. Ibid., fol. 101, First Lord to Prime Minister, 17 April 1941. Details of the naval action are in E. Grove, *Sea Battles in Close-Up: World War II*, vol. II (Ian Allan, Shepperton, 1993), pp. 53–4.
43. British Library, Cunningham Papers, Add. MS. 52567, Cunningham to Admiralty, 26 April 1941.
44. PRO CAB 79/9, COS (41) 132nd Meeting, 12 April 1941.
45. British Library, Cunningham Papers, Add. MS. 52567, Cunningham to Admiralty, 26 April 1941.
46. Playfair, *Mediterranean*, vol. I, p. 369.
47. Giorgerini, *Battaglia*, pp. 75, 134.
48. Gabriele, 'L'offensiva', p. 440.
49. Ibid.
50. Ibid., pp. 437–9.
51. General W. Warlimont, *Inside Hitler's Headquarters 1939–1945* (Presidio Press, Novato, California, n.d.), p. 131, and n. 59.
52. Ibid.
53. Schreiber, *Germany*, vol. III, p. 529.
54. Ibid., p. 671; see also Martiensson, *Conferences*, p. 185.
55. Gabriele, 'L'offensiva', pp. 442–3.
56. PRO AIR 8/499, Copy of DNI to SO(I) Malta, 18 January 1941.
57. Ibid., Copy of Vice-Admiral Malta to DNI, 18 January 1941.
58. PRO WO 106/3065, CIGS to Governor, 22 January 1941; copy of reply in PRO AIR 8/499, 23 January 1941.
59. PRO WO 106/3065, War Office to Governor, 30 January 1941.
60. PRO CAB 79/9, COS (41) 43rd Meeting, 6 February 1941; Governor's telegram of 5 February 1941 attached.
61. The full minute is reprinted in Churchill, *Second World War*, vol. III, p. 55.
62. PRO CAB 105/1, Principal Middle East Telegrams Nos 96 and 97, 7 and 8 February 1941.
63. Churchill, *Second World War*, vol. III, p. 687.
64. A Maltese eyewitness account is found in Attard, *Battle of Malta*, pp. 78–97.
65. PRO AIR 23/5706, Maynard to CAS, 16 February 1941.
66. Ibid., Copy of Vice-Admiral Malta to Cunningham, 27 February 1941.
67. Ibid., Governor to CAS, 7 March 1941.
68. British Library, Cunningham Papers, Add. MS. 52561, Cunningham to Pound, 18 January 1941.

69. PRO CAB 69/2, Defence Committee (Operations) (41) 6th Meeting, 20 January 1941; Prime Minister's Minute of 21 January 1941 annexed.
70. PRO AIR 23/5706, CAS to Governor, 8 March 1941.
71. PRO ADM 205/10, Prime Minister's Personal Minute D. 81/1, 9 March 1941.
72. PRO CAB 79/9, COS (41) 93rd Meeting, 11 March 1941.
73. PRO CAB 69/2, Defence Committee (Operations) (41) 10th Meeting, 27 March 1941.
74. British Library, Cunningham Papers, Add. MS. 52561, Pound to Cunningham, 28 March 1941.
75. PRO ADM 199/1932, Prime Minister's Directive D. 149/1, 30 April 1941.
76. Playfair, *Mediterranean*, vol. II, p. 48.
77. PRO AIR 8/500, Governor to CAS, 16 May 1941.
78. PRO PREM 3/266/10A, fol. 856, Vice-Admiral Malta to C-in-C Mediterranean and First Sea Lord, 15 May 1941.
79. British Library, Cunningham Papers, Add. MS. 52561, Cunningham to Pound, 18 May 1941.
80. PRO AIR 8/500, Governor to CAS, 8 May 1941.
81. PRO PREM 3/266/10A, fol. 841, Dobbie to Prime Minister, 17 May 1941.
82. Air Marshal Sir Hugh Lloyd, *Briefed to Attack: Malta's Part in African Victory* (Hodder & Stoughton, London, 1949), p. 13.
83. PRO PREM 3/266/10A, fol. 840, Prime Minister's Personal Telegram T. 195 to Dobbie, 18 May 1941. Maynard later received a CB.
84. Ibid., fols 858–9, CAS to Prime Minister, 16 May 1941.
85. Ibid., fol. 819, Governor to CIGS, 2 June 1941.

9: Malta's Contribution to 'Crusader'

1. Lloyd, *Briefed*, p. 13.
2. PRO AIR 8/500, Vice-Admiral Malta to C-in-C Mediterranean, 12 June 1941; see also Hinsley, *British Intelligence,* vol. II, p. 282.
3. PRO AIR 8/500, CAS Memorandum to Air Member for Personnel, and Air Member for Supply and Organisation, 14 May 1941.
4. Lloyd, *Briefed*, p. 26.
5. PRO AIR 8/500, Lloyd to Portal, 20 June 1941.
6. Playfair, *Mediterranean*, vol. II, p. 362.
7. PRO CAB 79/55, Lloyd to Air Ministry, 26 July 1941, annexed to minutes of COS (41) 22nd 'O' Meeting, 27 July 1941.
8. PRO AIR 8/500, Lloyd to Air Ministry, 31 May 1941.
9. PRO AIR 23/5744, 'Malta–Operational Intelligence Summary, 10 February 1941', Appendix D.
10. PRO AIR 8/500, Ludlow-Hewitt to Portal, 21 July 1941.
11. Playfair, *Mediterranean*, vol. II, p. 280.
12. These operations are fully described in Poolman, *Night Strike.*
13. PRO AIR 8/500, Air Ministry to Lloyd, 14 September 1941; see also Spooner, *Gallantry*, p. 71. These Wellingtons were formed into a Special Duties Flight commanded by Spooner.
14. For an account of Blenheim operations see R. Gillman, *The Shiphunters* (John Murray, London, 1976).
15. PRO AIR 8/500, Tedder to Air Ministry, 26 August 1941, and reply from Freeman, 27 August 1941.
16. Ibid., Portal to Tedder, 1 October 1941.
17. Ibid., Lloyd to Portal, 13 October 1941.
18. PRO AIR 8/506, 'Situation and Operational Reports, Malta, 1-3-41 to 28-12-41'.
19. British Library, Cunningham Papers, Add. MS. 52567, Cunningham to Pound, 3 June 1941.
20. Ibid., Add. MS. 52561, Pound to Cunningham, 3 September 1941.
21. Ibid., Add MS. 52561, Pound to Cunningham, 19 June 1941.
22. Reprinted in Churchill, *Second World War*, vol. III, p. 694.

NOTES

23. PRO PREM 3/274/1, fols 60–63, COS Memorandum to Prime Minister (n.d. early July 1941). Post-war records show that only 31 Axis supply ships of more than 500 tons were sunk in this period.
24. Ibid., fol. 57 has a copy of Pound's Memorandum from which the lower half is missing. A notation reads 'Torn off by Prime Minister'.
25. Ibid., fols 53–4, Ismay to Prime Minister, 22 August 1941. The figures given in this Memorandum are much higher than the reported Italian figures. These are shown later.
26. Reprinted in Churchill, *Second World War*, vol. III, p. 434.
27. Quoted in Hinsley, *British Intelligence*, vol. II, p. 286, fn. ‡.
28. PRO PREM 3/274/1, fols 23–4, C-in-C Mediterranean to Admiralty, 24 August 1941.
29. PRO CAB 79/55, COS (41) 27th 'O' Meeting, 25 August 1941.
30. Churchill, *Second World War*, vol. III, p. 435.
31. British Library, Cunningham Papers, Add. MS. 52561, Pound to Cunningham, 3 September 1941.
32. PRO PREM 3/274/1, fol. 8, Prime Minister Minute M. 960/1 to Pound, 5 October 1941.
33. Ibid., fols 6–7, Pound to Prime Minister, 5 October 1941.
34. PRO PREM 3/266/10A, fol. 786, Admiralty to C-in-C Mediterranean, 11 October 1941.
35. British Library, Cunningham Papers, Add. MS. 52561, Pound to Cunningham, 11 October 1941.
36. Figures in Knox, *Italian Allies*, pp. 25–7; see also L. Ceva, 'Italy', in I. Dear and F. Foot (eds), *The Oxford Companion to the Second World War* (Oxford University Press, Oxford, 1995), pp. 580–603.
37. Knox, *Italian Allies*, p. 79.
38. Van Creveld, *Supplying War*, p. 199.
39. Giorgerini, 'La guerra', pp. 405, 416–17.
40. Martiensson, *Conferences*, p. 226.
41. USMM, *Marina*, vol. VI, *La Difesa*, p. 197.
42. Knox, *Italian Allies*, pp. 70, 96.
43. Ibid., p. 98.
44. Giorgerini, 'La guerra', p. 418.
45. This account is based on Hinsley, *British Intelligence*, vol. II, pp. 277–340, and on Bennett, *Ultra*, pp. 68–108.
46. Hinsley, *British Intelligence*, vol. II, p. 279.
47. Ibid., vol. II, p. 22, fn. †.
48. Ibid., vol. II, p. 283.
49. Ibid., vol. I, pp. 570–72.
50. Ibid., vol. II, p. 319.
51. Lloyd described both these highly technical aircraft as 'temperamental' and added that they would not 'go into the air until they felt like it' (*Briefed*, p. 206).
52. Ibid., p. 52.
53. See the account in Spooner, *Gallantry*, pp. 74–87.
54. PRO ADM 186/801, *Mediterranean*, vol. II, p. 158.
55. Lloyd, *Briefed*, p. 105; Playfair, *Mediterranean*, vol. III, p. 18.
56. USMM, *Marina*, Vol. VI, *La Difesa*, p. 7.
57. Hinsley attributed this to the delay caused by the Admiralty's continued refusal to allow C38m intercepts to be decyphered at Malta (Hinsley, *British Intelligence*, vol. II, p. 319).
58. The British attacks on Axis convoys in November and December 1941 are described in Playfair, *Mediterranean*, vol. III, pp. 103–18, and in Grove, *Sea Battles*, pp. 56–74. For an Italian account see Giorgerini, *Battaglia*, pp. 163–71.
59. Hinsley, *British Intelligence*, vol. II, p. 321.
60. PRO PREM 3/274/2, fol. 408 records a Note by General Ismay, dated 24 November 1941, placed there on the instructions of the Prime Minister. It describes the signals sent on the previous day, including Pound's direct order to Vice-Admiral Ford at Malta to sail Force K to intercept the two German ships, 'all risks being accepted'.
61. Spooner, *Gallantry*, p. 90; Grove, *Sea Battles*, pp. 67–8.
62. Playfair, *Mediterranean*, vol. III, pp. 87, 110, 114; Grove, *Sea Battles*, pp. 72–4.
63. Hinsley, *British Intelligence*, vol. II, p. 324.

64. Giorgerini, *Battaglia*, pp. 171–3.
65. USMM, *Marina, Vol. VI, La Difesa*, p. 198.
66. Van Creveld, *Supplying War*, p. 185.
67. Playfair, *Mediterranean*, vol. III, pp. 70, 107.
68. Bragadin, *Italian Navy*, p. 72.
69. Hinsley, *British Intelligence*, vol. II, pp 302–4.
70. Details of Montezemolo's meeting with Rommel are in B. Pitt, *The Crucible of War: Western Desert 1941* (Jonathan Cape, London, 1980), p. 457.
71. G. Giorgerini, 'The Role of Malta in Italian Naval Operations, 1940–43', in US Naval Academy, Department of History (eds), *New Aspects of Naval History. Selected Papers from the 5th Naval History Symposium* (Nautical and Aviation Publishing Co. of America, Baltimore, MD, 1985), p. 190.
72. Gabriele, 'L'offensiva', p. 445.
73. Van Creveld, *Supplying War*, p. 199.
74. Admiral Simpson later wrote that, had Force K received its instructions after sailing, rather than at a briefing in Valletta, which he attended, the 40 minutes thereby saved might have led to the interception of the *Mongenevro* outside the Tripoli minefield. See Simpson, *Periscope View*, p. 181.
75. Churchill, *Second World War*, vol. III, p. 513.
76. Playfair, *Mediterranean*, vol. III, p. 108.
77. Bragadin, *Italian Navy*, p. 141.
78. Lloyd, *Briefed*, pp. 102–3; Spooner, *Gallantry*, p. 104.
79. Schreiber, *Germany*, vol. III, p. 712.
80. Trevor-Roper, *Directives*, p. 164.
81. Martiensson, *Conferences*, pp. 235, 245.
82. Ibid., p. 246.
83. Bennett, *Ultra*, p. 81.
84. Field Marshal Lord Carver, *Dilemmas of the Desert War: A New Look at the Libyan Campaign 1940–1942* (Batsford, London, 1986), p. 141.
85. J. Ferris, 'The "Usual Source": Signals Intelligence and Planning for the Eighth Army "Crusader" Offensive, 1941', in D. Alvarez (ed.), *Allied and Axis Signals Intelligence in World War II* (Frank Cass, London, 1999), p. 112.

10: *The 1942 Siege of Malta*

1. PRO CAB 79/56, COS (42) 2nd 'O' Meeting, 9 January 1942.
2. PRO CAB 80/34, Governor to War Office, 18 February 1942, annexed to COS Memorandum (42) 130, 'Supplies to Malta', 22 February 1942.
3. PRO CAB 79/18, COS (42) 62nd Meeting, 24 February 1942.
4. Ibid., draft telegram annexed to minutes of COS (42) 66th Meeting, 27 February 1942.
5. PRO CAB 105/9, Principal Middle East Telegrams, No. 43, 4 March 1942.
6. Reprinted in Churchill, *Second World War*, vol. IV, p. 261.
7. This is the view of his biographer. See J. Connell, *Auchinleck* (Cassell, London, 1959), p. 457.
8. PRO CAB 105/9, Principal Middle East Telegrams, No. 19, 17 February 1942.
9. Ibid., No. 23, 20 February 1942.
10. Quoted in Connell, *Auchinleck*, p. 454.
11. PRO CAB 105/16, 'Crusader' Series Telegrams, No. 240, 27 February 1942.
12. PRO CAB 80/61, COS 'O' Memorandum (42) 55 (O), 'Situation in Libya', 1 March 1942, Annex III.
13. Churchill, *Second World War*, vol. IV, p. 81.
14. PRO CAB 69/4, Defence Committee (Operations) (42) 7th Meeting, 2 March 1942.
15. PRO CAB 105/17, 'Crusader' Series Telegrams, No. 7, 3 March 1942.
16. Ibid., No. 13, 5 March 1942.
17. PRO CAB 69/4, Defence Committee (Operations) (42) 9th Meeting, 26 March 1942.
18. PRO CAB 79/19, COS (42) 99th Meeting, 30 March 1942.
19. PRO CAB 69/4, Defence Committee (Operations) (42) 12th Meeting, 22 April 1942.

NOTES

20. PRO CAB 66/24, War Cabinet Memorandum WP (42) 195, 'C-in-C Middle East to Chiefs of Staff', 7 May 1942.
21. PRO CAB 65/30, War Cabinet (42) 59th Meeting, 8 May 1942.
22. This telegram is reprinted in Churchill, *Second World War*, vol. IV, p. 275.
23. PRO CAB War Cabinet (42) 60th Meeting, 10 May 1942.
24. A. Danchev and D. Todman, *War Diaries 1939–1945: Field Marshal Lord Alanbrooke* (Weidenfeld & Nicolson, London, 2001); Diary entry 10 May 1942, p. 256.
25. PRO CAB 66/24, War Cabinet Memorandum WP (42) 196, 'Middle East Defence Committee to Chiefs of Staff', 10 May 1942.
26. Major-General Sir John Kennedy, *The Business of War: The War Narrative of Major-General Sir John Kennedy* (Hutchinson, London, 1957), p. 226.
27. The Prime Minister's telegram of 10 May 1942 and Auchinleck's reply of 19 May are reprinted in Churchill, *Second World War*, vol. IV, pp. 275–7.
28. Playfair, *Mediterranean*, vol. II, p. 362.
29. Ibid., vol. III, p. 458.
30. PRO CAB 79/20, COS Memorandum (42) (JP) 376, 'Relation of Strategy in Middle East and India', 8 April 1942, annexed to minutes of COS (42) 113th Meeting, 9 April 1942.
31. PRO CAB 79/20, COS Memorandum (42) (JP) 482, 'Supplies for Malta', 7 May 1942, annexed to minutes of COS (42) 145th Meeting, 9 May 1942.
32. PRO CAB 65/30, War Cabinet (42) 60th Meeting, 10 May 1942.
33. PRO CAB 79/21, COS (42) 194th Meeting, 1 July 1942.
34. PRO CAB 79/22, COS (42) 222nd Meeting, 30 July 1942.
35. These actions are fully described in Playfair, *Mediterranean*, vol. III, pp. 155–75.
36. Roskill, *War at Sea*, vol. II, pp. 50, 62.
37. Playfair, *Mediterranean*, vol. III, p. 174.
38. Roskill, *War at Sea*, vol. II, pp. 50, 59.
39. Simpson, *Periscope View*, p. 210.
40. Ibid., p. 222. Appendix 3, pp. 294–9, is the Report he submitted on the operations of the 10th Flotilla in the first five months of 1942.
41. Derived from Playfair, *Mediterranean*, vol. III, pp. 162–88.
42. Lloyd, *Briefed*, p. 141.
43. A daily account of these operations is set out in C. Shores, B. Cull with N. Malizia, *Malta: The Spitfire Year 1942* (Grub Street, London, 1991). See also Poolman, *Night Strike*, pp. 160–67.
44. There are many accounts of this battle. A contemporary account is given in Ministry of Information, *The Air Battle of Malta: The Official Account of the RAF in Malta, June 1940 to November 1942* (His Majesty's Stationery Office, London, 1944). A more recent narrative is given in L. Lucas, *Malta: The Thorn in Rommel's Side* (Stanley Paul, London, 1992).
45. PRO AIR 8/504, CAS to DCAS, 6 February 1942.
46. PRO PREM 3/266/4, fol. 509, CAS to Prime Minister, 20 May 1942.
47. Playfair, *Mediterranean*, vol. III, p. 188.
48. M. Gabriele, 'L'operazione "C3" (1942)', in R. Rainero and A. Biagini (eds), *Cinquant'anni dopo l'entrata dell'Italia nella 2a guerra mondiale. Aspetti e problema. L'Italia in guerra: il 3o anno–1942* (Gaeta, Rome, 1993), pp. 409–34.
49. Field-Marshal A. Kesselring, *The Memoirs of Field-Marshal Kesselring* (Greenhill Books, London, 1997), p. 122.
50. General W. Warlimont, 'The Decision in the Mediterranean 1942', in H-A. Jacobsen and J. Rohwer (eds), *Decisive Battles of World War II: The German View* (Andre Deutsch, London, 1965), p. 189.
51. Gabriele, 'L'operazione', p. 430.
52. A. Santoni and F. Mattesini, *La partecipazione Tedesca alla guerra aeronavale nel Mediterraneo (1940–1945)* (Edizioni dell'Ateneo & Bizzari, Rome, 1980), pp. 183–6.
53. PRO PREM 3/266/1, fol. 133, Middle East Defence Committee to Prime Minister and Chiefs of Staff, 20 April 1942.
54. Churchill, *Second World War*, vol. IV, p. 273.
55. In June 1942 two experts from the Ministry of Food, just returned from Malta, told the Chiefs of Staff of the increased fatigue of even young servicemen as a result of the severe rationing. PRO CAB 79/21, COS (42) 190th Meeting, 26 June 1942.

56. S. Dobbie, *Faith and Fortitude: The Life and Work of General Sir William Dobbie* (privately printed, 1979), p. 298.
57. The report of the Vice-Admiral Malta, Vice-Admiral Leatham, about the difficulties of unloading these ships is reprinted in Vella, *Malta*, pp. 65–7. See also Attard, *Battle of Malta*, pp. 160–62.
58. PRO AIR 8/500, HQ Middle East to Air Ministry, 28 March 1942.
59. Vella, *Malta*, p. 68.
60. Marshal of the Royal Air Force Lord Tedder, *With Prejudice* (Cassell, London, 1966), p. 264.
61. PRO CAB 69/4, Defence Committee (Operations) (42) 12th Meeting, 22 April 1942.
62. PRO PREM 3/266/1, fol. 129, Governor to Colonial Secretary, 23 April 1942.
63. Ibid., fols 125, 121, Prime Minister to Dobbie, and Prime Minister to Monckton, 24 April 1942.
64. Lord Casey, *Personal Experience 1939–1946* (Constable, London, 1962), p. 99.
65. PRO PREM 3/266/1, fols 82–3, Casey to Prime Minister, 3 May 1942.
66 Dobbie, *Faith*, p. 295.
67. J. Alexander, *Mabel Strickland* (Progress Press, Valletta, 1996), pp. 121–8.
68. Jellison, *Besieged*, pp. 213–14.
69. PRO PREM 3/266/10A, fol. 771, Governor to Prime Minister, 23 April 1942.
70. PRO PREM 3/266/1, fols 130–31, Cranborne to Prime Minister, 21 April 1942.
71. Casey, *Experience*, p. 99.

11: *Malta's Contribution to the Recovery of North Africa*

1. PRO CAB 79/21, COS (42) 190th Meeting, 26 June 1942; Report by Dr Drummond and Mr Wall.
2. Ibid. Prime Minister's Minute M. 261/2 annexed to minutes of COS (42) 180th Meeting, 16 June 1942.
3. Lloyd, *Briefed*, pp. 213–14.
4. PRO CAB 105/10, Principal Middle East Telegrams, No. 13, Governor to Chiefs of Staff, 4 July 1942.
5. PRO CAB 79/21, COS (42) 194th Meeting, 1 July 1942.
6. PRO CAB 105/10, Principal Middle East Telegrams, No. 84, Chiefs of Staff to Middle East C-in-Cs, 30 July 1942.
7. PRO CAB 79/22, COS (42) 222nd Meeting, 30 July 1942.
8. PRO CAB 79/57, COS (42) 94th 'O' Meeting, 19 August 1942; the Directive is in PRO CAB 105/10, Principal Middle East Telegrams, No. 131, 19 August 1942.
9. PRO CAB 80/37, COS Memorandum (42) 392, 'Malta: Petrol Supplies', 1 September 1942.
10. PRO CAB 79/23, COS (42) 271st Meeting, 25 September 1942.
11. PRO CAB 79/58, COS (42) 155th 'O' Meeting, 21 October 1942.
12. PRO CAB 79/57, COS (42) 130th 'O' Meeting, 28 September 1942.
13. These operations are described in Playfair, *Mediterranean*, vol. IV, pp. 196–200.
14. See D. Richards and H. St. G. Saunders, *Royal Air Force 1939–1945* (His Majesty's Stationery Office, London, 1954), vol. II, p. 232.
15. PRO DEFE 3/580, Enigma signal ZTPGM/211, 2 September 1942.
16. Liddell Hart, *Rommel*, pp. 243, 287, 290.
17. PRO CAB 146/21, EDS/Appreciation/11, 'The Axis Supply Situation in North Africa', Part III, p. 272.
18. Liddell Hart, *Rommel*, p. 266.
19. Hinsley, *British Intelligence*, vol. II, pp. 411–12.
20. Ibid., vol. II, p. 408.
21. Ibid., vol. II, p. 420.
22. Kesselring, *Memoirs*, p. 131; Liddell Hart, *Rommel*, p. 274.
23. PRO CAB 146/20, EDS/Appreciation/11, 'The Axis Supply Situation in North Africa', Part II, p. 214.
24. PRO DEFE 3/773, Enigma signals QT 585, 2 September, and QT 658, 3 September 1942.

NOTES

25. Ibid., Enigma signals QT 417, 505, 585, 604, 607, 630, 669, 844, between 30 August and 6 September 1942.
26. PRO CAB 146/16, EDS/Appreciation/9, 'Axis Operations in North Africa, 1 September–23 October 1942', Part V, pp. 35–9; Liddell Hart, *Rommel*, p. 283.
27. Kesselring, *Memoirs*, p. 131.
28. The Beaufort operations are described by its CO, Wing Commander P. Gibbs, in P. Gibbs, *Torpedo Leader* (Grub Street, London, 1992).
29. Liddell Hart, *Rommel*, p. 287.
30. Hinsley, *British Intelligence*, vol. II, pp. 425–9.
31. PRO CAB 146/21, EDS/Appreciation/11, 'The Axis Supply Situation in North Africa', Part III, p. 261.
32. PRO DEFE 3/780, Enigma signal QT 4077, 20 October 1942; Hinsley, *British Intelligence*, vol. II, p. 427.
33. Liddell Hart, *Rommel*, p. 313.
34. PRO DEFE 3/780, Enigma signal QT 4119, 23 October 1942.
35. PRO DEFE 3/781, Enigma signal QT 4599, 28 October 1942.
36. PRO CAB 146/16, EDS/Appreciation/9, 'Axis Operations in North Africa, 1 September–23 October 1942', Part V, pp. 34, 37; Liddell Hart, *Rommel*, p. 312.
37. See R. Nesbit, *The Armed Rovers: Beauforts and Beaufighters over the Mediterranean* (Airlife Publishing, Shrewsbury, 1995), pp. 88–103.
38. Giorgerini, 'La guerra', p. 414.
39. Knox, *Italian Allies*, p. 99.
40. F. Mattesini, *La battaglia aeronavale di mezzo agosto* (Edizioni dell'Ateneo, Rome, 1986), pp. 445–6; the sources for his Table are not given and cannot be reconciled with those presented here.
41. Van Creveld, *Supplying War*, p. 199.
42. See also Sadkovich, *Italian Navy*, pp. 302–13, for an analysis of the fuel deliveries at the various ports in North Africa.
43. See also PRO CAB 146/20 and 146/21, EDS/Appreciation/11 'The Axis Supply Situation in North Africa', Part II, March-August 1942, and Part III, September–December 1942.
44. Warlimont, 'Decision', p. 203.
45. Liddell Hart, *Rommel*, p. 233; see also D. Fraser, *Knight's Cross: A Life of Field Marshal Erwin Rommel* (HarperCollins, London, 1993), pp. 343-4.
46. Liddell Hart, *Rommel*, pp. 286–8.
47. The planning for 'Torch' is described in detail in M. Howard, *August 1942–September 1943*, vol. IV of *Grand Strategy*, 6 vols (Her Majesty's Stationery Office, London, 1970), pp. 111–39.
48. Hinsley, *British Intelligence*, vol. II, p. 463.
49. PRO CAB 121/491, 'Torch: Plans and Directives. Outline Plan, 20 September 1942'.
50. Hinsley, *British Intelligence*, vol. II, p. 474.
51. PRO CAB 79/57, COS (42) 131st 'O' Meeting, 29 September 1942.
52. PRO CAB 121/632, Admiralty to C-in-C Mediterranean, 19 September 1942.
53. PRO CAB 79/23, COS Memorandum JP (42) 862, 'Malta–Offensive Operations in Conjunction with a Certain Operation', 6 October 1942, annexed to minutes of COS (42) 283rd Meeting, 8 October 1942.
54. See Simpson, *Periscope View*, pp. 266–8.
55. Playfair, *Mediterranean*, vol. IV, p. 170, n. 1.
56. See A. Bryant, *The Turn of the Tide 1939–1943* (Collins, London, 1957), p. 503.
57. Warlimont, 'Decision', pp. 204–13.
58. Playfair, *Mediterranean*, vol. IV, pp. 170–73; Giorgerini, *Battaglia*, pp. 205–10.
59. PRO CAB 79/58, COS (42) 178th 'O' Meeting, 11 November 1942.
60. PRO CAB 121/632, COS Telegram (ME) 323 to Middle East C-in-Cs, 11 November 1942.
61. PRO CAB 79/58, Prime Minister's Minute D. 196/2, 12 November 1942, annexed to minutes of COS (42) 180th 'O' Meeting, 13 November 1942.
62. Simpson, *Periscope View*, pp. 268–9.
63. Ibid., pp. 268–9.
64. Quoted in Wingate, *Fighting Tenth*, p. 245.

65. Rear-Admiral Ben Bryant *Submarine Command*, (William Kimber, London, 1958), pp. 193–4.
66. PRO CAB 79/24, COS (42) 318th Meeting, 17 November 1942.
67. PRO CAB 69/4, Defence Committee (Operations) (42) 18th Meeting, 23 November 1942; the various signals are in PRO CAB 121/632, F/Malta/2, 'Offensive Operations', vol. I, September 1942–July 1943.
68. Reprinted in Churchill, *Second World War*, vol. IV, p. 808.
69. PRO ADM 205/27, Pound to Prime Minister, 9 December 1942.
70. PRO AIR 8/1011, 'Operation "Torch": Malta Air Contribution'.
71. Ibid., Deputy AOC-in-C Middle East to AOC Malta, 2 November 1942.
72. PRO CAB 79/4, COS (42) 322nd Meeting, 20 November 1942.
73. PRO AIR 41/33, Air Historical Branch Narrative, 'The North African Campaign, November 1942–May 1943', Appendix 6, 'Malta's Contribution to Torch'.
74. Tedder, *With Prejudice*, pp. 369–84.
75. Hinsley, *British Intelligence*, vol. II, pp. 493–6.
76. Giorgerini, *Battaglia*, pp. 205–10.
77. The Tunisian campaign is well covered in Levine, *The War*, and Playfair, *Mediterranean*, vol. IV.
78. Warlimont, *Hitler's Headquarters*, p. 311; Hinsley, *British Intelligence*, vol. II, p. 578.
79. Playfair, *Mediterranean*, vol. IV, p. 289, n. 1.
80. Details are in PRO AIR 41/33, Appendix 6, 'Malta's Contribution to Torch'.
81. Giorgerini, *Battaglia*, p. 209.
82. Bragadin, *Italian Navy*, p. 249.
83. Appendix V in Spooner, *Supreme Gallantry*, pp. 329–38, lists 247 ships sunk in the Tunisian campaign, dividing these between naval and air forces. He does not, however, identify those sunk by Malta-based forces.
84. Playfair, *Mediterranean*, vol. IV, pp. 262–3.
85. Vella, *Malta*, pp. 182–3.
86. Cunningham, *Odyssey*, p. 565.

12: Conclusion

1. Gabriele, *Operazione C3*, p. 25.
2. Shores, *Spitfire Year*, p. 645.
3. Ibid., p. 679.
4. F. Hinsley and A. Stripp, *Codebreakers: The Inside Story of Bletchley Park* (Oxford University Press, Oxford, 1993), p. 12.

References

RECORDS AT THE PUBLIC RECORD OFFICE, KEW

Admiralty Papers

ADM	1	Admiralty and Secretariat Files
	116	Admiralty and Secretariat Cases
	167	Board of Admiralty
	186	Admiralty Publications
	199	War History Cases and Papers
	205	First Sea Lord's Papers
	223	Naval Intelligence Division

Air Ministry Papers

AIR	2	Air Ministry Registered Files
	8	Chief of the Air Staff Papers
	9	Director of Plans Files
	20	Unregistered Files
	23	Overseas Commands
	41	Air Historical Branch: Narratives and Monographs

Cabinet Office and Cabinet Committee Papers

CAB	2, 4, 5	Committee of Imperial Defence
	7, 8	Oversea Defence Committee
	11/190	Malta Defence Scheme 1935
	16	Cabinet Sub-Committees
	16/105	Coast Defence Isnquiry
	16/109–12	Defence Requirements Committee
	16/121	Abyssinia Committee
	16/136–44	Defence Policy and Requirements Committee
	16/181–83B	Defence Plans (Policy) Committee

215

16/209	Strategical Appreciation Committee
21	Cabinet Registered Files
23, 24	Cabinet Papers to September 1939
27	Disarmament Conference Committee
36	Joint Oversea and Home Defence Committee
36/21	Defence of Ports Committee
44	Historical Section: Narratives
53, 54	Chiefs of Staff Committee to September 1939
55	Joint Planning Committee to September 1939
56	Joint Intelligence Committee to September 1939
63	Hankey Papers
65, 66	War Cabinet:
69	Defence Committee (Operations)
79, 80	Chiefs of Staff Committee
82	Deputy Chiefs of Staff Committee
83	Military Co-ordination Committee
84	Joint Planning Committee
95	Military Policy in the Middle East
99	Supreme War Council
105	War Cabinet: Principal Middle East Telegrams
106/481–510	Historical Section; Monographs on Malta
121	Special Secret Information Centre
146	Enemy Documents Section
PREM 1	Prime Minister's Papers to 1940
3	Prime Minister's Operational Papers
3/266/1–10A	Prime Minister's Operational Papers relating to Malta

Colonial, Intelligence, Foreign Office and Treasury Papers

CO 158	Malta: Original Correspondence
355	Malta: Registers of Correspondence
883	Malta: Confidential Print
DEFE 3	Intelligence from Enigma Intercepts
HW 3	GC&CS Histories and Personal Papers
FO 371	General Correspondence
850	General Correspondence: Communications
T 161	Supply Files
161/1459	Malta: Provision of Aerodromes, 1935–42

War Office Papers

WO 32	War Office Registered Files
32/2403–17	Registered Files Relating to Malta (Code 041)

REFERENCES

32/10211–14   Royal Malta Artillery
106   Directorate of Military Operations and Intelligence
106/3062–6   War Office–Governor of Malta Cables
190   Military Appreciations
196   Director of Artillery
196/24   Report on Coast Defence: 1928

UNPUBLISHED AIR HISTORICAL BRANCH NARRATIVE

The Middle East Campaigns; Vol. XI Malta (n.d.)

UNPUBLISHED PRIVATE PAPERS

Admiral of the Fleet Viscount Cunningham, British Library
Admiral of the Fleet Lord Chatfield, National Maritime Museum

PUBLISHED DOCUMENTS

Documenti diplomatici Italiani, Series IX, vols III–IV (Rome, 1952–53).
Documents on British Foreign Policy 1919–1939, 2nd Series, vol. XIV (Her Majesty's Stationery Office, London, 1976).
Documents on German Foreign Policy, Series D, vol. IX (Her Majesty's Stationery Office, London, 1956).
Parliamentary Debates, 5th Series, vol. 313.
Statement Relating to Defence, Cmd 5107 (His Majesty's Stationery Office, London, March 1936).
Treaty between the British Empire, France, Italy, Japan, and the United States of America for the Limitation of Naval Armaments, Cmd 2036 (His Majesty's Stationery Office, London, 1924).

BOOKS AND ARTICLES

Alexander, J. *Mabel Strickland* (Progress Press, Valletta, 1996).
Amery, L. S. *My Political Life, Vol. II, War and Peace 1914–1929* (Hutchinson, London, 1953).
Arnold-Forster, M. *The World at War* (Collins, London, 1975).
Attard, J. *The Battle of Malta* (Hamlyn Paperbacks, London, 1982).
——. *Britain and Malta: The Story of an Era* (Publishers Enterprises, Valletta, 1988).

Avon, Earl of, *The Eden Memoirs: Facing the Dictators* (Cassell, London, 1962).
Badoglio, P. *Italy in the Second World War: Memories and Documents* (Oxford University Press, London, 1948).
Baer, G. *The Coming of the Italian–Ethiopian War* (Harvard University Press, Cambridge, MA, 1967).
Barnett, C. *Engage the Enemy More Closely: The Royal Navy in the Second World War* (Penguin Books, London, 2000).
Beesly, P. *Very Special Intelligence: The Story of the Admiralty's Operational Intelligence Centre* (Hamish Hamilton, London, 1977).
Bell, P. H. M. *A Certain Eventuality . . . Britain and the Fall of France* (Saxon House, Farnborough, 1974).
Bennett, R. *Ultra and Mediterranean Strategy 1941–1945* (Hamish Hamilton, London, 1989).
Boffa, C. *The Second Great Siege: Malta 1940–1943* (Progress Press, Valletta, 1992).
Bond, B. (ed.), *Chief of Staff: The Diaries of Lt. Gen. Sir Henry Pownall, Vol. I, 1933–40* (Leo Cooper, London, 1972).
Bonham-Carter, V. *In a Liberal Tradition* (Constable, London, 1960).
Bragadin, Commander M'A. *The Italian Navy in World War II* (United States Naval Institute, Annapolis, MD, 1957).
Brodhurst, R. *Churchill's Anchor: Admiral of the Fleet Sir Dudley Pound* (Leo Cooper, Barnsley, 2000).
Bryant, A. *The Turn of the Tide 1939–1943* (Collins, London, 1957).
Bryant, Rear-Admiral Ben. *Submarine Command* (William Kimber, London, 1958).
Budden, M. 'British Policy towards Fascist Italy in the Early Stages of the Second World War' (PhD Thesis, King's College, University of London, 1999).
Cameron, I. *Red Duster, White Ensign: The Story of Malta and the Malta Convoys* (Bantam Books, London, 1983).
Carver, Field Marshal Lord, *Dilemmas of the Desert War: A New Look at the Libyan Campaign 1940–1942* (Batsford, London, 1986).
Casey, Lord, *Personal Experience 1939–1946* (Constable, London, 1962).
Cassels, A. *Mussolini's Early Diplomacy* (Princeton University Press, Princeton, NJ, 1970).
Ceva, L. 'Italy', in I. Dear and M. Foot (eds), *The Oxford Companion to the Second World War* (Oxford University Press, Oxford, 1995).
Chatfield, Admiral of the Fleet Lord, *It Might Happen Again, Vol. II, The Navy and Defence* (Heinemann, London, 1947).
Churchill, Sir W. *The Second World War*, 6 vols (Cassell, London, 1948–54).
Ciano, G. *Ciano's Diary 1937–1938* (Methuen, London, 1952).

REFERENCES

Connell, J. *Auchinleck* (Cassell, London, 1959).

——. *Wavell: Scholar and Soldier* (Collins, London, 1964).

Cunningham, Admiral of the Fleet Viscount, *A Sailor's Odyssey* (Hutchinson, London, 1951).

Danchev, A. and Todman, D. *War Diaries 1939–1945: Field Marshal Lord Alanbrooke* (Weidenfeld & Nicolson, London, 2001).

Dean, Sir Maurice. *The Royal Air Force and Two World Wars* (Cassell, London, 1979).

Dear, I. and Foot, M. (eds), *The Oxford Companion to the Second World War* (Oxford University Press, Oxford, 1995).

Dobbie, S. *Faith and Fortitude: The Life and Work of General Sir William Dobbie* (privately printed, 1979).

Ferris, J. 'The "Usual Source": Signals Intelligence and Planning for the Eighth Army "Crusader" Offensive, 1941', in D. Alvarez (ed.), *Allied and Axis Signals Intelligence in World War II* (Frank Cass, London, 1999).

Foss, Group Captain P. *Climbing Turns* (Linden Hall, Yeovil, 1990).

Fraser, D. *Knight's Cross: A Life of Field Marshal Erwin Rommel* (HarperCollins, London, 1993).

Frendo, H. *Party Politics in a Fortress Colony: The Maltese Experience* (Midsea Publications, Valletta, 1991).

Gabriele, M. *Operazione C3: Malta* (Ufficio Storico della Marina Militare, Rome, 1965).

——. 'L'offensiva su Malta (1941)', in R. Rainero and A. Biagini (eds), *Cinquant'anni dopo l'entrata dell'Italia nella 2a guerra mondiale. Aspetti e problema. L'Italia in guerra: il 2o anno–1941* (Gaeta, Rome, 1992).

——. 'L'operazione "C3" (1942)', in R. Rainero and A. Biagini (eds), *Cinquant'anni dopo l'entrata dell'Italia nella 2a guerra mondiale. Aspetti e problema. L'Italia in guerra: il 3o anno–1942* (Gaeta, Rome, 1993).

Gibbs, N. *Rearmament Policy*, vol. I (1976) of *Grand Strategy*, 6 vols (Her Majesty's Stationery Office, London, 1956–76).

Gibbs, Wing Commander P. *Torpedo Leader* (Grub Street, London, 1992).

Gilbert, M. *Winston S. Churchill, Vol. VI, Finest Hour 1939–1941* (Heinemann, London, 1983).

Gillman, R. *The Shiphunters* (John Murray, London, 1976)

Giorgerini, G. *La battaglia dei convogli in Mediterraneo* (Mursia, Milan, 1977).

——. 'The Role of Malta in Italian Naval Operations 1940–43', in Department of History, US Naval Academy (eds), *New Aspects of Naval History: Selected Papers from the 5th Naval History Symposium* (Nautical and Aviation Publishing Company of America, Baltimore, 1985).

——. 'La guerra per mare e il problema dei convogli', in R. Rainero and A. Biagini (eds), *Cinquant'anni dopo l'entrata dell'Italia nella 2a guerra mondiale. Aspetti e problema. L'Italia in guerra; il 2o anno–1941* (Gaeta, Rome, 1992).

Goldman, A. 'Sir Robert Vansittart's Search for Italian Cooperation against Hitler 1933–36', *Journal of Contemporary History*, vol. 9, no. 3 (July 1974), pp. 93–130.

Greene, J. and Massignani, A. *Rommel's North African Campaign: September 1940–November 1942* (Combined Publishing, Conshohocken, PA, USA, 1994).

——. *The Naval War in the Mediterranean 1940–1943* (Chatham Publishing, London, 1998).

Grove, E. *Sea Battles in Close-Up: World War II*, vol. 2 (Ian Allan, Shepperton, 1993).

——. *Vanguard to Trident: British Naval Policy since World War II* (Naval Institute Press, Annapolis, MD, 1987).

Halpern, P. (ed.). *The Keyes Papers, Vol. II, 1919–1938* (Navy Records Society, London, 1980).

——. *A Naval History of World War I* (University College London Press, London, 1995).

Hamlin, J. *Military Aviation in Malta G.C. 1915–1993* (GMS Enterprises, Peterborough, 1994).

Hancock, W. *Survey of British Commonwealth Affairs, Vol. I, Problems of Nationality* (Oxford University Press, London, 1937).

Hinsley, F. et al. *British Intelligence in the Second World War*, 5 vols (Her Majesty's Stationery Office, London, 1979–90).

Hinsley, F. and Stripp, A. *Codebreakers: The Inside Story of Bletchley Park* (Oxford University Press, Oxford, 1993).

Hoare, Sir Samuel (Viscount Templewood). *Nine Troubled Years* (Collins, London, 1954).

Howard, M. *August 1942–September*, vol. IV (1970) of *Grand Strategy*, 6 vols (Her Majesty's Stationery Office, London, 1956–76).

Jellison, C. *Besieged: The World War II Ordeal of Malta 1940–1942* (University Press of New England, Hanover, NH, 1984).

Jones, T. *A Diary with Letters 1931–1950* (Oxford University Press, London, 1954).

Kennedy, Major-General Sir John. *The Business of War: The War Narrative of Major-General Sir John Kennedy* (Hutchinson, London, 1957).

Kennedy, P. *The Rise and Fall of British Naval Mastery* (Fontana, London, 1991).

Kesselring, Field Marshal A. *The Memoirs of Field-Marshal Kesselring* (Greenhill Books, London, 1988).

Knox, M. *Mussolini Unleashed 1939–1941: Politics and Strategy in Fascist Italy's Last War* (Cambridge University Press, Cambridge, 1986).

REFERENCES

———. *Hitler's Italian Allies: Royal Armed Forces, Fascist Regime, and the War of 1940–1943* (Cambridge University Press, Cambridge, 2000).

Lamb, C. *War in a Stringbag* (Arrow Books, London, 1978).

Levine, A. *The War against Rommel's Supply Lines 1942–1943* (Praeger, Westport, CT, 1999).

Liddell Hart, B. *The Defence of Britain* (Faber & Faber, London, 1939).

——— (ed.), *The Rommel Papers* (Collins, London, 1955).

Lloyd, Air Marshal Sir Hugh *Briefed to Attack: Malta's Part in African Victory* (Hodder & Stoughton, London, 1949).

Lloyd's War Losses: The Second World War (Lloyd's of London Press Ltd, London, 1989).

Lucas, L. *Malta: The Thorn in Rommel's Side* (Stanley Paul, London, 1992).

Lukacs, J. *Five Days in London, May 1940* (Yale University Press, New Haven, CT, 1999).

Macintyre, D. *The Battle for the Mediterranean* (Batsford, London, 1964).

Mack Smith, D. *Mussolini's Roman Empire* (Longman, London, 1976).

Mallett, R. *The Italian Navy and Fascist Expansionism 1935–1940* (Frank Cass, London, 1998).

Marder, A. *From the Dardanelles to Oran: Studies of the Royal Navy in War and Peace 1915–1940* (Oxford University Press, London, 1974).

Martiensson, A. (ed.). *Fuehrer Conferences on Naval Affairs 1939–1945* (Greenhill Books, London, 1990).

Mattesini, F. *La battaglia aeronavale di mezzo agosto* (Edizioni dell'Ateneo, Rome, 1986).

Micaleff, J. *When Malta Stood Alone (1940–1943)* (Interprint, Valletta, 1981).

Ministry of Information, *The Air Battle of Malta: The Official Account of the RAF in Malta, June 1940 to November 1942* (His Majesty's Stationery Office, London, 1944).

Minney, R. *The Private Papers of Hore-Belisha* (Collins, London, 1960).

Muggeridge, M. (ed.). *Ciano's Diary 1939–1943* (Heinemann, London, 1947).

Nesbit, R. *The Armed Rovers: Beauforts and Beaufighters over the Mediterranean* (Airlife Publishing, Shrewsbury, 1995).

Perowne, S. *The Siege within the Walls: Malta 1940–1943* (Hodder & Stoughton, London, 1970).

Pile, General Sir Frederick, *ACK–ACK: Britain's Defence against Air Attack during the Second World War* (Harrap, London, 1949).

Pitt, B. *The Crucible of War: Western Desert 1941* (Jonathan Cape, London, 1980).

Playfair, General I. et al., *The Mediterranean and Middle East*, 6 vols (Her Majesty's Stationery Office, London, 1954–73).

Poolman, K. *Night Strike from Malta: 830 Squadron RN and Rommel's Convoys* (Jane's Publishing Co., London, 1980).

Postan, M., Hay, D. and Scott, J. *Design and Development of Weapons: Studies in Government and Industrial Organisation* (Her Majesty's Stationery Office, London, 1964).

Pratt, L. *East of Malta, West of Suez: Britain's Mediterranean Crisis 1936–1939* (Cambridge University Press, Cambridge, 1975).

Reynolds, D. 'Churchill and the British "Decision" to Fight on in 1940: Right Policy, Wrong Reason', in R. Langhorne (ed.), *Diplomacy and Intelligence during the Second World War* (Cambridge University Press, Cambridge, 1985).

Richards, D. and St. G. Saunders, H. *Royal Air Force 1939–1945*, 3 vols (Her Majesty's Stationery Office, London, 1953–54).

Roberts, A. *'The Holy Fox': A Biography of Lord Halifax* (Weidenfeld & Nicolson, London, 1991).

Rohwer, J. *Allied Submarine Attacks of World War Two: European Theatre of Operations 1939–1945* (Greenhill Books, London, 1997).

Rollo, D. *The Guns and Gunners of Malta* (Mondial Publishers, Malta, 1999).

Roskill, S. *The War at Sea*, 3 vols (Her Majesty's Stationery Office, London, 1954–61).

——. *The Navy at War 1939–1945* (Collins, London, 1960).

——. *Naval Policy between the Wars*, 2 vols (Collins, London, 1968, 1981).

——. *Churchill and the Admirals* (Collins, London, 1977).

Sadkovich, J. *The Italian Navy in World War II* (Greenwood Press, Westport, CT, 1994).

Santoni, A. and Mattesini, F. *La partecipazione Tedesca alla guerra aeronavale nel Mediterraneo (1940–1945)* (Edizioni dell'Ateneo & Bizzari, Rome, 1980).

Santoro, G. *L'Aeronautica Italiana nella seconda guerra mondiale*, 2 vols (Edizioni esse, Milan, 1966).

Schreiber, G. et al., *Germany and the Second World War*, vols III and VI (Clarendon Press, Oxford, 1995, 2001).

Shores, C. and Cull, B. with Malizia, N. *Malta: The Hurricane Years 1940–41* (Grub Street, London, 1987).

——. *Malta: The Spitfire Year 1942* (Grub Street, London, 1991).

Simpson, Rear-Admiral G. *Periscope View: A Professional Autobiography* (Macmillan, London, 1972).

Slessor, Marshal of the Royal Air Force Sir John. *The Central Blue* (Cassell, London, 1956).

Smith, H. and Koster, A. *Lord Strickland, Servant of the Crown*, vol. II (Progress Press, Valletta, 1986).

Smith, M. *British Air Strategy between The Wars* (Clarendon Press, Oxford, 1984).

REFERENCES

Spooner, T. *Supreme Gallantry: Malta's Role in the Allied Victory 1939–1945* (John Murray, London, 1996).

Strong, Major-General Sir Kenneth. *Intelligence at the Top: The Recollections of an Intelligence Officer* (Cassell, London, 1968).

Tedder, Marshal of the Royal Air Force Lord, *With Prejudice* (Cassell, London, 1966).

The Times of Malta, May–June 1940.

Thompson, Sir Geoffrey, *Front Line Diplomat* (Hutchinson, London, 1959).

Trevor–Roper, H. (ed.). *Hitler's War Directives 1939–1945* (Pan Books, London, 1966).

Ufficio Storico della Marina Militare, *La Marina Italiana nella seconda guerra mondiale*, 19 vols (USMM, Rome, 1950–72).

——. Vol. I, *Dati statistici*.

——. Vol. II, *Le azioni navali dal 10 Guigno 1940 al 31 Marzo 1941*.

——. Vol. VI, *La guerra nel Mediterraneo: La difesa del traffico coll'Africa settentrionale dal 10 Giugno 1940 al 30 Settembre 1941*.

——. Vol. VII, *La guerra nel Mediterraneo: La difesa del traffico coll'Africa settentrionale dal 1 Octobre 1941 al 30 Settembre 1942*.

——. Vol. VIII, *La guerra nel Mediterraneo: La difesa del traffico coll'Africa settentrionale dal 1 Octobre 1942 Alla Caduta Della Tunisia*.

——. Vol. XXI, *L'organizzazione delle Marina durante il conflitto: Tomo I: Efficienza all'apertura della ostilità*.

Van Creveld, M. *Supplying War: Logistics from Wallenstein to Patton* (Cambridge University Press, Cambridge, 1977).

Vella, P. *Malta: Blitzed but not Beaten* (Progress Press, Valletta, 1985).

Warlimont, General W. *Inside Hitler's Headquarters 1939–1945* (Presidio, Novato, CA, n.d.).

——. 'The Decision in the Mediterranean 1942', in H-A. Jacobsen and J. Rohwer (eds), *Decisive Battles of World War II: The German View* (Andre Deutsch, London, 1965).

West, N. *MI6: British Secret Intelligence Service Operations 1909–1945* (Weidenfeld & Nicolson, London, 1983).

Wheeler-Bennett, Sir J. (ed.), *Action This Day: Working with Churchill: Memoirs by Lord Normanbrook, John Colville, Sir John Martin, Sir Ian Jacob, Lord Bridges, Sir Leslie Rowan* (Macmillan, London, 1968).

Wingate, J. *The Fighting Tenth: The Tenth Submarine Flotilla and the Siege of Malta* (Leo Cooper, London, 1991).

Index

1st Submarine Flotilla: moves to Beirut (June 1942), 166; and 'Torch', 171
5th Destroyer Flotilla: at Malta, 114; withdrawn, 127
8th Army: assessments of fighting strength of, 141–2; forced back to Gazala, 143; and Alam Halfa, 161
10th Submarine Flotilla: at Malta, 112, 114, 133; withdrawn to Alexandria, 152; and 'Pedestal' convoy, 168; re-established at Malta, 167; successes in October 1942, 168; in support of 'Torch', 171; *see also* Admiralty, Cunningham, Pound, Simpson
14th Destroyer Flotilla: at Malta, 158–9
25-pounder guns: 67; requested for Malta (1940), 113–14
Abruzzi: damaged, 165
Abyssinian crisis: 4, 35–48, 52, 71, 73–4, 75, 82, 182
'Acrobat', Operation: 143
Aden: receives eight Bofors AA guns (1939), 63, 67; possible withdrawal of Mediterranean Fleet to, 70
Admiralty: decides to base Main Fleet at Malta (1923), 7–8; and war plans (1925) 7–9; concern for Malta, 14; critical of 3-inch AA guns, 15; rejects Admiral Fisher's AA proposals for Malta (1933), 23; and Abyssinian crisis (August 1935), 35; explains intended Mediterranean strategy in war with Italy (1935), 39; seeks improved defences at Malta (1937–9), 58–62; urges authorisation of Scale B defences at Malta (1939), 61–2; reinforces Mediterranean fleet (1940), 65; warns Cunningham of probable Italian declaration of war (May 1940), 66, 84; and plans for use of Malta, 95; sends more submarines to Malta, 112; orders 14th and 5th Destroyer Flotillas to Malta, 113–14; sends cruisers and destroyers to Malta (October 1941), 129, 134; withdraws 10th Submarine flotilla and surface ships from Malta (April 1942), 151–2; prepares for 'Torch', 161; orders Force K re-established at Malta and Force Q at Bône (November 1942), 174; *see also* Chatfield, Chiefs of Staff, Cunningham, Pound
aerial reconnaissance: 95; ineffective in Mediterranean in 1940, 97, 104, 112–113; over Sicily (February 1941), 117, 132; in support of Force K, 135; in Tunisian campaign, 177, 186–7; *see also* photo-reconnaissance
Air Defence of Great Britain (ADGB): 58–9; large deficiency in AA guns (1940), 99
Air Historical Branch (AHB), Ministry of Defence: assessment of absence of fighters at Malta in 1940, 71–2; analysis of Axis shipping losses, 191–2
air raids on Malta: first raids on 11 June 1940, 85; civilian reactions to, 85, 89; on diminishing scale (1940), 103–4; German raids (January-May 1941) 116; renewed in December 1941, 140; heaviest in April-May 1942, 152
Air Staff: assessments of Italian air threat to Malta in late 1920s, 14–15;

225

propose 5 1/2 squadrons to defend Malta (1928), 15, 24; re-assess Italian air threat (1931), 24; propose two squadrons for Malta (1933), 26; propose 'composite' squadron and new airfield at Takali (1934), 31–3; plan to defend Malta by counter-attacks on Italy and Sicily (1935), 37, 62; send two squadrons to Malta in Abyssinian crisis (1935), 40; secure Treasury consent for Luqa airfield (1936), 57; provide radar for Malta, 60; doubt value of four squadrons at Malta (July 1939), 61; refuse Longmore's request to hold six Hurricanes at Malta (June 1940), 70; despatch four Hurricanes to Malta (June 1940), 85; consider main value of Malta as staging post, 95–6; send Hurricane reinforcements to Malta, 100–1; order Blenheims to Malta (May 1941), 112; send Spitfires to Malta (May 1942), 148–53; *see also* Newall, Portal, Royal Air Force in Malta

Alam Halfa, battle of: 161, 165–6

Albacore aircraft: 125, 127

Albania: 79, 98, 101

Alexander, A. V.: 94, 111

Alexandria: 100, 107, 112, 136, 192; Mediterranean fleet moves to (1935), 1, 36, 43, 44, 52; decision to expand naval facilities at (1937), 52–3; 3.7-inch AA guns diverted to (1939), 63, 67; Pound requests Hurricanes to protect (May 1940), 70; six Hurricanes sent to (May 1940), 70; Mediterranean fleet retained at, 94; attack by Italian frogmen at (December 1941), 140; 10th Submarine flotilla withdrawn to (April 1942), 152; naval evacuation of (June 1942), 160, 166

Amery, L. S.: opinion on Malta's 1929 constitutional crisis, 18

Anderson, General: warns Foreign Office of weak Malta defences (1935), 36

Anglo-Japanese Treaty: not renewed in 1922, 7

Ankara: 136, 139, 192

anti-aircraft defences of Malta: reviewed by DOP (1928), 14–15; reviewed by JDC (1933–4), 22–7; 24-gun scheme approved (1933), 32; CID considers 48 AA guns 'desirable' (1937), 59; Cabinet releases twelve AA guns (1939), 60; CID authorises Scale B of 172 guns (July 1939), 62; 18 more heavy AA guns sent in 1939–40 period, 1, 4, 67–8, 94; AA comparison with other ports, 68; COS order completion of Scale B by April 1941, 97; additional AA guns ordered to Malta (July 1940), 99–100

anti-aircraft guns:
3-inch: 24 proposed for Malta (1928), 15, 23, 32, 58, 60; considered inadequate by Admiralty, 15, 16
3.7-inch: under development (1933), 23; Cabinet allocates all production to Home Defence (1937), 58; eight guns allocated to Malta (January 1939), 60; eight diverted to Alexandria (August 1939), 63; more delivered to Malta, 67–8, 99–100, 184
naval 4-inch: 23
naval 4.5-inch: adapted for ADGB (1938), 59; allocation of to Malta by DCOS (September 1939), 67–8, 184
4.7-inch: 15, development considered unsatisfactory (1933), 23
Bofors: eight diverted from Malta to Aden (August 1939), 63, 67; ten more reach Malta (August 1940), 100;

Ark Royal, HMS: ferries Hurricanes to Malta (April 1941), 120; sunk, 140

Arnim, General von: supply requirements (December 1942), 176; surrender of (May 1943), 179

Argus, HMS: 64, 100, 119

Asdic (British submarine detection equipment): 48

ASV (Air-to-Surface Vessel) radar: 111, 113, 125, 177, 186

Attlee, Clement: opposes suggested approach to Mussolini (May 1940), 91; 120

Auchinleck, General (later FM) Sir Claude: 129, 138; disagreement

INDEX

with Churchill and COS about importance of Malta (May 1942), 144–8; *see also* Brooke, Chiefs of Staff, Churchill, War Cabinet
Aurora, HMS: sent to Malta (October 1941), 129; *see also* Force K
Axis shipping: initial Italian losses (1940), 97, 105; and German ships, 105, 107; war-time construction, 105; losses in early 1941, 115; losses in mid-1941, 133–4; losses in November-December 1941, 135; losses in early 1942, 151; losses during autumn 1942 battles, 166–8; losses in the winter of 1942–3, 178–9; overall losses 188, 191–2; *see also* Italian convoys to North Africa
Axis supplies to North Africa: losses in 1940, 104; losses in early 1941, 115; losses in mid-1941, 134; losses in November–December 1941, 136; losses in early 1942, 150; losses in mid-1942, 164; shortages during autumn 1942 battles, 165–8; losses in the winter of 1942–3, 177; overall losses, 188, 191–2

Backhouse, Admiral Sir Roger: proposes early strike against Italy (1939), 56
Badoglio, General: advises Mussolini war plans ready (1935), 43; receives Mussolini's policy directive (1940), 76; fails to delay declaration of war, 78, 79; orders to Pricolo, 78, 83; and convoys to North Africa, 105; *see also* Italian Chiefs of Staff, Mussolini
Baldwin, Stanley: forms new Government (1924), 8; and financial policies (1924–8), 17; chairs Coast Defence Enquiry (1931–2), 21; warns COS of possibility of sanctions against Italy (July 1935), 35–6; chairs DPRC (August 1935), 38; fears large casualties at Malta (1935–6), 46; and Italy, 51
Baltimore aircraft: 132, 186
Banda Nere: sunk by British submarine, 151
Barbaro, Marquis; appointed Food Distribution Officer in Malta (1941), 89
'Barbarossa', Operation: 108
Barham, HMS: sunk, 140
Bari: attacked by Wellingtons from Malta (1940), 98
Bastico, General: 139
Battle of Britain: 97, 101–2; and Italian bombers, 130
Beatty, Admiral Sir David (later Lord): discloses War Plans in event of Japanese hostility (1925), 9; reaches agreement with Trenchard about 15-inch guns at Singapore (1926), 12
Beaufighter aircraft: 124, 127, 143, 175, 186
Beaufort aircraft: 95, 112, 124–5; shipping attacks (1942), 167, 175
Beda Fomm: 109
Belardinelli: convicted for spying in Malta (1935), 48
Benghazi: 136, 137, 162; captured by British (1941), 109; Axis recovery of airfields near, 143, 152
Bizerta: 79, 171, 177
Blenheim aircraft: 96, 123, 133; six ordered to Malta (1941), 112; low serviceability of, 124; suffer severe losses (1941), 125
bombardment trials: carried out at Malta and Portsmouth (1928–30), 16, 21
Bône: 171; and Force Q, 174
Bonham-Carter, General Sir Charles: appointed Governor of Malta (1935), 48, 50, 72; presents new defence proposals for Malta (1936), 50, 57–8; requests fifth battalion (1939), 66; raises four local defence companies for KOMR (1939), 66; and measures to strengthen British position in Malta (1935–39), 72–5, 185; and 'MacDonald Constitution' (1939), 74; and shelters at Malta, 86; *see also* Malta
Brauchitsch, Field Marshal von: and Rommel, 108
'Breastplate', Operation: plan for landings at Sousse, 172
Breconshire, HMS: 136, 143, 151, 155; sunk, 147
Brenner Pass: meeting at between

227

Mussolini and Hitler, 18 March 1940, 65, 76
Bridges, Lord: views about Churchill, 92
Brindisi: attacked by Wellingtons from Malta (1940), 98, 133
British Embassy in Rome: cyphers believed stolen by Italian Secret Service (1935), 42
Brooke, General Sir Alan (later FM Lord Alanbrooke): succeeds Dill as CIGS, (December 1941), 143; raises Malta's 'acute' food position with COS, 143; critical of Auchinleck, 148; and 'Torch', 171; *see also* Chiefs of Staff, Churchill, War Cabinet

'C3', Operation, (Italian plan for invasion of Malta), 153–4
C38m (Italian naval cypher): broken by CG&CS (June 1941), 132
Cabinet: authorises new naval base at Singapore (1921), 7; suspends work at Singapore (1924), 8; authorises Singapore resumption (1924), 8–9; accelerates completion of Singapore (1933), 26; prohibits defence expenditure against Italy (1933), 27, 34; scales down expenditure at Malta (1934), 32; orders emergency reinforcements for Malta (1935), 38; declares that British actions in Mediterranean are 'precautionary' (September 1935), 45; reserves all AA guns for Home Defence (1937), 59; releases twelve AA guns for Malta (January 1939), 60; *see also* Chamberlain, Committee of Imperial Defence, Chiefs of Staff, Defence Policy and Requirements Committee, War Cabinet
Calcutta, HMS: 100
Campbell, General Sir David: warns Colonial Office about bombing at Malta (1935), 46; succeeded as Governor of Malta by General Sir Charles Bonham-Carter (June 1936), 72
Cape Bon: 96, 174
Cape of Good Hope: alternative route to east, 7, 32, 96, 100

Casey, Richard (later Lord): and relief of General Dobbie (May 1942), 156–7
Castel Benito airfield, Tripoli: bombed by Malta-based Wellingtons (1940), 99
casualties in Malta: 85, 88
Catholic Church, Malta: and dispute with Strickland (1929–30), 18–19; withdraws opposition to Strickland (1932), 46
Cavagnari, Admiral: opposes attack on Malta in 1935, 43; rejects notion of invasion of Malta (1940), 78–81; considers Malta only of 'secondary importance' (1940), 81; and supply convoys to North Africa, 105; *see also* Italian navy
Cavallero, General: opposes withdrawal from Cyrenaica (December 1941), 139; and Operation C3, 153–4; promises supplies for North Africa (October 1942), 165, 167
Chamberlain, Sir Austen: does not anticipate aggression by Japan (1925), 8–9
Chamberlain, Joseph: considers Malta a 'fortress colony' (1902), 17
Chamberlain, Neville: 56; recommends no defence expenditure against Italy (1933), 29; proposes new formula regarding Italy (1937), 51–2; succeeds Baldwin as Prime Minister (May 1937), 51; meets Daladier (September 1939), 64; and possible approach to Mussolini (May 1940), 91
Chatfield, Admiral of the Fleet Sir Ernle (later Lord): rejects suggestion of new base for Mediterranean fleet (1933), 24–5; agrees priority for Singapore (1933), 26; accepts defences at Malta inadequate, 26–7; and Abyssinian crisis (August 1935), 35; moves Mediterranean fleet to Alexandria (1935), 36; views about value of Malta (1935), 39; outlines naval strategy in war with Italy (1935), 39; and possible loss of Malta (1937), 55; appointed Minister for Co-ordination of Defence (1938), 55; chairs

228

Strategical Appreciation Committee (1939), 55; critical of plan to 'knock out' Italy, 56; urges 48 AA guns for Malta (1937), 58–9; agrees move of Mediterranean fleet to Alexandria (1939), 63; chairs Military Co-ordination Committee (January 1940), 65, 67; *see also* Admiralty, Chiefs of Staff, Committee of Imperial Defence, Joint Defence Committee

Chiefs of Staff (COS): affirm need for strong defences at Malta (1933), 25; recommend acceleration of Singapore defences (1933), 26; warn that Mediterranean defences 'obsolete' (1933), 29; discuss strategy in Abyssinian crisis, 40–1; urge restoration of friendly relations with Italy (1936), 49–50; review Mediterranean and Middle East Appreciation (1937), 53; accept possible loss of Malta, 55; prepare European Appreciation (1939), 55; favour neutrality of Italy (1939), 56; instruct JDC to review Malta air defences (1939), 61; recommend 'administrative development' in Middle East (December 1939), 65; confirm Scale B defences to be completed at Malta (1940), 67; not able to 'increase power of resistance' of Malta (April 1940), 69; recommend fighter squadron for Malta (January 1940), 69; agree essential stocks at Malta to be built to eight months' level (1940), 88; consider strategy in event of French surrender (May 1940), 93; decide to retain Mediterranean fleet at Alexandria (June 1940), 94; order completion of Scale B AA defences at Malta by April 1941, 96, 101; approve plans to strengthen reconnaissance capability at Malta (October 1940), 98; agree AA and troop reinforcements for Malta (July 1940), 99–102; and Greece, 109; order two more battalions to Malta (February 1941), 118; and despatch of surface ships to Malta (August 1941), 128–9; and Auchinleck 144–8; and convoys to Malta, 144, 160; restrict offensive air operations from Malta (July 1942), 160; order maximum strike operations from Malta (August 1942), 160–1; discuss Malta's contribution to 'Torch' (October 1942), 171–2; and November convoy to Malta, 173; *see also* Admiralty, Air Staff, Brooke, Cabinet, Chatfield, Churchill, Committee of Imperial Defence, Portal, Pound, War Cabinet, War Office

Churchill, Sir Winston: attacks Admiralty plans when Chancellor (1925), 8, 17; supports plan to 'knock out' Italy (1939), 56; recommends completion of Scale A defences at Malta (February 1940), 67; opposes Halifax's suggested approach to Mussolini (May 1940), 91–2; orders retention of Mediterranean fleet at Alexandria (June 1940), 94; Directives of relating to Malta (July 1940), 99; recommends strengthening of Malta's garrison (1940), 101–2; and assistance to Greece, 109–10; issues Directive about stopping Axis convoys (April 1941), 111; urges surface ships and priority for fighters at Malta, 111–12; urges two more battalions for Malta (1941), 118; orders major air reinforcements for Malta (April 1941), 119–20; and relief of Maynard as AOC, Malta, 121–2; presses Pound to send surface ships to Malta (August 1941), 128–9; and operations of Force K (1941), 135; and dispute with Auchinleck about value of Malta (May 1942), 144–8; and relief of General Dobbie (May 1942), 154–8; urges August relief convoy for Malta, 159; and November 1942 convoy to Malta, 173; urges Force K be re-established at Malta (November 1942), 174–5; presses for stoppage of Tunisian convoys (December 1942), 175; influence of, 185, 190; *see also* Brooke, Chiefs of Staff,

Cunningham, Brooke, Portal, Pound, War Cabinet

Cianchi, Commander: confirms Italian reading of RN cyphers, 98

Ciano, Count Galeazzo: records Mussolini's 1935 threats to attack Malta, 45; records Mizzi's conversation with Mussolini (December 1937), 73; records Mussolini's intention to declare war (May 1940), 77–8; provides 'full information' on Italian intentions (June 1940), 84; *see also* Italy,Mussolini

Clarke, William: decyphering of Italian naval signals (1935), 43–4

Coast Defence Enquiry, 1931–2: favours guns over aircraft, 21–2, 71

coastal artillery at Malta: 14–15, 23, 32
9.2-inch: 15, 23, 32, 58, 184
6-inch: 15, 23, 32, 58
12-pounders: 15

Colonial Office: warned of possible unrest in Valletta dockyard (1926), 19; warned of effects of Italian bombing of Malta (1935), 46; appreciate Ede's reports (1935), 48

Committee of Imperial Defence (CID): considers possible Japanese threat (1925), 8; recommends no defences be provided against Italy (1933), 27; approves revised formula regarding Italy (1937), 50–1; refers European Appreciation to SAC (1939), 55; approves new airfield at Luqa (1936), 57; recommends 48 AA guns at Malta as 'desirable' (1938), 59; approves Scale B defence scheme at Malta (July 1939), 62, 184; *see also* Cabinet, Chatfield, Chiefs of Staff, Joint Defence Committee

Constitutional crises in Malta: (1929–30), 18; (1933), 46, 73

Constitutional Party, Malta: forms Government (1927), 18; wins six seats in 1939 election, 75; *see also* Malta, Strickland

Corfu: 7, 45, 82, 167

Coryton, Air Commodore: advises Air Staff unable to provide fighters for Malta (May 1940), 69–70, 72; *see also* Air Staff, Maynard

Cospicua, suburb of Valletta: air raids on (June 1940), 85

Courtney, AVM: gains Treasury approval for Takali airfield (August 1935), 37

Coventry, HMS: 100

Cranborne, Viscount: and relief of General Dobbie (April 1942), 155–8

Crete: 81, 84, 98, 102, 109, 118, 123; German assault on 117; British evacuation from, 127, 154

Cripps, Sir Stafford: visit to Cairo (March 1942), 147, 156

'Crusader', Operation: 123–42, 186

CSS (Chief of the Secret Service): advises absence of agents in Italian territories (1935), 44

Cunliffe-Lister, Sir Philip: 38–9

Cunningham, Admiral Sir Andrew (later Admiral of the Fleet Viscount): moves to Alexandria (May 1940), 65; warned of impending Italian declaration of war (June 1940), 66, 84; provides twelve Sea Gladiators to Maynard (April 1940), 70; tribute to General Dobbie, 86; resents Churchill's 'prodding' (May 1940), 93; opposes withdrawal of Mediterranean fleet to Gibraltar (June 1940), 94; transfers 830 FAA squadron to Maynard's command (June 1940), 95; urges strengthening of Malta's defences, 96; receives reinforcements (August 1940), 100; critical of weak air forces in Mediterranean (March 1941), 111; orders 14th Destroyer Flotilla to Malta (April 1941), 113; and difficulty of stopping Axis convoys, 114; advises Pound of deteriorating air situation at Malta (May 1941), 121; shortage of destroyers (June 1941), 127; receives two cruisers for Force K (October 1941), 129, 185; and loss of battleships, 140; orders Simpson to attack Tunisian supply route (November 1942), 174; establishes Force Q at Bône (November 1942), 174; receives surrender of Italian fleet at Malta (September 1943), 180;*see also*

INDEX

Admiralty, Chiefs of Staff, Churchill, Pound

Cyprus: naval base there rejected (1937), 52

Cyrenaica: 44, 136; British capture of, 106–7; Rommel recovers, 110, 120

Daladier, Edouard: meets Chamberlain, September 1939, 64

Defence Committee: *see War Cabinet Defence Committee*

Defence of Ports Committee (DOP): established by JDC, 10; considers defences of Malta (1928), 10, 14–15; *see also* Joint Defence Committee

Defence Plans (Policy) Committee (DPP): considers Eden's recommendations about Italy (1937), 51

Defence Policy and Requirements Committee (DPRC): orders reinforcements to Malta (1935), 38; orders 'every effort' to be made to defend Malta (September 1935), 41; postpones evacuation of service families from Malta (1935), 47; *see also* Baldwin, Cabinet, Chatfield, Chiefs of Staff

Defence Requirements Committee (DRC): established to consider defence deficiencies (November 1933), 30; first Report (1934), 30; proposals of 'impossible to carry out', 31; third Report (November 1935), 50; *see also* Cabinet, Committee of Imperial Defence

Defence Security Officer (DSO), Malta: *see* Ede, Strong

Delia, Professor: convicted for spying in Malta (1935), 48

Denniston, Alastair: 43–4; *see also* Clarke, Government Code and Cypher School

Deputy Chiefs of Staff (DCOS): 64, divert AA guns from Malta to Aden and Alexandria (1939), 63, 67; allocate eight 4.5-inch AA guns to Malta (September 1939), 67; recommend fighter squadron for Malta (November 1939), 69; unable to meet Dobbie's request for further reinforcements (May 1940), 72

detentions in Malta: about 60 Maltese detained under Defence Regulations (1939–40), 75, 86, 89, 185

Deutsches Afrika Korps (DAK): 110, 115; established in North Africa, 108; *see also* Rommel

Deverell, General (later FM) Sir Cyril: explains AA gun shortages (1937), 58–9, 66

Dill, General (later FM) Sir John: advised by Dobbie of conditions in Malta (1940), 85; authorises additional reinforcements for Malta (October 1940), 101–2; and assistance to Greece, 110; and further reinforcements for Malta (February 1941), 117–18

Director of Naval Intelligence (DNI): warns Governor of German forces in Sicily (January 1941), 117; *see also* Godfrey

Disarmament Conference (1933–4): 17, 27

District Councils: responsible in Malta for civil defence, 74

Dobbie, Lieutenant-General Sir William: warns of airborne attack on Malta (May 1940), 69, 83; becomes Acting Governor of Malta (May 1940), 72; request for further reinforcements denied by DCOS (May 1940), 72; warns General Dill of Maltese reactions to initial bombing (1940), 85, 89; and importance of teachers in emergency work (June 1940), 85; and shelter construction work, 87–8; advises Lord Lloyd of supply needs (September 1940), 88; requests additional reinforcements (October 1940), 99, 101–2; receives further substantial troop and air reinforcements (April-June 1941), 118–20; asks Portal for strengthened staff support for Maynard (May 1941), 121; reports worsening supply position (February 1942), 143; relief of recommended by Middle East Defence Committee (April 1942), 154–5; health and

231

heavy responsibilities of, 155;
succeeded as Governor by General
Gort (May 1942), 157; *see also*
Churchill, Malta, War Office

Dockyard Defence Battery, Malta: 89

Drummond, Sir Eric (later Lord Perth):
tells Mussolini British actions are
'precautionary' (September 1935),
45; warns of anti-British propaganda
(July 1937), 53

Duff Cooper, Alfred: opposes heavy
expenditure at Malta (1937), 51

Eagle, HMS: ferries Spitfires to Malta
(May 1942), 148, 153

Ede, Major (later Colonel) Bertram,
DSO in Malta: security operations in
Malta (1935–6), 48; surveillance
leads to dismissal of two Maltese
civil servants (1937), 73; warns of
possible consequences of heavy
bombing (June 1940), 85

Eden, Sir Anthony: and Abyssinian
crisis, 35–6; becomes Foreign
Secretary (December 1935), 49;
considers Italy a possible enemy
(1937), 51–2; Chairman of Middle
East Committee (July 1940), 96; and
assistance to Greece, 110

Egypt: 36, 53–5, 65, 72, 93–4, 96, 98,
100, 106, 168; invaded by Italian
army (September 1940), 97;
Rommel invades (June 1942), 154;
loss feared, 160

Eisenhower, General: 18, and 'Torch'
planning, 171–2; and possible
seizure of Sousse by troops from
Malta garrison, 172

El Alamein, battle of: 161, 168–70,
172, 187; *see also* Montgomery,
Rommel

Ellington, ACM (later MRA) Sir
Edward: complains about lack of
agreed strategy in Abyssinian crisis
(1935), 39; sends two squadrons to
Malta as emergency measure (1935),
40; *see also* Air Staff, Chatfield,
Chiefs of Staff

Enigma intercepts: 109, 123;
breakthrough in summer 1941, 132;
and operations of Force K
(November 1941), 135; and Alam

Halfa battle, 165; reach 4,000 per
month (June 1942), 167, 170, 186,
190

Essex: carries Hurricanes to Malta
(January 1941), 119

European Appreciation: 55, 61; *see also*
Chiefs of Staff

'Faith', 'Hope' and 'Charity'; 1, *see also*
Gladiator aircraft

Fascist Grand Council: Mussolini's
speech to (February 1939), 76

Ferrante: expelled from position as
Italian Consul General in Malta
(1935), 48

Fighter Command: 62, drawn into
battle in France (May 1940), 70;
Churchill visit to (September 1940),
101; and release of Spitfires, 158,
183

Fisher, Sir Warren: member of DRC
(1934–5), 30; approves finance for
Takali airfield (August 1935), 37

Fisher, Admiral Sir William: C-in-C
Mediterranean (1933), 23; proposal
of to install naval AA guns at Malta
rejected (1933), 23; urges stronger
defences at Malta (1933), 26;
confident of dealing with Italian fleet
(August 1935), 36, 38–9; *see also*
Admiralty, Chatfield

Fleet Air Arm (FAA) Squadrons at
Malta:
No. 830: 95, 104, 111, 125, 133
No. 828: 125
No. 821: 175

Fliegerkorps II: ordered to Sicily by
Hitler (November 1941), 140;
begins raids on Malta (December
1941), 140–1

Fliegerkorps X: ordered to Sicily by
Hitler (December 1940), 107;
attacks *Illustrious*, 108, 113, 114,
116; some squadrons of diverted to
Greece and North Africa (April
1941), 118, 119; departure of
remaining squadrons of from Sicily
(June 1941), 123; ordered by Hitler
to protect convoys (September
1941), 140

Floriana, suburb of Valletta: disused
railway tunnel at converted to
shelter (1939), 74, 87

INDEX

Force B: reinforces Force K, 135–6

Force K: operations from Malta, 133–6, 185; suffers losses on minefield, 136; impact on Axis supplies, 139; withdrawn from Malta (March 1942), 151; re-established at Malta (November 1942), 174

Force Q: operations from Bône (November 1942), 174–5

Ford, Vice-Admiral Sir Wilbraham, Vice-Admiral Malta (VAM): and shelter construction in Valletta, 87; recommends eight months' reserve of essential stocks (1940), 88; and Dockyard Defence Battery, 89; and shortage of mine-sweepers, 112; and Axis convoys, 113; and invasion threat, 117; advises Cunningham of deteriorating air situation at Malta (May 1941), 121; receives Enigma decrypts (August 1941), 132; receives Force K orders from Pound (November 1941), 135; *see also* Cunningham, Malta

Foreign Office: advises COS about Italian risks (1933), 28, 34; warned of Malta's weak defences (1935), 36–7; urges stronger defences at Gibraltar and Malta (April 1940), 68–9

France: no defences required against (1933), 27, 28–9; as possible base for air attacks against Italy (1934), 31; not prepared to attack Italy (1935), 41; Supreme War Council meeting of Daladier and Chamberlain (September 1939), 64; Reynaud's visit to London (May 1940), 91–2; collapse of (June 1940), 93, 185

Freeman, ACM Sir Wilfrid: 125

French, Vice-Admiral Sir Wilfrid: warns of anti-British sentiment in Malta dockyard (September 1935), 47

Funck, General von: 108

Galatea, HMS: sunk, 140

garrison of Malta: two under-strength battalions in 1925, 12; four battalions proposed by DOP (1928), 15; additional three battalions sent to Malta (September 1935), 41; fifth battalion sent (May 1940), 69, 83, 184; over-estimation of by Italian navy (1940), 80; Churchill urges additional troops (September 1940), 101–2; major reinforcements (1941), 117–8; plan for landings at Sousse, Tunisia (October 1942), 172; *see also* Bonham-Carter, Dobbie, Malta, War Office

gas: expected to be used in attack on Malta, 74, 84; used by Italy in Abyssinia, 74; not used at Malta, 86

Gazala: 137, 143, 148, 150, 166

George Cross: awarded to Malta (April 1942), 149, 186

Germany: admitted to League of Nations (1926), 17; withdraws from League of Nations and Disarmament Conference (1933), 27; 29, 34, 50, 54–6; at war with Britain and France (1939), 63; successes in Norway (April 1940), 77; intervention in North Africa, 107–10; and invasion of Russia, 109; *see also* Hitler, Kesselring, Rommel

Gibraltar: 10, 14, 25, 34, 38–9, 43, 76–7, 94, 100, 112, 114; overflow base for Mediterranean fleet, 8; Foreign Office urge stronger defences at (April 1940), 68–9; COS send additional troops to (April 1940), 69

Giulio Giordani: sunk November 1942, 178

Gladiator aircraft: flight of Sea Gladiators established at Malta (April 1940), 70; *see also* Maynard

Glengyle, HMS: 143, 151

Glorious, HMS: 70

Gloucester, HMS: 114

Godfrey, Rear-Admiral: comments on captured Italian document (1939), 82; *see also* Director of Naval Intelligence

Göring, Field Marshal: opposes invasion of Malta (March 1941), 117

Gort, General (later FM) Lord: explains cuts in Malta defence programmes (1938), 60; succeeds Dobbie as Governor of Malta (May 1942), 157

Government Code and Cypher School

(GC&CS): and attack on Italian cyphers (1935), 43–4, 82; unable to read Italian navy cyphers after July 1940, 97; read signals about Axis troop convoys (April 1941), 113; break C38m Italian cypher (June 1941), 132; read 4000 signals monthly (mid-1942), 167; *see also* Clarke, Denniston, Enigma intercepts

Governor of Malta: 12; *see also* Bonham-Carter, Campbell, Dobbie, Gort

Grand Harbour: 12, AA gun density over, 62; growing destruction in (March 1942), 151; *see also* Valletta

Graziani, Marshal: raises question of invasion of Malta (June 1940), 78; invades Egypt (September 1940), 97, 101; retreats into Cyrenaica (January 1941), 107

Greece: 6; invaded by Italy (October 1940), 98, 102–3; and Axis convoys to, 106; and British assistance to, 109–10; and evacuation of British forces from, 110, 120, 123

Greenwood, Arthur: opposes suggested approach to Mussolini (May 1940), 91

Gualdi: 165

'Gun v. Air' controversy: 20–2, 33; *see also* Coast Defence Enquiry

Haining, Colonel: member of JDC 1933–4, 23; warns of effect of Singapore expenditures on Malta (1933), 26

Hal Far: first airfield established at Malta (1923), 14, 57

Halder, General: opposes additional German army units for Libya (January 1941), 108

Halifax, Lord: supports Scale B defence scheme at Malta (July1939), 62; his suggested approach to Mussolini rejected by War Cabinet (May 1940), 91–2

Hankey, Sir Maurice (later Lord): Secretary of CID: reviews work on defence of ports (1926), 10; Chairman of JDC, 22; suggests 'go slow' on Malta's defences (1933), 26; and influence on defence formula agreed by CID in 1933, 29; Chairman of DRC (1934), 30; and Abyssinian crisis, 35; supports restoration of good relations with Italy (1936–7), 51

'Harpoon', Operation: failure of June 1942 Malta convoy, 159

Harris, Group Captain (later MRA Sir Arthur): presents amended proposals to JDC regarding Malta (1934), 31, 182

Harwood, Admiral Sir Henry: withdraws Mediterranean fleet from Alexandria (June 1942), 166; and 'Torch', 171; re-establishes Force K at Malta (November 1942), 174

'Hats', Operation, 100

Hitler, Adolf: becomes Chancellor (1933), 27; withdraws Germany from League of Nations and Disarmament Conference (1933), 27; meets Mussolini (March 1940), 65, 76; and Directives regarding Mediterranean, 107–8, 116; orders Rommel and German army units to North Africa, 108; orders *Fliegerkorps II* to Sicily under Kesselring's command (November 1941), 140; orders U-boats to Mediterranean (September 1941), 140; agrees invasion of Malta to be launched after capture of Tobruk, 153; persuades Mussolini to accept Rommel's plan to invade Egypt (June 1942), 154; orders Kesselring to occupy Tunisia (November 1942), 172

Hoare, Sir Samuel: 35–6, 47–8, warns of possible Italian 'mad dog' attack (August 1935), 38; urges improved defences at Malta (1936), 49–51

Home Fleet: 36, 38–9, 45, 49

Home Guard in Malta: 85, 89

Hong Kong: Washington Naval Treaty prevented expansion of docks at, 8

Hore-Belisha, Leslie: and reinforcements for Malta (1938), 66; and expansion of RMA, 66

Hurricane aircraft for Malta: 70–2, 85, 99; twelve flown from *Argus* (August 1940), 100; eight lost on delivery

INDEX

flight (November 1940), 100; Maynard request for Mark II version of, 119; major reinforcements of, 120

Imperial Conference, 1937: despatch of fleet to Singapore confirmed at, 53
Illustrious, HMS: 99; attacked at Malta (January 1941), 108, 116; Fulmar fighters disembarked from, 119
India: 9, 27, 29, 149
Inskip, Sir Thomas: supports Scale B defence scheme for Malta (1939), 62
Iraqi oilfields: strategic importance of, 7
Iridio Mantovani: sunk by Force K, 135
Ismay, General Sir Hastings (later Lord): 93, 128
Italian air force (*Regia Aeronautica*): believed to have 1000 modern aircraft in 1931, 23; plans to bomb Malta (1935), 43; attack by 276 bombers of assumed by Air Staff (1939), 61; and initial raids on Malta, 85; air offensive against Malta (June 1940), 103–4; losses, 103; and Battle of Britain, 130
Italian Chiefs of Staff: discuss plans for war with Britain (1935), 43; protest to Mussolini about lack of readiness (April 1940), 77–8; and movement of ships, 131; *see also* Badoglio, Cavagnari, Cavallero, Graziani, Mussolini, Pricolo, Valle
Italian convoys to North Africa: organisation of 105–6; suffer few losses in 1940, 104, 106; 'mini-convoy' system adopted, 105, 131, 187; battleship escorts for (December 1941–January 1942), 136–7, 150; diverted via Greece to avoid attack from Malta (August 1942), 162; achieve rapid build-up in Tunisia (November 1942), 173; suffer heavy losses on the Tunisian route, 176; *see also* Axis shipping, Axis supplies to North Africa, Italian navy
Italian navy: prepares plans for war with Britain (1935), 43, 79; fleet mobilised (April 1940), 77; plans regarding Malta, 79–81; new cyphers of unreadable (July 1940), 97; and convoys 105–6; and shortage of escort ships 131; provides battleship escort for convoys (December 1941), 136–7; damages British battleships at Alexandria, 140; develops improved anti-submarine techniques (November 1942), 174; *see also* Cavagnari, Italian convoys to North Africa
Italy: Corfu incident (1923), 7; growing air threat to Malta in late 1920s, 15; and Maltese Nationalist Party, 18; excluded from British defence planning by CID (1933), 27–8; and Abyssinian crisis (1935–6), 35–48; new defence planning formula applied to (1937), 50–2; intervenes in Spanish Civil War (1936), 50; increases forces in Libya (1937), 53; her neutrality sought by COS (1939), 56; and lack of preparations for war, 78–82; declares war 10 June 1940, 78; limited resources of, 130, 187; *see also* Mussolini

Jacob, Lieutenant-General Sir Ian: views about Churchill, 92
Japan: 29, 34, 42, 50, 54–5; Anglo-Japanese Treaty not renewed in 1922, 7; influence of on decision to base Main Fleet at Malta (1923), 7–9; invasion of Manchuria by (1931), 21, 27; believed to have task force ready to attack Singapore (1932), 25; declares war, 149
Joint Defence Committee (JDC): establishes DOP to examine ports defence, 10; suspends work on port defence (1929), 20; resumes enquiries into Malta's defences (1933–4), 22–7; considers Malta's defences in 'perilous' condition (1934), 32; considers plans to strengthen Malta's defences (1937), 56–8; urges completion of 24-gun AA scheme (January 1939), 60; offers CID choice between Scale A and B defence schemes for Malta (July 1939), 61–2; *see also* Admiralty, Air Staff, Chiefs of Staff, Defence of Ports Committee, Malta

Joint Intelligence Committee (JIC): considers fleet at Alexandria might be attacked (May 1940), 70; assessment of Italian intentions (June 1940), 83–4; underestimates German reaction to 'Torch' landings, 171

Joint Planning Committee (JPC): proposals to reinforce Malta during Abyssinian crisis (1935), 36; and Port X, 39, prepares Interim Mediterranean Appreciation (July1937), 53–4; recommends reinforcements and 48 AA guns for Malta (1937–8), 54; advises against withdrawal of Mediterranean fleet from Alexandria (June 1940), 94, reviews Future Strategy 96; assesses Malta's strategic value (February 1942), 144; and Malta's value as staging post for India, 149; and Malta's role in 'Torch' (October 1942), 171–2; considers request for landings at Sousse by Malta troops, 172

Kalafrana, seaplane base at Malta: 14, 44, 70, 98,

Kellogg-Briand Pact, 1928: 17

Kennedy, Major-General Sir John: critical of Auchinleck, 148

Kentucky: sunk, 160

Kesselring, Field Marshal: appointed C-in-C South (December 1941), 140; launches heavy air attacks on Malta, 150; urges capture of Malta (February 1942), 153; believes Malta neutralised (May 1942), 153; last attempt to neutralise Malta (October 1942), 162, 169, 187, gives priority to convoy escort work (September 1942), 162; promises to provide fuel to Rommel (August 1942), 165–6; later denies Alam Halfa defeat due to fuel shortages, 166; delivers fuel to Rommel by air (October 1942), 168; effects rapid Axis build-up in Tunisia (November 1942), 172–3, 174; *see also* Hitler, Rommel

Keyes, Admiral of the Fleet Sir Roger: and Mediterranean Fleet exercises to relieve Singapore (1925), 9; plans to attack Pantelleria, 96

King's Own Malta Regiment (KOMR): 12, 15, 89, 101, 184; addition of four local defence companies (1939), 66

Labour Party, Malta: in coalition with Constitutional Party (1927), 18; wins one seat in 1939 election, 75; *see also* Malta

Labour Government: suspends work at Singapore (1924), 8

Laferla, Dr., Director of Education in Malta: teachers vital in emergency work (June 1940), 85

League of Nations: admission of Germany to (1926), 18; withdrawal of Germany from (1933), 27; British obligations to, 28, 73; lifts sanctions against Italy, 49

Leatham, Vice-Admiral Sir Ralph: 156

Lehen is-Sewwa, Catholic Maltese language newspaper: 73

Libya: Italian forces there to be increased to 60,000 (1937), 53; possible French attack on (1939), 56; large Italian reinforcements to (March 1940), 65; supply route to, 82, 95; additional troops arrive (June 1940), 83; and port capacity, 105; Axis forces in, 108, resources needed in, 130

Liddell Hart, B.: 30

Lieutenant-Governor, Malta: warns of effect of dockyard discharges (1926), 19; *see also* Luke

Little, Admiral Sir Charles: warns Admiral Fisher of possible Italian surprise attack on Mediterranean fleet (August 1935), 37–8

Littorio: 78

Lloyd, Lord: advises War Cabinet of Malta's supply requirements (September 1940), 88; asks about offensive uses of Malta (July 1940), 96

Lloyd, AVM (later AM Sir Hugh): appointed AOC, Malta, June 1941, 121; organises ground dispersal of

INDEX

aircraft, 123–4; and improved fighter control, 124; expands offensive operations, 125–7; available aircraft, 127; and Wellington operations, 133; sends away Blenheims and Wellingtons (February-March 1942), 152; receives large Spitfire reinforcements (May 1942), 153; and relief of General Dobbie (April 1942), 155–6; 188; *see also* Air Staff, Malta, Portal

Locarno Treaty, 1925: 17

Longmore, ACM Sir Arthur: denied permission to hold six Hurricanes at Malta, (June 1940), 70–1; request for Beaufort squadron rejected (1940), 95; sends Hurricane reinforcements to Malta, 119; succeeded by Tedder, 125

Ludlow-Hewitt, AVM (later ACM Sir Edgar): recommends 'composite' squadron and new airfield at Takali (1934), 30, 37; reports to Portal on improvements at Malta (July 1941), 124, 183

Luftwaffe: 60, 89; raids on Malta, 107–8, 113, return to Sicily (December 1941), 140; losses, 187; *see also Fliegerkorps II, Fliegerkorps X,* Kesselring

Luke, Sir Harry: warns of growing pro-Italian sentiment (1935), 47

Luqa: new airfield at approved (1936–7), 57, 60; becomes operational (June 1940), 70, 80, 184; Wellington squadron based there (December 1940), 98; heavy raids on (April-May 1942), 150

Luisiana: sunk (October 1942), 168

Lyttleton, Oliver: 146

MacDonald, Malcolm: opposes evacuation of service families from Malta (1935), 47

MacDonald, Ramsay: accepts new defence formula regarding Italy (1933), 29; and economic policy, 33

'MacDonald Constitution', established at Malta (1939), 74

'mad dog attack': fears of (1935), 35, 38, 42–5

'Main Fleet': to be based at Malta (1923), 8–9, 30, 42, 52–3, 61, 182, 186; *see also* Mediterranean Fleet

Malaya, HMS: 65

Malta: *passim*: alleged to have been 'written off' before the war, 1, 4; decision to base Main Fleet there (1923), 7; and employment in dockyard, 12; garrison of two battalions (1925), 12; DOP reviews defences of (1928), 14–15; receives new Constitution (1921), 18; Constitution suspended (1929), 18; Royal Commission appointed (1930), 19; Constitution restored (1932), 46; and again suspended (1933), 46; JDC enquiry into defences of (1933–4), 22–7; threat of Italian attack on (1935), 35–42; and DPRC decision to defend (1935), 41; reinforced during Abyssinian crisis, 38–41, 47; Intelligence operations in (1935), 48; as base for light forces, 54, 56; Governor requests stronger defences for (1936), 57–8; reinforcements and 48 AA guns recommended (1937–8), 54; Scale B defence scheme approved by CID (July 1939), 62; first radar installed (1939), 1, 60; and expansion of RMA (1938), 66; Maltese constitute 44% of military garrison (1940), 66; more AA guns sent (1940), 67–8; fifth battalion sent (May 1940), 1, 69; flight of Sea Gladiators established at (April 1940), 70; and Constitutional developments 74–5; detention of Maltese citizens in 1939–40, 75, 86; first air raids 11 June 1940, 85; emergency plans activated, 85; shelter construction programme, 86–8; supplies and rationing, 88–9; possible cession to Italy rejected by War Cabinet (May 1940), 91–2; heavy bombing early 1941, 116; increase in garrison (June 1941), 118; receives more Hurricanes (April-June 1941), 120; arrival of Force K at (October 1941), 133–4; and 'Crusader', 137–42; suffers renewed German bombing

237

(December 1941), 140; and losses to February 1942 convoy, 143; and loss of supplies from March convoy, 147, 155; award of the George Cross to (April 1942), 149; suffers heaviest bombing (April-May 1942), 152; invasion threat to, 153–4; General Gort succeeds General Dobbie as Governor of (May 1942), 157; and arrival of 'Pedestal' convoy (August 1942), 160; and contribution to autumn battles in Egypt, 166–70; Force K re-established at (November 1942), 174; and air operations in support of 'Torch', 175; contribution to Tunisian campaign, 178–9; as base for invasion of Sicily and Italy (July-August 1943), 179; Italian fleet surrenders at (September 1943), 180; *see also* Bonham-Carter, Dobbie

Malta Defence Regulations: 105, 126

Malta, Italian language Maltese newspaper: 46; subject to press Ordinances (1937–8), 73; *see also* Mizzi

Manara: damaged and beached (August 1942), 167

Maritza; sunk (November 1941), 135

Maryland aircraft: 97, 98, 104, 113, 125, 186

Massy, General: 67

Mavity, Mr.: appointed to manage Shelter Construction Department in Malta (1940), 86–7

Maynard, Air Commodore (later AVM) F. H. M.: protests to Air Ministry about absence of fighter squadron (March 1940), 69; establishes flight of Sea Gladiators at Malta (April 1940), 70; receives four Hurricanes (June 1940), 85; given command of 830 FAA Squadron (June 1940), 95; and formation of second fighter squadron, 113; requests Mark II Hurricanes (February 1941), 119; lack of staff, 121; relief of, 121–2; *see also* Air Staff, Dobbie, Portal

Mediterranean Fleet: 1, 6–7, 9, 12, 23–4, 35; moved to Alexandria (1935–6), 36; returns to Malta (1936), 49, 54, concentrated at Alexandria (1939), 64; reinforced (May 1940), 65; decision to retain at Alexandria (June 1940), 94; reinforced in Operation 'Hats', August 1940, 100; suffers heavy losses in evacuations from Greece and Crete, 127; further losses, 140; leaves Alexandria (June 1942), 160; and Force K, 185

Mediterranean and Middle East Appreciation (1937): 53–4, 60

Medway, HMS: sunk (June 1942), 166

Mercieca, Arturo Sir: pro-Italian sympathies noted (1935), 48; Governor's wish to dismiss as Chief Justice refused by Colonial Office (1937), 73; detained under Defence Regulations (1940), 75

Mersa Matruh, Egypt: 102, 107

Middle East C-in-Cs: advised by COS that Mediterranean Fleet to be retained at Alexandria (June 1940), 94; and General Dobbie, 154–5; and 'Stoneage' convoy, 173; *see also* Auchinleck, Cunningham, Longmore, Montgomery, Tedder, Wavell

Middle East Committee: considers offensive use of Malta (July 1940), 96; *see also* Eden, Lord Lloyd

Middle East Defence Committee: recommends relief of General Dobbie (April 1942), 154–5

Middle East Intelligence Centre (MEIC): reports arrival of Italian bombers in Sicily (June 1940), 83

Military Co-ordination Committee: endorses COS Middle East policy (January 1940), 65; directs that completion of Scale A be 'immediate aim' at Malta (February 1940), 67; considers fighter squadron for Malta (January 1940), 69

Milne, Field Marshal Sir George: 28, 34

Mizzi, Enrico: editor of *Malta*, 46; visit to Mussolini (1937), 73; detained under Defence Regulations (1940), 75

Monckton, Sir Walter: recommends relief of General Dobbie (April 1942), 156

Mongenevro: 136, 139

Montezemolo, Colonel: advises Rommel of supply problems (December 1941), 139

Montgomery, General Sir Bernard (later FM Viscount): and Alam Halfa, 162–5; and El Alamein, 167; enjoys material superiority, 170; preparations for Alamein, 187

Montgomery-Massingberd, General (later FM) Sir Archibald: explains cost of Singapore defences (1933), 26; supports Chatfield's proposed strategy in Abyssinian crisis, 40

Moore, Captain: critical of 3-inch AA guns (1933–4), 23

Munich crisis: 55, 60

Mussolini, Benito: 16; speech in Sicily (1930), 19; fears of 'mad dog attack' by (1935), 42; becomes aware of British intentions from stolen cyphers (1935), 42; orders Italian COS to prepare for attack on Malta (1935), 43; threatens war against Britain, 45, 51; meeting with Mizzi (December 1937), 73; remains neutral (1939), 63–4; advises Hitler that Italy will be ready in 'three to four months' (March 1940), 65, 76; issues policy directive (March 1940), 76; advises Ciano and Badoglio of resolve to declare war (May 1940), 77; expects short war, 79; declares war (June 10 1940), 84, possible British approach to (May 1940), 91–2; orders Graziani to invade Egypt (September 1940), 97; and Malta, 101; Hitler's support for, 108; and Libyan supplies, 138; agrees to Rommel's request to invade Egypt (June 1942), 170; *see also* Hitler, Italy

Naiad, HMS: sunk, 151

Nationalist Party, Malta: Italian Government support for, 2, 18; successful in 1932 elections, 46; confronts British Government on language issue, 46; is dismissed from office (November 1933), 46; wins three seats in 1939 election, 75

Naval Intelligence Division, Admiralty: acquisition of Italian naval document (1939), 82; *see also* Godfrey

Navarino Bay, Greece: 39, 45; *see also* Port X

Neptune, HMS: 139

Newall, ACM Sir Cyril (later MRA Lord): opposes sending fighters abroad (May 1940), 70; provides twelve Hurricanes for Malta, 100; sends ground crews for four Hurricane squadrons to Malta (October 1940), 100

Nye, Lieutenant-General Archibald: visits Cairo, 147

O'Connor, General Sir Richard: 109

Olympus, HMS: lost, 152

Ordinances, Malta: enacted to control press (1935), 47, 73

Ormsby-Gore, William: refuses to allow dismissal of Merceica as Chief Justice (1937), 73; and Executive Council in Malta, 74

Oversea Defence Committee (ODC): responsible for defence of overseas ports, 9; examines vulnerability of Malta to air attack (1925), 14; considers army reinforcements for Malta in Abyssinian crisis (1935), 40–1; authorises large expenditures on shelters in Malta, (1939), 86; recommends six month supply of essential stocks at Malta (1939), 88; *see also* Chiefs of Staff, Joint Defence Committee, Malta

P247: HMS: 174

Palermo: 117, three ships sunk at (March 1942), 152; and 'Torch' operations, 176

Pampas: sunk in Grand Harbour (March 1942), 155

Panuco: damaged (October 1942), 167

Pargiter, Colonel: proposes completion of 24-gun AA defence scheme at Malta (1937), 53

'Pedestal', Operation: five ships arrive, 160, 186

Peirse, AVM (later ACM Sir Richard): explains radar to JDC (1938), 60; recommends fighter squadron for Malta (November 1939), 69

Penelope, HMS: sent to Malta (October 1941), 129; leaves Malta (April 1942), 151; *see also* Force K

Perth, Lord: *see* Drummond, Sir Eric

Phillips, Admiral Sir Tom: 67, 82, 94, 96, 114

Photo-reconnaissance (PR): and RAF operations during Abyssinian crisis (1935), 44–5; two PR Spitfires photograph southern Italy (June 1940), 83; need for current photographs, 95; inadequate resources at Malta, 104; operations (1941), 132; operations in support of 'Torch', 177, 186; *see also* aerial reconnaissance

Picci Fassio: sunk, 165, 167

Port X, Navarino Bay: 39, 42

Portal, Group Captain (later MRA Lord): JDC member (1933) 22, opposes exclusion of Italy from list of possible enemies (1933), 26; proposes two squadrons and two new airfields for Malta (1933), 27, 182; appointed CAS (December 1940), 98; establishes Wellington squadron at Malta (December 1940), 98; orders six Blenheims to Malta (May 1941), 112; and supply of Hurricanes to Malta, 119; and relief of Maynard by Lloyd (June 1941), 121–2; and importance of Malta, 123; expresses concern about Blenheim losses (October 1941), 125; orders suspension of transit flights through Malta (July 1942), 150, 154, 160; orders Spitfire Vs to Malta (May 1942), 153; and fuel shortages at Malta, 161

'Portcullis', Operation: December 1942 Malta convoy, 161

Pound, Admiral of the Fleet Sir Dudley: urges reinforcements for Middle East and Malta (1937), 58, 60; diverts AA guns from Malta to Aden and Alexandria (August 1939), 63; urges need for Hurricanes at Alexandria (May 1940), 70; his proposal to withdraw Mediterranean fleet to Gibraltar rejected (June 1940), 93–4; opposes Churchill's demand for despatch of merchant ship to Malta (July 1940), 100; employs *Argus* to fly 12 Hurricanes to Malta (August 1940), 100; and Axis convoys to North Africa, 111; sends more submarines to Mediterranean, 112; sends 'every available' submarine to Cunningham (September 1941), 127; refuses Churchill's request to send surface ships to Malta (August 1941), 128–9, 185; sends two cruisers to Malta (October 1941), 129; and Force K (November 1941), 135, 141; and Malta's contribution to 'Torch', 171; resists Churchill's pressure to employ surface ships by day (December 1942), 175

Pownall, Colonel: appointed Secretary of JDC and ODC (1933), 22; notes Malta's defence plans 'temporarily shelved' (1933), 26

Pozarica: damaged (August 1942), 167

Pricolo, General: considers there are 'too many illusions' about Italian prospects (April 1940), 77; instructed to prepare air attack on Malta (June 1940), 78, 83

Procida: sunk (November 1941), 135

Proserpina: sunk (October 1942), 168

Protection officers in Malta; assist with evacuation (June 1940), 85

Queen Elizabeth, HMS: damaged at Alexandria, 140

radar (RDF): plans for Malta outlined (April 1938), 60; first radar set established in Malta, January 1939, 60; two more radar sets established at Malta (1940), 70; improved facilities (June 1941), 124

Raeder, Admiral: 110; urges capture of Malta (1941), 117; and Italian merchant fleet, 131; ordered by Hitler to send U-boats to Mediterranean (September 1941), 140; again urges capture of Malta, (February 1942), 153

Regia Aeronautica: *see* Italian air force

Reynaud, Paul: visit to London (May 1940), 91–2; *see also* Churchill, Halifax, War Cabinet

Ritchie, General: 136, 139

Rommel, General (later FM): 2, 5; arrives in North Africa (February

INDEX

1941), 108, 116; first offensive, 110; and supply requirements (1941), 137–40, 186; withdraws from Cyrenaica (December 1941), 139; renews offensive (January 1942), 136–7, 143; attacks at Gazala (May 1942), 150; captures Tobruk (June 1942), 153–4; gains Hitler's approval for invasion of Egypt (June 1942), 154; and supply requirements autumn 1942, 162–4; and captured British supplies and lorries (June 1942), 164; and attack at Alam Halfa (August 1942), 165; loss of supply ships before El Alamein, 168; has limited ability to manoeuvre, 168; his assessment of his defeats in autumn 1942, 170; and Tunisian offensive, 176

Roosevelt, President: commitment to 'Torch', 170

Rorqual, HMS: 192

Rosalino Pilo: sunk, 167

Rowntree, Mr.: explains food situation in Malta to COS (September 1942), 161

Royal Air Force in Malta: has flight of six seaplanes in 1925, 14; air garrison of 5 1/2 squadrons proposed (1928), 15; 'composite' squadron proposed (1934), 42; Cabinet rejects plan for squadron for Malta (1934), 31; airfield at Takali approved (August 1935), 37; two squadrons temporarily based at Malta during Abyssinian crisis, 40; airfield at Luqa approved (1936–7), 57, 60; first radar installed January 1939, 60; force of four fighter squadrons approved (July 1939), 62; no modern fighters at Malta in June 1940, 69–70; Gladiator flight formed (April 1940), 70; first Hurricanes reach Malta (June 1940), 85; Wellington squadron formed (December 1940), 98; Hurricane reinforcements, 100, 120; relief of Maynard as AOC by Lloyd (June 1941), 121–2; expanded offensive operations, 125–7; faces *Fliegerkorps II* (December 1941), 140; receives large numbers of Spitfires (May 1942), 148; shortage of aviation fuel (July 1942), 160; maximum strike operations ordered (August 1942), 160; *see also* Air Staff, Lloyd, Maynard, Portal

Royal Air Force squadrons at Malta:
No. 202: 44
No. 228: 98
No. 148: 98–9
No. 69: 132, 177, 186
No. 37: 152
No. 39: 168, 175

Royal Commission: appointed in 1930, 19; recommends restoration of Malta Constitution (1932), 46

Royal Malta Artillery (RMA): re-organised in 1920s, 14; expansion of (1938), 66, 89, 184

Safari, HMS: 174

Salmond, ACM (later MRA) Sir John: gives evidence to Coast Defence Enquiry (1931–2), 21–2; does not believe AA fire will deter air attack, 24; urges Admiralty to seek alternative base in Mediterranean (1931), 24

San Andrea: sunk (August 1942), 165–7

Savoia S.81 Italian bomber: 37, 41

Secret Intelligence Service (SIS): 44

Senglea, suburb of Valletta: shelters dug at (1939), 74; air raids on (June 1940), 85; heavily damaged, 179

shelters in Malta; Governor urges more be constructed (1936), 57; further work carried out (1939–41), 74, 86–8; cost of construction an imperial responsibility, 87

Sicily: 15, 16, 19, 24, 36–7, 41, 44–5, 62, 63; arrival of Italian bombers in (June 1940), 83, 103; plans for invasion of, 96; arrival of *Fliegerkorps* X in (December 1940), 107; arrival of *Fliegerkorps II* in (December 1941), 140; Allied invasion of (July 1943), 179

Sidi Barrani: 97, 101

Simon, Sir John: supports Scale B defence scheme at Malta (1939), 62

Simpson, Commander (later Rear-Admiral): commands 10th Submarine Flotilla at Malta, 112; and 'Torch' operations, 174, 192; *see also* 10th

Submarine Flotilla, Admiralty, Cunningham, Pound
Sinclair, Admiral: Head of SIS and GC&CS (1935), 44
Sinclair, Sir Archibald: opposes suggested approach to Mussolini (May 1940), 91
Singapore: Cabinet authorises new naval base at (1921), 7; and Malta, 8; construction work suspended and recommenced (1924), 8; decision to install 15-inch guns at (1926), 12, 21; acceleration of construction urged by COS (1933), 26, 34; security jeopardised by weak defences at Malta (1934), 32; despatch of fleet to re-affirmed at Imperial Conference (1937), 53, 55; COS consider more important than Middle East (December 1939), 65; effect of its loss on Churchill, 146, 149
Slessor, Group Captain (later MRA Sir John): views on port defences, 22; makes proposals to JDC enquiry (1939), 61; after 1939 visit to Malta proposes formation of fighter squadron, 69; later admits underestimation of 'efficacy of fighter defence', 71; *see also* Air Staff, Joint Defence Committee
Smuts, Field Marshal: and assistance to Greece, 110
Somerville, Vice-Admiral (later Admiral of the Fleet) Sir James: 100
Spanish Civil War: 43, 50
Special Constables in Malta: 85
Special Liaison Unit (SLU): established at Malta (August 1941), 132
Spitfire aircraft: 70, 83; large reinforcements of for Malta (May 1942), 148; Spitfire Vs sent to Malta (May 1942), 153; and 'Torch' operations, 175, 186
Stanhope, Lord: opposes sending more than two battleships to Singapore (1938), 55
'Stoneage', Operation: November 1942 Malta convoy, 161; arrives, 173
Strategical Appreciation Committee (SAC): considers War Plans (March 1939), 55–6

Stresa Conference, April 1935: 28
Strickland, Sir Gerald (later Lord): becomes Prime Minister of Malta (1927), 18; in dispute with Catholic Church in Malta (1929–30), 18; opposes reversion to colonial rule, 48; wins six seats in 1939 election, 74–5
Strickland, Mabel: and relief of General Dobbie (April 1942), 156–7
Strong, Lieutenant (later Major-General Sir Kenneth): appointed Defence Security Officer at Malta (1930), 18; assesses security situation at Malta, 19; apprehensive about Mussolini's intentions, 19
Submarine losses in Mediterranean: losses in 1940, 97; losses in early 1942, 151–2; losses in late 1942, 174; *see also* 1st and 10th Submarine Flotillas, Admiralty, Cunningham, Pound, Simpson
Suda Bay, Crete: 98
Suez Canal: 6, 8, 10, 32, 43, 45, 70, 76, 77, 82, 107, 110
Sunderland aircraft: 97, 104, 112
Supreme War Council: 64
Swordfish aircraft: 95, 104, 105, 127
Syfret, Captain: opposes War Office's AA plans for Malta (1937), 58

T-class submarines: four sent to Malta (September 1940), 104, 192
Takali: new airfield proposed at (1934), 31; finance refused by Treasury (January 1935), 32–3; finance approved (August 1935), 37; airfield at, 57, 60
Takoradi air route: 96, 124, 150, 187
Talabot: sunk in Grand Harbour (March 1942), 155
tanks: mixed troop sent to Malta (October 1940), 102
Taranto: attacked by Wellingtons from Malta (December 1940), 98; attack on Italian fleet at, 104
Tarigo convoy: destroyed (April 1941), 114, 116
Tedder, ACM Sir Arthur (later MRA Lord): succeeds Longmore as AOC-in-C Middle East (June 1941), 125; and relief of General Dobbie (April

INDEX

1942), 155–6; offers more aircraft to Malta to support 'Torch', 175; takes command of Mediterranean air forces (February 1943), 175

'Ten Year Rule': effectively abandoned in 1932, 29

The Times of Malta: 89, 156

Tizard, Sir Henry: assists JDC enquiry into Malta's defences (1939), 62

Tobruk: 44, 109, 138; captured by Rommel (June 1942), 153–4

'Torch', Operation: 159, 161, 171–4

Treasury: opposes Air Staff proposals for Malta (1934), 31; refuses finance for Takali airfield (January 1935), 32–3; approves finance for Takali (August 1935), 37; approves finance for Luqa airfield (1936), 57; and gun production priorities (1940), 67

Trenchard, MRA Sir Hugh (later Lord): views of on proper function of air force, 11; favours bombers over fighters (1923), 11; advocates aircraft to replace guns in defence of ports, 11–12, 21; reluctantly agrees first three 15-inch guns at Singapore (1926), 12; submits views to Cabinet on retirement in 1929, 12

Tripoli: 48, 99, 108–9, 111, 113; suffers heavy air raids (June-October 1941), 133; suspension of convoys to (October 1941), 134; British advance to planned, 143

Tunisia: 1, 62–3, 70, 76; campaign in, 170–5; Axis surrender, 177

Turin: Air Staff proposal to bomb Italian aircraft factories at (1935), 37

Turkey: 6, 109–10

U-class submarines: first arrive at Malta, January 1941, 112; *see also* 10th Flotilla, Simpson

United States of America: 7, 27–8

Upholder, HMS: lost, 152

Urge, HMS: lost, 152

Upright, HMS: 136

USAAF: 164, 179

Valiant, HMS: 100, damaged at Alexandria, 140

Valle, General; prepares plans to bomb Malta (1935), 43

Valletta; dockyard dependent on Maltese workers, 2; dockyard facilities at, 6; floating dock established at, 8; dockyard discharges in 1926, 19; fears of sabotage at (1935), 47; shelters at, 74; floating dock sunk (1940), 95; heaviest air raid on 26 April 1942, 152

Vansittart, Sir Robert: recommends policy regarding Italy (1933), 28; becomes member of DRC (1934), 30; warns of dangers of Italian surprise attack (August 1935), 37; and Chatfield, 43; supports stronger defences at Malta (1938), 59

Vickers Predictor: 16

Victoria: sunk, 152

'Vigorous', Operation: failure of June 1942 Malta convoy, 159

Vittorio Veneto: 136

Vittoriosa, suburb of Valletta: air raids on (June 1940), 85

Wanklyn, Lt.-Cmdr. M.: 112; successes, 133; lost, 152

War Cabinet; considers Middle East plans, 65; approves eight months' supplies for Malta (September1940), 89; rejects Halifax's suggested approach to Mussolini (May 1940), 91–2; considers strategy in event of French surrender, 93; orders assistance to Greece (March 1941), 110; orders Auchinleck to launch offensive in Cyrenaica (May 1942), 148; *see also* Churchill, Chiefs of Staff, War Cabinet Defence Committee

War Cabinet Defence Committee: orders fifth battalion to Malta (May 1940), 69; endorses plans to strengthen Malta's defences (October 1940), 98; authorises additional reinforcements for Malta (October 1940), 102; orders aircraft carrier operations to supply fighters to Malta (March 1941), 119–20; and Auchinleck, 146–7; and General

Dobbie, 156; *see also* Chiefs of Staff, Churchill, War Cabinet

War Office: proposes new gun defences for Malta (1928), 15; proposes increase of garrison of Malta to four battalions (1928), 15; and bombardment trials (1928–30), 16, 21; new proposals for coastal and AA defences at Malta (1933), 23; sends reinforcements to Malta (September 1935), 36–7; proposes completion of 24-gun AA defences at Malta (1937), 58; expands RMA, 66; concerned about lack of adequate shelters in Malta (1940), 87; ordered by COS to complete Scale B AA defences at Malta by April 1941, 97; *see also* anti-aircraft defences of Malta, Bonham-Carter, Dobbie, garrison of Malta, Joint Defence Committee, Malta

Warlimont, General W.: and invasion of Malta (April 1941), 117; and Hitler's opposition to invasion of Malta, 154; assessment of Rommel's supply position (July 1942), 170; judges German position in North Africa a 'house of cards' (February 1943), 177, 179

Washington Naval Treaty, 1922: 7; prevents expansion of port facilities at Hong Kong, 8

Wasp, USS: ferries Spitfires to Malta (May 1942), 148, 153

Watson Watt, Professor Sir Robert: explains radar to JDC (1938), 60

Wavell, General Sir Archibald (later FM Lord): request for bombing of Italy from Malta rejected by Air Staff (July 1940), 96; and Egypt, 102; offensive in Egypt (December 1940), 106–7; and assistance to Greece, 109–10

Wellington aircraft: 96, 98, 111–12; three equipped with ASV arrive at Malta, 125, 132; raids on Italian ports (June-October 1941), 133, 137; raid on Palermo, 152; withdrawn from Malta (March 1942), 152; successes in October 1942, 168; operations against Tunisia (December 1942), 175, 177, 186

Welshman, HMS: carries food to Malta (October 1942), 161

'Winch', Operation, 120

Yugoslavia: 28, considered possible base for air attacks against Italy (1934), 31; possible Italian attack on (1940), 78; Italian supply convoys to, 106